Praise for American Phoenix

"Long before 'Barack and Michelle' or 'Bill and Hillary,' there were 'John and Louisa.' Leave it to my friend Jane to set us straight on America's first real power couple. And leave it to this incredible historian, to show how John Quincy and Louisa Adams not only took themselves to new heights, but this country to new heights as well. Just when I thought I knew everything about John, along comes Jane to whack me upside the head and complete the power picture . . . with Louisa. Great story. Great book. Great, period."

—NEIL CAVUTO, ANCHOR AND SR. VP, FOX NEWS AND FOX BUSINESS

"This wonderful book from Jane Hampton Cook goes a long way in shining a light on a compelling—and little known—woman in American history. British-born American Louisa Catherine Adams was a patriot and diplomat and did her part to secure America's sovereignty and power among nations at a time when America was a country in name only. With unending faith in the promise of our new nation, this future First Lady endured hardship, loneliness, illness, economic uncertainty and a heartbreaking separation from two of her children to help secure America's place on the world stage."

—ANITA McBRIDE, AMERICAN UNIVERSITY, AND FORMER ASSISTANT TO
PRESIDENT GEORGE W. BUSH AND CHIEF OF STAFF TO FIRST LADY LAURA BUSH

"Jane Hampton Cook's storyteller's narrative and penchant for detail vividly portrays John Quincy and Louisa Adams's watershed quest to establish America's sovereignty among nations. The couple's perseverance to diplomacy in the establishment of early America's free trade and to crossing European cultural divides to promote peace during wartime helped turn the tide of American and world history. Cook's glimpse, through diary entries, into the Adamses' sacrificial and loving devotion to one another amid scenes of political intrigue transcends time, inspiring reader and historian. A mesmerizing tale of two patriotic and focused faith-filled lives as needed and relevant today as it was 200 years ago."

—CATHY GOHLKE, CHRISTY AWARD–WINNING AUTHOR
OF PROMISE ME THIS AND BAND OF SISTERS

"Jane Hampton Cook's *American Phoenix* is a hugely entertaining and deep and dramatic portrait of America's sixth president and his wife Louisa, the only First Lady born outside of the United States. It tells the forgotten story of the Adamses in exile, when John Quincy was James Madison's minister to Russia, and how his diplomacy, with Louisa's assistance, helped to end the War of 1812, America's perilous second revolution. Cook creates vivid, cinematic scenarios, reminiscent of a David Lean epic set in Napoleonic Europe. The title is telling. If there is a better example of a political and historical comeback and a continuation of service to country than *American Phoenix*, I've yet to read it."

—KEVIN KNOBLOCK, WRITER, DIRECTOR, AND
DOCUMENTARY FILMMAKER, *A CITY UPON A HILL*

"John Quincy Adams has what it takes to obtain America's full sovereignty as an infant nation, but has no idea what that assignment will cost him. *American Phoenix* recounts the rise of JQA from the ashes of political irrelevancy to strategic obscurity. Caught in the life-altering wake of her husband's diplomatic service in St. Petersburg, Russia, Louisa Adams navigates through loneliness, loss, and depression. Along the way she is forced to face that which has sought to destroy her very heart, soul, mind, and marriage. What Jane Hampton Cook has unearthed in *American Phoenix* is a magnificent love story. John and Louisa Adams knew they deeply loved their country, but what they needed to find out when the ice of service and sacrifice melted, was if their love for one another would survive the ordeal. If you love America, a realistic love story, and cheering for the underdog, *American Phoenix* offers you an outlet for all three. You won't be disappointed!"

—DONNA TALLMAN, SCREENWRITER

"When Jane Hampton Cook brings history to life, she gives us what many don't: the full human experience behind the names of those long gone, textured with emotion, riddled with conflict, and surprisingly relevant to us today."

—JOCELYN GREEN, AUTHOR OF THE *HEROINES BEHIND THE LINES* SERIES

"*American Phoenix* by Jane Hampton Cook is an immaculate work of nonfiction, though it reads like a page-turning novel. Cook's attention to detail and historical accuracy transports us as readers back to the time of the War of 1812 and immerses us in the lives and drama that played out—much of it behind the scenes—at that time. If you like American history as told through the hearts and lives of those who lived it and sacrificed for its outcome, you will *love American Phoenix*!"

—KATHI MACIAS, MULTI-AWARD-WINNING AUTHOR OF NEARLY
40 BOOKS, INCLUDING THE GOLDEN SCROLLS 2011 NOVEL
OF THE YEAR, *RED INK* (WWW.KATHIMACIAS.COM)

American Phoenix

John Quincy and Louisa Adams, the War of 1812, and the Exile that Saved American Independence

JANE HAMPTON COOK

THOMAS NELSON
Since 1798

NASHVILLE   DALLAS   MEXICO CITY   RIO DE JANEIRO

In memory of my fiercely independent grandmother, Kathryn Jane McKewen Travis, who would have recognized some of herself—and her daughters and granddaughters—in Louisa Catherine Johnson Adams

Published in Nashville, Tennessee, by Thomas Nelson. Thomas Nelson is a registered trademark of Thomas Nelson, Inc.

Thomas Nelson, Inc., titles may be purchased in bulk for educational, business, fund-raising, or sales promotional use. For information, please e-mail SpecialMarkets@ThomasNelson.com.

Adams Family Papers, permission from the Massachusetts Historical Society.

Scripture quotations are taken from the King James Version (public domain).

Library of Congress Cataloging-in-Publication Data

Cook, Jane Hampton.
  American phoenix : John Quincy and Louisa Adams, the War of 1812, and the exile that saved American independence / Jane Hampton Cook.
    pages cm
  Includes bibliographical references and index.
  ISBN 978-1-59555-541-0
  1. Adams, John Quincy, 1767-1848. 2. Adams, Louisa Catherine, 1775-1852. 3. United States--History--War of 1812--Biography. 4. United States--History--War of 1812--Diplomatic history. 5. United States--History--War of 1812--Peace. 6. United States--Foreign relations--Russia. 7. Russia--Foreign relations--United States. 8. Diplomats--United States--Biography. 9. Presidents--United States--Biography. 10. Presidents' spouses--United States--Biography. I. Title.
  E377.C67 2013
  973.5'22092--dc23

2012039898

Printed in the United States of America

13 14 15 16 17 RRD 6 5 4 3 2 1

Contents

Contents

CONTENTS

Author's Note

RECALLING THE ONES WHO WERE

The phoenix riddle hath more wit. By us, we two being one, are it.
—JOHN DONNE, ENGLISH POET, CIRCA 1631

THOUGH HE OFTEN CONCEALED HIS TRUE FEELINGS FROM POLITE society, President John Quincy Adams kept detailed diaries throughout his life. Dipping a pen into his inkwell was as natural to him as breathing. In contrast his letters—particularly to his parents, brother, and wife—revealed this reserved man's deeper passions of love, justice, and a manly quest for honor.

An avid reader, John also understood the value of eyewitness accounts to historians. If his life proved influential at all—something he longed for—he suspected scholars just might collect his diaries and correspondence. He was right. Researchers throughout the years have published his writings in many volumes.

His wife, Louisa, also loved the written word. She, too, dared to dream that someone just might take an interest in her life. In her own Jane Austen–like way, she kept a diary and even dabbled in drafting fiction. When she wrote about one of the most dramatic times in her life, she hoped that one day, maybe—just maybe—her story could make a difference in someone else's life too.

"It may perhaps at some future day serve to recall the memory of one *who was*—and show that many undertakings which appear very difficult and arduous to my sex, are by no means so trying as imagination forever depicts them."

Writing was the key to being remembered in their generation. Photography didn't exist in their heyday, much less the concept of video. They understood the sentiment behind Benjamin Franklin's quip: "If you would not be forgotten, as soon as you are dead and rotten, either write things worth reading, or do things worth the writing." John Quincy and Louisa Adams did both.

Through this book I hope to bring to life the story of their honorable exile for you—a modern-day reader—in a way that resonates with your mind, heart, and soul. In scouring their diaries for main conflicts and combining their viewpoints, I sought to write a nonfiction book that also leverages the age-old fiction structure of conflict-setback-conflict-setback-climax-resolution. Their quotations come from their diaries and letters, updated only through modern spellings, corrected punctuation, and other essential editing elements required for modern publication standards. My desire is to portray the Adamses as they were—and as we all are—flawed human beings longing for love and respect.

Their journey also awakened me to the significance of the lesser-known War of 1812. Back then America was a country in name only and in desperate need of honor—much like John Quincy himself. We were a country whose national sovereignty was laughed at, spit upon, and joked about around the world. In 1776 independence depended, in part, on the senior John Adams. By 1812 independence depended again on an Adams—on two of them. John and Louisa Adams's sacrifices for their nation and the cause of liberty are as inspiring as those made during the American Revolution decades earlier.

Communication changes. Technology transforms time, but the human heart doesn't change. The need for honor, family, acceptance, justice, reunion, faith, hope, and love is as real today as it was from 1809 to 1815. From being down on your luck to rising stronger than before, *American Phoenix* shows "the ones who were" and the triumph that can come when anyone's life—yours, mine, or theirs—takes an unexpected journey.

Warmly,

Jane Hampton Cook

PART 1

Journey Interrupted

RUSSIA, FEBRUARY 1815

1

Murder Outside

LOUISA ADAMS EXPECTED TO DEAL WITH THE HAZARDS OF SNOW and ice as she said good-bye to St. Petersburg, Russia, in February 1815. She knew traveling by land to Paris in winter wouldn't be easy. The distance alone was overwhelming—sixteen hundred miles.

What she didn't expect to slow her down was the inconvenience of a murder.

Weather woes, however, were her first worry. When she left St. Petersburg, she traveled more than 330 miles southwest along an icy, winding road toward Mitau, the capital of Courland. Centuries earlier, Baltic merchants had used this pathway to transport their most abundant natural treasure—fossilized amber—to jewelry makers and medicinal healers throughout the Roman Empire. No matter the era, ice still ruled these roads in winter.

Not far from Mitau, her carriage became stuck in icy sludge, which had refrozen after a brief thaw. Today, Mitau is called Jelgava, a city in Latvia, an independent Baltic nation about the size of West Virginia. In Louisa's day the region was a rugged country of swamps, forests, hills, valleys, and crusty roads dimpled by deep holes—and stuck wheels.

When her carriage wouldn't budge, her hired post drivers rang bells to rally the locals for help. Several Russian farmers came to her aid by bringing pickaxes and shovels. As their amber-supplying ancestors had witnessed centuries earlier, so they also saw many coaches and wagons become stuck in refrozen slush. While offering their hands and brawn and hacking around the wheels, these men made a startling discovery.

Louisa was not Russian, as her carriage's insignia indicated. She was an American, and a female at that.

Few of them had seen an American, let alone a lady from that land. To most Europeans, Americans were Yankee Doodles—buffoons in beaver hats.

Others envisioned Native American chiefs with feathered headdresses and scantily clad wives who resembled Eve in buckskin fig leaf. Louisa was neither of these. What they didn't realize was this: she was more demure than Dolley Madison, the perfectly mannered, snuff-inhaling socialite wife of the president of the United States, and as sensible, opinionated, and observant as Jane Austen, the popular but still anonymous English novelist.

More than her sex, Louisa's aloneness plagued the propriety of these Russians that winter day. She was traveling to Paris without her husband, brother, or grown son. Gypsies did that—not a lady clad in clean clothing in the high-waist Empire style or riding in her own carriage. Then again, maybe American ladies were different—more independent—than European women.

With the skill of sculptors and the speed of dogs digging for bones, the farmers chiseled and shoveled until the carriage loosened and the icy sludge cracked. They cheered the instant the wheel broke free. Thanking them, Louisa resumed her journey.

When she arrived at the post house in Mitau later that day, she was emphatic. Her stay was to be short. She was already lagging behind her schedule, which was as realistic as chasing a comet. Rest, not recreate. Then resume.

"Here I stopped to rest for some hours, with a determination to proceed one stage more to sleep," she recalled.

Travelers were at the mercy of innkeepers, post house managers, and others who opened their houses to strangers. Unlike a modern voyager, Mrs. Adams couldn't use her smartphone to make hotel reservations via the Internet or call ahead by telephone. None of these advances, not even the telegraph, had been invented yet. All she had were hired drivers, called postilions. They were her communication network, the social media of the day. Postilions worked for post house managers, who furnished fresh horses and drivers from stage to stage for traveling carriages and post coaches.

For centuries Europe's postal systems were nothing more than messenger boys riding alone on horseback to carry letters to the next post or town. This system changed in the 1780s, when postal services, such as the one operated by the famed Thurn and Taxis family, began using coaches to carry both mail and passengers from post to post. Russia's postal system was similar. Louisa, however, was paying for post drivers and horses to transport her private carriage.

Russia's mammoth postal system differed in one significant way from the rest of Europe. In compact England postal stations were close together, allowing drivers to change horses every six to twelve miles. The Russians spurred their beasts much farther, forcing horses to pull a coach eighteen miles or more to the next station.

No matter the country, postal drivers were sometimes suspicious characters. One Englishman described a postal carrier as "an idle boy mounted on a worn-out hack, who so far from being able to defend himself against a robber, was more likely to be in league with him."

Despite this, local drivers knew these postal paths better than anyone and recommended places to stay. One thing was certain. Travelers could usually find shelter at post houses, but hospitality—especially along roads recently ripped by Napoleon's army and the czar's pursuing Cossacks—was no guarantee.

Louisa found an inn at Mitau, called upon its master, and ordered dinner for her party, which included her seven-year-old son, Charles; a nurse; and two servants. Everything was comfortable—at least for the first sixty minutes.

"In about an hour after my arrival, Countess Mengs, a lady with whom I was slightly acquainted at St. Petersburg, called and gave me a most kind and urgent invitation to her house entreating me to remain with her some days."

Word of this American's arrival traveled as quickly as the cook could serve soup. Countess Mengs remembered Louisa as the musical, French-fluent, intelligent wife of John Quincy Adams, the son of the former US president—whatever that meant to the countess's European understanding of America.

When Mengs realized her socialite friend was traveling alone, especially without her reserved, in-control husband, she immediately asked her to stay for a few days. She not only asked; she implored. Her demeanor suggested Louisa's life depended on it, while her words masked her true concerns. She claimed she simply wanted to introduce her to friends at her house nearby.

Though flattered, Louisa declined the kind offer. How could Mrs. Adams possibly stop to enjoy herself when her mission was so pressing? Didn't her papers imply her travels were urgent? Weren't these letters of introduction as glued to her person as her own hands? She had to get to Paris.

What her papers didn't reveal was how long it had been since she had taken a stroll with John Quincy by the river or heard him recite the most inspiring points of a sermon he had just read. Although she had dreaded the days when he would wake up with some new-fangled determination—such as scouring his floor-to-ceiling library of books to find the circumference of the earth—she now missed his calculations of trivia.

She even longed for those endless summer days when he would pull out his apothecary scales and compare the weights of European coins to American ones. Back then his weights and measurements obsession seemed a terribly boring way to tinker with time.

"Mr. Adams too often passed it [the evening] alone studying weights and measures practically that he might write a work on them," she had complained back then. Now she would trade anything for the pleasure of his most annoying habits.

Nearly a year had passed since their separation. Diligence, not entertainment, must guide each and every decision. How dare she even think of recreating while she traveled sans husband! What would people say? Worse, what would they *whisper*?

"I thought it my duty to decline an invitation which would have been very pleasant and agreeable, the countess being a lady of great respectability, and superior attainments."

Rest, not recreate. Resume. Then it happened, or rather *he* happened.

—✦—

Though Adams didn't know it at the time, his Eve left St. Petersburg on February 12, her fortieth birthday. While Louisa stopped in Mitau on her icy land journey around the Baltic Sea, John was in Paris—completely unaware of her whereabouts. He didn't know if she had chosen to leave St. Petersburg to join him or not. He had yet to receive the letter she wrote him the morning of her departure.

"I am this instant setting off," she hurriedly explained, "and have only time to say that nothing can equal my impatience to see you. . . . I could not celebrate my birthday in a manner more delightful than in making the first step towards that meeting for which my soul pants."

He had asked her to conduct several business transactions in St. Petersburg, but the way she saw it, his demands were as realistic as flying to Paris in an air machine. Worried he would disapprove of her ability to sell furnishings and settle accounts, she added, "I hope that you will forgive all that is not exactly correspondent to your wishes and receive me with as much affection as fills my heart."

She had every reason to fret over his disapproval. The last time they moved, he had made every arrangement—including the one that changed her life forever—*all* without consulting her.

Though she anticipated his desire to be reunited with her was mutual, after a nearly year long separation, she couldn't be sure. He couldn't be, either.

John arrived in Paris on February 4, 1815, after living in Belgium, where he grew fat on countless three-hour dinners and "great relaxation of my customary exercise [walking]." His first observation was that no one examined his baggage as he crossed the bridge into Paris. No inspection was the surest sign that peace had, indeed, come to Europe. One thing had not changed.

"The tendency to dissipation at Paris seems to be irresistible. There is a moral incapacity for industry and application," he wrote in his diary, remembering when he lived there as a youth with his father and elsewhere in Europe as a young diplomat. "I am as ill guarded . . . as I was at the age of twenty."

The nearly forty-eight-year-old Adams would never forget traveling to France with his father years earlier, during the American Revolution. Born July 11, 1767, to John and Abigail Adams, he was not yet eleven years old when he first visited France in April 1778. His father had hoped the trip would be an invaluable education for his son. He was right. From reading his father's French grammar books and attending an academy in Passy, young Johnny had learned French easily. He had taken to the language so quickly that he taught English to his father's new European acquaintances.

"The ambassador said he was astonished at my son's knowledge; that he was a master of his own language, like a professor," the senior Adams had boasted.

By watching his father and Benjamin Franklin implore the French king and other European leaders to aid the United States in its quest to cast off royalty, John had learned the rules of diplomacy—the dos and especially the don'ts of the game.

A more seasoned John Quincy Adams returned to Paris in February 1815. His sharply curved nose and high arched eyebrows, which he inherited from his mother, still made him look a bit like a bald eagle. No longer was he a youth with a full head of brown hair and his whole life ahead of him. Neither was he a man on a mission. He was navigating a transition with no solid assurance of where he would land. He both hoped and feared that a letter would soon arrive and forever change his destiny—and his family's—for the better.

While Louisa couldn't waste a minute socializing in Mitau, John couldn't stop chasing the muse of recreation in Paris. He didn't know which was more irresistible: the museum, the opera, or the new judicial court.

From his second-story chamber at the Hotel du Nord on the Rue de Richelieu, he could hear the clip-clopping of coaches along the cobblestones and the shouts of pedestrians walking the street below with someplace to go.

Then he had an idea. He put on his dark overcoat and walking boots. He sought to conquer the bricks with his own feet and get some exercise. Perhaps he could still find it. Maybe his memory would lead him to the other hotel, the Hôtel de Valois, "the same house where I lodged with my father in 1778, April, the first time I ever was in Paris." Maybe it would be more suitable for living in limbo and a better place to bring her.

After crisscrossing the city, he found his way back to the Valois. His memory of an elegantly furnished hotel suitable for properly dressed gentlemen was suddenly replaced by the ragged reality of time. The Valois was "altogether in decay, and scarcely furnished at all; yet the price of the apartments is as high as at the best hotels."

He knew, too, what it once meant to be vibrant and flourishing only to fall into an abyss of unpopularity. Isn't that how he had spent the past seven years since being booted from the US Senate in 1808? Isn't that what life in his so-called exile in Europe had been all about?

What he couldn't see as he stared at the decaying hotel was the possibility of his legacy: the banishment of this Adams and his Eve had just become the nation's salvation.

While waiting for fresh horses at the Mitau hotel, Louisa could not escape the countess's pleas to stay through a pretense to socialize. On top of this, Mrs. Adams came face-to-face with a mystery.

"Immediately after my dinner was removed, the master of the house, after carefully shutting the doors, watchfully noting that no intruders were near, said he wished much to speak to me upon a matter which he considered of vital importance to me."

The countess sent the innkeeper to talk with her or, more accurately, to talk some sense into her.

"I expressed my thanks . . . requested him to be seated and to inform me on what subject he had asked this interview."

She watched the man return to the door and give it a solid push, making sure it was closed. Then he sat knee-knockingly close to her, increasing her anxiety to provocative proportions. What stranger would dare get so close to a lady?

"I, however, assumed an air of great calmness. . . . He began by informing me that the last night a dreadful murder had been committed on the very road which I was about to take, and to urge me to wait until the next morning before I determined to proceed."

Murder! She knew crossing the frozen Russian tundra in winter would be a battle against nature's worst weather, but she wasn't prepared to battle the worst in man's nature. She had anticipated below-freezing temperatures by bringing several fur coats and blankets to keep everyone warm as they endured the carriage's clumsy clopping over pathetic paths from post to post. Expecting hours of fatigue, she had created a cozy bed for Charles in the front of the coach. Nonetheless, nothing could prepare her for this. The murder was proof of humanity's insanity. No matter the generation, Cain never dies.

"I told him very coolly and decidedly that the plan of my journey was fixed, and . . . I only intended to go four German miles [roughly eighteen English miles] farther that night, and was to start so early with two well-armed servants."

Nonetheless, the day was slipping away. Perhaps a morning ride would be safer than traveling at night on a road marked with fresh blood. After all she had experienced in St. Petersburg, she must move forward. Each mile put her farther away from her heartache, especially from the one she loved so very much, and closer to reunion.

2

Thief Inside

JOHN PICKED UP HIS PEN. "AFTER INFORMING YOU BY MY LAST LETter of my arrival in this city," he wrote her, "and of the hotel where I had taken up my abode, I have suspended my communication to you."

He did not have a choice. Writing to Louisa again was as impractical as it was painful. If she had left as he hoped, then he did not need to write. Because they had been separated for ten months, he could not be sure of her choice or desire to see him.

Paris was a place to recreate, to take one's mind off all worries. He had already visited the National Museum many times, spending hours among its halls. Above all the magnificent sculptures and paintings, the Apollo and Venus de Milo attracted his attention. They "absorb the consideration of everything else; the eye of the enquirer begins and ends with them."

Though he attended the museum several times, he visited the theater more often. Tonight would be no different. He was looking forward to watching the female lead, an actress he had seen perform in Russia. "She has improved since I saw her at St. Petersburg," he recorded in his diary.

The ends of the plays were just as notable as the actresses and performances. To close the show, the orchestra dutifully struck up "Vive Henri IV," France's national song, which celebrated the first king from the Bourbon family, Henry IV, who took power and brought peace to France in the 1590s. Unlike the dramas before them, this royal anthem and tribute to their newly restored Bourbon-family monarch, Louis XVIII, received lukewarm receptions. The audience "applauded a little."

Paris may have been at peace again in 1815, but the people were clearly bored with their king.

"I conceived I had nothing to apprehend, as the postilions must be in the habit of passing the road constantly, which was a very public one, and that I should reach the place of my destination by nine or ten o'clock that night."

Louisa watched the innkeeper shake his head grimly in disbelief at her stubbornness. He didn't mean to alarm her. His voice softened as he spoke of his daughters, women he loved and wanted to protect. He was not a man to be feared or to force his way upon anyone. With tenderness he noted that she was alone. Suddenly he couldn't handle it any longer. He must open her eyes to the true danger of her circumstances—a most intimate one.

"He then informed me that the French servant who I had with me was well known in Mitau; that he was a soldier in Napoleon's army and had remained in that city two years, that he was known to be a desperate villain of the very worst character, and that he did not consider my life safe with him if I suffered him to proceed with me."

The news was as surprising as Napoleon's unquenchable thirst to conquer Europe. Louisa suspected as much about Baptiste. She had hired him and another servant, likely a relative, to travel with her. She did not refer to the other man by name in her memoirs, but noted that he moved at a slow, limping pace.

At one point Louisa questioned her recollection of Baptiste's name, writing: "Baptiste, I believe that was his name (but no matter)." Her Russian passport, dated January 28, 1815, documented her servants as Englebert and John Fulling. The apparent discrepancy can be explained by Louisa's linguistic abilities. The *Oxford English Dictionary* defines *fulling* as an English word meaning "to baptize" or "to consecrate fully." Because she spoke French fluently, she likely thought in French, which explains why she remembered the French name *Baptiste* instead of the English name of *Fulling*.

She had also arranged for Madame Babet, a nurse who had worked thirty years for one of her best friends in St. Petersburg, to help care for Charles. Baptiste was to oversee day-to-day arrangements. As a woman traveling without a husband, brother, or father, Louisa needed the pretense of masculine protection that her servants gave her.

Baptiste had suffered from Napoleon's wanderlust. As with Madame Babet and the other servant, he seemed to want nothing more than to go home to his native country. Mrs. Adams, however, had recently begun to doubt his honesty. When they left St. Petersburg, Louisa, Charles, and Madame Babet rode inside the carriage, which required runners to glide over iced roads. Her servants endured in a *kibitka*, a canvas-covered wagon on skis.

Before traveling to Mitau, they stopped for four days in Riga to fix a mechanical problem. While there, she discovered that all her provisions had frozen. Even her stashes of Madeira wine had become solid ice. Because of its alcohol content, wine freezes more slowly than water.

Frozen wine was not her only problem. A thaw then took over the countryside. The iced roads suddenly turned to slush, forcing her to dispose of her ice-sliding kibitka. Louisa had never faced such problems. Then again, she had never traveled such a great distance under so many extreme conditions—at least, not by land and not without her husband as the leader of her entourage.

The kibitka's loss forced her servants to ride on the carriage's backside, which made the vehicle even heavier and more costly. The drivers charged her a rate of a coach and six horses, not a coach of three, the Russian troika, or even four, the English model, as she preferred. Would John have been able to negotiate a better deal? Was she being taken advantage of because she was a woman? She fretted over the likelihood.

"Here for the first time I had some reason to doubt the honesty of my servant [Baptiste]," she wrote about her stop in Riga, where she first began feeling insecure from within. "A silver cup presented . . . as a parting keepsake to my little boy, was taken from the carriage; and there was little doubt that he had made free with it."

John and Louisa were friends with many diplomats, including the Baron de Bussche, who gave Charles the cup. For years John's propriety and fear of bribery forbade Louisa from accepting gifts from anyone. Easter eggs were the exception. From the peasants on the pavement to princesses at the palace, everyone gave and received Easter eggs in Russia. The custom of trading hard-boiled, glass, or porcelain eggs at Easter was so prevalent that Adams broke his no-gift rule only once a year.

Louisa and Charles's departure from St. Petersburg, not to mention her husband's absence, finally gave her the freedom to do something she had long wanted to do: accept a gift that wasn't an egg. Now that gift was gone.

Baptiste had probably disposed of the silver cup by selling it when she wasn't watching. No sooner had she discovered the theft than the governor of Riga appeared. He invited her party to stay at his home. She refused. Relax, not recreate. She must get to Paris. If she was lucky, she would make the journey in forty days.

Now the hotel manager before her in Mitau warned of a murder on the very road she was about to take and, perhaps worst of all, confirmed the truth. She was traveling with a thief.

"At the same time he begged most earnestly that I would not dismiss him [Baptiste] at Mitau, for fear he, the servant, should suspect that I had received information there, and he might burn the house over his head."

"I told him that the man had behaved very well so far," Louisa responded pretentiously. "That I had felt a mistrust of him and did not like him, but that the gentleman who had engaged him had entered into a bond that he should be taken to his own country, and that I was not to part with him unless he behaved improperly."

Without proof, she couldn't charge Baptiste with robbery. Their contract was binding—absolute. She was obligated to take him to Paris in exchange for his service. So far he had adequately managed their arrangements. The other man was good and honest but timid, a contrast to Baptiste, who often took charge. At times she needed Baptiste's aggressive, if slightly Napoleonic ways.

The innkeeper said her situation was difficult. She shouldn't even hint to Baptiste that she doubted his character. Appearing to place unlimited confidence in his services, she ought to rely on him in any emergency and welcome his advice. But if the opportunity came, she would be smart to part with him faster than a flintlock fowler could shoot a fox.

The man apologized for delaying her. He begged her to keep their conversation quiet. Whispers wouldn't be wise but would merely endanger both of them.

"I promised a perfect silence . . . that I would willingly postpone my departure; but as the hour had arrived for that departure, and the carriage would be at the door directly, I was fearful that a sudden change of purpose would excite suspicion, and do more harm than good," she said, promising to adopt his excellent advice.

As he stood to leave, Countess Mengs returned. With more urgency than before, she begged Louisa to change her mind and stay.

"All this I declined, I fear, from a proud and foolhardy spirit, and the conviction that, however retarded, the difficulties of my path must be conquered, and it was as well to face them at once," Louisa recalled.

The countess and the innkeeper probably wondered why Louisa was in such a hurry to get to Paris. The battlefields were finally silent, strewn with skeletons, not the sounds of soldiers. The war was over. Napoleon wasn't dead, but he was no longer a threat, either. He was locked up, exiled to Elba, an island off the Italian coast of Tuscany.

Although the countess and the hotel manager had lived through unspeakable difficulties on land that became the front lines of the war, they had no idea how depressed Louisa had become and what she had endured in St. Petersburg. Her sorrows were private. They truly didn't know why she was in such a hurry to leave Russia. They didn't understand why she refused to socialize with the countess, particularly when she might not have another opportunity to do so. They didn't realize that as much as she longed to see her husband, it broke her heart to say good-bye to the one who would never leave Russia. They didn't know that she had been living in exile. St. Petersburg was Louisa's Elba. Like Napoleon, she realized that reunion was the only remedy for her broken heart.

They really didn't know Louisa Adams.

3

Lost

THE SECOND OF EIGHT CHILDREN, LOUISA CATHERINE JOHNSON Adams was born on February 12, 1775, in London, England, the same year and country as novelist Jane Austen. Unlike Jane, Louisa was half-American. Her father, Joshua Johnson, was born in Calvert County, Maryland, while her mother, Catherine Nuth Johnson, was born in London. Also unlike Miss Austen, Mrs. Adams found wedded love, until politics came along and broke her heart.

Though she was too young to remember it, Louisa had lived previously in a form of exile. Decades earlier her father had moved to London from the colonies to make a living as a merchant representing an Annapolis shipping company. When the American Revolution broke out, he'd sided with the Patriots and fled with his family to Nantes, France, in 1778. She couldn't remember the agony her parents felt while being captives in a foreign country during a devastating war, one that might forever separate them from their homeland. Little did she realize that years later she, too, would find herself again living away from home, only to be trapped by the most destructive worldwide war humanity had ever witnessed.

Being exiled to France had one big benefit. She'd spent her earliest school years under the tutelage of French nuns. These women had unknowingly given her the most useful gift for a future envoy's wife—the ability to speak French, the language of diplomacy. She'd absorbed the language as naturally as a native French child. Not only did Louisa speak French correctly, but she also spoke it without an American or English accent. Some thought she spoke French better than English.

After the Revolutionary War officially ended in 1783, Mr. Johnson and his family returned to London, where he had later served as the American consul. Their home became the nucleus of social life for Americans doing business in England—whether in trade or diplomacy. Her family was so pro-American that she never expected to have anything in common with the dictatorial Napoleon, other than speaking fluent French.

Now here she was alone and on the road. She understood the pains of exile that her parents had felt years earlier. Though she loathed the exiled French emperor as much as her father-in-law, John Adams, had despised Britain's King George III a generation earlier, she understood the sorrow of separation from a spouse, children, and homeland.

Louisa's exile became even more agonizing in April 1814, when John Quincy traveled to Belgium, leaving her alone with Charles in St. Petersburg. Ironically, he left at the same time the kings of Europe sent the conquered Napoleon to Elba. Being exiled from America with John Quincy had been unbearable, but living without him in St. Petersburg during the greatest threat to America since the Revolutionary War was worse than she could have ever imagined.

By February 1815 it was impossible to know who wanted reunion more—Louisa to her family or Napoleon to his throne. One thing was certain: both would do anything to go home. Both would make any decision, no matter how impulsive or rash, to be reunited with the passions of their hearts. For Louisa anything now meant traveling with a thief and taking a road marked by murder. While at the inn in Mitau, she thanked the countess for her concern.

"Finding me determined, she took a very kind leave of me, and I got into the carriage and began my ride under the most uneasy impressions."

Her party departed in late afternoon, when the amber hues of daylight vanished into black, with only torches or lanterns to light the road. Travel was slow. Unless paved by the order of a king or emperor, most roads lacked any foundation other than dirt, dust, or mud. Given the conditions, she expected to reach the next post by ten o'clock in the evening.

The innkeeper's words may have haunted her as she hugged her carriage's seat and endured the terrain's tossing and tussling. A *dreadful murder* had been committed on the very ground beneath her.

Who was killed? Why? Was it over money? What should she do with her bags of coins? They were already hidden in the best place possible—under her seat. She made certain that no one, not even Charles or Madame Babet, knew of their whereabouts. The innkeeper's warning now left her as uneasy as a fortune-teller after reading a palm. Had Baptiste discovered her gold? She would have to be as sly as a thief whenever she withdrew coins from her stash.

Perhaps the murder was over something else, maybe ethnicity. Depravity often leads to dastardly deeds. Did a gang of peasants stop a carriage and drag the poor soul into the forest? Suddenly each boulder on the road became a suspicious hiding place; each beggar, a criminal. The farther she traveled from St. Petersburg, the less protection she received from the Russian minister of interior, who gave her introductory papers.

"I was likewise furnished with a letter from the [Russian] government recommending me to the protection of all whom I called on; and, that any complaint should immediately be attended to."

Louisa displayed these letters in her coach's window or concealed them on her person. They were her shield, her crest. Just as masked medieval knights relied on coats of arms to identify and protect them from accidental death by a knight from the same family or tribe, so Louisa relied on her papers from the land of the czar. Such letters have one major flaw. Their interpretation depends on the perspective and true loyalties of the viewer.

As she traveled that night, Louisa probably also worried as much—if not more—about Baptiste. She may have hugged Charles closer, placing him in her lap before encouraging him to get some sleep. She had already failed his siblings. She couldn't fail him now. She may have stroked his hair, pulling it past his oversized ears under the pretense of reassurance, but the gesture was really an attempt to pacify her conscience. Charles was likely oblivious to the murder outside and the danger within. How she wished to relieve Baptiste of his post! But a bond was a bond.

When the time grew closer to ten, Louisa relaxed. They were nearly there. Then she felt the abrupt backward jolting of the carriage. Her pulse quickened.

"After riding about four miles, the postilion suddenly stopped and informed us that he had missed the road; that the man who was accustomed to drive was sick; that he had never been on that road before; and that he could not tell where he was."

Now her circumstances were worse than before. She was lost in the woods at the hands of a novice driver. What if the rookie was the criminal? The driver took them through rough terrain. Paths jerked the coach at each and every hole and rock, spitting them suddenly forward and sometimes throwing them from their seats. Nature tripped them with the same teasing as a ship caught in a storm's fury, something she knew all too well. Their problem was made worse by clouds. Absent from the sky were a bright moon and delicate stars to brighten their path.

"Until eleven o'clock at night we were jolted over hills, through swamps and holes, and into valleys into which no carriage had surely ever passed before; and my whole heart was filled with unspeakable terrors for the safety of my child, for whom I offered the most ardent prayers to the ever protecting father of his creatures."

Taking charge, Baptiste halted the carriage. Because of the uneven terrain, the vehicle might overturn. Mindful of the innkeeper's advice to appear to place unlimited confidence in Baptiste, Louisa agreed. If this wasn't an emergency, what was?

"At twelve o'clock at night, the horses being utterly worn out, and scarce a twinkling star to teach of living light, we determined that Baptiste should ride one of the horses and endeavor to find a road through which we might be extricated from our perilous situation."

Louisa snugly tucked Charles into his bed. The scene around them was as dark as the fur on a Russian bear. She gathered all their blankets and made sure everyone was as warm as possible. Questions in her mind haunted her as much as the sounds from the swamp surrounding them. Would Baptiste return, or would they freeze to death? Would they die at the hands of a wandering murderer? How her pulse raced!

4

The Crossing

FOOLHARDY! WHY HADN'T SHE STAYED IN MITAU? THE COUNTESS
would have kept her company. Perhaps she should have delayed her journey.
She could have saved herself heartache and worry over Charles. Now she would
have to wait for the sun to rescue her, unless a beast of the forest or the worst of
man found her first. Then she heard it— voices and the trampling of a horse
at a short distance. Man or monster?

"The palpitation of my heart increased until I thought it would have burst.
My child lay sweetly sleeping on his little bed in the front of the carriage,
unsusceptible of fear and utterly unconscious of danger."

Then she heard his familiar voice. She didn't record whether it was raspy or
mellow, high-pitched, or deep toned, but she recognized his unmistakable voice.
Even if Baptiste was a thief, his voice gave her instant comfort in that frightful
moment, while his perspiration-stained frock shirt suddenly smelled sweet.

"Baptiste rode hastily up to the carriage door and informed me that he had
found a house quite near."

Accompanying Baptiste was a Russian officer, who saw him riding from
the house. The man "offered his services to take us into the road, as it required
great skill to keep the carriage out of the gullies by which we were surrounded."
Louisa agreed to let the Russian officer escort them to the house. Confirming
her fears, he told her that murder had recently taken place on that road. Not
to worry. He brought lanterns and fresh torches to light their path to shelter.

"One of my men mounted the officer's horse and we proceeded at a foot
pace." They arrived at the house at half past one, three hours later than she
expected. "He [the officer] accepted a handsome present, made many polite
speeches, and took leave, recommending the innkeeper to be attentive, and to see
that horses should be ready at any hour I might want them, [and] he departed."

Though the post driver was at fault for missing the road and accepting a job to ride to a place he had never been before, and at night at that, Baptiste and the other servant performed their duty with honor. She was not mangled or murdered in the forest. Neither was her carriage sunk in a swamp. Though shaken, she was alive. More important, so was her child.

"I therefore expressed my satisfaction to my domestics for the prudence and discretion which they had shown through this singular accident, and bade them be ready at an early hour with the carriage and horses," she explained, determining to get out of there as soon as possible.

Louisa retired to a small room with Madame Babet and Charles. Before she closed her eyes, she did something the French nuns taught her to do many years ago. Grateful for God's guardian angels, she prayed.

"After thanking most devoutly the Almighty for His protection through this hour of trial, I sought repose with renewed confidence in the persons attached to my service, and determined not to listen to any more bugbears to alarm my nerves and weaken my understanding."

⁕

While Louisa zigzagged through dark forests, John calmly walked into the ornate Palais-Royal, "[w]here I was presented to the Duke of Orleans [Louis Philippe]."

Though not the king—Adams had already been introduced to Louis XVIII—this man was a French royal nonetheless. And in postrevolutionary France, one never knew when the throne would change again.

"He asked me whether I was the son of Mr. Adams who had been president of the United States when he [the duke] was in America."

"*Oui*," John replied.

"He saw the resemblance between me and my father, but did not recollect having seen me in America."

Adams had heard the comparison many times. To avoid confusion with his father, he often signed his name *JQA*.

"I was at that time in Europe," he explained about why they did not meet during the Frenchman's introduction to his father. John Quincy was an envoy to Berlin while his father was president.

"He had a very grateful remembrance of the hospitality with which he had been treated in America, and was very happy to make my acquaintance."

The Duke of Orleans was unique among the Frenchmen Adams had met recently. Louis Philippe based his opinion of the United States on what he had witnessed, not on negative stereotypes.

The greatest struggle America faced in the early 1800s was acceptance as a legitimate sovereign nation. Though the United States had won its independence from Great Britain during the Revolutionary War, most Europeans believed the son never left the father. America and England were still one and the same power in their view. The gravest dangers facing the nation were failing to establish free trade in Europe—the surest sign of actual acceptance of US sovereignty—and risking independence by losing a new war with England. Independence once again depended, in part, on an Adams.

As enjoyable as it was to meet a French royal who favored the United States, pressing most on Adams's mind was his daily obsession—the post. When would the president's letter arrive? Would he receive the orders he longed for? Would he finally be free to go home to America? Would he receive an honorable appointment? The position of secretary of state was vacant. Or would he be stuck—eternally in "exile" in Europe? Tremendous strife still existed between the United States and England.

"The British will take care to inflict some signal stroke of vengeance to redeem their reputation," he predicted to Louisa in a January 1815 letter. "Its darkest shade is that it has settled no one subject of dispute between the two nations." He still worried that the future would be worse than the past.

"My visit here [in Paris] has not hitherto given me much satisfaction," he confessed. Something was missing no matter where he lived. That something was his wife. As much as he loved the theater, such excursions felt empty without Louisa sharing them with him.

"But life here is a perpetual tumult, the forms and manner of the society are contrary to all my habits," he complained, adding, "I find myself as much a stranger as the first day."

The reason he had stopped writing to her was as simple as it was practical. Adams longed to embrace his wife. More than anything he hoped that she had dared to risk winter to leave St. Petersburg and be reunited with him. Though he offered for her to wait until spring, when travel was safer, he prayed that she had left frosty St. Petersburg and was en route to meet him. Because they were nearly the same height, theirs was a comfortable embrace, no hunching over for him or stretching up on tiptoes for her. At five feet seven inches, he was an inch taller than his wife. He missed her more than he would ever admit to the Marquis de Lafayette, the Frenchman who aided the American Revolution years ago, and others he dined with in Paris.

He sent this letter by post to Königsberg in East Prussia and another copy to Berlin. Maybe she would reach one of those places soon. How he dared to hope!

———

Finally, Mrs. Adams and her entourage broke free, riding five hundred miles without incident toward the Vistula River, the Baltic Sea's main basin and Poland's largest river, stretching more than six hundred miles.

They likely passed many pleasant sights, such as the area's fourteenth-century storehouses, which held salt, timber, grain, building stones, and other raw materials. Because the Baltic's shores boast the largest and richest deposits of amber in the world, they likely saw bits of this fossilized resin sprinkled along the way.

No matter how attractive the antique amber or quaint the ancient granaries, when they arrived at the Vistula's shores, Louisa made an alarming discovery: the ice was thin. Help from the locals was even thinner. The ice was in such a critical state that she had trouble finding drivers who were willing to risk crossing it.

How solid was the ice? Could the frozen river hold the weight of her carriage? The ice was iffy, she learned. Even iffier was finding an inn nearby. The locals—likely ice fishermen or traders—gave her the bad news. If she didn't cross, she would have to make a long, winding detour around the river with no guarantee of finding shelter for the evening. The time was four o'clock in the afternoon. Because it was winter, the sun would disappear very soon. Time was the enemy too.

Her choice was clear: cross the iffy ice or risk a night without shelter, a reminder of getting lost in the woods outside Mitau. The men gave her a variable. If she had the courage to cross, they would attach the horses to the far end of long poles and tap the ice ahead of her.

An hour passed. Night was awakening. She made her choice: cross.

They started at five o'clock. The men went forward a few feet, beating their poles to find the firmest path. They tapped, listened, and watched for cracking. The ice was secure enough to start. Then they attached the long poles to the horses pulling the carriage. Inch by inch Louisa and her party slowly slid over the uncertain ice. Just as the coach reached the border—a few feet from land—the ice cracked and gave way.

The first jolt probably sounded like a crunch. Then suddenly the coach punched through the ice, tossing the passengers from their seats. Madame Babet started screaming. Charles was locked by fear. Louisa heard the severe cracking of the whip as the driver yelled at the horses to pull the sinking carriage to shore.

Is this how it was to end? After all she had suffered, she now faced the worst possibility. If the carriage continued to sink, she and Charles would be permanently separated from John and their family—exiled into a frozen river forever.

What Louisa did not realize in that moment was historical hindsight: her Russian destination had just changed US destiny.

PART 2

Journey Begins

Six years earlier, Boston, July 4, 1809

THE *HORACE*, COURTESY OF THE PORTSMOUTH ATHENAEUM.

5

Fireworks

Let fame to the world sound America's voice;
No intrigue can her sons from their government sever;
Her pride is her Adams—her laws are his choice,
And shall flourish till liberty slumbers forever.
Then unite, heart and hand,
Like Leonidas' band,
And swear to the God of the ocean and land,
That ne'er shall the sons of Columbia be slaves,
While the earth bears a plant or the sea rolls in its waves.

—"The Boston Patriotic Song" also
called "Adams and Liberty"

As Americans celebrated their independence on July 4, 1809, Louisa learned she was going into captivity. At the same time John realized his political resurrection just might become a reality—so he secretly wished.

John had planned to spend Independence Day quietly at his parents' home in Quincy, just outside Boston. A few days before the nation's birthday, he received an invitation to attend the Bunker Hill Association dinner instead. As a down-on-his-luck politician turned Harvard professor and local attorney, he couldn't resist the opportunity to mingle with five hundred of Boston's most prominent men and veterans. He accepted. Former president John Adams acquiesced. He rode to Boston early the morning of July 4 to meet his son so they could attend the morning's official festivities together.

John's Boston home was located at the corner of Frog Lane and Nassau Street, which today are Boylston and Tremont Streets. Not far from the

Central Burying Ground, his house, which he bought in 1806, was part of an expanding metropolis. The town of Boston, America's fourth largest city, would soon boast a population of more than thirty-three thousand in the 1810 US census, up from twenty-five thousand in 1800.

Adams lived in a trade town known for its harbor and commerce, not agriculture. His neighbors made candles, shoes, saddles, clocks, watches, and bells, among many other products. Belonging to Suffolk County, Bostonians now produced more than one million gallons of "distilled spirits made from molasses" and more than six hundred thousand gallons of beer each year. They also made eleven thousand fur hats and ten thousand spectacles.

While many Boston tradesmen preferred to travel by carriage or horseback, Adams and his father enjoyed walking. The pair likely discussed the happenings of the past few days as they strolled down the street and turned to pass the tombstones. John might have talked about how boring life had been recently in the city, as he revealed in his diary a few days earlier when June 1809 came to a close:

> A multitude of little occupations distract my attention and my time to such a degree that I can scarcely observe any of my intended purposes. . . . But instead of reading with [eight-year-old] George, I pass my time until breakfast in arranging books and assorting pamphlets, or writing upon transient topics. I seldom get to my office until 11 or twelve o'clock, and pass most of my afternoons at home. . . . George's instruction and my own have almost entirely failed.

He probably told his father about the most significant occupation of his time: attending the district court, which was hearing cases from the Embargo Act. The proceedings only reminded them of why John was now a professor and attorney in Boston and not a senator in Washington. John Quincy's support of Jefferson's embargo ultimately had forced him to resign his US Senate seat a year earlier, in 1808. The senior John Adams understood his son's dilemma. Returning to private life was as embarrassing as it was boring.

While they walked through the mall toward Beacon Hill, the younger Adams may have broken the unexpected news to his father. He had learned of it the night before, after he accompanied Louisa and her younger sister Kitty to a dinner party at a friend's home.

"After I came home, about 10 in the evening a couple of boys came to my house," he reported in his diary of the tap on his door, which was unusual unless accompanied by a cry of fire. More mysterious was the mission behind the knocking. John explained that the boys "left me with a *National Intelligencer* of 28 June, requesting me after I should have looked over it, to send it to the *Palladium* Office."

Founded in 1800 by publishers who supported Jefferson's administration, the *National Intelligencer* was a prominent Washington City newspaper. The editors of the *New England Palladium* and other Boston newspapers often reprinted national news from the latest *Intelligencer*, which usually arrived in Boston several days after publication. Adams was naturally curious. Someone thought he needed to read the *National Intelligencer* at 10:00 p.m. before Boston's leaders gathered the next day to hear orations commemorating July 4. He quickly discovered why.

"I found in it a paragraph, that on the day before, that is, the 27th of June, the Senate had confirmed the nomination of John Quincy Adams, as Minister Plenipotentiary to the Court of St. Petersburg [Russia]."

Minister plenipotentiary was an official title for the highest-ranking diplomatic position available to a US envoy at the time. His mission was to establish diplomatic ties with Russia and represent the entire US relationship with the mammoth nation.

After attending President James Madison's inauguration in March 1809, John concluded that Madison, who had been Jefferson's secretary of state, was as likely to nominate him for a domestic administration position as Boston's Federalists were to select him again for the US Senate.

Though he was a reserved man, John's letters to his parents frequently revealed his deeper opinions and feelings, which he often concealed from official letters on similar topics to government officials. Because he was close to his father, he most likely shared his conflicting opinions and emotions about the appointment that day and the surprising timing.

The duo probably discussed the cons of accepting the nomination as they walked tirelessly through the Boston Common. Both knew John could promote his personal popularity more with the Federalists by refusing the position because it was offered by Madison, a Jeffersonian Republican. They felt some disappointment, too, because both believed he could have contributed more at home than abroad. They also knew the truth: John's retirement to private life did not shelter him from "the most virulent and unrelenting" persecution by their enemies. Perhaps that alone was reason enough to say yes to the St. Petersburg mission.

As they passed key sights, such as the artillery preparing to launch fireworks later that night, they may have discussed the greater significance of the appointment. At the time the US government boasted only "sixty consuls" serving throughout the world. Though a large number, these low-ranking consuls enjoyed little influence over their foreign hosts. Breadth did not equal depth and certainly not power or overwhelming support. Only three other nations had accepted an American envoy at the higher rank of minister: England, France, and Portugal. The only diplomatic rank higher than minister was ambassador, and America didn't have any of those.

In 1809 the United States was largely a country in name only, with minimal recognition that was often dismissed as England's long-lost prodigal. Not only was it not a superpower, but it was hardly a power at all.

However, if Russia's czar accepted an American minister's credentials— which had never been done before—then the United States would possess official diplomatic ties with the largest country in Europe. On top of that, a true trade alliance with Russia just might force England to abandon its abusive commerce policies against the United States. An alliance with Russia would prove to France's Napoleon once and for all that the United States was no longer a child of Great Britain but a grown-up in its own right. America deserved to be treated as an independent nation. In order to survive, America needed to thrive.

The arguments in favor of accepting Madison's nomination may have soared higher as the two easily climbed Beacon Hill to the State House. The senior Adams would have instantly seen the honor of his son serving as the president's top representative to Russia. The younger Adams looked to "the vague hope of rendering to my country, some important service, as intended by the mission." Topping the list for saying yes was his duty to obey the call of his country.

They both knew the reality that John Quincy faced. Though he could live comfortably the rest of his life as a lawyer and professor, his ambition, like his father's, longed for the public stage. This was the biggest opportunity to do so, the last chance to resurrect his dead political career. Not only that, but serving abroad as one of the nation's top diplomats could also lead to future service on the public square, whether as secretary of state—or, maybe, just maybe—an even higher position back home.

The Adams pair arrived at the State House, whose dome was originally painted gray, not glittering gold as it later became. Both were buoyed by John's sudden change of fortune. They knew word of his appointment would spread throughout Boston just as quickly as the artillery would shoot fireworks from the mall. What could be better than revealing John's new appointment to their friends, Boston's selectmen, and government leaders during the city's revelry of reflections on the American Revolution?

They entered the State House's Senate chamber. From there they processed with the governor, state representatives, senators, and other guests to the Old South Church, where they listened to the town oration commemorating independence and liberty. John Quincy recorded: "While in the church, and immediately after the delivery of the oration, Mr. Shaw gave me several letters, one of which was from the secretary of state, enclosing the commission to St. Petersburg."

Just the day before, he had visited attorney William Smith Shaw, his cousin on his mother's side. Shaw most likely received Adams's commission and letters from the nation's capital after Adams left his office; otherwise John wouldn't have been so surprised when the boys brought him the *National Intelligencer* later that evening. Because Shaw had served as a private secretary to the senior Adams when he was president, he remained loyal to his kin and maintained ties to Washington City. Included in the packet was a letter from John Quincy's friend, Ezekiel Bacon, a Massachusetts congressman.

"So far as your public sentiments and conduct may have an influence on the public mind, your friends would certainly have preferred that the theater of your employments should have been on American ground," the congressman wrote. "Though your friends will not probably accede to the position that it was the best thing, yet they will very readily agree that it was a very good thing."

Bacon put it bluntly: "A mission to the court of St. Petersburg is, to a man of active talents, somewhat like an honorable exile."

Indeed it was.

After the morning ceremonies, John and his father parted ways for the rest of the day. While the senior Adams returned to his son's home, John walked with a friend in the parade to the Bunker Hill dinner.

John loved the parade. If anyone dared heckle him, which was always a possibility among the embargo-hating merchants, he didn't record it. Instead he was caught up in the ambience and pageantry of a Boston Independence Day celebration: "The procession, with various emblems of agriculture, commerce and manufacturers, and consisting of about 500 persons, including those militia companies went through the town, over Charles River bridge, to Bunker Hill, where a dinner was prepared under an arbor covered with a tent and four rows of tables for the company." The grand feast was complete with pastry and an endless number of toasts to Boston, independence, and the nation.

News of his appointment spread quickly. His friend Mr. Austin approached him with an urgent suggestion. His son would be glad to serve as his secretary in St. Petersburg.

"But the application was too late," the flattered Adams commented. Included in the packet of papers that Shaw gave him just hours earlier was a letter of application from William Steuben Smith, the twenty-two-year-old son of John's older sister Nabby. Smith wanted to serve as John's private secretary. Adams already had Smith in mind, but smiled at the compliment Austin paid him by inquiring for his son.

John had one more brief obligation to fulfill before returning home. He and his friend left Bunker Hill so he could "pay a visit to young republicans assembled at the Exchange Hotel." Though far from a declared member of Jefferson's party, this former Federalist knew the political benefits of a bipartisan Independence Day celebration. "We stayed there only a few minutes to reciprocate salutations and give toasts after which we retired."

Then it was time to face his wife.

Louisa loved music. She was an accomplished and passionate pianist, singer, and harpist. Five nights earlier, she had entertained her husband and sister after dinner. Neither she nor John Quincy documented the songs she played that late June evening. She would have been familiar with the era's most popular music, including "The Boston Patriotic Song," also called the "Adams and Liberty" song. Through lyrics such as "Let fame to the world sound America's voice. No intrigue can her sons from her government sever" and "her pride is her Adams, his laws are her choice," Robert Treat Paine Jr. of Massachusetts paid tribute to President Adams in 1799. Paine's father, Robert Treat Paine Sr., was a signer of the Declaration of Independence and member of the first Continental Congress with Adams. Like many other songs, this was sung to a popular English melody, "To Anacreon in Heaven," the tune later adopted for "The Star-Spangled Banner," whose lyrics had yet to be written.

Because it was Independence Day, Louisa may have dressed in a fashionable red or blue Empire-style dress with a high waistline under her bosom and a white linen wrapper around her shoulders. With her light brown hair likely piled high on her head in Grecian style, she may have played this and several other patriotic songs on that Fourth of July, which she spent at home with Kitty. Both watched intently over Charles, Louisa and John's youngest son. Not quite two years old, he was recovering from the measles. Between his large ears was a cherubic oval face dotted with spots.

Their oldest son was George, a tall, slim lad resembling Louisa. He was spending as much time as he could that summer in leisure, except when his father insisted that they read together or he practice his penmanship, expectations the eight-year-old struggled to meet.

She likely kept a most observant eye on their middle son, John, the spitting image of his father. John was celebrating his sixth birthday that day. He was also mischievous. A few days earlier he had run away, forcing Adams to spend an entire afternoon walking Boston's cobblestones and searching until he found him.

Exactly how she learned about her husband's nomination that July 4 is a bit of a mystery.

"This day the news arrived of Mr. Adams's appointment to Russia," she wrote.

John may have given her the news. Or her father-in-law may have told her when he returned to her home from the morning's oration after his son received the official paperwork from Shaw. Another possibility is that she found out accidentally. Mr. Everett, one of John's law students, may have broken the news when he dropped a letter by their house that day. Like Mr. Austin at Bunker Hill, as soon as Everett heard of Adams's appointment, he wanted to be the first to apply for the position of secretary.

When Everett gave her his letter of request to pass along to her husband, Louisa may have wondered: *Secretary? For what?* Imagine the hurt she felt if she found out through someone other than her husband. Regardless of who told her, the news was as hard to take as hearing of someone's death.

"I do not know which was the more stunned with the shock," she recorded in her diary, comparing her distress to Kitty's ashen face.

Any joyful singing was instantly replaced with melancholy shock. The idea of moving a family of five to Russia and enduring a sixty-day or longer ocean voyage was enough to make anyone wallow in the tune of a funeral dirge.

Louisa was not surprised to hear about the appointment. Rather, she was shocked because the possibility of John's going to Russia had died an absolute death months earlier. The US Senate had considered him for the post earlier in the year. The senators had not only rejected his nomination but also passed a resolution against the idea. In the minds of the senators, sending any diplomat to Russia—much less one holding the high rank of minister plenipotentiary and also named Adams—was a waste of money and time. What could a faraway place like Russia possibly offer when America's foreign troubles rested squarely with England and France?

Declining a nominee is one thing; refusing to appoint anyone is the same as shoveling dirt on a grave. Such tombstone opposition understandably lured Louisa into completely releasing her worries about moving to St. Petersburg. Someone found a way to resurrect the mission. But who?

That person was none other than Emperor Alexander, Russia's czar. When he followed through on his promise to send an envoy to the United States, Congress had no choice but to act quickly in return. In June 1809 President Madison could not accept the credentials of the recently arrived Russian chargé d'affaires or look him in the eye without making good on the US government's promise to send an envoy to Russia in kind.

The news was a stunner for other reasons too: party politics. By this time a two-party political system was firmly anchored in America. The term *federalist* initially characterized supporters of the new US Constitution in 1787. When the first federal administration began two years later, political "parties were generally deplored." Many thought a republican government should avoid a party system. As a result "President George Washington was able to exercise nonpartisan leadership during the first few years of the new government."

Disagreements over fiscal policies and the French Revolution split Washington's administration, pitting treasury secretary Alexander Hamilton against secretary of state Thomas Jefferson, among others. The Federalists became a solid party by 1796 and elected vice president John Adams to the presidency. Jefferson founded another party, the Republican Party, which was later called the Democratic-Republican Party and Jeffersonian Republicans. This party eventually became today's Democratic Party. John Quincy Adams did not refer to this party as Jeffersonian Republicans or Democratic-Republicans. He used the terms Federalists and Republicans. Though similar in name to Jefferson's party, the modern Republican Party grew out of an anti-slavery movement embodied by Abraham Lincoln.

Despite John's dropping by the Republican celebration that day, Louisa knew her husband was far from a sold-out supporter of the party that had defeated his father. Yet he was no longer a devoted Federalist, either. A politician without a party, Adams was as independent as a boulder between two intersecting streams.

John was aware that the Senate's prior rejection of the post and his nomination had greatly relieved his anxious wife.

"I believe you will not be much disappointed at the failure of the proposition to go to Russia," he understatedly, if not sarcastically, wrote to her in March 1809 from the nation's capital, where he presented arguments to the Supreme Court for a legal case. He strategically leveraged the proceeding's timing to attend Madison's inauguration and ball with Louisa's oldest sister, Nancy, and her husband, who lived on K Street. This gave him an opportunity to see if any other nomination from Madison was possible. It was not.

In that same March 1809 letter, John wrote that he had little "expectation of that or any other appointment; and although I feel myself obliged to the president for his nomination, I shall be better pleased to stay at home than I should have been to go to Russia."

His lack of interest buried the possibility even further. Now he was singing a different but patriotic tune, one of duty and acceptance. All this—Adams's attitude, the political dynamics, and the Senate's reversal—left Louisa feeling betrayed.

"I had been so grossly deceived, every apprehension lulled—And now to come on me with such a shock!" she wailed. The timing was ironic. While celebrating *Independence* Day, Mrs. Adams discovered that she would soon be shackled into a type of diplomatic captivity.

⁓

John could not decline the opportunity to serve his country, especially after his failure in the Senate. What would people think? He could not show any hesitation or coolness to the idea.

"I have determined to go," he confided to a friend in Congress. "I have yet acquiesced in the judgment of those to whom the Constitution has left it, and who have thought best to place me abroad."

Two constitutional organs now called him to duty: the president and the Senate. He could not decline the post any more than he could an appointment to the US Supreme Court. Adams's ambition prevented him from saying no.

"The public service, to a man of independent patriotism, is neither to be solicited nor refused," he later reflected.

⁓

Regardless of feeling deceived, deep in her heart, Louisa knew the truth. Madison had made a wise choice. Her husband was the most qualified citizen to represent the United States in Russia. More than anyone else, he had the experience, skills, and intellect to succeed there.

She also understood the stresses of diplomatic life. Her path had first crossed with Johnny Adams's when they were children. Johnny and his father had visited Louisa's family in Nantes, France, in 1779 before the Adams duo returned to America. Louisa and Johnny had met again in London in 1783 when she was eight years old. He was sixteen.

Louisa didn't get to know John Quincy the man until years later, in London in 1795. By the time he met Louisa again, he was living on his own. He had caught the attention of President Washington, who was so impressed with young John's grasp of international affairs that he named him minister in residence to the Netherlands. Adams later traveled to London for the temporary assignment of exchanging ratifications for a treaty. There he spent many hours at the Johnson household. She was twenty; he was twenty-eight. Assuming at first that he was interested in her older sister Nancy, Louisa felt free to be herself. She played the piano, sang, and revealed her other passions. They fell in love and married two years later.

When the senior Adams became president in 1797, he appointed his son as minister to Prussia. For four years John Quincy and Louisa enjoyed the pleasures and challenges of diplomatic life in Berlin. Their early marriage was set against a backdrop of parties and pretension. They saw both the wickedness and wellspring of European courts. When John Adams lost the presidential election to Jefferson in 1800, the curtain closed on John Quincy's court life in Berlin. Not wanting to give Jefferson the chance to fire or embarrass his son, President Adams recalled Minister Adams from Europe. John and Louisa exited the diplomatic stage and returned home in 1801.

By the time of her husband's Russian appointment in July 1809, Louisa was sufficiently past her newlywed days. The Declaration of Independence was thirty-three years old; Louisa, thirty-four. She was too old to be seduced by the romance of court life.

"I had passed the age when courts are alluring." So she thought.

Louisa knew, too, that if her husband represented America well in Russia, he might reverse his political fortunes at home, something he longed to do more than he would ever admit.

No Independence Day is complete without fireworks, which was how Louisa and John concluded their day. Adams returned to their house about 10:00 p.m., only to discover that his father had already taken his son John back to Quincy—perhaps to give the recent runaway the freedom to roam on an open farm. Everyone else went to a neighbor's home to watch the fireworks from the rooftop.

"They [the fireworks] were principally from the gun house, and the rockets sent up, came down in blazing paper and burning sticks upon a house itself and several of the neighboring houses and yards including mine—in a manner which I thought dangerous," John observed.

What neither John nor Louisa realized at the time was another hazardous possibility. The fireworks between them were just beginning, as intense and equally threatening to their home, marriage, and romance as those blazing paper sticks.

"No accidents of fire however ensued," he recorded of the literal fireworks.

6

Good-bye, Boston Birches

JOHN HANDLED ALL THE ARRANGEMENTS FOR THEIR VOYAGE TO St. Petersburg, including packing and cataloging crates and crates of books, transferring his law cases to his brother Thomas, settling his finances, delivering his last lecture, resigning from Harvard, and drawing up his final will and testament. Although it was not unusual for a husband to make such business decisions, many choices bothered Louisa's more liberal leanings about the capabilities of the female sex.

"Every preparation was made without the slightest consultation with me," she wrote in her diary. Worst of all, John made the most important decision affecting her life and their marriage: he chose to leave their oldest boys behind in Boston.

"And even the disposal of my children and my sister was fixed without my knowledge until it was too late to change," Louisa lamented over the man-made earthquake breaking up her family. The plan was as carved in stone as an epitaph on a grave—Louisa's. At least that's how it felt to her.

The decision came just two weeks before their departure. On July 22 Abigail Adams dined with John Quincy in Boston. John Quincy took George with him so the youngster could return with his grandmother to Peacefield, the family homestead in Quincy. His father had named this estate *Peacefield* in 1796 as a reminder of the peace between England and America that he'd helped broker to end the Revolutionary War in 1783. With such a name, Peacefield was a continual reminder of John Adams's unsurpassable legacy.

The younger John had been with his grandparents since July 4. Perhaps assuming that her boys would feel trapped by the ship on such a long ocean voyage, Louisa probably didn't mind if they spent a few more days with their grandparents at the farm.

The next day Adams and his father visited a local teacher, who agreed to educate George. Then he paid Aunt and Uncle Cranch to board his sons at their nearby home. The senior Adams had known Richard Cranch for years. He attended Cranch's wedding to Mary Smith in 1762. John later courted Mary's young sister, Abigail, and married her in 1764. Because Abigail had maintained a close relationship with her sister, John Quincy knew his sons would be in good hands. Thus the Adams men implemented the plan. The older boys would stay behind in America under the care of their grandparents and great-aunt and -uncle, while Louisa and toddler Charles accompanied Minister Adams to Russia.

"Judge Adams was commissioned to inform me of all this as it admitted of no change," she documented of her brother-in-law's role in giving her the news.

No matter the customs of the day dictating male-female decision making, Louisa felt betrayed. Perhaps she saw her marriage differently. Hadn't he chosen the Genesis model to leave his family and cleave to her? Out of courtesy to her and her role as mother, why didn't he consult her? If he loved her, why didn't he tell her instead of sending Thomas? Was he cold? Cowardly? Or was his heart too sensitive to be the one to break the news to her?

Louisa pleaded. As in the case of death, no amount of mourning could change the outcome. Without recourse, legal or otherwise, she quickly descended into depression.

"O it was too hard! Not a soul entered into my feelings and all laughed to scorn my suffering at crying out that it was affectation."

Affectation means "pretension" or "pretending." How dare they insinuate her reaction was an act of theatrical emotion! She was experiencing the genuine heartache of a mother losing her children and her God-given responsibility to raise them. The Adams men knew of her previous losses. She was no Shakespeare. She was not drafting a drama or acting out a part but merely pouring out her heart.

Louisa's in-laws had made similar sacrifices. John and Abigail had lived apart for most of the Revolutionary War. Abigail had cared for four children in Massachusetts while he served in the Continental Congress in Philadelphia and later abroad.

The senior Adams knew all too well the temptations of European court life. He had witnessed the ways of the French court when he lobbied for the

American cause. Perhaps forgetting the academic education John Quincy had received in Paris, he wanted to shield his grandsons from the depraved morals of similar circles. Or maybe the old man was simply prioritizing his lineage's survival. If something happened to John, Louisa, and Charles on their travels, then at least the Adams line would continue through the male heirs left behind.

"On the 4 of August we sailed for Boston. I having been taken to Quincy to see my two boys and not being permitted to speak with the old gentleman alone, lest I should excite his pity and he allow me to take my boys with me."

Louisa was permitted to say good-bye to her sons but not to her father-in-law. He couldn't bear to hear the cracking of her voice as she tried to reassure George and John that she loved them. He couldn't watch the torrent of tears streaming from her doelike eyes. Her journal might have given him a heart attack, had he been privileged enough to read it.

"Oh this agony of agonies! Can ambition repay such sacrifices? Never!!" she wrote.

Her sons would grow tall and strong, like the birches of Boston, in her absence. As she bid adieu to America, Louisa's paper diary proved her safest refuge for weeping. She wrote with abandon, as if the pages were her best friend. And they were. Here she felt safe to pour out her deepest feelings, her dark thoughts. No matter that others thought the choice was logical; she understandably lacked hope for her future and her sons.

"And from that hour to the end of time life to me will be a succession of miseries only to cease with existence," she wrote. No reasonable arguments could erase reality. Louisa was being separated from her children against her will—a heartbreaking way to start a dangerous journey into the unknown.

———

With the conspiracy unraveled and the plan fixed, a captive Mrs. Adams and her husband bid adieu to America on August 5, 1809. Closing the door of their home at Frog Lane and Nassau Street, they traveled by carriage a little more than two miles to Gray's Wharf, owned by William Gray. There they boarded the *Horace,* one of Gray's merchant vessels assigned to take them all the way to St. Petersburg. Built in Durham, New Hampshire, in 1800, the

Horace weighed 382 tons. They departed in this three-mast, square-sailed boat just as the church bells rang at one o'clock in the afternoon.

John feared they had already left too late. After Gray told him the waters leading to St. Petersburg could freeze as early as October, Adams decided to embark no later than the end of July. Several logistical delays stalled their departure. Finally they had all they needed to set sail by August 5.

Fanfare followed them from the wharf. Ships in the Navy Yard saluted them. A garrison from Fort Independence marched and paraded as they passed. When the captain of a revenue cutter saw them, he sent an officer in a rowboat to extend well wishes for a safe intercontinental journey. The crew of the six-gun *Horace* returned these salutes. Guided by fair wind supported by fresh breezes, they couldn't have asked for a better bon voyage as they left the bonds and birch trees of Boston and sailed toward a Russian destination.

No sooner did she step onto the deck's wooden planks than Louisa regretted leaving her oldest boys behind. Guilt consumed her faster than seasickness.

"A man can take care of himself—And if he abandons one part of his family he soon learns that he might as well leave them all—I do not mean to suggest the smallest reproach—It was thought right and judicious by wiser heads than mine but I alone suffered the penalty—They are known only to God," Louisa recorded of her heartache. This was her way of forgiving her father-in-law and husband, or at least an attempt at it.

Though he often hid his passions from public view, Adams was not indifferent to leaving his children behind; far from it.

"It is with a deep sense of the stormy and dangerous career upon which I enter; of the heavy responsibility that will press upon it, and of the unpromising prospect which it presents in perspective," he wrote in his diary on July 5, 1809, after sending his acceptance letter to President Madison.

"My personal motives for staying at home are of the strongest kind; the age of my parents, and of the infancy of my children, both urge to the same result," he reflected on why he ought to turn down the appointment.

Nevertheless, he could not say no to his country's call. Because he believed the president's motive was for the "welfare of the whole union," he intended to devote all his powers to earning Madison's trust.

He bade good-bye to his sons in a separate visit at his parents' home.

Though he claimed he was too busy making preparations—and his diary is full of the many details he finalized before leaving—he may have hidden the truth from his journal. Knowing they were not unified in the decision, he likely couldn't bear to accompany Louisa to Quincy and say good-bye together.

Worrying that they might not survive the voyage, he also implored "the blessings of Almighty God, upon this my undertaking . . . and prepared alike for whatever event his Providence destines for its termination."

John, Louisa, and Charles were not the only players on this nautical stage set. Joining them was Catherine, nicknamed Kitty. The presence of Kitty, too, was forced upon Louisa. Of the seven daughters and one son in the Johnson clan, Louisa was second oldest; Kitty, the third youngest. In preparing for the voyage, John asked Thomas for advice on what to do about his sister-in-law: "I also enquired of him if Catherine Johnson should not go with us."

Thomas and John's sister, Nabby, had accompanied their mother to England and France years earlier in 1784. Thomas agreed that Louisa would benefit from the company of an American female companion. Louisa most assuredly loved Kitty, but she did not want to parent her. With their father deceased and their mother impoverished, Kitty needed Louisa to take care of her. Thus societal customs thrust Mrs. Adams into a chaperone for a very flirtatious woman in her early twenties on a ship filled with single men.

As planned from the beginning, nephew William Smith served as John's secretary. Nine other men applied or inquired on behalf of a son or other male relative for the position of secretary to the new minister to Russia. While keeping his outer reserve in check, John was flattered by the attention. Everyone wanted to accompany him to St. Petersburg except one person—his wife.

Though he couldn't solve that problem, he found a way to satisfy the demand and fill a need. With permission from the secretary of state, he allowed a few of these men, those with the greatest character and loyalty to country, to go as attachés. John made sure, however, that they would not drain the US Treasury. He informed them: "[T]hey should go altogether at their own expense and occasion no charge to the government." Three agreed: Francis Gray, Alexander Everett, and John Spear Smith.

Francis was Mr. Gray's son. The richest man in America at the time, Gray owned the *Horace* among thirty or more ships. He was one of the few who had stood by Adams when he resigned in defeat from the Senate. He trusted John so much that he was willing to send his son with him to Russia. There Francis could see the Baltic trade world with his own eyes and return to Boston to steer the family business.

A recent graduate, Everett had been studying law under John's tutelage at his Boston law office. Joining them later and traveling separately was John Spear Smith, nephew of secretary of state Robert Smith. Adams also brought with him two servants: Nelson, a free black domestic from Trinidad, and Martha Godfrey, Louisa's chambermaid.

"Our voyage was very tedious—All but Mr. Adams and Mr. Smith very sick and as usual I having the whole care of the child, who suffered as much as any of us," Louisa wrote from her nautical prison somewhere across the Atlantic Ocean.

The rolling of the boat as it rocked in the waves and winds was too much. At first the most common smell aboard ship was vomit, whose putrid fumes permeated their cabins as motion sickness got the better of them. No matter the delightful sighting of dolphins or the abundant catch of cod off the coast of Newfoundland—seasickness abounded.

Louisa became seasick the first time she traveled by ship with her husband. Leaving London in 1797 a few months after their wedding, the newlyweds crossed the North Sea toward the mouth of the Elbe River on their journey to Berlin, where Adams was to be a diplomatic minister. Back then she had an added excuse for her nausea; she was pregnant. Many disappointments had come since, but some things remained as constant as the stars. No matter her condition, beginning an ocean voyage still made her seasick; John always had the stomach of a seasoned sailor.

"I scarcely perceive that we are at sea," John wrote. Such thoughts were a sharp contrast to his wife's. Their opinions were so opposite, they seemed to be taking different trips. To him, the open ocean was an oasis. He spent his days reading and scouring sermons, the Bible, and books on geography and fish. "There is much time for study and meditation," he observed. "The rest of mankind seem to be inhabitants of another planet."

John played cards and daily recorded the temperature, latitude, and longitude as they crossed the Atlantic toward Scotland. He loved his thermometer so much that he called it his "amusement." But he longed for more. He decided a celestial globe would have been an "agreeable companion" for such a voyage. Dating from ancient Greece, celestial globes depicted stars and constellations as they appear in the sky. These decorative ornaments were also useful for astronomical calculations.

What he really needed was a device to heal his wife's heart and the foresight to turn around and take his boys with him. In his journal John called the enterprise before him "perhaps the most important of any that I have ever in the course of my life been engaged in." He again implored the blessings of Providence on his mission, for the benefit of his country and family.

While John vanished into his books, an unwell, headache-prone Louisa poured herself into caring for Charles. Both were sick night and day. How did a two-year-old react to seasickness? Vomiting is unpleasant to anyone, but at least an adult knows what's going on. Unlike a baby who spits up on occasion, a two-year-old is aware that something awful, uncomfortable, and frightening is happening.

As ill as her son was, Louisa was grateful just to be able to hug him. He was the last child she had. "Broken hearted miserable, *alone* in every feeling; my boy was my only comfort," she reflected.

Louisa carried one hope: this venture would be a one-act or two-act play at the most. "I had thought that one year would have been the extent of my stay," she later wrote. If all went well and Russia's emperor accepted her husband's credentials, then she would remove her costume as a diplomat's wife and return home in year to give a thousand kisses to George and John.

While hope of reunion kept Louisa sane, John focused on the immediate outlook. Though mindful of the difficulties of sea travel, he basked in the distinctive difference from this journey and the ocean voyages he undertook during the height of the American Revolution. Concluding that England had revoked its policies and now recognized American trade rights after recent negotiations, President Madison had recently reopened trade with England.

By June 1809 more than six hundred American merchant ships had embarked for Europe.

"The dangers of war . . . do not threaten us now," John wrote of the policy change.

So he thought.

———

Wind direction is critical for a sailing ship's success. Wonderful weather followed the *Horace* from Boston across the Atlantic, around Scotland, and into the North Sea. Their voyage progressed without interruption until they reached the Norwegian coast on September 17, 1809.

Although the day had started with a picturesque panorama of steep, rugged mountains, Louisa noticed they hadn't passed a vessel since leaving the previous port. The sea was empty of ships. She soon discovered the reason when a tempest rolled in and stole the scenic show.

With sharklike speed, a storm seized the *Horace* and shook its sails. Clouds hovered. Heavy winds blew the ship across the water. Louisa described the swell or rising waves as "frightful." The water seemed to climb as high as Norway's nearby mountains before suddenly toppling the ship's sides.

"It was dusk, the wind blowing in squalls like a gale with a very heavy sea," Louisa recorded. How did she keep Charles calm during the tempest and lightning flashes? This situation wasn't pretend. These storms were real. While tightly hugging Charles, Louisa thought continually of the boys she had abandoned.

"If it was to do again nothing on earth could induce me to make such a sacrifice and my conviction is that if domestic separation is absolutely necessary, cling as a mother to those innocent and helpless creatures whom God himself has given to your charge."

In the midst of this turbulence, she heard an explosion—cannon fire from a nearby brig. Captain Beckford responded by ordering his crew to hoist the colors. Within an hour the firing brig was within signaling distance and hailed the *Horace*. Beckford answered their questions with customary signals. The brig's commander doubted that they hailed from Boston and were traveling to St. Petersburg on a diplomatic voyage. He twice signaled the *Horace* to send

Beckford to his ship. With no response, he reinforced his order by hurling a musket ball into the *Horace*'s side.

Beckford was hot. The brig had yet to show her colors. Such arrogance! He rightly feared his rowboat wouldn't survive the storm's swell. Ordering him to row to the brig was akin to expecting a modern skydiver to jump out of a plane in low visibility with twenty-mile-an-hour or stronger winds. Both are death wishes.

Not wanting a fight, Beckford and four sailors boarded the small boat and began rowing toward the brig. Within ten minutes they realized they couldn't reach it and doubted they could safely return to the *Horace*. The rowboat was half full of water.

Suddenly a large wave crashed over the rowboat's side. Louisa trembled as she heard them cry out that they "could not live."

7

Danish Prey

THE STORM CONTINUED, THROWING WAVES OVER THE ROWBOAT. Captain Beckford's clarity of thinking prevailed. Abandoning the ridiculous scheme of trying to reach the brig, he reversed course and safely returned the rowboat to the *Horace.*

"All this time the boat and people were in the most imminent danger but got on board at last," Louisa wrote with relief.

From the *Horace's* helm, a thoroughly soaked captain hailed the brig again. No answer. Within a few minutes, the anonymous boat gave up. Beckford waited until the ship was as far away as the moon before resuming the *Horace's* route.

Mystery lurked behind the masts in Norway, which was then ruled by Denmark. Because this brig never hoisted its colors, they were left to question its identity. Was it Danish or English? English, John decided, because no other armed ships would dare monitor that particular coast. He knew British nautical ways all too well. In fact, it was an English ship that had exiled him from the US Senate, at least indirectly.

———✦———

Two years earlier, the HMS *Leopard* had caused a major international incident when it bombarded the USS *Chesapeake,* an American naval vessel, off the coast of Norfolk, Virginia. Three Americans were killed, eighteen wounded. "The *Chesapeake-Leopard* incident was the most important naval confrontation between the United States and Britain" since the American Revolution. Though on a different scale of destruction, the emotional impact on the nation was similar to the attack on Pearl Harbor on December 7, 1941, and the terrorist attacks on the World Trade Center and Pentagon on September 11, 2001.

The British seized four sailors from the *Chesapeake* on June 22, 1807. Claiming a right to do so, the *Leopard*'s captain said he was merely recovering British navy deserters. Americans viewed his actions very differently, believing his real aim was to impress or take Americans from the *Chesapeake* and force them to serve in the British navy—potentially against their homeland.

How dare the British spit on American sovereignty! President Thomas Jefferson secretly retaliated by asking Congress to pass an embargo preventing US merchant ships from trading with Great Britain and other European nations. New England merchants traded with English merchants more than any other foreign entity. Already suffering from the war between commercial Britain and agricultural France, those Americans dependent on the shipping trade for income would lose their livelihoods from an embargo.

In addition Jefferson learned that the British government released a proclamation to continue its policy of impressment. This allowed British captains and generals to seize English subjects or anyone that they thought was English and force them to serve in the British military. Thus they could ignore a sailor's citizenship papers from America.

John was a US senator from Massachusetts at the time and a member of the committee that recommended the embargo to the full Senate. When he read the committee's intelligence reports, he knew what he must do. Impressment must stop. He concluded that an embargo on foreign trade—all of it—would save the lives of hundreds of merchant sailors. Supporting Jefferson's embargo was the most agonizing decision of his public career.

Many people in Massachusetts were so angry about the embargo that they threatened to secede from the Union. Federalists couldn't understand why John—one of their most favorite native sons—supported *Jefferson's* embargo. After all, Jefferson defeated his father for the presidency in 1800.

Adams wrote his mother, saying these trials "have been severe beyond any that I ever was before called to meet." He was more concerned about keeping the American people safe than angering Boston merchants or aligning himself with his father's political rival.

"I was sworn to support the Constitution of the United States, and I thought it was my duty to support the existing administration in every measure that my impartial judgment could approve." John later told a friend that he needed to take a stand against the English bullies and their kidnapping ways. He put the greater needs of the Union ahead of the economic needs of his commonwealth. The *Chesapeake-Leopard* affair turned a topsy-turvy trade situation into a trajectory for future battles. If successful, the embargo might prevent war.

John's decision cost him. Back then citizens did not vote directly for their US senators; instead, members of state legislatures made the choice. When the Massachusetts legislature decided not to support his reelection in June 1808 and chose someone else, John immediately resigned his Senate seat rather than wait out his term.

As he explained in his resignation letter, he supported the embargo "to preserve from seizure and depredation the persons and property of our citizens." He also wanted to "vindicate the rights essential to the independence of our country, against the unjust pretensions and aggressions of all foreign powers."

Revenge for his father did not play a role.

"I have been obliged to act upon principles exclusively my own," he confessed to Abigail, "and without having any aid from the party in power have made myself the very mark of the most envenomed shafts from their opponents."

He could not sacrifice the peace of the nation or "the personal liberties of our seamen or the neutral rights of our commerce" for the sake of party politics. "I discharged my duty to my country, but I committed the unpardonable sin against *party*." Union and independence, not allegiance to party, guided his choice.

"It was not without a painful sacrifice of feeling that I withdrew from the public service at a moment of difficulty and danger," he wrote. They abandoned him, "discarded me for the future, and required me to aid them in promoting measures tending to dissolve the Union."

He faced his fate. "I was no representative for *them*. These were the immediate causes of my retirement from public life."

Indeed his father's views on a man's conscience fit his son's situation. "Upon common theaters, indeed, the applause of the audience is of more importance to the actors than their own approbation," the senior John Adams wrote to a friend years earlier. "But upon the stage of life, while conscience claps, let the world hiss! On the contrary if conscience disapproves, the loudest applauses of the world are of little value."

A significant change, however, took place between John Quincy's resignation in June 1808 and his Russian appointment in June 1809. Just before Jefferson left office, he altered his embargo policy. Congress overturned the Embargo Act and replaced it with the Non-Intercourse Act, which allowed American merchant ships to trade with any nation except Britain and France. Jefferson and the newly elected Madison hoped to keep American trade neutral between those two competing powers while opening the United States to other trading partners such as Portugal, Prussia, and Russia.

———

Nature does not care about the supremacy of nations or conflicts over trade. She freely throws waves on ships no matter their country of origin.

Thus, the *Horace* sailed along Norway in weather duress. Its captive passengers endured a storm for more than twenty-four hours, an eternity for a heartbroken woman caring for a two-year-old child. The ship rolled and pitched so much that Louisa rightfully feared the *Horace* would overturn.

The next day gave them the weather break they needed. From a narrow nook, they relaxed and enjoyed the reflection of the morning dew on the pink-and-gray granite rock of the sea mountains towering over them. Norway features hundreds of these fjords, U-shaped valleys cut into the land by enormous glaciers eons earlier. The glaciers polished the rocks, licking them clean of soil. As the glaciers receded, the ocean filled the void, leaving fjords. The deepest fjord in Norway plunges more than four thousand feet. By noon they settled snugly on top of one of these deep sleeves.

At this time they were traveling east between the coasts of Norway and Jutland, Denmark's mainland peninsula. Norway was to their north; Jutland south. The North Sea, where they had just passed, was west. To their immediate east was the Kattegat Sea, the narrow water separating Denmark from Sweden.

Captain Beckford's plan was to swoop southeast through the Kattegat and the straits of Denmark, which connected to the Baltic Sea. From there they would travel hundreds of miles northeast through the Baltic and into the Gulf of Finland. St. Petersburg rested at the far eastern corner of the Gulf of

Finland. They had a long way to go but had made good time so far. For now they were safely tucked in a narrow Norwegian nook.

"We had a quiet night," Louisa wrote with relief. She soon discovered why she saw so few ships the day before: "We were awakened this morning with the news that an English Cruiser was near us."

No matter the beauty of Norway, a nuisance now appeared from nowhere. An eighteen-gun brig suddenly lay alongside the *Horace*. Unlike the previous ship, this new character's identity was quite clear. She boldly displayed English colors and soon sent a rowboat to the *Horace*. Four men boarded with so much confidence that they marched around the wooden barrels and riggings as if they were the owners, not guests. After examining Beckford's papers, an officer said, "I suppose you may proceed."

Such a statement proved to be truly generous.

"He said it was fortunate that he had not seen us last night, as he should have fired into us supposing it [the *Horace*] was [a Danish ship]," Louisa noted.

The officer boasted that his English brig chased not one, but two, Danish men-of-war the previous day.

John's prediction that war did not threaten their voyage was mistaken. Although the United States was not at war, the English and the Danish obviously were. The reason stemmed from a significant event two years earlier, when the British navy captured more than forty large Danish-Norwegian ships and bombarded Copenhagen. Instead of turning the Danes into forced allies as the English hoped, the outcome turned Denmark into an enemy of England and a friend of France. The British navy responded by blockading the water route connecting Denmark and Norway.

Jefferson's and Madison's policies of neutrality didn't matter in these waters. With the US flag topping her rigging, the *Horace* ventured around Norway with little assurance. Two great white sharks were chasing a red, white, and bluefin tuna.

⤙⤚

Sailing with uneasiness, the captain couldn't dismiss the British officer's confession that he had nearly fired on the *Horace* after mistaking her for a Danish ship. To fire without knowing a ship's colors was as cheeky as it was reckless. Then again, what else could he expect from the likes of the British?

Captain Benjamin Beckford of Beverly, Massachusetts, would never forget the first time he witnessed English arrogance. He was a mere lad, not quite seventeen, when his company, along with William Gray, rushed to Lexington to keep British soldiers from seizing the town's military supplies. He would always remember the sulfurous smell of gunpowder clouding the rising sun that day, April 19, 1775. Ask anyone from Beverly. It was the redcoats who'd fired those first shots at Lexington and Concord launching the Revolutionary War. As a Massachusetts newspaper recorded, "The troops of His Britannic Majesty commenced hostilities upon the people of this province."

Two years later Beckford married. In between nearly a dozen voyages to St. Petersburg, he sired eight children. William Gray often paid captains like Beckford a monthly wage of twenty-five dollars with a commission from the sale of cargo. As experienced as the captain was at age fifty-one, he had never carried such valuable cargo as the son of a former US president.

For two hours Beckford sailed the *Horace* along the Norwegian coast. Finally he saw it. Another ship came within view. Would she fire freely?

Her colors were Danish. Full speed ahead, he ordered. Before he could flee, the brig fired a signal requesting to inspect the *Horace*. Beckford's impatience increased with each passing second as the curious ship took thirty minutes to pass the stern. She hailed the usual questions: Where are you from? Why are you in these waters? Where are you going?

After receiving Beckford's answers, the ship suddenly lowered her Danish flag and hoisted English colors instead. Such mast maneuvering made her even more mysterious—and possibly dangerous. Not believing Beckford's answer or understanding his signals, the mysterious ship's captain sent a boat over to the *Horace*.

When an officer and four men boarded, they confirmed their ship's identity. The sounds of a British accent were obvious in the officer's voice. After examining Beckford's papers, the Englishman notified his captain of the *Horace*'s identity and mission.

"The boat soon returned with an answer that we might proceed without interruption having a minister onboard," Louisa documented.

They were allowed to proceed for one reason: John's position as an envoy. Because the *Horace*'s mission was to deliver a diplomat to a distant shore, the British captain honored the law of customs and allowed them to continue. How many more times would they have to endure such inspections and intrusions? Would John's paperwork continue to be their best olive branch? They could only hope.

Beckford's wavy hair tightly framed his face as if wearing a bowl on his head. Under such duress, the sweat from his brow must have crusted his hair to his forehead as he worried about encountering a ship too cavalier to hold its fire.

Soon they came within sight of Kristiansand, Norway. Beckford made a decision. The horizon again looked troublesome, blackened by another storm.

Sailing ships with square sails must head into the wind from forty-five- to sixty-degree angles. Because the process of going into the wind is labor-intensive, Beckford decided that they should put in there or go into the harbor to replenish their supplies while they waited for the storm to pass and catch a more favorable wind. Seeing the shallow waters, he decided to hire help.

"We sent for a pilot," Louisa wrote in her diary. In the preindustrial nautical world, a *pilot* was someone who knew the local waters. Just as regional drivers directed a coach on land from post to post, so pilots temporarily boarded and steered ships through their hometown's shallow ports and channels, which were also called canals or grounds. The *Oxford English Dictionary* traces the term *pilot* to 1481.

A pilot quickly responded to Beckford's signal and rowed out to the ship, but so did another vessel. Sweeping alongside the *Horace* was a smaller two-mast boat with a swivel gun. On board were twenty armed sailors.

The swivel boat signaled. Beckford complied. A Danish lieutenant came onto the *Horace*'s quarterdeck, the area reserved for officers. Instead of asking questions, he issued commands, ordering Beckford to go to Kristiansand.

"The captain became alarmed and declared he would not put [in] anywhere," Louisa observed.

Volunteering to go to Kristiansand was one thing; being ordered to do so was another. Beckford directed his crew to turn the *Horace* around toward the sea.

The lieutenant countersignaled, ordering the twenty armed men on the swivel boat to board and take possession of the *Horace*. Carrying pikes in their tentacles, these sailors crept onto the deck.

Beckford signaled. The *Horace*'s crew drew their swords. Soon clear-eyed Danes and Norwegians stared into angry-eyed Americans. Sword to sword. Axe to axe. Pike to pike.

"I was perfectly indignant at being taken by this boat," Louisa said.

What would it have been like for her in this moment? She certainly felt anxious for her own life, but as a mother, she felt even more protective of her son, the only one she had left to care for. Most likely she, Kitty, and Martha made sure the toddler was secured in their cabin. There they could hide him from the intruders. Charles likely didn't see the drawn swords, but he must have heard the piratelike shouts above him.

Although shielding her six- and eight-year-old boys would have been even more challenging, Louisa would have gladly done so with the fierceness of the sirens of the sea just to have George and John with her. As single women, Kitty and Martha were at risk of assault. Under these circumstances, their cabin was the safest place of refuge.

"The lieutenant, however, made a signal to them to withdraw—He and the pilot were afraid the captain would carry them out to sea," she noted.

Beckford was angry enough to drag those Danes into the deep. A near-international incident came within a pike's pointed tip. Imagine what might have happened had the Danes captured or worse, sunk, the very ship carrying the newly appointed minister to Russia and the son of a former US president. War! Indeed.

The confrontation revealed the root problem of American-European relations. Though America was technically an independent power completely separate from England, it was hardly a power, much less a superpower. It was a country in name only, if that. Aye, there was the rub.

Years earlier as a young diplomat to Prussia, which was a German-run kingdom that included Germany and portions of Poland, John experienced a similar dilemma firsthand. When he and Louisa arrived at the gates of Berlin in 1797, a German soldier accosted him. He wouldn't let them pass because he didn't know "who the United States of America were." Another soldier intervened, allowing them to enter Berlin. European perceptions apparently had not changed much since then.

The United States had lived under its Constitution only twenty years. Didn't Americans and Britons speak the King's English? Of course! Though the accents were different even at this early time, most Europeans considered anyone who spoke English to be British. This was the justification that English captains used to impress American sailors into the British navy and why the Danes were suspicious of US merchant ships.

The Danish lieutenant didn't believe Beckford's story for one simple reason. He feared that the *Horace*'s crew members, mostly local boys from Boston, were really English sailors in disguise.

As clear as the lens of a spyglass, this latest clash revealed the truth that John and Louisa now faced. Storms were not the only danger that might prevent them from reaching St. Petersburg. Pretension was just as powerful a force. Too many English ships paraded as American ones, hoisting the Stars and Stripes instead of Great Britain's Union Jack flag. Though the *Horace* was as independent as the bald eagle, to Danish and English sharks, this eagle might as well have been a seagull—prey to be devoured, not respected as an independent creature.

8

Three Hundred Americans

As soon as the Danish swivel boat sped away, Captain Beckford set sail again, traveling southwest a mere four more miles and docking safely in Flekkerøy. Before them was an oasis: a fishing village set among jagged rocks, white sailing boats, and neat red-and-white wooden houses topped by steep red roofs. The charming sight was a welcome relief from the danger they had just faced.

The next morning Beckford and a few crew members boarded their rowboat and paddled to Kristiansand to present the ship's papers to local authorities there. Though he returned to the *Horace* with a pass to proceed, he also brought Adams disturbing news from a man named Isaacson.

"They found the captains of nearly thirty American vessels, which have been brought into Kristiansand since last May by privateers, and are detained for adjudication," John recorded of the outrage.

Using private boats to capture them, Danish authorities were detaining three hundred American sailors and captains against their will. "I went immediately to Mr. Isaacson's."

⌁

Mr. Isaacson lived in one of Kristiansand's neat wooden fishing houses. Friendly to the Americans detained there, he explained to John what had happened. Over four months, the Danes had captured dozens of US merchant vessels and put their captains and crew on trial. A Danish lower court condemned half of their cargoes. They were waiting on their appeal to the admiralty court. The rest had yet to undergo a trial. Though not imprisoned or chained, no one was allowed to leave.

The reality was strong and clear. No wonder the Danish swivel boat officer ordered them to Kristiansand. That was why he was so quick to command his men to draw swords against them. He wanted to impound the *Horace* too. Capturing American ships and their valuable colonial cargo was as commonplace in Danish-controlled Norway as ice fishing in winter.

Adams also learned that the detained Americans were waiting for *him*. After reading about his appointment in newspapers, the captains sent letters addressed to Minister Adams in St. Petersburg. Anticipating he would stop in Norway or Denmark on his voyage, the captains also sent him letters to the US consul in Elsinore, about 250 miles away. In addition they mailed copies of their papers to Levitt Harris, the US consul in St. Petersburg, and to President Madison in Washington.

Adams's banishment might be their salvation. He was their best hope.

The lawyer in John emerged with all deliberate speed and due process. With the help of his attachés Gray, Everett, and Smith, he immediately sent messages to the governor of the city, the commandant of the garrison, and the admiral of the nearby naval force. He tried to talk to any authority who would listen.

By dusk the final answer came. No one was available for a meeting. That night the Adams party dined at Isaacson's house.

"Mr. Isaacson, an agent for American seamen, a very gentlemanly man," Louisa wrote of her refreshing break from her nautical prison cell. "We all had a charming dinner in this little nook in Norway."

Twenty of the detained Americans joined them that night, which allowed John to see the problem with his own eyes. What he saw horrified him, gripping his patriotic heart as much as the bombardment of the *Chesapeake* had two years earlier.

Possibly while drinking ale and eating mackerel, a fish common to the area, the captains showed John their condemnation sentences and minutes of their proceedings in the Danish courts. Esquire Adams peppered them with questions, such as:

Did you understand the charges against you?

No.

Did you have a translator?

No.

Did they think you were British in disguise?

Yes.

"The sight of so many of my countrymen, in circumstances so distressing, is very painful and each of them has a story to tell of their peculiar aggravations of ill treatment which he has received," John wrote of his anguish.

He was indignant. What crime had these US sailors committed? Practicing the merchant trade? He expected to hear of such atrocities by the Brits, but not the Danes. These American sailors were merely guilty of speaking in their native tongue.

What also emerged was the evil side of economics. The Danes were requiring them to pay for their detainment, including their lodging, food, and ship-harboring expenses. All conveniently boosted the local economy.

The detainment of these three hundred Americans underscored the great overarching reality. Until the United States was allowed to freely trade with other nations, it would remain a country without true sovereignty.

"The desire of contributing to their relief is so strong in me, that I shall, without waiting for express authority from the government of the United States, use every effort of my power on their behalf to however little purpose it may be as to its success." John concluded that if their cases were heard on their merits and appropriately translated, then the captains and crews should be freed from Kristiansand and allowed to resume their trade business.

At dinner he made a decision. He would stop in Elsinore along their planned route through the Kattegat. From there he would travel to Copenhagen by coach. No matter the delay. As much as he needed to reach St. Petersburg, he absolutely must go to Copenhagen.

"They request my interposition with the Danish government in their behalf, and although having no authority from my government to speak officially to the court of Denmark, my good offices may probably be of little or no avail to them. I propose, however, to attempt a representation in their favor at Copenhagen."

John could hardly wait. He didn't have to be in St. Petersburg to duel in diplomacy. This protagonist had a new mission: advocate for his fellow countrymen in Denmark.

"We are ready to proceed upon our voyage, and I shall put to sea the first moment that wind and weather will permit," John wrote with captain-like control.

Louisa was also touched by their plight. She may have been going to St. Petersburg against the wishes of her heart, but the stories of these sailors reminded her of a different truth: she was not under legal confinement. She wasn't in jeopardy of losing her cargo and only source of income. She wasn't in danger of becoming a beggar on the street without enough money to pay for a return voyage home.

Weather would not permit an immediate voyage to Elsinore, however. The date was September 21, 1809, near the day "when the sun crosses the line." This was the autumn equinox, the time of year when the days and nights grow closer and closer in length until equal. Then they slowly switch, with nights becoming longer and days shorter. Unfavorable sailing winds or "equinoctial gales" prohibited the *Horace* from sailing immediately. Heavy wind and continual rain confined them. As anxious as they were to leave Norway, nature now imprisoned them.

"Mr. Isaacson to his great inconvenience accommodated us all with lodgings, where we were compelled to stay until the next evening," Louisa explained.

John was so ready to sail that by 2:00 p.m. the next day, he decided they were leaving Isaacson's house anyway, despite the wily weather.

"Mr. Adams obliged us to return to the ship in a heavy gale, and that night we sailed," she wrote of his Noah-like determination.

Hence they set sail under poor weather conditions into one of the most difficult waterways in the world, the Kattegat Sea. The name comes from the Dutch words for cat and hole, called a *gat*. *Kattegat* simply means "cat hole." During medieval times captains described these straits and their many reefs as so narrow and shallow that not even a cat could squeeze through them.

Not long after their departure, Louisa made an interesting observation: "We saw four or five vessels ashore."

No one else was out gallivanting in the cat hole. She was not surprised at her husband's skipper-like decision to go forward. Public service was more important to him than anything else. John was as predictable as his timepiece. His purpose in life, his very existence, was to be useful to mankind. Serving the public, especially seeking justice for others, was paramount. Mrs. Adams understood her husband's motivation to get to Copenhagen. Justice was a respectable ambition, something the son of John Adams could not refuse.

⌁

As the *Horace* sailed for Elsinore, the pounding of the ship was greater than at any previous time in their voyage. The ship rolled, pitched, and heaved all at the same time. Once again turbulence tossed them about as if they were as light as sand. Unknown to the impassioned diplomat, whose wife's anxiety and physical suffering increased with each crashing wave, a more stubborn headache was ahead.

"In the midst of the passage of the sound, we saw a ship of war at anchor— And a sloop with several other vessels anchored near them," Louisa recorded.

Instead of waiting to be stopped, Beckford hailed the man-of-war. Soon a British officer and a few sailors rowed to them. "And a lieutenant from her soon came on board."

With the audacity of a pirate, the English officer ordered the crew of the *Horace* to line the deck. One by one as if inspecting prisoners, he compared each sailor with the ship's paperwork and written descriptions of the crew. Cameras, of course, did not exist in 1809. The sailors didn't carry photographic identification cards or even pencil sketches of their faces.

One of Beckford's written descriptions didn't match, at least in the lieutenant's view. Silence filled the boat as the Brit questioned the young sailor.

Where are you from? Charlestown, the young man may have answered. Charlestown was the hallowed site of the Battle of Bunker Hill during the Revolutionary War, which John watched burn from a distance when he was eight years old. No matter if the towns were adjacent, if the paperwork said Boston and the lad answered Charlestown, then the lieutenant had what he wanted—a discrepancy and justification to haul off the young man.

The interrogation could have continued with more "discrepancies." What, blond hair? Says here, brown. Say that again? Your English smacks of Liverpool.

"[The lieutenant]—who on examining the papers of the crew was very troublesome and threatened to take one of them off," Louisa recalled.

They were witnessing the practice of impressment. For all they had endured, so far no one had questioned the nationality of an individual sailor or threatened to kidnap him.

Would the crewman from Charlestown be taken off? Hadn't his hair simply lightened with exposure to the sun? Worse, would he be impressed to serve in the British navy? Is this what the crew of the USS *Chesapeake* had suffered?

Seeing Mr. Adams, suddenly the lieutenant had a bigger fish to catch than a freckled-face crab from Charlestown. The officer became even more indignant as he questioned John.

What? No passport? An American commission to Russia? Hardly a substitute. A diplomatic mission? The smell of coffee beans below deck is stronger than your pathetic story. Why would a merchant ship be going to Russia on a diplomatic mission? Didn't the United States have military boats for that purpose? All are highly suspicious.

John's paperwork seemed as foreign to this English officer as the Russian alphabet. As he bombarded John with questions and threatened them with a pirate's pike, all the passengers could do was watch, wait, and pray.

9

Caricature vs. Character

"I HAVE FRIENDS WHO WOULD DOUBTLESS DRAW A FLATTERING likeness of my character, and enemies who would perhaps be ready enough to show me in caricature," John wrote to a family acquaintance before leaving Boston in 1809.

What sketch would his enemies have drawn as the English lieutenant questioned Adams's credentials while threatening to kidnap a crew member from the *Horace?* In that moment of extreme urgency under the threat of impressment, would they have better understood why an *Adams* supported *Jefferson's* embargo? Would they have painted him as a man who stood by and did nothing, a cowardly actor? Or would they have seen the fire in his brown eyes and the stern look of his eagle-like face?

Adams was all too aware of the gloating of his enemies, particularly from Timothy Pickering, his former fellow senator from Massachusetts.

John Quincy's confirmation to St. Petersburg was not unanimous. The Senate voted in favor nineteen to seven. Pickering and four others voted against the man. Two voted against the nomination because they opposed the mission, not Adams.

The dynamics between Pickering and the Adams family were complicated. Before serving in the Senate, Pickering was secretary of state for President Adams. Because John Quincy was a diplomat in Berlin at the time, Pickering was his boss, and his father was Pickering's boss. As a result John sent official correspondence to Pickering and then wrote openly and personally about the same matters to his father. Pickering ultimately parted ways with President Adams over his policies toward England and France. Siding with the Federalists and England, Pickering refused to resign, as Adams requested. Hence the president dismissed him. Pickering had resented anyone named Adams ever since.

By the time of Jefferson's embargo, Pickering and John were no longer boss and employee but colleagues. As the senior senator from Massachusetts, Pickering publicly opposed junior Senator Adams's support of Jefferson's embargo. Sending a letter to the Massachusetts governor, Pickering claimed that not only did Adams support the embargo, but he also abandoned Senate deliberation on the matter.

Pickering was correct. The US Senate met behind closed doors, where they debated fewer than four hours before passing the embargo to the House of Representatives. John Quincy opposed a long deliberation in the Senate but not to kiss up to Jefferson. Hardly. He simply thought a prolonged debate would put more sailors at risk. As soon as news of the embargo leaked to the public, ships would flee the wharfs of Baltimore, Boston, Philadelphia, and New York to make one final outward-bound voyage to British and French ports before the embargo went into effect. Adams believed a long Senate deliberation would have put more American sailors in jeopardy of impressment by English captains.

"For the instant it should be known in the commercial cities that an embargo was impending, the spirit of desperate adventure would have rushed to sea, with every plank that could have been made to float," he later reflected.

"And the delay of a week in deliberation, instead of sheltering the property of our merchants from depredation, would only have cast it forth upon the waters to be intercepted by the cruisers of both the combating nations [France and England]."

John could not overcome Pickering's public distortion of him. Though no moral scandal led to his departure, Adams's stand on the embargo cost him his job. Failing in the US Senate killed his political career. At the time his prospects for returning to public service appeared as dead as the cod on his dinner plate.

The rivalry took a personally vindictive turn on June 27, 1809. After the US Senate voted on Adams's appointment to Russia, Pickering quipped, "[T]he best thing that could be done" was to send him "out of the country." Pickering hated John so much that he was willing to deny him the honor of a unanimous confirmation. The political bee sting was potent compared to the sweetness of Adams's first confirmation. In 1794 the Senate unanimously confirmed his appointment by President Washington as a special envoy to the Netherlands. Much had changed since then—too much.

Louisa may have felt that a succession of miseries had fallen on her since leaving her older boys in Boston, but she was not the only one struggling with this so-called exile. The truth was as fixed as the stars above them. John had been living in a political exile at Harvard, sent there by the likes of political enemies, especially Timothy Pickering.

While Adams faced the English lieutenant on the planks of the *Horace* that September day in 1809, the question facing him was more complex than his wife's. She was clearly going into exile from her children and country. But was he journeying farther into exile, or was he coming out of one? Would success in Russia resurrect his political career? Or would an undertaker merely inscribe his epitaph with the words: *Harvard professor and local lawyer?* Though respectable, these were failed labels for a man named Adams.

The English lieutenant continued nit-picking John Quincy's commission. The anxiety level of the captain and passengers increased with each skeptical glance from the British officer. Suddenly John had enough. Standing up to this English bully, he explained his appointment. The pair went back and forth. Neither yielded. The lieutenant punted.

"The officer not understanding Mr. Adams's commission told him he had better go on board the admiral's ship and see him himself," Louisa exclaimed.

John and Beckford left the *Horace* and rowed three miles to the admiral's ship, the *Stately.*

"We were left under the protection of the officer," she fearfully added.

When Adams and Beckford boarded the *Stately,* they visited Admiral Bertie in his stateroom. Without offering them a seat, Bertie began his interrogation.

Why would the US government send an envoy on a ship laden with coffee, sugar, and cotton? Shouldn't a diplomat be carried by a military vessel? Or at least, travel in a merchant ship under ballast with no cargo at all? And where is your passport?

Bertie bombarded them with such questions. Invoking his lawyerly instincts, Adams unemotionally explained that he did not have time to procure a passport or military vessel from his government. His commission papers should suffice.

Bertie would not bend. Passport aside, he simply couldn't allow the *Horace* to pass. The British were blockading Denmark. His instructions were as firm as the bars of a prison cell: no one was to pass. Not even a supposed neutral vessel. His directive came from Britain's Orders in Council. At first the Orders in Council banned trade with ships coming from ports controlled by France or France's allies. Then the orders required ships, including neutral ships not allied with France or Britain, to first call at British ports to receive a license to trade. The instructions also allowed British authorities to search ships.

The problem for the passengers of the *Horace* was timing. Months earlier Parliament rejected President Madison's peace agreement with a British negotiator, who exceeded his instructions and promised too much to Madison. Instead of revoking the restrictive Orders in Council as Madison expected, British authorities imposed new orders, which included a paper blockade throughout European ports. This allowed them to capture any of the hundreds of American merchant vessels that left US shores in June 1809 under the mistaken understanding that Britain had revoked its policies against America. This was one reason John did not believe war would threaten their voyage to St. Petersburg. In mid-July Madison received "thunder clap news . . . London had repudiated the . . . agreement and thus restored the discriminatory Orders against American trade." Unknown to Adams, just days after the *Horace* left Boston, a fuming President Madison reinstated the embargo against England.

Instead of seizing the *Horace*, Admiral Bertie offered another solution. He said they should go around the island and take the belt.

The Danish straits connect the North Sea southward to the Baltic Sea. These alternating bodies of water and land resemble uneven blue-and-green diagonal bands on a map. Each island sits between two stripes of water. The broader stripe is called the belt; the narrower stripe is called the sound. John didn't have time to backtrack around to the belt, which would have taken him farther away from advocating for the Americans in Copenhagen and put him in greater jeopardy of failing to reach St. Petersburg before winter froze the water.

The date was September 25, 1809. They had sailed nearly four thousand miles in seven weeks. However, in the past seven days, they had traveled fewer than two hundred miles. The nights were starting to get longer. Winter would not wait.

Lacking the reserve of Adams, a passionate Beckford explained that he didn't have maps of the belt or a pilot on board who knew how to maneuver through it. Bertie didn't budge. They should hire an additional pilot who knew the belt, no matter the cost.

John was getting worried. In that moment this diplomat found himself serving as his own defense attorney. He called upon the usages of nations, customary standards followed by civilized countries. He became more and more desperate to find something to soften Bertie's iron heart.

The anchored admiral asked Adams another question. Did you have prior knowledge of the English blockade in Denmark?

"No," he answered, "but if I had, as our only object was passage [not trading and making money] I should still have relied on the usages of nations, that I should not be obstructed."

Back and forth they went. John made an interesting observation. The admiral had failed to offer him or Beckford a place to sit. They stood like attorneys in a courtroom; the admiral sat behind his desk like a judge. Refusing to bow to Bertie's power play, Adams continued to argue his position and circumstances.

"And you say, sir, you have your family on board?" Bertie asked.

"Yes, sir. My wife, her sister, and an infant child."

Finally Adams found the soft spot. Family. Louisa and Charles's presence made all the difference.

Calling it an exception to the blockade, Bertie permitted the *Horace* to pursue its voyage through the Kattegat because Louisa and Charles were aboard. He issued a pass on one condition: Adams must give his word that his ship would not violate the blockade by going into Copenhagen.

John said he would not *voluntarily* violate their agreement. Because Adams was willing to go forward in the face of such risks, Bertie issued the pass.

They returned to the *Horace*. Upon hearing of the admiral's acquiescence, the lieutenant left the ship without taking the sailor from Charlestown. It was so late in the day that Beckford decided to spend the night where they were, anchored three miles from the admiral's ship.

Instead, they became even cozier with the cruiser.

10

All the World's a Stage

LOUISA NOTICED THE PROBLEM ABOUT ELEVEN O'CLOCK THAT NIGHT. Likely while wearing a nightgown, with her hair long and loose about her long neck and shoulders, she probably heard the whistling and rustling in her cabin. Although the wind was fair, it was also freshly blowing, strengthening with every gust. The *Horace* was drifting, a movement caused by tide flows, wind, and other currents. By morning the *Horace* had floated within a mile of the *Stately*.

"We put down another small anchor which, however, did not arrest the drift," Louisa noted.

Small anchors were poor men's tugs. A ship could sometimes stop its drifting by dragging an anchor on the leeway, the side away from the wind. The crew dropped their third and final anchor—their heaviest elephant—on the leeway.

"We had drifted within the ship's length of a large brig whose bowsprit was threatening our cabin windows and we were within a mile of the shore," Louisa observed with fright. The bowsprit was a long piece of wood extending from the bow of the ship, where it held ropes leading to the foremast.

Louisa became concerned about Charles, Kitty, and Martha: "I was anxious to send the ladies and child ashore for which purpose a signal was made at the masthead—but none came out."

Although they were within a mile of land, their distress signal went unanswered. With no one willing to take them to shore, Louisa probably did what only a prudent mother would do with a bowsprit so close to her cabin window. She moved her child to the other side of the ship.

"[A] boat from the British man-of-war came out to us and gave some advice to the captain—He told him that one good anchor would be better than three."

Sailors used wooden devices such as sea anchors or drag anchors to keep the ship's head to the wind and diminish drifting. Three anchors can cause many problems, such as fouling each other, striking another ship's anchor, or getting caught in rocks. If any anchor fouled in any way, the crew would have to cut the anchor's line, thus losing it forever.

The *Horace*'s heaviest anchor proved a fouler as the weather worsened. The wind and rain hovered, pounding for hours. With dawn came a new order from Beckford: all hands on deck—passengers too.

"All the morning was employed in weighing [retrieving] the anchors; two of them were successfully got on board," Louisa said, indicating they lost the third anchor.

As they tried to sail again, the wind changed direction. The *Horace*'s stern would not turn through the strong wind. Three times Beckford ordered his crew to move the ship, but they couldn't do it. Then he "lashed down the helm" and tied the steering wheel toward the wind so the stern would go through the airstream.

Finally they sailed. As they voyaged through the Kattegat toward Elsinore, they understood why ancient captains called it a cat hole. The channel was quickly narrowing.

"We were between the shores in a narrow sea and expecting every instant to be dashed on Kohl Point, a fearful spot in the history of wrecks," Louisa noted.

The Sunday before their departure from Boston, Louisa and Kitty attended church while John visited his mother and sons in Quincy. The ladies heard a sermon by Pastor Emerson, a longtime friend, who preached about guardian angels.

John later reflected that his wife and sister-in-law were very affected by the message and the "pleasing and not improbable doctrine of a guardian angel, which Christians have often supposed to be assigned to every individual to watch over him, and as far as is consistent with the general designs of Providence, to guide his conduct, and to preserve him from extraordinary dangers."

As they headed toward one of the deadliest places in the Kattegat, they needed an angel more than ever.

The weather calmed. The temperature wasn't too cold, and they still had enough daylight to aid them. No waves or crosscurrents troubled them, at least for now. Making progress, they passed the dangerous point without incident. Soon, however, their good fortune changed.

"The light in the binnacle went out and there was not a light to be had in the ship," Louisa explained of the candle that lit the ship's compass.

Facing the nineteenth-century version of a power failure, the crew urgently searched for a substitute. No luck. John then sorted through his tinderbox and found another candle. The delay came with a price. The blackout cost them their course. They had drifted, going backward by as many as five miles and passing Bertie's ship *again*.

"To go through the horrors of this most terrible and tedious voyage is beyond my strength," she recorded.

Where had their guardian angel gone?

Passengers often feel like prisoners. Indeed. That is the confining nature of ship travel. Such Noah-like venturing is enough to strangle the humanity in anyone. Mrs. Noah was more than ready for a new dove to take them to land.

Louisa carried with her deep ache something intensely personal, writing that the "long voyage [was] to me painful in every possible shape for many more reasons than I can mention."

Something drove her to reach for her medicine chest tonics. What was too painful that she could not mention it in her diary? She did not hide her sorrow over leaving behind her boys. What backstory did she choose to conceal, even from her own pen? She did not withhold her anger over her father-in-law's and husband's decision to keep her from George and John. She did not hide her fears of chaperoning her unmarried younger sister. What was so personal that not even her journal could absorb the blow?

Prudence was passport in this era of extreme manners, so acutely observed by novelist Jane Austen. Discretion dictated Louisa's pen, which freely flowed about common health problems such as seasickness. Nevertheless she struggled with something too delicate for a lady to put into print. Unlike today, describing female health matters back then was considered unladylike and vulgar.

Although miscarriage and infant death were very common in this era, Louisa had experienced more than her share of maternal woes. She had lost more pregnancies than she had successfully delivered. Between the births of John and Charles, she delivered a son who soon died. Such heartache only made leaving George and John more traumatic. Most mothers would have felt extreme anguish over abandoning their children, but Louisa's struggle just to become a mother was so seismic that leaving her children behind was a much greater earthquake as a result.

On top of her guilt and private pain, she was enduring the physical toll of a ship tossed about by powers beyond her control. She expected to see a few waves. She anticipated the literal headaches that accompany sea travel. What she didn't expect was to be chased by both Danish and English sharks.

Louisa also knew that something else tugged on her husband as the boat drifted back toward Bertie's boat. His mind was adrift. The plight of the Americans detained at Kristiansand weighed on his heart like a thousand anchors, fouling his need to get to St. Petersburg. Their youth reminded him of his own boys. Their exile reminded him of his duty to serve his country, and of his previous voyages.

———

Adams had endured separation from his closest loved ones at other times in his life. This was the fourth time he left family members behind and sailed for Europe.

"The separation from my family and friends has always been painful; but never to the degree which I feel it now," he wrote of this voyage. The mathematics of life expectancy made this trip more difficult than his previous adventures. His parents were older. John Adams was nearly seventy-four; Abigail, nearly sixty-five. Would he ever see them again?

"The age of my parents awakens, both in them and me, *the hopes* [not certainty] of our meeting again and I now leave two of my own infant children behind. My father and mother are also deeply affected by my departure," he confessed in his diary. One letter from his mother was so moving that it "would have melted the heart of a stoic."

Miles before the *Horace* passed through Bertie's blockade, John wrote a special letter to his boys. Although they were only six and eight years of age, he wanted to prepare them for an early departure from childhood. In this letter to his sons, John referred to the most famous passage of William Shakespeare's play *As You Like It*: "All the world's a stage, and all the men and women merely players. They have their exits and their entrances, and one man in his time plays many parts."

Indeed John was a very minor player on his first ocean voyage with his father; now he held the leading role. He wanted his children to understand his motives and embrace the same philosophy.

"You should each of you consider yourself as placed here to *act a part*—that is to have some single great end or object to accomplish, towards which all the views and labors of your existence should be directed," he wrote with emphasis to George and John.

When they entered the threshold of life, they must first supply their own wants. As he did years before when he graduated from Harvard, they must receive training to support themselves through employment. Civil society depended on men pursuing "some mechanical art or laborious profession." Adams practiced law as a young man. Once they were successful, they could advance to the next stage: marriage.

"As a great portion of the enjoyment of life consists in the society of the sexes, there is an obligation upon you to share your pleasures with a partner." John believed the stages of a man's life progressed in this order: providing for oneself, comfortably providing for a wife, nurturing and educating children, and serving the public, life's paramount stage.

Perhaps John worried that this letter was his last opportunity to impart wisdom to his boys. Death was a real danger to an intercontinental traveler in the early nineteenth century. Ships wrecked. Ships sank. Sickness attacked. Souls passed.

If he or Louisa was unable to return to them in Boston, then at least these words would provide a script for the rest of their lives. He also needed to explain what was so important that he was willing to cast aside normal family life and leave them behind. Some call it ambition. To John, it was public service. Life's responsibilities didn't end with intimate family ties. Prosperity multiplied a man's duties and magnified his obligations. Successful men served society. Man held a responsibility to pursue "justice and fidelity to others." Self-preservation was not enough. Life was more than individuals and families.

"The relations of man are no longer confined to his own family but extend to his neighbors and fellow citizens," he explained. Without the poetry, he became Shakespeare to his sons. "There are also the duties of a citizen to his country, which are binding upon all, and more forcibly binding in a republican government than in any other." Under republican principles, "every individual has a stake, an interest, and a voice in the common stock of society."

America's form of government and belief that rights come from God required individuals to promote the common interest. This was to be done "to the utmost of his power, compatibly with the discharge of his more immediate duties of self-preservation and preservation of his kind [family]."

Though he professed to be imparting wisdom to his boys, John revealed the motivation that drove his heart: "Finally, let the uniform principle of your life, the 'frontlet between your eyes,' be how to make your talents and your knowledge most beneficial to your country and *most useful to mankind*."

As they sailed through the Kattegat, John's eyes switched to those other boys, the three hundred captive sailors from thirty ships held at Kristiansand. No matter the cost, he must get to Copenhagen and try to do something, anything, for his countrymen. Diplomacy was now his greatest duty.

——

Another storm brewed as they sailed through the seas. Beckford may have been the ship's captain, but John was exerting his authority with each towering gale and new danger. They disagreed over their arrangement with Bertie. The question between them was whether or not Bertie's pass allowed them to stop in Elsinore and go to Copenhagen.

Beckford's view was simple: no landing. He didn't think Bertie permitted them to stop at all. John countered. Yes, of course the *Horace* could land. They just couldn't sell cargo there. Surely they could stop for customary manners, such as resupplying. As the boat drifted, so did Beckford's and Adams's opinions.

They arrived at the narrowest part of the sound between Denmark and Sweden, which was only 2.4 miles wide. This spot marked the place in Denmark known as Helsingør—or Elsinore, the name Shakespeare made famous in *Hamlet*. Within their view was the magnificent Kronborg castle, a fortress monitoring ships heading for the Baltic Sea. The question for John and the captain was not "to be, or not to be?" but "to dock, or not to dock?"

Their debate abruptly abated. The Danes decided for them. A mile from Kronborg, a Danish boat fired a shot "and immediately after boarded us, and took us into Elsinore Roads." The local gatekeepers quickly accepted John's commission.

"Mr. Adams was prevailed upon to go to Copenhagen by the Americans to make some effort in their cause and we continued on shore until their return, anything was better than sea as we could at least sleep without alarm," Louisa explained.

While her husband traveled to Copenhagen, Louisa showed a sign of accepting her new role as a diplomatic minister's wife. After tidying their haggard appearance aboard the ship, she and Kitty donned their best and cleanest Jane Austen–style dresses and went shopping.

Worried that their American hats were too small for European society, they bought some larger beaver bonnets, which they hoped would be appropriate for St. Petersburg's fashionable diplomatic circles. Along the streets of Elsinore, they probably tasted the pleasantries of pastries, treasured luxuries to nautical captives. They also went sightseeing. Louisa noted that the Hamlet gardens "as they were still called [were] ornamented with heavy leaden statues [and] were the great object of curiosity."

Meanwhile John traveled twenty-eight miles by stagecoach in about five hours. He tried to visit appropriate authorities in Copenhagen. After several failures and an overnight stay at a hotel, he met with Mr. Saabye, a Dane who had represented the Americans before the Danish government.

Adams put forward his finest legal arguments. Assuring him that he had done his best, Saabye suggested that Adams talk with Count Bernstorff, a top government official who would be at his home until three in the afternoon that day. The count's house was not far off the route back to Elsinore. Time was now the enemy. Adams boarded a stagecoach and headed for the count's home. He arrived at 2:00 p.m., but Bernstorff wasn't there. John learned that the count would not return until later that evening.

This American diplomat now faced a dilemma. This constantly observant, weather-obsessed Bostonian knew the winds were favorable that day. The longer he stayed, the more time the *Horace* lost for grabbing a good wind for sailing into the Baltic. Time was ticking. Winter could come early. What should he do? Wait? Or take advantage of the good winds and sail immediately?

He considered his dilemma. Had he presented his best arguments on behalf of the American sailors to Mr. Saabye? Yes. Had he made it clear that a language barrier was the problem and they needed a translator? Yes. Had Mr. Saabye seen his passion? Yes. Would waiting for the count make a significant difference? Yes, very possibly, but there was no guarantee.

Which was his greatest obligation, getting to St. Petersburg or waiting on the count to help the stranded Americans? Suddenly Adams faced the greatest internal dilemma of his voyage. He debated in agony. Not even Shakespeare could have crafted this quandary.

11

Baltic Circle

To go or not to go? That was the question. Adams contemplated his circumstances in Denmark with Hamlet-like angst. How he longed to advocate for those trapped Americans. If only he could speak to Count Bernstorff, he might be able to secure a fairer trial. However, if he waited for the count to return, would he miss the best sailing wind for the Baltic? If he didn't reach Russia before winter, his mission to establish free trade with the largest country in Europe would be delayed by months, and Louisa's return to their boys would be extended even longer.

His practical side, the Yankee in him, prevailed. He left the count's home and returned to his ship with the bitter taste of failure in his mouth. The next morning, October 2, 1809, the *Horace* resumed its voyage.

"We all embarked again on our dismal course," Louisa wrote.

Though the weather was bearable, her heart was as depressed as ever. Shopping did not lift her spirits for long. Within half an hour after their departure, the wind changed, forcing them to anchor a mere half mile from where they started. What to do? Because they were sandwiched between two opposite shores, they needed not just any wind to take them out, but a very brisk one.

They waited as long as Jonah stayed in the belly of the whale. For three days wind was as absent as summer. Finally the air currents changed, and they gained enough gusts to get going. With good wind and clear skies, they peacefully journeyed through the straits. Because they were close to both the Danish and the Swedish shores, they enjoyed parallel scenery of spires and steeples.

Suddenly a signal came. Cannon fired at them unexpectedly—another headache-producing explosion. They heard the blast as they passed a battery near a palace, which was built on three sunken ships—a bad sign.

Though surprised, Beckford decided it was merely a customary signal.

They saluted by striking their top gallant sail. Then a big gun fired an even larger cannonball, which landed a few feet ahead of the *Horace*. Because the water was too shallow to come to shore, Beckford ordered his crew to lower their anchors in the middle of the channel. A Danish boat came out to them. Once again local authorities searched their ship. The incident cost them an hour's time, a precious sacrifice of fair wind.

Then another boat stopped them, and another. Each examination slowed their progress through the low waters. Just before sunset, a fourth ship inspected them. Because the water was shallow and narrow, they dared not go through the rest of the grounds at night. Throwing their iron elephant overboard, they anchored, hoping for a guardian angel.

Weather smiled on them the next day. They effortlessly traveled seventy nautical miles and came within site of Bornholm, a two-hundred-square-mile island. The Baltic proved a much safer place than the Kattegat, at least from the dangers of man. No one forced them to take a detour. No one fired at them. No officers searched their crew and cargo. But soon they realized that the Baltic offered something more maddening: monotony.

"For three days we have been beating half the day about southeast, and half the day northwest, without advancing a league in our course," Adams wrote on October 9, more than a week after leaving Elsinore.

They were traveling in a circle. Mother Nature was flirting with them. Just as she gave them hope, she snatched it away. The wind took them in one direction in the morning, and back to where they'd started by evening. The turbulence at night was so great, they couldn't sleep. It was enough to drive them mad. Louisa was already on the brink. Would this push her over?

"Thus we went on day after day—beating about and worn down with fatigue and anxiety," she recorded. How she longed to wash her soiled skirts in fresh water.

Then Mother Nature threw in some special effects, as John noted: "The night was moderate, and the day has been so, with the exception of a constant succession of squalls, with rain, hail, sleet, snow, and sometimes wind."

Winter was emerging from hibernation. How long would it blow snowy kisses before making its presence fully known? After all that they had faced, now the simple change of seasons threatened to keep them from their destination.

"Dangers accumulated every moment . . . and now we had cold added to our burdens," Louisa commented.

The Gulf of Finland is a shallow body of water and freezes more quickly than the Baltic, sealing St. Petersburg from ship travel. If they didn't reach the gulf before it iced over, then they wouldn't make it to St. Petersburg. Their mission to Russia would be delayed for half a year at least, shackling John with enough failure to make Federalist rival Timothy Pickering smile.

Beckford grimly assessed the situation. Though they were only six hundred miles away, he told Adams it would take a miracle to get them to Russia before winter. Their best hope was to turn around and dock at Kiel for the winter. Kiel, in present-day Germany, was more than one thousand miles from St. Petersburg by land. Perhaps they could travel in spring via carriage.

Adams decided he needed time to think about Beckford's solution, at least a day. He mulled over the monotony. Had they truly reached a crisis? Yes. The cold, wet taste of snow on their tongues was evidence enough. Were they facing an emergency? Obviously. The sleet on the ship's bow spoke louder than any of the captain's words. John knew it was true. All he had to do was skim his recent journal entries.

While crossing the Atlantic, he read sermons and the classics. Since then he had scarcely cracked a book. The way he spent his time was the best testimony of their trials. His diary revealed the truth: weather, wind, the Danish, the English, and the detained Americans—all kept him from his books and now, possibly reaching his destination in time. He had spent most of his days administering, trying to solve each and every problem. Captain Beckford may have commanded the ship, but John had been in charge of their course.

After a sleepless night of contemplation, he proposed to the captain that they should try to get as close as possible to Kronstadt, the island fortress guarding St. Petersburg.

No. Beckford disagreed. The winds were not cooperating. Winter was coming. It was too late. John described the captain as worrying about endangering the ship: "The prospect of reaching Kronstadt before the formation of the ice, which will make it impracticable, has now become desperate."

Adams was more frustrated than at any other time in this fateful voyage to date. He had not come all this way to stop because of some silly snow. He was from Boston, for heaven's sake! Sleet and snow were as common there as cod was to the Atlantic Ocean.

Weighing on his mind, too, was his mission: to be the first person to establish official ties between the United States and Russia. Strong US relations with the largest nation in Europe could give America the leverage it needed with England and France over trade rights. Before Adams could make another suggestion, the captain refused to come out of his quarters. He was not angry, but ill. Quite ill.

With his earthly captain unable to lead, John looked to his heavenly captain for hope. Their success was now "in better hands than mine" he wrote, praying for Providence to send a much-needed angel. A simple glimpse of Gabriel would do.

Beckford stayed confined to his bed several days. The squalls continued. Wind and rain hailed upon them. At one time the wind pushed them dangerously close to the island of Bornholm, nearly wrecking them. Having earlier lost an anchor, the *Horace* was out of options for contending with drift. It was as if Poscidon were blowing them to the brink with his bad breath.

"They were no imaginary dangers that assailed us, and our sufferings were pitiable," Louisa wrote.

Their problems were as real as the bread they ate. By October 13 they faced another danger: low supplies and the stench of spoiled food.

"Thus we continued with every variety of bad weather and at last provisions began to give out and Mr. Adams began to think that we could land somewhere and go the rest of the way by land but the captain would not agree for fear of the British," Louisa explained in exasperation.

Because of the searches and interrogations they had endured, Beckford feared the British would impound the *Horace* and his crew if John Quincy and his delegation left them and took a route by land.

They headed for Christiansø, Denmark's eastern most island, about twelve miles northeast of Bornholm, to buy supplies and make a final decision about what to do.

As they arrived, they hoisted their flag. A guard at the stone fortress raised a flag in return. A representative rowed out to them but failed to bring supplies as their signals suggested. Disappointed, they were not surprised. The reason was highly familiar. The authorities protecting Christiansø, sometimes called Ertholmene, feared the *Horace* was an English ship in disguise and with good reason. Nearly a year earlier on October 24, 1808, a battle took place between the island's fortress and an English flotilla of twenty-five ships. The fight left seven killed and many others wounded.

After reviewing their papers, the relieved man agreed to help. Because the weather was fair, smaller boats carrying supplies easily came to them throughout the day. But when the *Horace* pushed out away from the land, the wind and sea were as rough as could be. They just couldn't get a break.

While they battled the weather again, John and a recovered captain continued discussing their future course. Louisa knew her husband well. He was an Adams. Perseverance was planted as firmly in him as any tree in the ground of the family's Peacefield farm. "I knew that Mr. Adams would never give up and we were obliged to make the best of our miserable condition."

As they reached the climax of their nautical drama, a messenger rowed out to the *Horace* and interrupted them with exciting news. Christiansø's governor was inviting the ladies to a ball.

"We received an invitation to a ball at the governor's on the island of 'Burnt Hollum' as our captain named it, for eight o'clock in the evening while the vessel was rocking rolling and pitching as if she would go to pieces—We were obliged to decline the honor," Louisa politely quipped.

The invitation seemed as out of place as a waltz at a funeral. They could not taste cake's sweetness or wine's fruitiness while making the most crucial decision of their voyage. This was no time to rest or recreate. They must resume.

Finally John could no longer dance around the issue. He had to make a final choice. He capitulated to the captain, agreeing to change course toward Kiel on one condition: if the weather changed—if favorable winds came upon them as they sailed for Kiel—then they would turn around and try one last time to catch a fair wind for St. Petersburg.

Though Yankee ingenuity prevailed, the Adams in him scolded him for giving in. "I cannot but reproach myself for this momentary compliance, as it indicated a flexibility which ought not to belong to me," he later confessed.

He saw the fatigue, and likely tantrums, of his two-year-old. He watched the tired lines grow wider on his wife's ashen face. Her brown eyes stopped dancing, and her wavy, light brown hair became limp and lifeless from the sea air. Though he lacked a physician's ability to diagnose her troubles and treat her symptoms, he had compassion for her. He, too, felt imprisoned by the ship, captive to their constantly changing hardships. They had endured far more dangers than he expected.

"But I had objects on board more precious to me than my own life, and there was some reason for shrinking from a risk of the ship and cargo, which was not mine and which was the special trust of the captain."

———

They headed for Kiel on October 14. The wind bore them away at a good clip, enabling John to return to reading books.

Beckford may have longed for Kiel's shores, but he bore integrity as often as he donned his captain's cap. Unwilling to deceive the diplomat under his charge, he alerted John the next day that the weather was about to change. They would try one more time to sail to St. Petersburg.

The crew protested. They were "desponding under the long succession and continued prospect of adverse winds" and "alarmed at navigating the Baltic so late in the season," John described the men.

Standing out in the open away from shore for a whole day, the *Horace* waited for the wind to change. To no avail! The water was as still as a dead man. Beckford was ready to sail again for Kiel, while John implored him to wait just a little longer. Back and forth they argued. Their battle lacked the violence of pirates standing with swords drawn, but not the passion. Each frankly put forward his reasons.

As an attorney, Adams knew that forensic evidence was on the captain's side. Freezing rain. Falling temperatures. Rocky reefs. John was armed with principles, namely, that he owed it to his government to reach Russia through the cheapest, most direct way possible.

No matter the succession of miseries that had imprisoned them the past month, what was past was past. He was the only one charged by the president to establish official ties with Russia. He alone represented the mission's failure or success to Congress. He was the only one who needed a successful mission to bring him out of his so-called exile.

"Yet, in the pursuit of a public trust, I cannot abandon, upon any motive less than that of absolute necessity, the endeavor to reach the place of my destination by the shortest course possible," John explained.

While the *Horace* waited, Adams soon made an interesting observation. They were not alone. Like a school of fish, four other ships pulled out from the port.

Forty-eight hours after giving up, they received a second wind. Literally. The *Horace* caught a swift gust and headed toward the Gulf of Finland. Heaven smiled on them with an angelic gale. Fair breezes carried them for three days.

Then the pilot gave Beckford and John a worrisome verdict. He feared that a recent fog caused him to miss a crucial turning point into the Gulf of Finland, Gotland island, a sizable landmark. Because of the fog, he couldn't see the end of their bowsprit, much less an island.

Heaven, however, hastened again and sent another angel. When the fog cleared, they saw a ship. They hailed it. She raised her colors. Was it an English flag? No. Whew. Danish? No—thank goodness. The Stars and Stripes topped her sails. Her presence was as helpful as backup troops to a losing general. Called the *Ocean,* this New York–based ship was also bound for St. Petersburg. The *Ocean's* captain gave them good news. Yes, they missed the island, but they were headed in the right direction after all.

The captains of both ships agreed to help each other. Staying within yelling distance, they took advantage of each other's sailing force, and if necessary, the ability to rescue the other in case of a wreck along a rocky Russian reef.

As they entered the Gulf of Finland, the water felt smooth. They glided with ease as if going over ice, though the water was not yet frozen. Fair winds blew strong. They quickly passed lighthouse after lighthouse, each keeping them on course with the precision of following the stars. More incredible was the brilliance of an October moon, which enabled them to travel continuously at night. On the morning of October 22, 1809, the *Horace* and *Ocean* arrived in Kronstadt's shallow waters.

"At last we reached our destination though some distance from the land," Louisa wrote with relief.

Before them was Kronstadt, an island fortress twenty miles from St. Petersburg by water and at the head of the gulf. When Peter the Great began building St. Petersburg in 1703, he ordered stone fortifications, or moles, to dissect Kronstadt's low waters. No boat could get to St. Petersburg without going through Kronstadt's stone canals or the Russian navy's Baltic fleet.

After surveying the area, Beckford ordered the *Horace* to anchor near one of the guard ships, about two miles away from the mole. A Russian officer rowed out to them and inspected their paperwork. At 1:00 p.m. they signaled for a pilot to take them into the mole. They waited. And they waited. An hour passed. Then two. Three. Finally a Russian pilot came out to them, but it was so late in the day that Beckford and John came to the same conclusion. Both rightfully feared they would damage the *Horace* by taking it into the mole in the dark.

"My objective was merely to land and get a lodging for the night at an inn," John determined practically.

A guard boat officer offered a solution. The *Horace* could stay where she was until daylight, when a pilot could better guide her through Kronstadt's channels to St. Petersburg. In the meantime, the lieutenant would take the passengers to Kronstadt island in a Russian government boat. Because the imperial government required all foreigners to pass an examination by the admiral, he would escort them to the admiral's house. John agreed. His primary goal was to get his wife and child onto land.

The government boat, however, was barely big enough for their large party: John, Louisa, Kitty, Charles, their two domestic servants, and three attachés. Seeing the dilemma, Mr. Smith offered to stay with the *Horace*. Everyone, however, would have to leave clothing and trunks behind. Because it was for one night only, the plan seemed plausible.

"We dressed ourselves and accompanying him [the officer] left everything in the vessel," Louisa wrote, explaining that they took what she thought would be appropriate attire for a Russian admiral's house. "[We] landed perfect beggars though supposing that our trunks would follow us immediately."

The small boat took them to the mole. From there they walked a mile to the main mansion. They were "ushered into an immense saloon at the admiral's house full of elegantly dressed ladies and gentlemen staring aghast at the figures just introduced."

Appalled. Horrified. These Russians stared at them as if they were wearing buckskin fig leaves.

"My sister and myself wore hats which had been chosen at Copenhagen that we might appear fashionable—and we could scarcely look at one another for laughing: immense brown beaver of the most vulgar imaginable as much too large as our American bonnets were too small."

Shakespeare could not have written a better farce. Not even new beaver hats could conceal the fact that they had just disembarked after a long journey. Their American simplicity shocked this society of sophistication. The Russian women's dresses were most likely silk, trimmed around the edges with intricate, expensive embroidery. Louisa's plain white linen wrapper and her equally plain skirt could not have contrasted more with the Russian ladies' embroidered dresses. The Adamses' attire stood out as plain brown boulders against a coral reef's pretty delicate lace of red, pink, and orange hues.

"It [the admiral's house] was exquisite beyond all description and too ridiculous in the first moments to be mortifying as we naturally supposed it would only be momentary," a highly embarrassed Louisa noted.

When the Russian admiral realized that the dirty, plainly dressed, wigless man standing before him was the designated US minister to Russia, he was shocked. He quickly arranged for Mr. Sparrow, an English gentleman, to escort these stragglers to an inn, which turned out to be full.

"Not a place could be found to put our heads in (bonnets not excepted)," Louisa wrote, finding some humor in their Mary and Joseph–like dilemma.

Although the admiral offered his home, John and Louisa could not accept. These American aborigines were much too embarrassed of their plight. Mr. Sparrow took them to his house for the night.

Worse than being underdressed was having no clothes at all. Louisa took comfort in knowing the rest of their belongings would soon arrive. She fully expected the *Horace* to "warp into the mole" the next morning. However, there would be no warping for the *Horace* at Kronstadt. The reason was simple. By morning there was no *Horace*. The ship was gone.

Eighty days after saying good-bye to the birches of Boston, the Adams party arrived in St. Petersburg on October 23, 1809, with only the clothes on their backs. Facing a new challenge, they were trading a Shakespearean farce for a Danish fable. This diplomat and his wife needed new clothes. After all, they couldn't very well meet the emperor wearing nothing at all.

12

Fig Leaves

ADAMS AND HIS EVE WERE NOT NAKED WHEN THEY LANDED IN Russia, but they were ashamed nonetheless—of their fig leaves.

"[We] did appear quite in the garb of the aboriginals of our land," Louisa wrote with embarrassment. She didn't expect to arrive like a queen, but she never dreamed of showing up like the wife of the very first Adam, either.

Suddenly they regretted leaving their clothing on the *Horace*. So starved were they to sleep on land and reach their destination after nearly three months at sea that they were willing to go without their trunks for a day.

"At breakfast Mr. Sparrow informed us that a heavy [gale] had sprung up; the vessel been blown many miles down . . . and she probably would not get back for ten days."

Had they realized that their choice would keep them from their clothing for so long, they might have stayed aboard, enduring Beckford's crankiness a little longer. With all they had faced, they never imagined arriving without their belongings. They felt like beggars from Boston.

"Here was a position agreeably defined—myself [wearing] a white cambric wrapper [a thin white linen shawl]; my sister the same; [a] child of little more than two-years old with only the suit on his back, and the minister with the shirt he had on; solus!!"

Solus is a stage direction indicating that a character is alone onstage. Louisa clearly saw her husband playing the leading role in this farce. What to do? Should they wait for the *Horace*? Or go to St. Petersburg? Yes. That was the best option. The admiral offered them a government boat for the remaining twenty miles.

Their voyage along the ship channel was unmercifully slow, a staccato stint. Louisa paid the price of the stop-start motion of the smaller boat while it continuously changed its tack to get through the winding channel. She felt so much nausea, she could not enjoy some of St. Petersburg's most magnificent sights, such as the fountains at Peterhof Palace facing the water not far from Kronstadt.

As they landed, a golden spire did inspire. Topped with a gilded angel, the Peter and Paul Fortress pointed, needlelike, toward heaven, a reminder of guardian angels.

"A beneficent Providence, whether operating by general laws or by the subordinate energy and care of a guardian angel, did conduct us safely through all these perils," Adams later wrote his mother.

Perhaps no one noticed their aboriginal American fig leaves as they stepped from the rocking Russian boat onto St. Petersburg's sturdy wharf. They docked about four o'clock in the afternoon under a bridge on the Neva River's south bank not far from Peter the Great's grand equestrian statue, the symbol of St. Petersburg.

Weak with nausea and dysentery, Louisa couldn't use her normally appreciative artistic eye to admire the statue's grandeur. In addition to this, if two boys were playing chase around the statue's base or on the wharf, such a tear-inducing sight would have reminded her of leaving George and John behind in Boston.

Adams needed to find lodging. After what seemed like a hundred days to his suffering wife, he finally chose a hotel on the broad Nevsky Prospective. He arranged for a carriage to escort Charles and the ladies, while his aides and servants walked to the Hôtel de Londres.

Extending before them as they entered the Nevsky Prospective were dozens of three- and four-story baroque-style buildings. Just as gold embroidery brilliantly stood out against the rich-colored fabrics of Russian women's dresses at Kronstadt, so the bright white columns and trim sharply contrasted with the buildings' deep painted colors of green, turquoise, blue, and yellow.

Adams rented five chambers at the Hôtel de Londres. No one would trouble them for a while. At last they could remove their perspiration-soaked clothes and go fig leafless in private. They could live in seclusion for ten days or so until the *Horace* delivered their belongings. Then Adams could get down to the business of diplomacy.

Word of their arrival spread quickly. Levett Harris, the American consul, scurried to their hotel the next day. John's presence gave him something he did not have in St. Petersburg—a boss. As the US minister, Adams outranked Harris—if the czar accepted his credentials, that is.

John was well aware of Harris. US Secretary of state, Robert Smith, had instructed him to expect Harris's assistance. He also carried a letter from Smith to Harris with identical instructions. Adams was anxious to meet Levett and learn the ins and outs of Russian diplomatic life.

Harris quickly sized up their situation. John and Louisa had no time to rest and wait for their clothing. They must get down to business. Had Adams been a merchant in a similar fig-leaf situation, he could have easily taken a few days to hide until his clothing arrived. No such luck. As the top American diplomat responsible for the entire US relationship with Russia, he couldn't risk offending the emperor by concealing his presence. Kronstadt's admiral had alerted his superiors of their arrival.

Count Nicolas Romanzoff, Harris explained, was *the* man. John must be introduced to him without delay. Similar to the role of the US secretary of state, Chancellor Romanzoff oversaw foreign affairs for Emperor Alexander. Before Adams could officially be accepted by the emperor, he must first meet Romanzoff. No matter that his clothing was afloat; Adams must dress to impress the chancellor.

Although he had not been able to indulge in his love for long walks while voyaging, John was naturally robust and muscular. In contrast Harris was petite and athletically deficient. What he lacked in a sturdy physique, Harris made up in neatness and know-how, as he quickly revealed.

Harris had greeted many a merchantman fresh from the sea. He saw the soiled shirts of sailors, smelled their sweat, and chewed with delight on the exotic cigars they brought him. Nonetheless, the scruffy appearance of this new American diplomat made this neatnik panic. Harris knew the expectations for a gentleman in the czar's court—from polished gold buttons lining the center of a gold-embroidered waistcoat to spotless silk stockings tied tightly under the knees.

One glance at John's sagging, stained stockings, pathetically plain waistcoat, and wigless head led Harris to a quick conclusion. This new diplomat needed new clothes. If Adams's fig leaves were similar to the suits he'd left behind on the boat, then he needed significant help to fit into Russia's lavish diplomatic circles. From Harris's perspective, the *Horace's* delay provided a golden apple of opportunity. In this way he could help Adams find better suits without insulting his old ones.

Harris did not know that for years Abigail and John had fretted over their son's slovenliness. When John Quincy became a senator, she begged him to purchase a new coat. She didn't want him to become a dandy but feared his sloppiness would stand out on the Senate floor. When President Washington appointed Adams to be minister in residence to the Netherlands in May 1794, Vice President Adams gave his son many instructions on how to prepare for the role, including what to study and how to dress. "[N]o man alive is more attentive to these things than the President [Washington]—neat at least and handsome." Harris also realized he needed to turn his boss into a beau—quickly.

"Immediately after dinner Mr. Harris the consul came and all the shopkeepers were set in motion to procure the requisites for ready use," Louisa chronicled.

Thus John Quincy and Harris stepped out of the hotel and onto the Nevsky Prospective, St. Petersburg's signature street. Because it is broad even by modern standards, this was probably one of the widest boulevards that John ever walked. Today's streets generally range from twenty-foot alleys to sixty-four-foot or wider main avenues. The nearly three-mile-long Nevsky reaches two hundred feet in width, two-thirds the length of a modern football field. As the widest of the three avenues radiating from the navy shipyard, the Nevsky was the main vein of the leaflike layout, dividing the city in one direction lengthwise, with canals bisecting it crossways.

John and Harris crossed two canals before reaching a long line of clothing shops called the silver row arcade. John probably bought a new suit there. Although he didn't record what he purchased, he most likely bought a velvet or silk suit, appropriate fabrics for a full court suit, as it was called. What distinguished European court clothes from American suits were fabric, details, and embroidery.

Breeches, or pants ending at the knees, were in vogue. Collars were turned up, not down. Because John was not a dandy, he would have passed on buying something exotic, such as pink-and-brown-striped silk breeches with a matching coat. Solid blue, brown, and black were safer colors for a man of Adams's taste, not to mention his republican principles. For his vest or waistcoat, he needed tasteful and elegant fabric, such as white silk edged with embroidery. Likewise bands of embroidery were stitched on the stockings—and in Russia, stockings were often lined with fur. A plain John Adams became a gentleman of finery.

"And the minister was dressed from top to toe much to his discomfiture in a superb style wig and all to be presented to the chancellor of the empire when he should be ready to receive him," Louisa observed.

With Adams transformed, Harris sent a note to Romanzoff, who immediately invited them to call the next evening, October 25.

"Mr. Harris dined with us [and] gave Mr. Adams much instruction as to how many bows he must make—almost what to say; and told him to be careful not to dwell upon business but to be careful to introduce something light and pleasant into the conversation as the Russians must be amused."

By this time in his life, John Quincy was nearly bald. Although a wig was useful—not to mention warm—he preferred to go wigless. In Europe wigs were a fashion necessity regardless of how much hair grew from one's scalp. The sight of her husband with an abundance of hair—something she hadn't seen in a while—amused Louisa.

"At seven o clock [sic] in the evening they departed—Mr. Adams looking very handsome," Louisa remarked, an outward sign that their strained relationship had healed somewhat.

While his threads flattered him, one feature detracted from his physique, in his wife's opinion: [A]ll but the wig. O horrid! which entirely disfigured his countenance and not to his advantage."

While it warped his appearance, the wig worked. Pleased to see the finely dressed gentlemen standing before him, Romanzoff asked for Adams's commission. John handed him his papers along with a French translation that he had prepared.

"The count received us with courtly state and politeness," Adams reported of the brief but successful meeting.

The most important question, however, remained unresolved. What of the emperor? When would Adams meet him? Wait, the count replied. Emperor Alexander was indisposed with inflammation in his legs. He would be up and about soon.

"He [the count] assured me that the information of my appointment had been very agreeable to him [the emperor]."

Was Romanzoff telling the truth? Or was he beginning a series of put-offs? The new American minister could not know for sure. He had seen the Russian penchant for delay before—years earlier.

Harris spent the rest of the evening with the Adamses at their hotel. With each after-dinner drink, he dished more advice to his pupil-boss. Harris insisted that Adams purchase a carriage and travel to the other diplomats' homes, where he was expected to leave customary cards of introduction. On top of that he must make the rounds wearing his "full court dress." The diplomats, however, were not obligated to receive him and rarely did. Failing to perform the seemingly pointless tradition was not merely rude; it could jeopardize his credibility among his new colleagues. John hated this initiation ritual—especially while wearing silk threads—but agreed.

⌒

The next day brought a welcome sight: a bag from the boat.

"Mr. Smith arrived with only a small part of the baggage," Louisa noted.

No sooner had he delivered the goods than he carried them away to the customhouse, as the imperial government required.

Word of their arrival continued to spread. Hearing of Louisa's fig-leaf plight, Mrs. Annette Krehmer, the court banker's wife, called on her.

"She entered fully into our situation and appeared to take great interest in the child who was sitting on my knee when she came in." An hour after her departure, Annette sent Louisa and Charles several garments and encouraged her to use them as long as convenient. "[The] whole business was so elegantly performed that I felt very grateful and readily used the favor for the child."

Within a couple of days, Adams and his Eve had another reason to feel ashamed. "We this day received our clothes and baggage from the custom house, every article plumbed."

Plumbed meant "searched." Custom officials examined their belongings much more thoroughly than she would have preferred. Even her most intimate delicate slips and gowns were scrutinized by faceless Russian men working at the customhouse. What could she do? Nothing. At least she had her belongings, including her much-needed medicine chest.

"I was quite ill[.] The water was dreadful in its effects and both the child and myself suffered everything," she wrote of her ill health, which drove her to reach for whatever tonic she could find in her medicine chest to relieve her hemorrhaging bowels. They were all suffering from dysentery, common for newcomers adjusting to the water.

Their lodging was also contributing to their ills. "The chamber I lodged in was a stone hole entered by stone passages."

Such stone quays were foundational to the city. After capturing this flat delta from Sweden, Peter the Great founded St. Petersburg in 1703. Determined to turn the swamp into a capital city rivaling Venice, he used more than forty thousand Swedish prisoners to fill in the bog with imported rock and turn streams into canals. Because so many died in the process, the city was built on bones. Lining these waterways were barriers. These stone quays not only siphoned off water, but they also bred pests.

The passageway at Louisa's hotel was "so full of rats that they would drag the braid from the table by my bedside, which I kept for the child, and fight all night long." The braid was a toy she had given Charles. "My nerves became perfectly shattered with the constant fright least they should attack the child— we were all more or less sick."

———✦———

Realizing his hotel was far from a garden of Eden and wanting to satisfy his Eve's need for peace, Adams scoured the city of his Russian banishment for new housing.

Then it happened. A uniformed messenger arrived at their rat-infested hotel. The sight of gold fringe dangling from the coachman's shoulders could mean only one thing. He hailed from the palace. Could it be? Had the emperor agreed to accept his credentials?

Alas, no. The paper was an invitation from Romanzoff for dinner at his house the evening of October 28. John would go with Mr. Harris. Uninvited, Louisa would stay behind, fighting nausea and driving rats from her chamber while longing to be reunited with her sons.

Time for the dinner came. With his wig firmly in place and his silk stockings tied tightly under his knees, Adams set out. As soon as he stepped his polished buckled shoes into the large hall of Romanzoff's Russian mansion, John experienced true-blue déjà vu. He had been there before.

13

Déjà Vu

"I HAD IN THE YEAR 1781 DINED AT THE SAME HOUSE, MUCH IN THE same style, with . . . then the French minister at this court."

Decades earlier a teenage Johnny had briefly journeyed to St. Petersburg. Thirty-eight-year-old Francis Dana had served so ably as secretary to Adams's father in France that the Continental Congress commissioned Dana to secure Russia's official recognition of the United States. Young Johnny's ability to speak French impressed Dana so much that he asked for his help. Just days before his fourteenth birthday, Johnny left his father to accompany Dana as his secretary and interpreter. They traveled by land to St. Petersburg.

While his father negotiated peace to end the American Revolution, Johnny watched a different diplomatic drama unfold. The president of the Continental Congress wrote Dana that "the great object of your negotiation is to engage Her Imperial Majesty to favor and support the sovereignty and independence of these United States."

Russia's leader at the time was Catherine the Great. Of German descent, Catherine came to power after the murder of her husband, Peter III, in 1762. She brought many cultural changes to Russia and acquired much land, including annexing Courland and parts of Poland. She also issued the Great Instruction or the Bolshoi Nakaz, which among many others decrees declared in 1767 that Russia was a *European* power. Because she projected an image of Russia as an enlightened and progressive place, her favor and acceptance were valuable. If Catherine recognized America as an independent nation, then the rest of Europe would surely follow.

Adams watched hope fade from Dana's eyes as each day passed without receiving an invitation to meet Russia's empress. On one of those days in waiting, they dined with the French minister to Russia. He lived in the house now occupied by Romanzoff.

When Catherine refused to accept Dana's credentials—and thus officially ignored the sovereignty of the United States—Johnny left, traveling without Dana by land in a postal coach across Europe to join his father in the Netherlands. Years later he thought so highly of his patron Francis Dana that he gave Charles the middle name of Francis.

Now he was experiencing déjà vu. Not only had he sat previously for dinner in the highly ornate house, but the grandeur of the scene was also identical to his memory. "This was a diplomatic dinner, in the style of the highest splendor; about forty-five persons at table." The guests included diplomats of various ranks from France, Sweden, Bavaria, Holland, and Portugal, among others. Absent was an English envoy. Though once an ally, Great Britain and Russia were at odds because of their opposite relationships with France. Just as he had experienced years before, John did not know a foreign soul in the room. If Emperor Alexander accepted his credentials, then—unlike Dana—he would soon be an equal among the men at the table—so he hoped.

Something new, however, caught his attention.

"The rest of the company were strangers to me. But they were all covered in stars and ribbons—beyond anything that I had ever seen." Some of these were eight-pointed embroidered silver stars, the Order of Saint Andrew, which resembled diamonds superimposed on squares. Others were medals and bold ribbons signifying victorious battles from the native nations of these diplomats. Right then and there John made a decision. He would not be wearing stars or ribbons. A wig and a little waistcoat embroidery were all the fuss he could fashion. After all, they represented royalties; Adams represented a republic.

Romanzoff took an interest in his newest guest. He showed off his collections, including superb Parisian porcelain vases. One of his favorites was a splendid bound edition of French poems. John wasn't sure which meant more to Romanzoff, the book or the fact that Napoleon, the French emperor, gave it to him.

John Quincy's father had experienced diplomatic déjà vu too. When John Adams left Philadelphia at the end of the first Continental Congress in 1774, he didn't expect to return and wrote: "Took our departure, in a very great rain, from the happy, the peaceful, the elegant, the hospitable, and polite city of Philadelphia. It is not very likely that I shall ever see this part of the world again, but I shall ever retain a most grateful, pleasing sense of the many civilities I have received in it." Not only did his father return to Philadelphia, but he also lived there—in an exile of sorts from Boston—to build a nation.

Now John was experiencing the same phenomenon but halfway around the world. He certainly never dreamed he would return to St. Petersburg to face the same challenge that Dana faced—acceptance of American independence by the Russian government. As Adams studied the splendor surrounding him at Romanzoff's dinner, the lonely reality of his circumstances sank in as well.

"The house—the company—the exhibitions . . . led my mind so forcibly to the mutability of human fortunes, that it shared but little in the gorgeous scene around me."

Unlike prison, at least this was an honorable exile, as his friend Ezekiel Bacon had put it. But where would his mission lead? How could politely praising gifts of Napoleon in a baroque Russian mansion help solve America's problems? How could any American rise to prominence in the United States by way of Europe, especially in remote Russia? His mission felt like an exile, no matter how honorable.

An important piece of political news soon distracted him from his worries. "We heard this day that the peace between Austria and France was concluded." Romanzoff announced the accord, a boon to Russia, at the diplomatic dinner.

The problems began years earlier when French general Napoleon Bonaparte took power in a coup and became the first consul of France in 1799. Renewing the French war against England in 1803, he made himself France's emperor a year later. In response Great Britain, Russia, Prussia, and Austria formed a coalition against him in 1806. Napoleon's army, however, defeated the Prussians in a significant battle at Jena, Prussia, in October 1806, which allowed him to march 135 miles more and occupy Berlin.

In a dramatic turn, Napoleon sought to isolate British trade throughout Europe by issuing his infamous Berlin Decree in 1806. Because he could not defeat the English militarily, he sought to destroy them economically. He forbade France, countries under his conquering military influence, and his allies from trading with British ships, whether they embarked from British ports or British colonial ports, such as those in the Bahamas southeast of Florida. This exclusion included so-called British products carried by neutral ships, such as American trade vessels. Thus, Napoleon's Continental System began in earnest.

In 1807 Russia and Prussia, without Austria, came to terms with France through the Treaties of Tilsit. Napoleon took control of Prussian Poland. Alexander reluctantly agreed to join Napoleon's Continental System, which forced him to let go of long-standing trade ties with England. In return Napoleon agreed to underwrite Alexander's quest to capture Finland away from the Swedes.

Now Austria was finally at peace with both France and Russia. Under the clinking of glasses, Romanzoff toasted the new accord as beneficial to his country and the stability of Europe.

With the weight of Austria's alliance lifted from his mind, now maybe Emperor Alexander was ready to receive his newest diplomat. So John hoped. Before the evening ended, the chancellor pulled Adams aside. His demeanor was direct.

Ah, hope vanished from John's heart as soon as Romanzoff began speaking French. The message was clear. The emperor was still confined. He would not be able to receive Adams's credentials for several more days at least. "But he [Count Romanzoff] repeated that the mission was agreeable to him."

With his introduction to the czar postponed, John spent the next day leaving cards of introductions at diplomatic mansions. "The formalities of these court presentations are so trifling and insignificant in themselves, and so important in the eyes of princes and courtiers, that they are much more embarrassing to an American than business of real importance," John reflected on the ruffling of his republican principles.

Precisely following Harris's directions, he performed the door-to-door ritual, which was as monotonous as a Baltic sailing wind: "It is not safe or prudent to despise them [the customs], nor practical for a person of rational understanding to value them."

At the same time, John tried to rescue his wife from the rats.

"The style of expense is so terrible here it seems as if it would be impossible for us to stay here—we are in pursuit of lodgings but can procure none," Louisa moaned. Within a few days, another palace messenger boasting gold fringe on his shoulders arrived at their hotel.

"The emperor signified . . . that he would receive Mr. Adams," Louisa wrote in relief.

The wait was over. As John put his arm through his silk waistcoat and buttoned his jacket to prepare for the meeting, he may have wondered about the mysterious Emperor Alexander. Was the grandson of Catherine the Great wise and benevolent or prickly and petty? Did he have character, or was he a caricature of royalty? Who were his allies? His friends? Did he keep his friends close and his enemies closer?

John did not know the answers to these questions as he rolled his silk stockings to his knees and buckled his shoes, but he knew one thing for sure. Twelve years after the deed, one question lingered under the cigar smoke of taverns throughout Russia. Was Alexander involved in the mad murder of his foolish father, Paul? Because so many Russian nobles—as many as eighty—were aware of the conspiracy at the time, it was impossible to believe that the prince was completely ignorant of the plot. However, Alexander was so likable—and powerful—that no one wanted to believe he was involved, either.

Soon the moment arrived. A carriage whisked John away from the hotel and took him to the Winter Palace, a mint-green giant towering above the Neva River. Greeting him was a medieval-looking man dressed in a dark velvet robe with a wide white collar and feather in his black velvet cap. The master of ceremonies resembled a cross between an American pilgrim and a monk. He escorted John along the palace's checkerboard parquet floors and white marble columns to the emperor's cabinet room.

John stood stock-still as the ceremonial monk announced "the minister plenipotentiary from the United States of America to His Imperial Majesty the emperor of all Russia."

Standing before him was thirty-two-year-old Emperor Alexander, a tall, blondish red-headed man with cheery apple cheeks dotting his long oval face. The emperor stepped forward to greet him.

"Sir, I am happy to see you here," Alexander said in French.

Adams bowed according to his instructions and presented his credential letters.

"The president of the United States hopes His Imperial Majesty would consider the mission as a proof of the president's respect for His Majesty's person and character, and of his desire to multiply and to strengthen the relations of friendship and commerce between His Majesty's provinces and the United States," Adams said, delivering his most important and rehearsed lines.

The emperor dished out compliments, noting, "The system of the United States was wise and just."

Just as quickly as the formalities began, so they ended. The emperor suddenly led John away from the door to a window overlooking the Neva River. He mysteriously lowered his tone "to avoid being overheard." Without servants or courtiers standing nearby, Alexander could now freely talk business. That meant politics. He was ready to reveal who was a friend and who was not.

England was clearly a foe. In Alexander's view the only obstacle to peace across Europe was "the obstinate adherence of England to a system of maritime pretensions which was neither liberal nor just."

English stubbornness was none other than Britain's 1807 Orders in Council, a response to Napoleon's Berlin Decree in 1806. The Orders in Council declared an English blockade of the whole continent of Europe. The purpose was to prevent France and its allies from trading with anyone without first going through Britain. Napoleon retaliated further with the Milan Decree in 1807, which allowed authorities at French-controlled ports to seize any ship that first called at a British port. Thus, any merchant boat entering a British port could be taken by a French vessel. Any ship entering a Continental port, or one under Napoleon's military influence, could be taken by a British ship. The result was a power struggle, a tug-of-war at sea.

In Alexander's mind, as he told Adams that day, the only objective now was to bring England "to reasonable terms on the subject."

Who was a friend? Alexander explained that Russia's friendship with France was essential to security throughout Europe. Napoleon had assured Alexander that he was not trying to conquer England but "make her recognize the only fair and equitable principles of neutral navigation in time of war."

Adams responded by saying that America sought neutrality among Europe's quarrels. Despite problems between France and England, he hoped His Majesty could offer the United States assurances of fair trade. The emperor agreed, indicating that Russia and America could be useful to each other.

Alexander explained that this new relationship with America gave him great pleasure and "everything that depended on him he should be happy to contribute towards increasing the friendly intercourse between them."

The emperor relaxed even more. Business aside. Now it was time to get to know the latest addition to his diplomatic corps. He peppered John with questions. Had he been in St. Petersburg before?

Explaining his role as translator for Dana, John poured on the diplomatic charm. "I had then admired the city as the most magnificent I had ever seen."

The czar's curiosity continued unabashed. What were the largest US cities? Populations? What did they look like?

Adams boasted that New York and Philadelphia were the largest in America. New York's population was ninety-six thousand. Philadelphia's was nearly fifty-four thousand. Both were elegant cities with buildings three and four stories high. They formed "handsome and convenient dwelling houses suitable to the citizens of a republic but which in point of splendor and magnificence could not vie with the buildings of St. Petersburg, which to the eye of a stranger appeared like a city of princes."

Topping his compliments, John added that St. Petersburg was the most magnificent city of Europe and the world. The emperor smiled, confessing that he had not visited Vienna or Paris. Dresden was small. Berlin's modern parts were beautiful, but not the ancient ones.

"Petersburg had the advantage of being a city entirely modern and built upon a plan," he replied, asking his new friend about the weather in his hometown of Boston.

Adams explained that Massachusetts experienced six months of winter.

"Then, we have two months more here," Alexander said.

All the gravel, stone, or iron in the world could not make a road better than a few hours of frost, boasted Alexander. Such natural roads were an advantage to Russia's mammoth size. But size was also one of its greatest evils.

"It was very difficult to hold together so great a body as this empire," the emperor confessed.

Bluntness nearly burst from John's mouth in response. He wanted to point out that the czar recently increased this evil by acquiring Finland. The diplomat in Adams, however, demurred on this topic and the problem with the American sailors detained in Denmark. He needed to build trust with Alexander, which would take time, before he could successfully broach such a sensitive subject.

Saying he was pleased that the choice of minister had fallen on Adams, the emperor closed their cordial conversation. He added that he hoped Adams should find his residence there agreeable. At the moment John would have been happy to simply find an affordable hotel sans rats, but again, he kept his mouth shut.

Whisked away by the monk, Adams left the palace and boarded his carriage.

No doubt this reserved man concealed his pride as he walked into the hotel lobby. As soon as he closed the door of his chamber, he may have embraced Louisa with joy, telling his best friend the good news.

He did it. Without wearing obnoxious ribbons and stars, he donned the suit of a diplomat just the same. He had accomplished something no other American had done. Adams had just established diplomatic ties with Russia at the level of minister—a high rank respected by European countries.

His father had accomplished a similar feat. As the first American minister to England, the senior Adams was similarly introduced to King George III. England's acceptance of Adams's credentials was a colossal triumph for independence. While Russia was not an enemy, the country was not a friend, either. Now it was. On the world stage, this was an opening curtain moment for the United States, which longed to be treated for what it was—a sovereign nation completely independent of England.

With such a stellar starting point, perhaps envoy Adams could soon have enough success to put him back on track, allowing him to return to America within a year.

Though proud of her husband's Prince Charming start, all was not well with Louisa. Her nausea had subsided, but she made a startling discovery. She was going to be more alone in St. Petersburg than she expected.

"Madame de Bray was young and very pretty and the only lady of the corps diplomatic besides myself," she observed sadly.

Louisa and the Bavarian minister's wife were the only wives who had accompanied their ministerial husbands to St. Petersburg. The other diplomats who held the same rank of minister were either unmarried or left their wives behind in their native countries. Why couldn't John have done the same?

Here Louisa had given up her God-given responsibility to her sons, endured the worst ocean voyage of her life, and landed with only the clothes on her back, only to discover that she was not expected to come after all.

Had communication been faster, John and his father might have written letters inquiring of the expectations of diplomats' wives of Adams's rank in Russia. However, the Internet in 1809 was as inconceivable as traveling to the moon. Neither did they have time to write letters to the US envoys in France or England to inquire about corresponding customs in Russia. Yet the Adams men also saw something in Louisa that she could not see. As a British-born American, she could act like a princess and a republican at the same time—excellent qualities for a woman unofficially representing the United States in Europe.

So far the Russian government had ignored her, except to rummage through her clothing during customs inspections. While her husband reveled in his achievement, Louisa hoped to hide behind her plain white cambric shawl and other clothes from her trunks. She could be content to stay at home with Charles while her husband spent the next year at diplomatic dinners.

No such luck.

Three days later, the ceremonial monk jubilantly called on them. Adams's meeting with the czar went so well that it was time for both of them to be introduced to the czar's leading ladies. The emphasis was on Mrs. Adams. While she could act like a princess, Louisa now urgently needed a Cinderella gown.

14

Eve's Leaves

"This morning Monsieur de Maisonneuve called and informed me that I must write a note to the chancellor requesting to be presented to the empress mother and to the reigning empress," Louisa noted.

The date was set for Sunday, after the imperial family attended liturgy at the palace. She had only a few days to prepare for the greatest introductions of her life. What should she wear? What should she say?

Mrs. Krehmer rescued her, taking Louisa to several hat and dressmaker shops at the silver row arcade. Milliners there knew how to dress to impress the empresses.

Thick, luxurious velvet. Rich crimson. Intricate embroidery. Hoops. Diamonds. The textures were as varied as fur is to netting. While she felt the smoothness of silks with her fingers and marveled over the intricate embroidery trim, her heart sank. The satins, silks, velvets, and accessories were as beautiful to behold as the apple was to Eve. Mrs. Adams worried about indulging in extravagance. John's commitment to living within his means was as firmly attached to him as his head. As the gold thread glistened from the light beaming through the store's windows, the pain of not being able to afford what she truly wanted was very real.

"I had no vanity to gratify and experience had taught me years before the meanness of an American minister's position at a European court." *Meanness* meant "meager." The US government did not provide its diplomats with a sufficient purse to compete with other countries. America had traded royalty for representation. Diplomats from a republic were to dress and act differently than those from a monarchy. As an American newlywed living among Berlin's diplomatic elite, Louisa had learned to live on a shoe-buckle budget.

Her financial fears came from deep roots. When her parents met with unfortunate circumstances years earlier, they fled their London creditors just weeks after Louisa and John's London wedding, which denied the newlyweds Louisa's dowry. The Johnsons voyaged to America and settled in Washington City. Her father later died in 1802, leaving her mother and siblings with little. As a result, Kitty was completely dependent on Louisa, "without one six-pence in the world" and "not even clothed properly."

Seeing so many rich dress fabrics worried Louisa. Would she have to supply herself with silks and satins suitable for queens? Such a budget strain was something the Adams men had failed to consider. Had the decision been hers, she would have skipped the extravagance altogether and stayed home.

The Jane Austen in Louisa knew what smelled strongest among such social circles. Pretension perfumed European courts more than any colognes or powder puffs. Empress Elizabeth, Russia's mid-1700s ruler, owned more than "fifteen thousand ball gowns" and thousands of pairs of shoes. No matter that imitation is the highest form of flattery, she refused to allow another woman in her court to wear her hairstyle. Extreme extravagance continued to dominate this empire. Clothing was more than ornamented fig leaves. Hats, wigs, jewels, and hoops weren't just accessories. They were props. Clothing was costume.

Those seeking success with the czar must dress the part. Failure—especially for a woman—was not merely a fashion mistake but a fatal yarn, the unstitching of a minister's mission. Louisa could not afford for her threads to become loose, but neither could she afford lavish threads. Dresses cost from seven hundred to sixteen hundred rubles, or two hundred to five hundred dollars, a significant sum in 1809.

Tossing temptation aside, Louisa picked a dress made of silver tissue, a cheap but pretty gauzy woven material. Her choice reflected America's egalitarian principles while also being tasteful and elegant. She hoped it was not too simple for the czarinas or too expensive for her frugal husband.

The next question was protocol. Was she to bow to the empresses? Curtsy? Kiss hands? Storms may sink ships, but a missed kiss could cause a pretentious royal stink. She asked for help.

"In the evening we went by appointment to the Bavarian Minister's." Because John had dutifully left introduction cards with the other diplomats, he and Louisa could now call upon the Baron de Bray and Madame de Bray.

As the only other wife of a diplomatic minister, Madame de Bray had also been introduced to the imperial family. Surely she could relay the palace's expectations—woman to woman. However, her etiquette descriptions—such as whether or not to kiss their hands—didn't match the ceremonial monk's instructions.

"Her account of the forms of presentation differed very much from those we had heard before."

Whom should Louisa believe? The master of ceremonies? Or the only other woman who had recently experienced the same presentation? Louisa was as confused as ever. She took comfort in one fact: she would not face the introduction alone. John would be at her side.

In the midst of this, Adams gave his beloved something she needed: new quarters. They moved to the Hôtel de la Ville de Bordeaux. Gone were the rats. "Somewhat better but very bad at the Hôtel de Londres," Louisa wryly observed.

The master of ceremonies gave them one final instruction. The night before their introduction, they were to visit Countess Litta. The gossip about her was not as mysterious as the rumors about Emperor Alexander, but somewhat salacious nonetheless. Litta held a high position by virtue of heredity stemming from a less-than-virtuous history. She was the niece of Prince Potyomkin, a Russian general who was Catherine the Great's de facto, and possibly secret, husband. Litta inherited his wealth and stature, becoming the emperor's first dame of honor.

As their carriage clip-clopped from their new hotel over the cobblestones to the woman's exquisite mansion, their situation was fairy tale–like. Countess Litta received them "very politely" but not warmly as Louisa recalled. "Very handsome and very fat," she resembled a fairy godmother, not a witch—a good sign.

When the countess explained the ceremony, relief swept over Louisa faster than Cinderella's pumpkin could turn into a carriage. Litta's description aligned perfectly with the monk's instructions, not Madame de Bray's. Although the plump countess had waved her proverbial magic wand, she left open a worrisome possibility. Litta was not sure which the empresses preferred, joint or separate introductions.

"The countess told me that I was to be presented the next day directly after mass to the empress mother—But she did not know if I was to be presented to the Empress Elizabeth [Alexander's wife] or [if] Mr. Adams [was to be presented too]," Louisa wrote, worried about entering the palace solus or sans husband.

The next morning Adams and his Eve began donning their glistening fig leaves. By 11:00 a.m., with his wig secure, John was ready for mass and meeting the empresses. Then he heard it. The sound of trotting horses came to a sudden stop outside their hotel. A uniformed messenger gave him a message. He sighed and returned to their chamber to tell his half-dressed wife the news.

The empresses were delaying Louisa's presentation until half past two. Adams's orders to attend the liturgy were as solid as the stone quay lining the river. He had no choice. Neither did she. They would be introduced separately. The imperial family directed this performance, and all the Adamses could do was wear their costumes, rehearse their lines, and hope for graceful entrances and exits.

"Of this Mr. Adams informed me, and I was left alone to go through all the fears and frights of the presentation perfectly alone at the most magnificent court in Europe."

At least she had more time. For a woman in that century, putting on a full court dress was not simply pulling a dress over one's head. The process was multilayered from inside out and top to bottom. Executing the art of dressing took precision, patience, and a partner. With the aid of chambermaid Martha Godfrey, Louisa likely slipped on her chemise, an undergarment, first. Because her white bodice was heavily trimmed with curly blond material on the sleeves and fit tightly around her bust and shoulders, she probably relied on Martha to gently ease it over her so the bodice's details would remain uncrushed.

As she dressed, all she could do was worry, wondering if she would ascend as effortlessly as Cinderella to the palace or slink away sadly like a stepsister with ill-fitting slippers.

⌐⌐⌐

Meanwhile John and Mr. Harris rode to the Winter Palace, where they joined the diplomatic corps in the chapel's antechamber. While they waited, an attendant approached Adams. The empress mother wanted to meet him before liturgy.

Adams greeted Alexander's mother, Maria Fedorovna, the wife of the assassinated Paul. What struck him the most was not her oval face framed by tightly curled gray-brown ringlets but her curiosity about America.

"She asked whether there was not a great number of emigrants arriving there from Europe," John recorded, explaining that migration to America had recently decreased.

"How so? I thought there were even in these times more than ever," she replied with condescension.

Since Jefferson's embargo and Britain's Orders in Council, immigration had slowed.

"But it is freely admitted here," she said, referring to Russia's openness to trade with the United States.

"Yes, I hoped we should continue in the enjoyment of this advantage, which was important to the interests of both countries."

As they spoke about a variety of subjects, Adams couldn't help noticing the woman's obvious contradictions. She was friendly and patronizing at the same time.

Concluding their conversation, he rejoined the diplomatic corps in the hall. Then he saw him, a dashing, dark-haired man with sideburns stretching from his ears to the bottom of his jaw line. Though the man was Armand Augustin Louis, marquis de Caulaincourt, his official French title was much longer: the Duc de Vicence, Grand Ecuyer de France, Ambassadeur Extraordinaire près de S. M. l'Empereur de toutes les Russies.

Wanting to clear up some confusion, Adams approached Monsieur de Caulaincourt, the French ambassador to Russia. John explained that he was sorry to have missed him when he dropped a card by his home. The Frenchman replied that he had also called upon Adams but did not find him at his hotel. Given the time that Caulaincourt said he called, John knew the Frenchman was mistaken. He had been at his hotel.

Was it miscommunication? Or pretension? Adams feared the French ambassador was starting their relationship on a lie.

⌁

Meanwhile horses left the palace and headed for Louisa's hotel again. For the second time, one of the empresses notified her of a time change.

The confusing messages only increased Louisa's anxiety. She slipped on her satin slippers and prepared for the next layer—stepping into her skirt, which would dominate her frame. This was the era of the Empire waist, where skirts began just below the bust and gracefully flowed to the floor. Slipping on the skirt was not as easy as sliding a leg through breeches. Men did not have to worry about whale bone hoops. Fortunately this skirt was already attached to the hoop, which made it easier to step into.

Although Louisa worried about her presentation, English ladies wore silver tissue to the British court. Surely it was a safe choice here as well. What made this fabric beautiful were its intricately woven contrasting threads. With her bodice and skirt in place, she could relax a little and take her time with the next layers, unless another palace messenger arrived to change the time again.

⌁

John had attended many church services in Boston and Quincy, where he was accustomed to sitting in a pew. The church in Russia was the Orthodox Church, which he called the Greek Church in his diary. Except for kneeling once, the diplomatic corps stood throughout the entire Orthodox liturgy at the palace chapel. Following the mass was a Te Deum, a special praise service. This ceremony gave thanks to God for France's and Austria's new peace. The Te Deum began with a bang, literally. Cannon fired over the Neva River from the admiralty. John watched the service unfold, which included the emperor kissing the crucifix and the archbishop kissing the emperor's hand. What also stood out was the music, which was entirely vocal without instrument—quite unlike Congregational hymns accompanied by organs in Boston.

⌁

Louisa probably heard the cannon fire, though the sound of horses outside the hotel bothered her more. The time for her presentation changed again.

Martha hurriedly attached a train to Louisa's backside. The material was heavy crimson, a strong contrasting color to her silver skirt and white bodice. Because heavy trains were several feet in length, women often felt they were carting a curtain behind them. On top of this Louisa added a velvet robe, which also included a train.

The sound of horses halting at the hotel haunted her again. Now her presentation was moved up, not pushed back. "And I was obliged to hurry as the last ordered me to be at the palace at 1/2 past one."

To finish, she needed accessories. Gloves covering the forearms were popular. Fans were functional. She fastened a diamond arrow ornament in her Grecian-style hair, an up-do.

"And thus accoutered I appeared before the gentlemen of our party who could not refrain from laughter at my appearance."

Snickering was not the confidence boost she needed, but who could blame them? After all, Messieurs Smith, Gray, and Everett spent eighty days with her dressed as a plain, floor-washing Cinderella on the deck of the *Horace*. Despite laughing at her fig leaves fit for a princess, they could see what Edward Savage captured in an 1801 painting, which was painted four years after Louisa and John wed. He depicted Mrs. Adams as woman with a tiny waist, attractive figure, oval face, abundant hair, and large eyes that danced above a slender nose and lips.

"And over all this luggage my fur cloak," Louisa joked of the arctic addition. Two footmen eased her into the carriage, where she sat uncomfortably with her hoop bowing underneath her. "Off I went with a fluttered pulse quite alone in this foreign [place] among people whom I had never seen."

Twenty days after arriving in St. Petersburg and wearing only the clothes on her back, Louisa Adams wore enough material to outfit five women. However, by dressing in full court couture, she complimented the culture's customs.

The carriage drove through the streets toward the mammoth green Winter Palace, embellished with sixteen different opulent window designs. The powerful-looking edifice was the crowning achievement for French architect

Bartolomeo Rastrelli. The palace was two tiered, with a columned bodice on top and columned skirt on bottom. Just as its occupants wore heavy layers of clothing, so the exterior was weighed down with four hundred white columns and decorative sculptures. Such was the style of extravagance, whether in architecture or in clothing fashions.

Louisa was likely too nervous to admire the palace's exterior. What may have been beautiful to the Italian architect created great stress for Louisa. After all, Rastrelli never needed to climb the grand multiple steps while wearing two heavy trains.

"Arrived at the palace after ascending with great difficulty in the adjustment of my trappings."

At least she made it on time.

"I was received by a gentleman and shown in a long and large hall in which I found Countess Litta superbly dressed and covered with diamonds. . . . She received me very kindly—Told me that I was to be presented to the reigning empress first."

Empress Elizabeth was married to Emperor Alexander. Putting Louisa in the center of a hall, which faced a large folding door, Litta told her what to expect. "[She] informed me that the empress would enter by that door and that I must stand unmoved until Her Imperial Majesty walked up to me."

Cue number one was simple: stand as still as one of the palace's marble pillars and then move when the empress moves. The next cue was pretentious.

"When she came up I must affect to kiss her hand which Her Majesty would not permit." While merely pretending to kiss the empress's hand, she must make it look real by removing her glove. She must also "take care in raising my head not to touch Her Majesty."

After telling her to practice, Litta sat next to a window to watch.

"Naturally timid I felt as if I was losing all my composure and with difficulty could command the tremor."

The room was ornamented with marble columns kissed with gilding on top. Standing at the door were two turbaned African servants dressed "a la Turk with splendid uniforms." They were "stationed at the doors with drawn sabers with gold handles."

Then the doors opened, revealing a long suite of rooms, two more African servants, and the grand marshal, who also wore a brilliant costume. As they started walking toward her, she saw a regal strawberry blond man in a splendid uniform next to the empress, and a slender brunette boasting brown, Grecian-style hair. Behind them was a long train of ladies and gentlemen.

Who was the man next to the empress? The closer they came toward her, the more reality set in. She couldn't believe it. She was being introduced to Alexander too. No message, no note, no one could prepare her for this.

"As their imperial Majesties passed the door the grand marshal fell back and the doors were nearly closed and they approached me."

Louisa stood stock-still while the royal pair approached. A quick glance at the empress's dress, of the same style but grander, made her relax. She had chosen the right attire. A longer stare might have made her feel as if she were looking in a mirror. With light brown hair and large eyes, Empress Elizabeth looked a lot like Louisa.

"The emperor was in uniform and the empress like myself in a rich court dress."

She pretended to kiss their hands and dared not lift her head lest she accidentally touch them. When the ceremonial bowing was over, she relaxed a little and followed her hosts' cues. The emperor took charge of the conversation.

Louisa spoke to him in French.

"I think the audience was of about fifteen minutes ending with some complimentary words and they withdrew as they came and I remained in the same position until the doors were re-closed—And thus ended act the first."

In that moment she probably wanted to throw off her costume's trappings, especially her train, but her introductions were not quite complete.

"Countess Litta who had never approached during the ceremony came up and congratulated me on the success of introduction and said the rest of it would be more simple."

Much more relaxed for the next introduction, Louisa reflected, "We then went to the apartments of the empress mother, everything superb but not so elaborate and there, knowing my lesson, I was more at my ease."

The empress mother tested her knowledge of St. Petersburg. Louisa also detected condescension in the woman's questions.

"She received me very graciously and evidently expected to quiz my ignorance, putting many questions to me."

The empress mother didn't realize that although Louisa represented America, she had seen much of Europe's grandeur.

"I expressed in strong language my admiration of everything and mentioned that I had seen London, Paris, Berlin, and Dresden, &cc but that I had certainly [seen] no city that equaled St. Petersburg in beauty."

The empress responded, "*Ah mon Dieu vous avez tout vue,*" meaning, "My God, you have seen it all!"

The empress mother said she hoped to see Louisa again soon. After meeting the emperor's teenage sister, Louisa's Cinderella moment ended.

"At last I returned home with an additional budget of new ideas almost as oppressive and unsuitable as my robes—I was very much fatigued with all this variety of agitation but Madame Litta gratified me by intimating that I had got through very well."

Louisa recorded with amusement in her journal that "the savage had been expected!!" by the empress mother.

No sooner did she remove her fancy fig leaves than another invitation from the palace arrived. They were summoned to a ball.

Suddenly their new reality was clear. With successful introductions behind them, the relationship between the United States and Russia next hinged on whether or not John and Louisa could survive the first ball of St. Petersburg's social season.

15

Loneliness and Splendor

Loneliness and splendor danced before their eyes as they entered the large hall, though it wasn't clear which was in the lead. Yet they were hardly alone. More than 250 people attended this ball, which Count Romanzoff gave for the empress mother at his Winter Palace Square mansion on November 14, 1809.

"I did not know a creature in the room," Louisa wrote of the scene.

Privilege followed presentation. After being formally introduced, the Adamses could now officially socialize with the imperial family and their court. Louisa started the evening with more confidence than a few days earlier, when her husband's attachés laughed at her attire before she met the empresses. Although she wore the same dress for this ball, she had it altered.

"I was dressed in a silver tissue which was all fixed on me by a French dressmaker," Louisa recalled of trying to make her only formal dress look different than it had for her presentation. "And when I appeared before our young party it was approved."

Such a reassuring response eased her insecurity faster than a chocolate truffle could satisfy her sweet tooth. "I started in tolerable spirits."

As she saw the empress mother at the ball, she couldn't help fretting. Did the condescending woman notice that she was wearing the same dress?

At first the scene before them rang familiar. Though not true déjà vu, the sight of guests glittering in their finest garments was as recognizable as the golden carriages lining the street outside.

"But it resembled in every respect the parties of a similar kind which we often attended in Berlin, where the king and royal family of Prussia were present," John described.

Nonetheless the exiled Americans still felt as out of place as a tuba in a string quartet. They looked closely at the strangers surrounding them. The attire of the other guests simply shocked their senses. John and Louisa had seen splendor before, but they had never seen anything like this. In Prussia they may have seen one or two Cinderellas at a ball. Here they saw at least a hundred fairy-tale princesses.

Louisa zeroed in on the key difference immediately: texture versus sparkle. Her gauzelike silver tissue dress was pretty. In contrast many ladies were so covered in diamonds that their dresses seemed to disappear from the blinding bling.

John noticed that diamonds weren't just for females: "At this, however, the dresses were more splendid; and the profusion of diamonds and other precious stones worn both by the men and women, as well as of ribbons, blue and red, was greater than I have ever witnessed anywhere."

How could they possibly fit into so much extravagance? Moving to another city isn't easy, no matter the century or continent. Loneliness is a common denominator for newcomers. Unless the ball is a masquerade, few enjoy being strangers at a party.

Not only were they new, but they were also foreigners—savage Americans at that. Europeans vacillated between stereotyping Americans as either Indians or Britons. No amount of wine could numb their minds from their new reality. John and Louisa were simultaneously newcomers, strangers, and native English speakers.

As they compared their simple formal fig leaves to the splendor surrounding them, they had no choice but to dive into the water. Would their ability to speak French suffice? Would the other guests be as warm as the palace's fifteen thousand wax candles? Or would they be as cold as the Neva River in the arctic winter?

"As almost total strangers we found this ball somewhat tedious," John noted.

Louisa felt more isolated than her husband, who no longer played Prince Charming by dancing with her as he did till 5:00 a.m. during their courtship at her birthday ball in London. Romance was not on his mind. Tonight John had a job to do. After spending hours dropping cards at their homes, he needed to get to know his fellow diplomats. Putting aside his giant mind, he engaged in small talk. He needed his wife to do the same.

While John conversed, Louisa desperately scanned the room for a familiar face. She could count on one hand the number of people she had ever spoken with before: her husband, the emperor, the empress, and the empress mother—hardly enough to occupy her time.

Suddenly she saw her. Louisa recognized one woman, an English-speaking lady she'd met previously at Madame de Bray's. Seeing Louisa, the woman invited her to join some ladies in another room. Not long after she entered, the room suddenly grew quiet.

"The emperor followed us." Not only did Alexander join them, but he also "politely offered us wine." Because he could do so without violating any customs, he took advantage of the moment and spoke to Louisa.

"He entered into conversation with me."

What a thrill! Although it wasn't exactly like Prince Charming dancing with Cinderella, Russia's reigning czar took a polite but pleasant interest in the wife of the new US minister. She may have felt alone, but at least she spoke to the most important person in the room. He made her feel at ease.

A Russian countess of the day described Alexander's appearance, benevolence, and charisma this way: "[He] won all hearts and instantly inspired confidence. His tall, noble majestic figure, often stooping graciously like the pose of an ancient statue, was already threatening to become stout, but he was perfectly formed."

The emperor's gregarious nature; fresh, ruddy complexion; deep-set, blue, mysterious eyes; straight nose; and boyish grin were as appealing and intoxicating as his best wine. The countess's description elevated him to near Greek-god status. "His forehead was slightly bald, giving to his whole countenance an open and serene expression, and his hair—which was golden blond in color—was carefully groomed as on the heads of classical cameos or medallions so that it seemed made to receive a triple crown of laurel, myrtle, or olive."

After briefly conversing with His Majesty, Louisa returned to the ballroom, where she saw another familiar face, Mr. Harris, whose demeanor was more uptight than usual. "Mr. Harris at last arrived—He [his carriage] had been upset [overturned] and was obliged to return home and dress."

With John busy conversing, Harris rescued lonely Louisa.

"He asked me to dance a polonaise." This dance's noble elegance made it popular. Each partner maintains a straight upright posture as the pair processes up and down the room. Smooth and graceful hand gestures add grace to their movements. The couples proudly hold their heads high and bow as each passes under the lead couple's elevated hands.

As the newcomer, Louisa was all too aware that the moment she started dancing with Harris, people would whisper, wondering who she was. Because she wasn't fluent in Russian, she wouldn't have the advantage of understanding them. All she could do was count the music's triple time and hope her feet followed.

"I was much afraid I should blunder but I soon fell into the step and made out without mortifying my fastidious partner."

Louisa had not forgotten Berlin's or Boston's best ballrooms, where her brother-in-law Thomas often danced with her in place of her dance-averse husband. From the babble and banter of different languages to the polonaise's melodies, the noise echoed throughout the halls. The crowd was having a good time, and John was finding some social success too. "The emperor and empress mother spoke, I believe, to all the foreign ministers," he observed.

This was still not the time to ask the czar to help the Americans stranded in Denmark. The work of a new diplomat at a party was to socialize. By doing so, he could possibly make a good first impression and, just maybe, build a little trust.

"He [the emperor] asked me some questions about my former visit to St. Petersburg," John recalled. "I told him that I had been attached to a legation from the United States, which was not received here, it being in the time of the American war."

The emperor said that "must have been an interesting period of our history."

In different ways Alexander's friendliness eased both Louisa's and John's loneliness. One person who hardly seemed lonely was the French ambassador. The dashing Caulaincourt's gait was cool and easy. He wore confidence as splendidly as he bore ribbons from Napoleon on his gilded coat. While Adams found the diplomats from Holland and Spain cordial and pleasant, he detected aloofness in Caulaincourt's superficial charms.

Until now loneliness led this dance with splendor, but dinner reversed the course. The smell of food literally fit for a king lured them to the most abundant supper they had ever beheld. Magnificence reigned above all. Louisa did not record whether the meat was dry or moist, the bread was crusty on the outside and gooey on the inside, or the fruit was tart or sweet. What stood out to her was the splendor of the service—the trays. "There were fifteen supper tables . . . that of the corps diplomatique with silver."

Silver service, however, would not do for a king. "That of the emperor ornamented and served on solid gold." Outnumbering the guests, more than three hundred servants waited on them. More than half wore magnificent liveries according to rank. Gold-braided appliqués covered their rich velvet coats.

In less than a week John witnessed two contrasts. At the palace chapel he heard quiet monotone chanting and a cappella music, as blended and smooth as if one person were singing. Now he was attending an event on the same block with some of the same people but in a completely different atmosphere. While the liturgy silently whispered solemnity, the ball screamed splendor. Russia reveled in its extreme contrasts.

By the end of dinner, Louisa was introduced to the entire diplomatic corps. Though far from content, the Adamses were less lonely than when they arrived. They soon discovered, however, that splendor led the last dance, holding these liberty lovers captive. No matter how strong the need for fresh air or a warm bed, nothing changed one fact: protocol dictated departure. Guests could not come and go as they pleased.

"No one was allowed to depart before the emperor," Louisa wrote, noting with relief that the party broke up at 1:00 a.m. "I was glad to get home—all this was too much like a fairy tale."

~——~

"I was seized with violent illness and a Dr. Galloway was sent for—who ordered that I should be confined to my bed until he came again," Louisa wrote two days later after struggling to recover from fatigue after the dance.

Her medicine chest tonics were not enough. She needed a supportive doctor, who gave her the painkiller laudanum. "[The] voyage: the excitement and the uneasiness of Mr. Adams at the expense entailed upon us bore me down," she wrote of her anxiety and homesickness.

Worried about his wife's condition, John checked the thermometer outside. From their front windows at the Hôtel de la Ville de Bordeaux they could see the Moika Canal, the closest one to the Neva River. With the Moika nearly frozen, the Neva was not far behind.

Although they had no intention of returning to America immediately, as long as the water was passable, a voyage was possible. If the czar had denied John's credentials, they could have caught a boat and headed home. The falling temperature indicated the onset of long-term confinement. Once the Neva froze, no ships carrying mail or passengers would reach or leave St. Petersburg until the thaw. Land travel was the only option.

As the temperature dipped, so did Louisa's loneliness. Soon her separation would be sealed by thick ice for six to eight months. Within hours she reached a depth of depression that no ball—no matter how fairy tale–like—could cure.

"And again I sadly regretted that I had not stayed at home," she wrote in her diary of her longing for George and John. Nothing could replace what she was sacrificing for her country.

Weighing on them, too, was the new reality. Social life in the emperor's court was far more extravagant than they'd experienced in Berlin. How could they possibly survive the lavish social pressure? They certainly could not compete on an American diplomat's salary.

⚊⚊

Social life in America was radically different. A mere nine months earlier, John had attended the president's inaugural ball at a Capitol Hill hotel on March 4, 1809. Splendor was as absent from America's first inaugural ball as the British flag. Discarding diamonds, Dolley Madison, the president's wife, opted for pearls to accent her buff-colored velvet dress, a much heavier and more modest fabric than silk or satin. Absent, too, were ribbons and stars from President Madison's coat.

"The crowd [of four hundred] there was excessive; the rooms suffocating and the entertainment bad," John explained to Louisa in a letter. "Your sister

[Nancy] Hellen literally took me with her, for I should not have gone but at [a] special invitation that I would attend her. The President and his family were also there, and also Mr. Jefferson."

Adams's conversations focused on small talk, not politics. When the outgoing president saw him, the courteous Jefferson reflected on their shared time in Paris—not the embargo. "He [Jefferson] asked me whether I continued as fond of poetry as I was in my youth. I told him, yes. . . . He said he was still fond of reading Homer, but did not take much delight in Virgil."

Adams knew that Jefferson abhorred the European royal practice of having nearly as many servants as guests. The reason? The presence of too many servants created too great an opportunity for eavesdropping. Jefferson preferred the silent waiter, dumbwaiters, or cabinets prepacked with food and utensils.

The sharpest difference, however, between an American president and the emperor of Russia or the king of France was rank. Jefferson hated rank, insisting that all guests at the president's table were equals. Torn up were seating charts. No matter the expectations of European diplomats assigned to Washington City, Jefferson thought rank reeked of royalty.

"When brought together in society all are perfectly equal, whether foreign or domestic, title or untitled, in or out of office," Jefferson wrote.

John knew the America he represented in Europe. He understood the principles behind Jefferson's and now Madison's protocol. With the presentation to the emperor and the first ball behind him, his practical side emerged. He had to get to work. No more small talk. He must make progress, no matter how incremental, on his mission: firmly establishing trade with Russia—and thus thwarting England's madness against US independence.

———

"I was much better," Louisa wrote by week's end.

While his wife was up and about, a relieved John noticed a significant change.

"The River Neva has been these two or three days freezing, and is this day passable on foot upon the ice," he wrote. With the river inaccessible by boat, the people of St. Petersburg skated over it as easily as crossing the street. Thus, Adams's "honorable exile," as Congressman Bacon called it, was sealed until spring.

16

When in Rome . . .

FRUSTRATED BY THE EXPECTATIONS OF SPENDING NIGHT AFTER night socializing, John set an appointment with the count to discuss business between America and Russia.

Though not old enough to be a father figure, Romanzoff was fourteen years older than Adams. What very possibly stood out about the count at their meeting was his broad, white collar on his monklike chancellor's robe. It was so large that it fanned across his chest and halfway down his sleeve. On the left side of his robe was the eight-pointed leaf-shaped star of St. Alexander Nevsky, the city's patron saint.

While both men wore wigs, Romanzoff's receding hairline was not nearly as severe as Adams's. Where John's nose was triangular, the chancellor's was long and slender. Both had unusually arched eyebrows. Romanzoff's were even more distinctly arched than Adams's, giving the count an austere appearance.

With remarkable detail, Adams recorded this conversation with the chancellor and many others soon after they took place. Though much of his diary writings were personal, he copied official business entries into reports to the US secretary of state and other government officials. Hence, his pen and daily recordings were among his best tools for conducting diplomacy.

At this meeting, Adams wanted to talk trade. Romanzoff immediately made his position clear. England's foolish commerce practices were usurping other nations. Britain's obstinate maritime policies, namely Parliament's orders to blockade all Western Europe, were leading all countries to ruin. Such unchecked power needed a rival. Who should fill that role? Why, America, of course. A man of reserve, Adams concealed his pleasure at Romanzoff's suggestion.

"That some great commercial state should be supported as their rival, that the United States of America were such a state, and the highest interest of Russia was to support and favor them," John recorded.

Nonetheless, the chancellor's proposal was an idea, not official Russian imperial policy. The reason? Emperor Alexander had yet to reach the same conclusion, as Romanzoff explained.

Yes, the czar wanted to trade with America. But how far was he willing to give the United States the necessary preferential treatment to make free and fair trade happen? The count did not know.

John kept his poker face. He could hide his disappointment better than the best cigar-smoking gambler in St. Petersburg taverns.

What about France? Romanzoff believed the quick-thinking French emperor's military judgment was sound. However, Napoleon's trade policies were as confusing as trying to dance triple time while the string quartet played a double rhythm.

Ah. Adams relaxed a little. The chancellor was not as friendly to France as he seemed the night he boasted about Napoleon's gifts at the déjà vu diplomatic dinner.

Next came a change of subject: Did Adams have the power to negotiate treaties? John evaded. Instead he effusively affirmed US government policy. America "favored a course equally independent of both [France and England]."

Keeping the captive Americans in Denmark in mind, John made it very clear. Commercial trade meant *free* trade, not just trade.

America wanted "freedom to their commerce, freedom of admission and departure for ships, freedom of purchase and sale for goods, the more completely they could obtain this, the better."

Adams continued, saying that both France's and England's trade practices were "unjust and impolitic." He then complimented his host: "The more liberal system established under the auspices by Russia was not only of great advantage to both countries, but would very much increase the commerce already existing between them [America and Russia]."

Smiling at the accolade, a less austere Romanzoff changed the subject. Though barely acquainted, the pair found themselves easily chitchatting about politics in Sweden and other places.

Then John left. Free trade with Russia seemed closer to reality than it had before. In contrast as he stepped into the below-freezing temperatures to return to his hotel, he also knew that winter had a say in America's success.

US ships would have to wait until spring to reach Russia's ports. Much could happen between now and then. Too much.

While professing friendliness with the United States, Alexander needed more convincing to become a true-blue ally. As a blacksmith strikes an anvil, over the next few months, Adams would have to hammer his free trade message to any diplomat who would listen—but especially to the emperor. John's mettle—his conscience—was heating up too. He had yet to confront the problem with the Americans detained by the Danes. Doing so would risk his tender relationship with Romanzoff.

<hr>

John continued to meet the other diplomats. One in particular stood out, the Baron de Bussche Hunnefeldt of Westphalia. When he stopped by John's hotel to pay a customary visit, he made a startling proclamation.

"'Tis universal," the baron said. "There is the emperor and Romanzoff on one side, and the whole people on the other." The baron believed that everyone else in Russia, except Alexander and Romanzoff, hated the French. Pretension was absent from his opinion—something Adams admired. Bussche was partially correct. Many of the more conservative Russian nobles opposed their country's recent war with Sweden and acquisition of Finland. They feared their czar was a puppet for Napoleon, an unpleasing outcome of the 1807 Treaties of Tilsit.

The baron had good reason to detest Napoleon, who had conquered his beloved northwestern German province and renamed it Westphalia. King Jerome, Napoleon's brother, gave Bussche two choices: go to Russia as Westphalia's minister, or watch his house burn. The baron chose a Russian exile.

King Jerome's situation was not great, either. He had fled to the United States, where he married a prominent woman from Baltimore. The woman's father smartly insisted that Jerome marry his daughter in the Catholic Church under an American archbishop's authority. When the couple tried to return to France, Napoleon had Jerome arrested and refused his pregnant wife's entry into any French-controlled port in Europe. Ordering Jerome to rule over Westphalia, Napoleon forced him into marriage with a German princess.

The Catholic Church refused to grant Jerome a divorce. Napoleon paid the American woman, who gave birth to her child after the English let her into a British port, a severance for the rest of her life.

The baron's anti-French views were understandable. How many other diplomats shared the same sentiments? Did others merely pretend to admire Napoleon, or was worship of Emperor Bonaparte sincere? Adams might soon find out. The French ambassador had just invited all the diplomats to a party at his house.

By December John and Louisa were finding their footing among the Russian revelers. In a week's time they dined twice at the de Brays, attended a children's ball, and visited the theater, where they sat in the Italian minister's box. Sharing these events together brought them closer together as a couple.

To Louisa's relief the invitations to the de Brays came *sans cérémonie*, or without ceremonial trappings, which meant she didn't have to worry about what she wore. The balls and theater outings were another matter.

"My sister was quite enchanted with all these parties, but the want of variety of toilets [attire] was a dreadful drawback—what would have dressed one modestly was by no means competent for two, more especially for a younger lady."

She knew St. Petersburg would be expensive. The past week's social outings proved it.

"We had much to endure from the rigid parsimony of the salary, our expenses were very heavy and our difficulties increased every hour at a court so showy and every way extravagant."

Fashion-savvy Harris came to their rescue. He gave Louisa and Kitty elegant Turkish shawls.

"Mr. Harris had suffered agonies at the idea that American ladies should appear without such indispensables."

While a thrilled Mrs. Adams draped the exotic fashionable wrap around her shoulders, John was indignant. He could not accept such an expensive gift, particularly from a subordinate. He made it clear to Harris that *Louisa* received it, not him.

"Mr. Adams allowed *me* to accept it."

Adams wanted no hint at bribery, but even the most innocent events challenged his principles against accepting gifts. One particular occasion was the children's ball.

"We took Charles, who I had dressed as an Indian chief to gratify the taste for savages, and there was a general burst of applause when he marched in," Louisa said, noting that her two-year-old boy was "much surprised" at the attention.

Ranging from ages two to twelve, forty children wore costumes, danced, and dined. Children also did as the adult Russians did. There were "oceans of champagne for the little people." The extravagance did not end there. No matter the era, children's balls were not complete without a parting party favor.

"When supper was finished there was a lottery of choice and expensive toys—but Mr. Adams hurried us away when the child left the table and would not permit him to take a chance."

He couldn't let the Russians spoil the one Boston birch in his immediate charge. More than that, Adams could not allow anyone to take an axe to his deeply rooted principle against accepting gifts. Bribery, indeed.

⌒

Louisa needed her Turkish shawl for the many invitations issued by the French ambassador too. No sooner had they stepped inside his residence for one party than they realized that Baron de Bussche was not bluffing about French extravagance. "We were struck with the splendor of the ambassadorial residence, which is quite regal," she observed.

The French minister lived at an imperial palace, a mansion owned by Alexander. The two nations had struck a diplomatic exchange. The Russian minister to France lived in an elegant estate owned by the French government and vice versa. Housing a theater and chapel, Caulaincourt's imperial residence easily hosted forty guests.

This particular party lacked palace formality. Conversations were as free-flowing as the wine. Louisa and John Quincy could easily see that Bussche was wrong on one point. The Russian elite may have despised the French, but the diplomats seemed more relaxed at the French ambassador's than at the czar's palace. They appeared to love everything French—the food, the wine, and especially the theatrical entertainment.

Lips were looser too. Louisa learned more from the ladies at the party about Caulaincourt than she wanted to know. Her stomach's sudden queasiness had nothing to do with the water and everything to do with the French ambassador's stallion reputation.

Soon Caulaincourt cornered her in conversation, confirming the catty chitchat. His thick, wavy hair and upturned metallic gold collar made him every bit as handsome as a fairy-tale prince. He was a cad clad with the authority of Napoleon.

"The ambassador told me I was too serious for a pretty woman; and that when 'we were at Rome, we must do as Rome.'"

"If I should go to Rome perhaps I might," Louisa said, politely but playfully pushing back.

She would not be conquered: "The party was small divested of all ceremony—but I was not fitted for the sphere and 'could not do as Rome does.' The liaison of the ambassador was notorious."

Thus Louisa left the party unscathed but wiser than she wanted to be.

A special occasion is special when it's unique, not routine. For the Adamses, attending lavish events became as commonplace as hearing a rooster crow on a Boston farm. Parties seldom broke up before 4:00 a.m. As a result, John rarely awoke before nine in the morning. This social routine offended his sense of responsibility as a US government official.

Adams read Scripture for an hour, took breakfast at ten, and began work around eleven or noon. Then he received guests, wrote in his journal, and conducted business until three in the afternoon. The late-afternoon hours provided time for exercise. He walked for an hour or two, occasionally passing Emperor Alexander as he strolled. If a late-night party was on the docket, he ate dinner at 4:00 p.m. Devoting only a few hours each day to business and spending too many evenings socializing frustrated his industrious Boston work ethic and republican principles.

The lack of daylight also bothered John and Louisa. Near the Arctic Circle, St. Petersburg suffers from seasonal extremes. In winter nighttime consumes as many as eighteen hours a day. John recorded that on December 21 the sun rose at 9:14 a.m. and set at 2:46 p.m.—a mere five and a half hours of daylight. During those few hours, clouds often covered the sun, further suppressing natural light and depressing their homesick spirits.

"It is a life of such irregularity and dissipation as I cannot and will not continue to lead," he wrote in his diary.

The truth was simple. When in Russia, these Americans must do as the Russians did. The questions facing them were more complex. How far would they have to go to succeed? Could they secure free trade without compromising their integrity?

As Adams sarcastically wrote to his mother: "extravagance and dissipation" have "become a public duty."

He was worried, too, about his nephew, William, and his sister-in-law Kitty: "I hope . . . not only myself but all the younger part of my family will preserve steadiness of brain in this sudden and violent whirl, to come out of it still in possession of our purses and our reason."

Compared with the Roman temptations facing everyone in their household, their ocean voyage now seemed as easy as sailing across Boston Harbor. Pandora's box released a stream of enticements, including wealth, greed, power, and ambition.

"But we all, to begin with myself, need the care of the guardian angel, more than we did in the Baltic or the Gulf of Finland," he explained to his mother.

Little did he know that the social pressure had just begun.

⸺⸺

"Between 3 and 4 when we got home—I was quite knocked up," Louisa wrote after what seemed like the thousandth late night since arriving in St. Petersburg.

The nineteenth-century meaning of *knocked up* is different from today's vulgar slang. The *Oxford English Dictionary* dates the term from the 1740s and defines it as "overcome or made ill with fatigue." Louisa's body and mind were spent. She had danced enough polonaises to spoil a closetful of princess slippers. She had devoured enough delicacies to satisfy her sweet tooth for a lifetime.

Louisa's insecurity about her wardrobe weighed on her each time she received a new invitation. She eventually tried every experiment to change her gown's appearance, even of dressing in mourning, but "it would not answer, and our motive was suspected—What mortifications attend an American Mission!!!"

The expectation and frequency of formal attire became so oppressive that by December 23, Louisa could no longer do as the Russians did. When she opened the next imperial invitation, she knew what she must do.

"Received a notification for Mr. Adams and myself to attend at the celebration tomorrow evening of the emperor's birthday by the empress mother—to a ball." She had worn silver tissue too many times.

"Having but one dress in which I had already appeared several times, I declined on the plea of ill health." Saying no to the empress mother was as risky as sailing along St. Petersburg's shallow sandbar without a local pilot. She didn't know whether her choice would go unnoticed or wreck her reputation with the royals. For the moment, an exhausted Louisa didn't care.

John experienced the strain of suitable attire too. "Not a particle of the clothing I brought with me have I been able to present myself in, and the cost of a lady's dress is far more expensive, and must be more diversified than that of a man," Adams complained in a letter to Abigail.

Having witnessed his wife's heartache and delicate health over the years, he understood her reasons for declining. The next night John went alone to the palace, and he was able to report, "The ball was very splendid."

At the party one of the other diplomats, who had lived in St. Petersburg for years, revealed that the imperial family usually spent about eighteen thousand rubles on each ball. The thought of spending that much money on a party was enough to make the frugal republican choke on a leg of lamb. As usual the reserved Adams concealed his frankness in polite company.

"The empress mother, who did the honors of her house, went round all the tables, and spoke to every guest. She spoke to the foreign ministers before, at, and after supper [which began at midnight] and during the whole evening was very gracious in her manner."

The empress mother didn't appear to be disappointed by Louisa's absence. Free from wearing full court dress and being confined at the palace until the czar took his last drink, Mrs. Adams spent a quiet evening with a new friend, whose husband held the lower rank of consul, the same as Mr. Harris. Her health was the better for it.

"Went to take tea with Colombi, wife of the Spanish consul, and a lovely woman who we visited most sociably—We passed a delightful evening and I had gone to rest long before Mr. Adams came from the ball."

Was the empress mother truly as understanding of her absence as she seemed? In a world of pretension, neither John nor Louisa could be sure.

17

French Économie

NAPOLEON WAS GOD. SO SOME DIPLOMATS TO RUSSIA THOUGHT.

"The Emperor Napoleon is his idol," John recorded of a most revealing conversation with the Baron of Six d'Oterbeck, then the Dutch minister to Russia. Mr. Six, as Adams called him in his diary, believed that the French ruler would "demand the adoration of mankind, as being something superhuman." Mr. Six added, "This idea was entertained by the whole family of the Bonapartes."

Adams realized how opposite Six's sentiments were from Baron de Bussche's belief that only Alexander and Romanzoff favored Napoleon. Though Bonaparte had also conquered his country, this Dutchman's devotion was genuine.

"I do not know whether Napoleon will ever assume the god or not, but if he should, Mr. Six would be one of the most devout of his priests," Adams wryly wrote.

Although he didn't admire Six's idol worship, he found the Dutchman to be a man with great political expertise, long experience, and "better principles than most statesmen of this or any other day."

Six also told Adams how much the French ambassador spent annually in St. Petersburg: a gross sum of four hundred thousand rubles a year. The other ministers spent a mere fifty thousand rubles. Napoleon didn't want his subordinates to be too independent from him. He encouraged lavish spending, giving ambassadors, especially Caulaincourt, a large purse to keep him—and the host country—in line.

"He [Napoleon] confines his rewards to very few persons, but heaps them in profusion," the Dutch minister remarked.

By visiting one-on-one with these envoys, Adams was doing as the diplomats did. He was trying to make the most of the expectations. Despite his efforts, the more he settled into his role, the more unsettled he became about the global politics threatening his mission and country. Napoleon was becoming an increasing menace.

―――――

"About nine this morning I went out with Mr. Smith to see the emperor at the parade, a review of which he makes of his troops every Sunday, excepting when the frost is too severe," Adams wrote one December morning.

Hundreds of uniformed Russian soldiers marched in perfect sync, forming a line from the Palace Square to the Neva River's main bridge. It was the most impressive example of military might that Adams had ever seen. Nevertheless, the most revealing show was down below.

"The emperor, accompanied by [his brother] the Grand Duke Constantine and several officers, among whom is the French ambassador, galloped round in front of the troops and back again; after which the troops filed off before him in front of the palace."

John couldn't help noticing the obvious. Caulaincourt was the only non-Russian among the czar's reviewers. His French uniform, if he wore it, was impressive. The gold-fringed epaulets on his shoulders likely glistened in the sun while a dashing cloak covered his back. On his chest's left side was a five-sided white star symbolizing France's five orders. In the star's center was a blue-trimmed circle depicting a golden image of France's first king of the Bourbon line, Henry IV. A former officer, Caulaincourt bore this *Légion d'honneur*, Napoleon's highest decoration, with distinction.

What was Alexander up to? By including Caulaincourt in this ceremony, was he declaring his friendship with France? Or was he showing off Russia's military strength to a country he didn't truly trust? Both, most likely.

Regardless of the reason, Adams was uncomfortable with the preferential treatment that the czar gave the French ambassador. He first noticed it at a palace court meeting. Alexander signaled through Romanzoff that he wanted Mr. Smith and Mr. Everett to be presented to him after the diplomatic circle.

Adams, Smith, and Everett, along with the other diplomats, attended liturgy at the palace. Afterward they went to the throne room for the diplomatic circle.

What stood out were the favorable treatment that Caulaincourt received and the uneasiness it caused at least one of the diplomats.

"The French ambassador took his station nearest the door, and the corps diplomatique stood in succession after him," John observed of the strict arrangement. Caulaincourt's title of ambassador placed him closest to the czar's entrance, making him the first diplomat in the receiving line.

Although he arrived in St. Petersburg a mere seven weeks earlier, John was no longer the newest minister in Alexander's court. France's and Austria's recent peace treaty led Austria to send Count St. Julien to Russia. When St. Julien saw Caulaincourt's superior position at this circle, he purposefully positioned himself out of the range of the other foreign ministers. The reason? He did not want to appear below Caulaincourt's rank.

As an ambassador, Caulaincourt was the highest-ranking diplomat in the czar's circle. Most of the rest were second-ranking ministers like Adams, or lower-ranking envoys, such as Mr. Navarro from Portugal, who held the position of chargé d'affaires. Others were consuls, like Mr. Harris. Count St. Julien was not officially an ambassador, but he clearly saw himself as an equal with Caulaincourt.

So did Adams, at least in capabilities.

Starting with the French ambassador, the emperor, the empress, and the empress mother spoke to all the first- and second-rank diplomats at the circle.

"The empress asked me how my wife supported the climate of the country; and the empress mother whether I had heard from my children that I left in America." No, he had not heard from his children since their departure. His wife admired St. Petersburg. He could not possibly tell her the truth about Louisa's state of being.

The diplomatic signs were adding up with the exactness of a math equation. Caulaincourt's influence on Alexander seemed exponentially stronger than Adams initially calculated.

By late December John was ready to throw off his trappings and find a more favorable solution for the United States. He could not do as the Russians did. Nor could he do as the French did. This American must do something. Realizing he couldn't break the chains of his so-called exile solely by socializing, he decided to take a hammer to the anvil. It was time to test the new US relationship with Russia by calling for action on a matter that had weighed on him since Norway.

⟡

Adams made an appointment to see Romanzoff. As he entered the chancellor's cabinet room the evening of December 26, he ran into the Danish minister to Russia, the Baron de Blome. The two exchanged cool pleasantries. The sight of the departing Dane immediately increased the stakes. Regardless of what Blome had just told Romanzoff, Adams must strike the iron. He needed just enough heat to precisely shape his argument without melting his fledgling relationship with the foreign minister.

"I came at the request of a number of my countrymen," Adams began, "whose property had been arrested in a very extraordinary manner, by an order of the Danish government."

Adams forged his arguments. Their cargo was "unquestionably neutral, direct from America, and after having passed through every examination required by the law in Denmark, had now been arrested." He tied the problem to Russia. Much of the seized property was purchased on credit in St. Petersburg and nearby Riga. After presenting his points, he fired up his courage and made his request.

"I had flattered myself that by the exertion of His Imperial Majesty's influence with the Danish government, something might be done to obtain the release of this American property, and to relieve my countrymen, the owners of it, from their distress."

He reminded the count of the emperor's goodwill toward America. If Alexander was truly serious about trading with the United States, he needed to intervene with the Danes and call for releasing the sailors and their cargo.

Romanzoff replied with equal diplomacy. The emperor's dispositions toward the United States were as friendly as possible.

"General peace depended on England alone," Romanzoff declared, regretting the loss of the US commerce while blaming Britain. Until England could be reduced to reasonable peace terms, it was impossible for such cargo to avoid "rigorous inspections."

The count relayed a tidbit from his conversation with the Danish minister. Blome said seizing the cargo was "not a voluntary act on the part of the Danish government—it had been exacted by France, whose force at their gates was such as Denmark had no means of resisting."

Suspecting that Denmark was conniving with England, Napoleon accused the Danes of violating his policy, which prohibited France's allies from trading with England.

Adams was stunned. He saw the hostility between the Danes and the English with his own eyes while aboard the *Horace*. They could not possibly be secret allies. Regardless, Napoleon's suspicions put tight-fisted pressure on Denmark to halt American cargo as well as British goods under the cover of his Berlin and Milan decrees. Tiny Denmark was too weak to stand up to the Goliath Bonaparte.

While his expression remained reserved, sparks flew in John's mind. America and England were no longer welded together in law. He could understand if the French and the Danish were confused about American identity in 1776, when the Declaration of Independence was born. He could understand if some confusion remained after the peace treaty with Britain was forged in 1783. Yet to most Europeans, the United States and Great Britain still remained as joined together as an iron handle is to the base of its shovel—especially when it came to trade. Adams's mission was to correct the misperception.

John assured Romanzoff that, with the exception of coffee from Spain's Caribbean islands, all the items confiscated in Denmark were produced in America.

"Is not the produce of the United States in these articles of inferior quality? Cotton, for instance?" the count countered after showing some surprise.

Though hard to imagine, America was not known for producing cotton in 1809. Adams calmly responded to Romanzoff's mistaken impression.

"The United States produced the best of cotton, and in immense quantities, . . . in all of the Southern states, as well as in Louisiana, the cultivation of this article within the last twenty years had flourished beyond imagination."

The 1810 US census would later confirm Adams's assertion. American families produced more than 16 million yards of cotton while mills produced

146,000 yards of cotton. Americans produced more than 2.5 million yards of cotton-blend fabrics and 21 million yards of flaxen cloth.

Without these statistics, which were not published until 1813, Adams nonetheless pounded his point. Because the Danish government sanctioned these imports, the Danes could not lawfully seize them. By capitulating to France, they were breaking their own laws. Alexander's influence was the best chance for changing the Danish government's policy and freeing the detained Americans. If the czar was truly serious about trading with America, then he could start by intervening.

"If this was a French measure, of which the Government of Denmark was only the passive instrument, I trusted that the influence of a sovereign so powerful as the emperor of Russia, and in relations so close to France, would not be exerted without effect at Paris," noted Adams.

What mattered most to Adams in that moment were justice for his countrymen and the restoration of their property. "The active commerce of all other nations, thanks to France, was annihilated," John boldly asserted. "France herself, Holland, Sweden, and Denmark had nothing that would bear the name of commerce left in their own ships."

The United States had scarcely any commerce left. After Madison's debacle that failed to get a treaty with England, the president reinstated an embargo against Britain. Merchant trade was suspended with nearly every nation in Europe, save Russia and Sweden. Denmark controlled a major waterway to Russia. Without passing through Danish waters, American merchants, such as Captain Beckford, could not easily reach Russian ports or return safely home.

With the authority of a gavel-banging judge, Romanzoff told John that he agreed with him on his reasoning. Yes, commerce should benefit both parties. But it would be better to suspend all trade in Europe for ten years than to abandon it to the sole control of England. Romanzoff believed that Britain would dominate if Napoleon backed off his trade practices.

Adams disagreed.

The count then tossed Adams a few rubles of hope. He would bring up the matter with Alexander after he returned from a trip to Moscow. Because Napoleon's politics were involved, he doubted the emperor would dare interfere. "As this was a measure emanating from the personal disposition of the emperor of France," he didn't think any "influence in the world" would "shake his determination."

When he returned home, Adams recorded their meeting in his diary. His observation skills were so sharp that he was able to recall information with the accuracy of the yet-to-be invented camera.

"The general impression upon my mind was that the count was fully persuaded of the truth of my representations; and that he really disapproved of these measures, but that Russia would not interfere in the case."

—✦—

Seeing the French ambassador riding among the emperor's intimate circle at the military review and watching him take his top spot in diplomatic circles showed the dynamics of John's situation. His conversation with the count confirmed his conclusion. He may have been assigned to Russia, but he was really battling the French économie.

How could he find success under such political duress? How could he take on Caulaincourt, much less Napoleon? Romanzoff seemed more interested in adding to the French equation, not subtracting from it. Finding success in these circumstances was as impossible as leaving St. Petersburg by boat in winter. Quitting was a simpler solution, but not a viable one, certainly not for an Adams.

With the mettle of his arguments as frozen in the count's mind as the Neva River, John also faced a new reality of his exile: his physique might also soon freeze in the chill of extreme social pressure.

18

Ice Hills

"WE ALL HAD INVITATIONS FROM THE FRENCH AMBASSADOR TO the ice-hills, at his country seat at the Kamenny Ostrov. The company were to meet at noon, and pass the day and evening there," John wrote in his diary.

Fewer than five miles from the Winter Palace, Kamenny Ostrov was one of the two northernmost islands of the Neva River's delta. Traveling an hour by carriage in below-freezing temperatures and crossing two waterways in the process—much less spending an entire day with Caulaincourt—were about as appealing to Louisa as repeating their ocean voyage to St. Petersburg. She could not possibly do as the diplomats were going to do. Sliding down an ice hill in a sled was just too much for her delicate health. The headache-prone Louisa and her sister invoked the era's most acceptable excuse for ladies.

"Mrs. Adams and Catherine, being unwell, could not go," John recorded. As he prepared for the ice hills party the morning of December 29, depression irritated him more than his scratchy wool undershirt. He wished something would warm the Russian government into intervening on America's behalf in Denmark.

"Just as I was on the point of setting out, I received a note from Count Romanzoff requesting me to call upon him at two o'clock; I was therefore obliged to postpone my ride to the ice-hills until three."

While he didn't want to insult Caulaincourt by missing half of the outing, he certainly couldn't say no to the Russian chancellor. Why had Romanzoff requested the meeting? What was so urgent? He knew about the French ambassador's party. John mulled the matter while his servant Nelson drove William and him to the chancellor's Palace Square home.

Romanzoff's demeanor seemed different, less confident and austere—something Adams had not seen in him before. The count confessed he had made a mistake in judgment. The emperor held a different opinion. He had agreed to intervene on behalf of the United States with the Danish government after all.

"He had ordered him [the count] immediately to represent to the Danish government his wish that an examination might be expedited, and the American property might be restored as soon as possible; which order he had already executed," Adams joyfully wrote of their conversation.

Alexander opportunistically saw this as "proving his friendly dispositions towards the United States."

John was delighted for his countrymen to "have the benefit of His Majesty's powerful intercession." He would inform his government of this "fresh instance of the emperor's benevolence."

With his boss overturning his decision, the count was worried that he had lost some goodwill with his new American friend. Adams reassured the count that his confidence was "already as strong as possible." Romanzoff told Adams to notify the Danish minister of the emperor's decision the next time he saw him.

At two thirty in the afternoon, just before sunset in winter, Nelson drove Adams and William to Caulaincourt's country estate. Russian czars historically encouraged their favorite nobles to keep homes on the luscious Kamenny green belt, which was full of birch trees and great river views. Hence, Caulaincourt did as the wealthiest Russians did. He entertained at an estate there.

"We got there about half an hour before dinner, just in time to see a little of the sliding down the hills and to take part in the amusement."

While the faces of the other fifty guests were familiar, their attire was quite different from their usual fancy clothes. The men wore fur-lined spencers and caps, pantaloons over their boots, and thick leather mittens. The women were dressed just as warmly but in fur-lined riding habits. They needed every inch of fleece for an evening of sledding, a nineteenth-century extreme sport.

"The cold, which had been all day very severe, towards evening increased to fifteen degrees below Fahrenheit's zero."

While he froze on the outside, Adams was as warm as ever on the inside, secretly celebrating the emperor's decision to intervene on America's behalf in Denmark.

"I saw Baron Blome at the ice-hills, and had a long conversation with him on the detention of American property." While many danced, slid down the hills, played cards, or gambled with dice in the house, Adams and Blome found a place to talk, most likely as far away from Caulaincourt as possible. Gazing over the sloping ice hills, which were now lit by torches and lanterns, Adams took a chisel to the ice between them. He told Blome about the czar's decision.

Was the Danish minister disappointed? Angry? Hardly. Blome seemed as relieved over the news as the other guests were to thaw by the fireplace after their final romp down the hills.

Blome then bloomed. Opening up, he revealed that Denmark "had been goaded by France; that it was more injurious to themselves than to us." He confessed that "this little trade in American vessels, which had given them an opportunity of laying a transit duty, was the only source of revenue left [to] them."

The Danish minister boasted that many European nations were jealous of Denmark's supreme location on trade routes. Greedy merchants had convinced some French officials that the "Danes were carrying on a contraband trade with the English." When France threatened to stop trading with them, the Danish government issued orders to search and seize all American cargo as well as English contraband to prove to Bonaparte they were serious about supporting France. This fit perfectly with Napoleon's Milan Decree.

Blome's explanation added to the economic equation that Adams had formulated. Though officially France was a friend, Napoleon's economic policies were threatening America's ability to trade and establish itself as a respectable player on the world stage—and thus a sovereign power.

What to do about Blome? Educate him. Find common ground. Adams told Blome he believed Denmark and America wanted the same thing: free trade.

"I hoped the day would soon come when they might freely pursue those interests without reproach from any quarter."

Napoleon was blind. England was more prosperous than ever because the English were able to dominate the seas through their blockade while other European trade ceased. Napoleon was too good a general to continue on a course that advanced his enemy. The paradox perplexed Adams. Blome agreed.

In sharp contrast to the initial chill between them, the men parted with summertime in their steps.

———

When the New Year began in 1810, Adams reflected in his diary on the year that just ended: "It has witnessed another great change in my condition—brought me to face new trials, dangers and temptations."

His new post had relieved him from his embarrassment over resigning from the Senate in 1808. Despite this, the extravagance and social pressure of diplomatic life tested his principles of frugality, honesty, justice, and morality. He could not possibly subtract, much less divide, the formula of French influence over the Russian government. Each new incident multiplied his fears of failure for himself and his country.

"It has changed also the nature of my obligations and duties, and required the exertion of other virtues and the suppression of other passions." He turned to faith for hope: "From this new conflict may the favor of Heaven continue its assistance, to issue pure and victorious, as from the past. May it enable me better to discharge all my social duties, and to serve my country and fellow-men, with zeal, fidelity, and effect."

The New Year also brought surprising news and a new attaché. Mr. John Spear Smith arrived by land. He carried a letter from his uncle, Secretary of State Robert Smith, dated July 31, 1809, to John. He had offered John passports and a government boat to Russia.

"These dispatches it appears arrived at Boston the day after we had sailed. Had they reached Boston the day before, I should have availed myself of the permission to take passage in the *Essex*; and although it must have delayed my departure for several days, probably we should have accomplished the voyage in less time than we did on board the *Horace*," he concluded in a reply to Smith.

Unlike the six-gun *Horace*, the *Essex* was a hefty, thirty-two-gun military vessel. Congress authorized private citizens to loan the US government money at 6 percent interest through subscriptions to build this frigate and thus enlarge the nation's naval capabilities. William Gray was one of the major contributors for the *Essex,* which was completed in 1799.

"It [the *Essex*] would undoubtedly have had a more favorable effect, than the arrival of a public minister in a merchant vessel, upon the opinions of a court addicted to official parade beyond any other in Europe."

———

Louisa faced her own trial as the year began. Her health was worse. She not only turned down social engagements from the elite but also struggled to make it through daily pleasures, such as dinner. Whatever plagued her, whether a sudden burst of nausea, female health woes, or headaches from a feverish flu, Louisa was not well.

"Went with Mr. Adams to a small party at Mrs. Krehmer's but was so sick I was obliged to return home."

The New Year brought a custom she could not decline no matter how she felt. As one of only two diplomatic ministers' wives in St. Petersburg, she was obliged to call on the ladies of the Russian court.

"On this day I went with Madame de Bray and paid my visits," Louisa recorded on January 1, 1810. Charles spent the day with Mrs. Krehmer.

Paying social visits came with a price. She came face-to-face with the worst side effect of such social calls: gossip.

"I was informed that Her Majesty the Empress Mother having heard of my being out at tea with a friend the evening of the ball to which I had been invited, intimated that it must not occur again or I should be *omitted* on future occasions," she wrote with emphasis in her diary.

The empress mother had learned of Louisa's decision to spend that evening with Madame Colombi instead of attending the czar's birthday ball. Louisa had shammed sickness, so it seemed to Her Royal Highness.

"This was charming pour l'économie!! more especially as I had heard her [the empress mother] tell a lady who had worn the same gown several times that she 'wished that *she* would get another for that she was tired of seeing the same color so often.'"

Louisa knew good and well the empress was tired of seeing her in silver tissue. Had Mrs. Adams faked her illness? After all, pretending to be sick to avoid attending social events was common. Mr. Six told John that before the peace treaty with France and Austria, many Austrian women "shammed sickness" to avoid social events at the French ambassador's. Now Caulaincourt's parties overflowed, rivaling Alexander's.

Louisa wasn't shamming sickness.

She was pregnant.

Years earlier, in Berlin, she had miscarried four times before successfully delivering George Washington Adams. If her husband's success didn't depend in part on the imperial family having a good opinion of her, too, Louisa would not have cared what the empress mother thought. Now she had a more significant reason to decline invitations.

19

Divorce

WEARING THE EMPRESS MOTHER'S ADMONISHMENT LIKE A SHACKLE around her wrist, Louisa felt compelled to attend the many events launching the New Year. A slave of socializing no matter the cost to her health, she prayed for stamina to make it through the first ten days of January.

The events were as different as French champagne was from German beer. Up first were the de Brays, who hosted a traditional Bavarian-style ball in their home.

"Everybody felt at home and at ease there," Louisa observed.

Chevalier de Bray was full of hospitality with a genuine eye on making his guests comfortable. He didn't need fifteen thousand wax candles to impress his guests or extreme sports for entertainment. The event was "a total banishment of all pretention—It was the house of réunion of the whole corps who in Petersburg live much together."

On January 8, 1810, John and Louisa attended a ball hosted by Caulaincourt in honor of a Russian princess. No sooner had Adams taken off his hat and Louisa removed her Turkish shawl than they immediately noticed this extravaganza was much larger than the de Brays' ball. While they recognized the faces of the fifty members of the diplomatic corps, they did not know the eighty other guests, who were Russian nobility and French elite. The presence of so many Russian officials was purposeful. Absent, however, were Alexander and the imperial family. When they sat down for dinner at 2:00 a.m., the Adamses met a special guest.

"He was one of the handsomest men I ever saw," Louisa wrote of her pleasure in dining next to twenty-five-year-old Count Czernicheff, a "favorite of Alexander."

They quickly figured out why Czernicheff was so highly favored. Alexander had sent him on several special missions with the emperor of France. He was an open spy, of sorts.

"He has been during the whole of the last campaign with Napoleon, and in his immediate family—constantly the companion of his table, and sleeping in his tent," Adams explained.

"I asked him if he [Napoleon] was subject to epilepsy. He [Czernicheff] hesitated about answering, but finally said, not to his knowledge. Then, casting his eyes on both sides, as if fearful over being overheard, he said, 'il a la galle rentrée.'"

In other words Czernicheff believed Napoleon's thirst for conquest remained unquenched. Bonaparte also "slept little, waked often in the night, and would rise in his bed, speak, give some order, and then go to sleep again." Czernicheff's insights turned out to be timely. Indeed, big news about Bonaparte broke at the ball.

"Heard of the Empress Josephine's divorce—rumor says to marry the Princess of Saxony," Louisa wrote of Napoleon's divorce.

Though absent from the ball, Napoleon was talked about so much that he seemed to be the guest of honor. His wife, Josephine, could not give him a son, and he needed someone who could. "I still love you, but in politics there is no heart, only head," he told her. Bonaparte arranged a nullification of their marriage, saying their 1804 church ceremony took place without oversight by a parish priest.

Speculation about his next bride dominated the social parlors of St. Petersburg for days. Would he marry a Russian princess? Many in the Russian elite hoped that he would.

The day after the French ball, Adams called upon Mr. Six, who weighed in on the matter: "It is certainly not a Russian princess that the emperor [Napoleon] is to marry, . . . the imperial family here, and especially the empress mother would never consent to it."

Two years earlier, Napoleon expressed interest in marrying Russia's Grand Duchess Catherine. Unlike her brother Alexander, the duchess "detests the French."

"Though the most ambitious woman in the world [she] absolutely refused to have him. The Grand Duchess Catherine is her grandmother all over again," Six observed.

The Dutchman then praised his idol: "The Emperor Napoleon has been unanimously advised by all the persons in his confidence to this divorce of the empress. He is going to make his empire of the west, and will incorporate the whole of Holland in it. How wonderfully and how steadily he is favored by fortune."

By this time Louisa had formed her ironic opinion of Six: "A real plain spoken Dutchman shrewd, keen and very caustic—An enthusiastic admirer of Napoleon—Proud of his station, while he lives in perpetual fear of losing it."

For the Adamses, the first ten days of the year were full of enough social activity to fill a year. So far none of these events involved the imperial family, which made them less formal and more enjoyable. When a messenger from the palace delivered the latest round of invitations, Louisa felt the social shackles tighten once again.

"Received tickets for the ball and supper at the palace," she wrote. "This was a masquerade ball and ten tickets were sent besides the three for Mr. Adams, Mr. Harris, and myself."

Because she had just attended the French ambassador's ball, she could not say no to an imperial ball in spite of the difference in scale. Doing so would be an act of social suicide by indicating that America preferred France over Russia. No matter how much the smell of meat might make her nauseous or how imprisoned she felt, she could not refuse the invitation to the largest soirée of the year. She had already raised the ire of the imperial mother once and could not afford a fatal blow.

"It is a very difficult thing for Americans to conceive of the restraints exacted by European society, and what are termed delicate proprieties—But I have found that we cannot reason upon mere forms . . . and if we break thro' them we must submit to evil construction. . . . Custom is the law," Louisa reflected.

The ball took place January 13 (by the Gregorian calendar), the Russian New Year, a day of great "festivity and solemnity," as Adams described it. At nine o'clock in the evening, their carriage clip-clopped toward the palace's museum, the Hermitage. "It is called a masquerade; but there are no masques."

What distinguished this from previous imperial events was scale. Sixteen thousand had been invited, more than fifty times the size of the first ball they attended. The guests came from localities across Russia. "All the apartments of the palace are crowded with every description, and in all the dresses of the several provinces of the empire." John noted.

What stood out to John was the headgear. "The gentlemen wearing black Venetian hats with large plumes of feathers and cloaks and the ladies rich dresses of the most splendid style." Gone were tricornes, the three-sided hats of his father's generation. The new hat style was cone shaped. More impressive than the fashions of the guests were the museum's showpieces.

"Here is one of the most magnificent collections of masterpieces in many of the arts that the world can furnish—pictures, antique statues, medals, coins, engraved stones, minerals, libraries, porcelain, marble; and the catalogue seemed without end," John reflected. Admiring the Hermitage's collections was one activity that John and Louisa could comfortably do as the Russians did. The paintings so captivated him that he could have spent years studying them.

Louisa agreed: "It is impossible to describe the splendor of the scene—All the palace, that is the two united the imperial and the Hermitage, with all its magnificent embellishments are laid open to the public."

She particularly admired the Hermitage's labyrinth of art and architecture: "The illuminations exceed all description and the pictures, vases and rich ornaments of every description produce an effect perfectly dazzling to the eyes and the imagination."

America didn't have anything like the Hermitage in size, scale, or substance. Boston's and New York's city streets were lined with taverns and shops, not museums. American portrait artist Charles Willson Peale had only recently expanded his museum of art and odd curiosities in Philadelphia by moving into new space in Independence Hall in 1802. His collection featured crude novelties from western explorers such as Meriwether Lewis, William Clark, and Zebulon Pike, paintings by Peale and his sons, and donations ranging from dead weasels to a piece of a meteor that fell in Connecticut in 1808. As much as John and Louisa loved America, visiting the Hermitage was one European pleasure their principles fully embraced.

John saw another sign of French strength at the Hermitage. While few paintings came from Italian artists, the collection was rich in paintings from the French and Flemish schools.

Though thousands packed the palace like ants at a picnic that night, only two hundred were privileged enough to take dinner with the imperial family. The Adamses and their party left the crowds to join this elite group. While taking a stroll among the paintings, Louisa saw the empress mother.

"I . . . was gazing at the pictures when I observed the empress mother make a sign to me to come to her."

Insecurity swelled worse than nausea as she remembered the woman's admonishment. How could she possibly explain why she missed the previous ball? Her true reasons were too impolite to reveal. Regardless of her misgivings, she could not ignore the empress. Her husband's success depended on it.

"I immediately walked up to her and she told me that she wanted to introduce her sons to *me*." Louisa prepared for an exchange of pretension. "[The empress mother] then presented the Grand Duke Nicholas, then about 16 and the Grand Duke Michaal, a year or two younger—Nicholas was the most beautiful boy I ever looked on—His manner was elegant and he addressed me in a style of the most polished breeding."

Because Alexander did not have a legitimate heir, one of those boys would become the next emperor of Russia. Louisa smartly issued compliments. "I believe that my *astonished* admiration gratified the empress [mother] more than any words could have done."

The empress mother seemed to be introducing her sons as any proud mother would do. She was so gracious that Louisa felt absolved from her prior social sin of omission.

Dinner was served at 11:00 p.m. In the center of the room was the head table, where the emperor took his supper. The sign of French strength was as obvious as the meat on the serving trays. Caulaincourt sat conspicuously at the emperor's table—the only foreign diplomat with the privilege.

"The other foreign ministers had the second table to themselves," John noted.

While Emperor Alexander played favorites with Caulaincourt, he made it a point to greet everyone at the second table. "To me he was very courteous and seemed pleased at my expressions of admiration of the scene," Louisa happily reflected.

When the imperial family retired at one in the morning, the Adamses left. With signs of French influence visible everywhere he went, John made an important decision, a resolution of sorts, on that Russian New Year's Day. Before the ball, he had visited the French ambassador's home and asked for an appointment. The meeting was set for three days later. He could not rely on Alexander's intervention alone to solve America's trade problems. He needed to confront the French économie, face-to-face.

20

Water

WATER. WHETHER DRINKING FROM A ROYAL CHALICE OR A THIN TIN cup, no one can live without it. Water is as essential to a king's well-being as it is to the survival of the poorest serf. And when winter awakens in the Arctic, water becomes the enemy of both.

"On this day was performed the usual solemnity of the benediction of the waters of the Neva," John reported.

Just as late nights shortchanged his need for rest, so spontaneity also frustrated his sensibilities. Invitations for royal events, even annual traditions, often arrived at their hotel the day before they occurred. Such unpredictability was sheer madness. After all, he had business to conduct. Worried he was behind in sending reports to his government, he lacked a reliable way to transport his correspondence. Ships were stalled until spring. Land couriers were expensive. Such realities frustrated him as much as the short notice to attend palace events.

John answered the latest imperial summons by joining the other diplomats at the palace the morning of January 18 for the annual "Blessing of the Waters" celebration. Sealing the city with such a powerful grip by prohibiting travel for six to eight months, the Neva River was the natural focal point of this tradition in St. Petersburg.

"It is a grand ceremony of the church which takes place on the Neva right opposite to the palace in the presence of the imperial family," Louisa recorded.

"The foreign ministers, excepting the French Ambassador, who attended the emperor on horseback, were first received in the apartments of the Hermitage," John noted. Once again Caulaincourt received preferential treatment.

Not invited to watch from the palace, Louisa and Kitty observed the ceremony from a mansion on Palace Square, which was crowded with onlookers. "We obtained a seat in a window of a house in the square and saw the procession of priests with the archbishop at their head performing the ceremony."

With the imperial family gathered around, the archbishop performed the rituals and blessed the frozen river. Even with all his power, Alexander could not break nature's prison. He was trapped too. The exiled Americans might have felt shackled by French and Russian politics, but nature, the fiercest foe, chained everyone. No one could conquer the frozen river.

Through this blessing, all looked to Providence. How they longed to hear the ice crack and see the sun glisten on summer's free-flowing water.

"After the ceremony, the two empresses . . . returned to the palace, and went upon a balcony which overlooks the river," John recalled.

With Caulaincourt by his side, the emperor stayed behind at the river's edge. The court attendants and foreign ministers joined the empresses on the balcony to watch the military review. "Magnificent furs covered the balcony" and "all the imperial family attended by the grandees with all the foreign corps in superb costumes accompanied them," Louisa observed.

While the other diplomats donned uniforms representing their countries, Adams proudly wore a plain American suit. From their separate vantage points, Louisa and John watched something they would never see in the United States. Thirty-two thousand men wearing full uniforms paraded before Alexander and Caulaincourt. The soldiers were mostly serfs taken from wealthy landowners for the Russian army.

By reviewing the troops after blessing the waters, the emperor showed the superiority of his military. He could not conquer nature, but he could conquer another nation. Perhaps that was why he gave the French ambassador a front-row seat for the ceremonial review.

The precision of the troops impressed Louisa, and their splendid horses, which not "deviating the breadth of a hair from the line" displayed amazing accuracy. "This is the most splendid sight that can be imagined."

The United States did not have anything like it. The Continental Army mostly dissolved after the Revolutionary War ended in 1783. When George Washington became president in 1789, military personnel numbered fewer than eight hundred. Instead of organizing a large standing army, many statesmen preferred the militia approach, where men took up arms to fight only as needed.

Despite this philosophy, the military's numbers increased over the years. By 1809 the US Army reached nearly six thousand, the Navy six thousand, and the Marines more than five hundred. Though the military was the strongest in its history, these numbers were weak compared to France's Grande Armée and Russia's Cossacks. A pack of dogs was no match for a forest swarming with wolves.

Though exhausted from the ceremonies, John and Louisa met their social obligations that night, the nineteenth-century version of Mardi Gras. They attended a ball at the Krehmers' home. Once again custom confronted Adams's conservatism. He found the celebrated bean in his slice of cake.

"At supper the 12th cake was cut and Mr. Adams was made king; but declined the honor being a republican," Louisa wrote with amusement.

What would the newspapers have printed if Adams had been made a king? Knowing what his political enemies back home would say, he passed the honor to another guest.

"We danced, and it was past five o clock when we got home," Louisa wrote. The activity was too much. Once again a fatigued Louisa took to her bed.

Adams was more exhausted from a battle of wills. Two days before the blessing of the river, he had visited the French ambassador as planned by appointment. While he fastened his waistcoat's buttons and straightened his wig in a looking glass, he likely couldn't help stewing about French politics. Napoleon didn't care whether American ships were victimized in the process of conquering the British. They were one and the same to Bonaparte, so it seemed. John wasted no time when he arrived at Caulaincourt's.

"I told him the object upon which I wished particularly to converse . . . was the order of the King of Denmark," Adams explained of the American property sequestered by the Danes.

"[T]his measure was . . . intended only for . . . suppressing an illicit trade between these ports and the English . . . but in reality it had fallen most oppressively upon American citizens and American property," he continued.

Caulaincourt countered coolly. If Denmark's purpose was to keep British goods from entering other ports, then yes. Napoleon's government may have interfered to urge compliance.

Those sailors were not British, and neither was their cargo. Adams wanted the Frenchman to ask his government to stand on the side of justice for the Americans. Caulaincourt doubted whether he could do anything but promised to relay their conversation to his government. Was his assurance real or a pretense? Adams did not know. While doubting that anything would come of it, all he could do was take the man's word—a matter of honor.

Adams then steered their conversation toward the general topic of trade. Perhaps he could open Caulaincourt's eyes to the bigger picture. Careful not to blame Napoleon, he used his best persuasion techniques. The current Continental System seemed to embolden the English, did it not? The British were not as damaged as the French government intended.

Just as he began to engage Caulaincourt, a servant interrupted, introducing Count Schenk, the minister from Würtemberg. The men exchanged pleasantries, but Schenk's presence stifled further talk. John understood why. The politics behind the countries that Schenk and Caulaincourt represented were behind the most significant change in recent European history: the fall of the Holy Roman Empire. For ten centuries starting with the Franks, the origin of the French people, followed by the Germans, this Christian empire dominated Europe. After Napoleon humiliated Russia and Austria in 1805 at the Battle of Austerlitz in Moravia, he dissolved the Holy Roman Empire. Napoleon subsequently reorganized the states of Germany. As a result Würtemberg changed from a state into a kingdom in 1806, which left Count Schenk dependent on Caulaincourt for favors.

At three in the afternoon, with evening fast approaching, Caulaincourt had no more time for business. He was hosting another ice-hills party in the country. Once again it was time for the diplomats to play. Ice sledding turned the tables on nature's nemesis. While winter's greatest woe trapped them in St. Petersburg, they could at least frolic among its icy glory.

By trying to confront the problem, John had a clear conscience. France could no longer claim ignorance. If nothing else, maybe his conversation with Caulaincourt would reduce interference by France in Denmark. He felt failure nonetheless. Adams took out his frustrations with his pen in his diary: "My time hitherto has been wasted almost entirely."

⌇

Louisa became so exhausted that she could not bear another party. Fewer than ten days after making amends with the empress mother at the Russian New Year's ball, she received another invitation to the palace. The next festivities honored Empress Elizabeth.

Every inch of Mrs. Adams's body cried out for rest. This type of fatigue comes only with pregnancy. Though she wouldn't have known exactly what was happening—such medicine was still in its infancy—she could feel the changes women have felt since the beginning of time. Her body was working double time, ramping up its blood flow and hormone production.

Years earlier, when Louisa miscarried several times in Berlin, her mother-in-law meddled. Abigail concluded that her daughter-in-law's constitution was so delicate that she would live a short life. Wondering whether Louisa's propensity to miscarriage stemmed from Prussia's social swirl, Abigail blamed one of Louisa's miscarriages on her imprudent decision to attend a party in Berlin. When the hostess fell and broke her leg, Louisa helped the woman and strained herself in the process. Someone's lifestyle becomes an easy—though often misinformed—target for pregnancy problems. With such messages coming from Abigail, Louisa easily blamed herself for her lost pregnancies.

What should she do about the latest imperial invitation from the empress mother? She chose to stay home but avoided spending a quiet evening with a friend instead. Louisa knew the reality. If the empress mother didn't believe she was ill, she just might permanently cross her name off the palace invitation list—a fatal embarrassment to her husband. More than fearing the empress mother, Louisa feared for the life within. She may have been an absent mother to her two oldest children, but she would not let an empress rule or ruin her chance of becoming a mother again.

Her understanding husband attended the ball alone. "As usual inquired of

Mr. Adams why I was not there—He informed that I was quite ill and unable to attend being confined to my bed," Louisa wrote in her diary on January 24, 1810.

Then her pen went silent, her journal empty of activity.

Whether Louisa felt her womb contract or saw twinges of blood, hints of a miscarriage sent her to bed. With each cramp ricocheting across her lower back, she may have worried. Had she pushed her body too far?

Meanwhile Adams wrote, "We have at length got through the continual series of invitations which have so long kept us in a state of dissipation and absorbed my time in a manner the most opposite to my wishes and judgment."

With his wife ill in bed, Adams turned his attention to business. His letter writing greatly troubled him. Although the frozen river prevented sending correspondence by sea, he desperately needed to update his government on what he had accomplished—no matter how insignificant it seemed to him. "My correspondence, however, continues greatly in arrear, and I know not whether I shall ever bring it up."

Three days later John wrote a letter to the secretary of state. His dispatching options were to hire an expensive land courier or find someone traveling in that direction to take his letter to the American ministry in Paris, where a ship could take it to Washington City. Whom could he trust with official US government business? To avoid Napoleon's spies, he would have to write certain passages in the US secret code that the secretary of state had given him.

"I have sent to Holland, France and England, dispatches and letters for America, without knowing how or when they would find a conveyance," he wrote his mother. "It is not improbable that this, which is the first I have written you from this place, and which I yet know not how I shall send, will find its way to Quincy as soon as any of the rest."

Although the frozen water hindered communication, Adams was growing more fearful of what would happen after the water thawed in spring.

John had welcomed numerous American merchants into his meager quarters, including Captain Beckford, who, like the other captains there, was waiting to return the *Horace* to America when the ice broke. Beckford earned $115,000 by selling his cargo in St. Petersburg. John listened to his and the others' fears that summer would see war upon the seas.

"The expectation of an immediate war between the United States and England has given great alarm not only to the Americans who are here, but to all the commercial part of this city," Adams reported of their fears in a letter to Secretary of State Smith.

"This however is not their only apprehension. On the one hand it is generally believed that the emperor of France . . . will persist in renewing the experiment of totally annihilating the commerce between the British Islands and the continent of Europe." Because the United States and England were conducting diplomatic talks, Adams doubted that an immediate war between America and Britain would begin soon.

"On the other it is feared that the British government will at the opening of the spring declare all the ports of the Baltic in a state of blockade." While Adams did not believe the bluster about war, he feared that trade would worsen, not improve, in the upcoming season. He fretted about the catastrophic effects of Napoleon's policies on American commerce.

"Much of all this is undoubtedly commercial speculation. There is every appearance that during the present year the shackles and the oppressions upon commerce will be still greater than they have been during the two last."

⌒

By the first of February, Louisa needed help. "Mrs. Krehmer sent for Charles and she kept him until after ten at night—This lady is particularly kind and we are under great obligations to her."

How would this pregnancy end? She had been pregnant at least eight times by that point in her life, with only three successful outcomes. Why was she so prone to miscarriage? Why was she not as hearty as other women, such as her mother-in-law? Such thoughts possibly echoed in her mind while contractions tightened nooselike around her belly.

Just as the frozen water trapped her, so her body held her prisoner. The slightest cramping sent a shock wave of fear through her heart. All she could do was wait, wondering if the tremors would fade or erupt into an earthquake.

"This mode of life is dreadful to me and the trial is beyond my strength."

Had she the advantage of modern medical science to explain her condition, she would have known that 15 percent of confirmed pregnancies end in miscarriage. Most losses occur within the first trimester, before week ten of pregnancy. She might have learned that women suffering from endometriosis, an infertility condition where tissue inside the uterus escapes and latches onto tissue outside the uterus, are more prone to "repetitive miscarriages" and "migraine headaches" than other women. Louisa did not know why she miscarried so often, but she knew the signs all too well.

"My illness increased very rapidly and again I was afflicted by suffering and disappointment," Louisa wrote on February 3, 1810.

She miscarried. Another Adams child lost. As she grieved, how she wished to be able to embrace all her children again. Yet Russia's frozen water held her captive.

21

Winter Woes

WHILE LOUISA RECOVERED, JOHN RANTED. THE BURDENS OF HIS meager annual salary of nine thousand dollars—which he had not hitherto received from the US government—exploded through the writings of his pen. Many winter woes, such as the need to stay warm, cost him plenty.

"You are acquainted with the difficulty and the expense of forming a suitable domestic establishment for an American minister in other parts of Europe," John complained in a letter to his mother, who had lived in London in diplomatic quarters years earlier.

"Here they are greater than anywhere else. We are still indifferently lodged at a public house, and very expensively."

Some rental fees were as much as two thousand dollars a year. In addition, as the leader of a diplomatic delegation, he was expected to keep three times as many servants as he did in Boston.

"These are burdens from which no resolution can escape. . . . The tone of society among us is almost universally marked by an excess of expenses over income."

While the diplomats around him spent lavishly, many were also deep in debt and living beyond their means. His inability to compete with their extravagance was enough to make him quit or at least find some honorable way out of his assignment. How he longed to keep his bank ledger intact.

"You will readily conceive the embarrassment in which I find myself, and of the desire which I feel to get out of a situation irksome beyond expression," he wrote, reasoning that his mother would understand.

Forgetting her weakness for meddling, he would later regret sharing that particular rant with her.

The Adamses didn't mind showing their quarters to the soiled-shirted American merchants and expatriates who came to their hotel. John had also grown comfortable welcoming fellow diplomats, those who came for good conversation, not pretension, such as Mr. Pardo, the Spanish minister.

Pardo often called on John because he enjoyed their intellectual chats about classical literature and scientific discoveries. Louisa had become so comfortable with the cheery-cheeked Mrs. Krehmer that she eagerly welcomed the woman's spur-of-the-moment arrivals.

Thus, the sound of a driver signaling his two horses to stop was as common outside their hotel windows as the howling winter wind. On one particular February day in 1810, the whinnying of horses was much louder. A peek through the window sent a shock through Louisa, who was still recovering from her miscarriage.

"Count Romanzoff came in state to visit me," Louisa wrote in her journal as if telling her best friend. "He was in his state coach with six horses, outriders, three footmen with flambeaus all in full dress."

What should she do? Her house dress reflected Boston plainness, not a Russian princess. Their hotel quarters could not compare to Romanzoff's imperial mansion. Embarrassment gripped her heart. Pride got the best of her.

"Not being aware of the intended honor and our apartments very mean, I did not receive, which was as great an oversight as that of politeness as could have been committed," she wrote of another social sin against the law of custom.

Why did Romanzoff want to visit *her*? The surprising attention lingered in her mind like an unsolved mystery.

⤙•⤚

Within three weeks of miscarrying, Louisa regained her strength. No sooner had she felt well enough to resume a normal life—whatever that meant for an American trapped in St. Petersburg—than John became sick. "Just getting about when Mr. Adams was seized with a violent cold and was quite ill—Sent for Dr. Galloway who ordered him to bed and to keep very quiet."

Ignoring his doctor's orders, Adams would not be still. He wrote letters, this time complaining to his brother. Unlike Thomas's comfy spot of dirt in Boston, St. Petersburg felt like a trap to John. He bellowed that because of the "thick ribbed ice" they were "imprisoned almost constantly from the time of our arrival and still for six months."

Next he complained about France and England: "Unhappily for mankind the present state of the world exhibits the singular phenomenon of two great powers, oppressing the whole species under the color of a war against each other."

John realized that a huge change had taken place since Thomas joined him in Berlin a decade ago: "When we were last in Europe a sort of republican or democratic spirit was prevalent, not only in the official pretensions and varying constitutions of France, but in the political and literary character of the times."

Napoleon's empire was a mere mask for a monarchy. The French emperor was a kingmaker, not a liberator. European power players cared more for their individual wealth than the God-given rights of the individuals they ruled.

The evidence was all around him—in the conversations he heard with other diplomats on the ice hills or playing cards during Mardi Gras. Which woman would bear Napoleon's heir was of greater concern than how the French people would overcome their grain shortage.

"There is not a republic left in Europe," John sadly concluded.

As soon as she saw the commotion outside their window, Louisa felt déjà vu. An elegant coach pulled by six horses and footmen signaled the arrival of another unexpected imperial guest. Had Romanzoff come to call again? No. This passenger was a woman. The empress mother? No, thank goodness. The lady through the glass window was much younger.

"Princess Amalia, the sister of the reigning empress, came to take tea and spend the evening with me," Louisa wrote on March 3. "And the same blunder occurred—neither my husband or myself ever having expected such distinctions."

No matter how kind they viewed the German princess's gesture or how easily they could have conversed about Berlin, the Adamses remained ashamed of their fig leaves. Their hotel was no garden of Eden. Louisa put on a proper pretense. As gently and respectfully as she could, she turned down the princess's visit.

Princess Amalia's call was as unusual to these exiled Americans as seeing the sun set by 3:00 p.m. each arctic winter afternoon. Why were members of the imperial family and the czar's right-hand man trying to socialize with them?

The princess's gesture gave Louisa at least some satisfaction. Her decision to decline the last imperial ball had not been fatal. Far from having her name omitted from royal guest lists, she was obviously receiving favorable treatment.

What had she done to deserve such attention? Surely they could tell by her wardrobe that she did not have the purse strings to entertain in kind? Louisa must do something. She asked a reliable source.

Madame de Bray gave her perspective. She explained that Louisa's presentation to the court was "of the usual line." However, because John was leading the first US mission accepted by the Russian emperor, Louisa was receiving increased attention too.

Alexander's desire to develop a relationship with the United States seemed sincere. He was using his inner circle to reach out to them. In addition, because the river was frozen, members of the imperial family, such as Princess Amalia, spent more time at the Winter Palace in winter. In the summer, they fled St. Petersburg and retreated to countryside palaces. Winter was the best time to socialize in St. Petersburg. Such was the effect of the frozen Neva River.

Although John believed that serving as a diplomat in Russia was a waste of time, the opposite was emerging, even if he could not see it. The visits of Romanzoff and Princess Amelia were high honors. These modest Bostonians may have despised staying up until the wee hours of the morning at a ball, but by doing so, they were building their personal relationships and thus strengthening the relationship of the United States with Russia—and perhaps all Europe—as a result.

"I presume these honors were offered as compliments to the country this being the first regular mission from America," Louisa concluded in her journal.

The palace imperials proved as persistent as they were crafty. They tried again, this time through a back channel.

"Received a notification through Mrs. Krehmer to send my boy to the Princess Amalia's room in the palace to see the emperor and empress, who would be there on Monday morning at twelve o clock," Louisa wrote.

Why did they want to see her two-and-a-half-year-old son and her chambermaid?

"Thus I was obliged to make him [Charles] a suitable dress," Louisa wrote.

What does a toddler wear to meet royalty? White was the most angelic and stately color imaginable. Louisa took advantage of its appropriateness.

"[His clothes] consisted of a white satin frock," she wrote of his sleeveless top. His "pantelets" were made of the same material. Satin ribbon tied the frock to his shoulders, while a white satin sash fastened his waist. His slippers were white satin too.

Mrs. Krehmer also explained that Louisa was not to accompany Charles.

"Martha Godfrey attended him. They [the imperial family] were all anxious to see her," Louisa noted, wondering why they were interested in meeting a German chambermaid.

The moment gave her satisfaction. She may not have been able to host Romanzoff or Princess Amalia, but she could at least please the imperial family by sending Charles to the palace, no matter how strange their request to see Martha seemed. Though Empress Elizabeth and Martha shared the same country of origin—Germanic Prussia—they couldn't be farther apart in social status.

The visit was a success. The imperial majesties played with Charles for nearly an hour. The empress even got on her knees and showed him some pictures. Louisa later bragged to Abigail that Charles was the "admiration of Petersburg" and a most charming child. He was tall for his age too.

———⟶———

Though Adams recovered from his cold, he soon came down with a severe illness. "Mr. Adams . . . was confined by a violent Erysipelas in one of his legs," Louisa wrote of the painful skin infection on March 7.

Also called St. Anthony's fire, erysipelas is an inflammation of the skin caused by group A *Streptococcus* bacteria, the same chain bacteria behind scarlet fever and strep throat. Erysipelas patients suffered from painful, deep red skin lesions and blisters. In John's day, the disease could be life-threatening or, if in the legs, lead to gangrene, requiring amputation.

Once the initial fright passed, John assessed his situation. He wasn't going to die or lose his limbs, but he was too ill to fulfill his most pressing obligation: attend a ball hosted by the British. Though the British government did not have a minister in Russia, the local English elite were giving a gala honoring Emperor Alexander anyway.

Adams discussed the dilemma with his wife. International politics were involved. The French ambassador was also hosting a ball. With America now officially recognized by the Russians, someone from the US legation needed to attend both events. They could not go to one and snub the other. The fear of America not being represented at these parties was so strong in him that he made an unusual decision. He couldn't trust his nephew or Mr. Harris to replace him.

"[John] insisted that I should go to a ball given by the English Club to the emperor and empresses," Louisa wrote.

No, she didn't want to go.

Yes, she must.

The more she protested, the more he insisted.

Yes. No. Yes. No. The tug-of-war ensued. Louisa bowed to reality, agreeing to lead the American delegation at both events. After twice declining imperial invitations, she owed it to her husband to attend in his place.

"But no excuse could be offered and I went with my sister and the gentlemen of the legation and we could not return home until two in the morning."

She may not have realized it at the time, but by asking her to go in his place, John was showing his increasing confidence in her social and political savvy, a compliment to her abilities.

"The imperial family received me with the usual distinction and expressed their regret at Mr. Adams's indisposition—It was an elegant ball."

The next night Louisa went sans John to Caulaincourt's soirée. "Obliged to go to a ball at the French Ambassador's, escorted by the gentlemen of the legation." The event was "brilliant as usual." Suddenly Louisa was the top diplomat in the family.

As soon as he could, a recovered John visited Romanzoff by appointment. He needed to make amends for his wife's rejecting the man's social call at their hotel. More than that, he owed him a huge thank-you.

"I again returned him my thanks for the care of my packets forwarded by his courier to Paris, and of those which had come by his courier and he had sent me," John wrote of their conversation.

With water travel frozen, the Russian government relied on private couriers to travel by land to cities throughout Europe to conduct business in winter. Romanzoff had suggested earlier that John send his letters through the czar's courier to Paris. The messenger took Adams's letters, both official and personal, to General Armstrong, the American minister to France. Armstrong then forwarded their letters to America by ship. Romanzoff's offer expanded to anyone affiliated with the US ministry in St. Petersburg, from William Smith to Martha Godfrey. The courier, in kind, forwarded letters that came to them by way of the American legation in Paris.

Unable to refuse an offer that filled such a great need, Adams considered the gesture as "one of the numerous marks of attention" from the Russians. He also updated the count on America's problems with Denmark. The captive sailors and captains there had received their merchandise and were free to go. "I had also letters . . . expressing the gratitude of my countrymen there for the interposition of the emperor with the court of Denmark, and the effect which many of them had already experienced from it, in the liberation of their property."

The count was glad that the emperor was able to show his friendship for the United States. Nonetheless, until England made peace and ceased its forgeries, American commerce was at risk. Intimately aware of the British penchant for fraudulently hoisting US flags, Adams agreed.

John's extended illness presented a bit of a social quandary, at least in the eyes of protocol-prone Harris, who escorted Louisa to many functions in place of her husband.

"Nothing amused me so much as the instructions of our Consul Levett Harris," Louisa observed in her diary as if whispering gossip to her best girlfriend.

"He would favor me with instructions as to my conduct and deportment." When he escorted her into a room at a party, Harris said she could "take his arm on the stairway where nobody could see it . . . lest our acquaintance should seem too familiar."

The rules continued. "That a lady must not go to the theater with a gentleman but only under the protection of her footmen."

Most of all Harris hoped he would not have to wait with her for their carriage too long at the end of a ball "lest it should [appear] that we had an improper liaison!!"

Louisa could not hold back her amusement in her diary: "This was quite too much for my gravity and I laughed in his face, assuring him that whatever fears he might have for his reputation, I had none whatever for my own and this entretien put an end to such discourse."

A romantic entanglement with Harris was the last thought on her mind. Yet he could see what she couldn't. Louisa was not only the wife of the American minister but also the *attractive* woman who spoke French fluently and could converse with kings as easily as servants. He feared the damage that could come from gossiping lips.

22

Contradictions

THOUGH THE RIVER REMAINED FROZEN, THE ROADS WERE MORE easily traveled by April 1810. A fully recovered John took advantage of winter's loosening chains. With mixed motives, he decided to make a few field trips. Part of him wanted to escape the Russian high life and see how the other side lived. The other part wanted to see Russian manufacturing, particularly factories using steam machines. If US merchants wanted to trade with Russian distributors, then he needed to see Russia's best exports.

The US economic system was colonial, not industrial. Because most Americans held unfavorable opinions about manufacturing and industrialization, President Madison and Congress strategically leveraged the 1810 US census to gather better information about what products Americans were making and where. The resulting data revealed much about the US economy in 1810. For example, only two of twelve counties in Massachusetts could boast of grist- and sawmills. Though not a surprise, absent from Adams's mercantile hometown were iron forgeries, naileries, and mills. Southerners, however, were producing more raw cotton than ever but mostly without the benefit of machines. Spinning wheels and carding machines were run by hand at fulling mills, which spun, cleaned, and thickened cotton.

Census analysts concluded: "The prosperity of the cotton manufacture" was taking place "with little assistance from labor-saving machinery." That needed to change, according to the government report. "To neglect, in our country, the due use of such an advantage, would evince a destitution of common sense." Labor-saving machines would also improve the manufacture of many Northern-produced products, such as shoes, hats, and candles.

British blockades and Napoleon's trade abuses largely confined American crops to domestic consumption. For this reason many farmers and tradesmen saw no need to move to machine labor. In contrast, some in the US government believed that machine manufacturing would improve American textiles, lessening the country's dependence on Europe for manufactured products. Others realized that machinery would lead to better American exports, far beyond raw cotton, sugar, and indigo. If America could secure free trade, foreign commerce would also greatly promote the "wealth of the United States " by bringing cheap products to US ports and selling additional US goods to other markets.

In contrast Russia produced few raw materials to sell to anyone. Manufactured goods were its best assets. Adams was determined to find out what Russian factories could offer his countrymen. He visited Alexandrofsk, a yarn- and fabric-making manufactory five miles from St. Petersburg along the Neva River.

The factory boasted four hundred carding, spinning, and winding machines. They were powered by the latest technology—three steam engines, "[a]ccording to the recent improvements on that great invention," he noted in his diary.

The factory was under the empress mother's patronage. Yarn- and fabric-making was her business. *Patronage* was merely a nice-sounding word for employing child laborers. About five hundred boys and girls—all orphans—worked there. The youngest workers were eight years old. The boys remained at the factory until age twenty-one; the girls, age twenty-five. The only way to escape any earlier was to get married. The factory also provided quarters for twenty-five married couples who chose to stay.

"In two of the family apartments, I saw Russian cradles, which are a sort of hammock suspended by four small cords from the end of an elastic pole, fastened by the other end near the head of the bed," he observed of the devices, which hung four feet from the floor. The contraptions allowed mothers to reach their hands to the poles and rock the cradles from their beds.

"It is a very clumsy contrivance, and the child must always be in danger of falling to the floor, an accident which four times in five must prove fatal."

Adams inquired about the infant mortality rate. "Of the earliest, almost all the children died, and even now a small portion of those that are born are likely to live. . . . This mortality is attributed to the ignorance of the parents."

He then visited the dining hall, where the girls "looked for the most part wretchedly and very unwholesome."

They were taking their dinner at long, wooden tables with benches.

Hanging on the wall in front of them was a picture of the Virgin Mary. In unison they chanted grace before eating. Adams noted the tiniest details. The girls ate off wooden plates, while the boys ate from pewter plates. Despite the dinnerware disparity, both ate thin turnip soup, boiled buckwheat, and rye bread. They also drank *quas*, a kind of beer.

"I scarcely saw one that could be called handsome, and very few not positively ugly."

When he visited the children's bedchambers, Adams could scarcely breathe. His guide explained that their quarters were not ventilated during winter because of the cold. No wonder they looked so unhealthy.

"But the confinement of the chambers allowed to the families, their extreme poverty, the want of cleanliness, and the almost pestilential air which I found in them, sufficiently accounted in my mind for the fact [high child mortality]."

The contradiction was enough to make any liberty lover vomit. The empress mother complained over trivial matters, such as when guests wore the same silk gown several times to court functions. Yet this same woman was a patron over a factory employing orphaned children laboring twelve hours a day only to enjoy the privilege of breathing unventilated air while sleeping. Was she aware of their conditions? If she was, she chose to ignore them.

The visit sobered him. His tour guide boasted that no accident had occurred with the machines in the factory. An unimpressed Adams sarcastically questioned in his diary which of these miseries had led to such a perfect track record. Was it the continuous cold, hard labor, extreme poverty, or "perfection of subserviency?" Though not as bad off as slaves—a practice Adams detested—these Russian child laborers faced poorer prospects than America's indentured servants, who worked under contracts for a specified number of years until freed from their debt and allowed to start a new life.

How could Adams complain about his own fleeting finances while these children gnawed on buckwheat, with little chance of experiencing a better way of life? As much as he admired Alexander, visiting the factory underscored the revelation he shared with his brother Thomas in a letter. Republicanism was dead in Europe. The hope for liberty, so vibrant a decade earlier in Europe, was as frozen as the Arctic Circle.

John made more field trips that April to see the other side of St. Petersburg. He attended a Russian service at St. Nicolas Church on Good Friday. As customary in Orthodox churches, the interior formed the shape of an equal-sided cross. The resulting worship area was smaller than longer Latin-style churches. Though in church, he felt he was at a theater.

"The multitude of self-crossings, the profound and constantly repeated bows, the prostrations upon the earth and kissing of the floor," he noted of why the room was empty of chairs and benches.

With the span of an eagle's wing, worshippers fully extended their arms wide while bending completely over the cold stone floors. Compared to the reserved manner of US Episcopal and Congregational churches, these theatrics seemed almost superstitious to Adams. He also noticed that several trophies from Russia's enemies hung in the center of the city's churches. Among the trinkets were captured English flags, a sign that imperial Russia equated religion with political power.

"In the meantime beggars are circulating through the crowd to catch the critical moment of charitable feeling and receive the donation of his copeck."

Churches were also filled with the begging lower class, called mujiks. "I saw one this day of the most squalid appearance, in tatters which scarcely hung together upon his body, but with a leather bag half full of the alms he was receiving, and giving single copecks in exchange for two copeck pieces." This beggar was doing so well that he was able to make change.

"But the donors themselves appeared as much objects for charity as those to whom they gave it."

Even on the happiest occasions, Adams couldn't help noticing Russia's contradictions: "Easter Sunday; the greatest holiday of the Russian calendar. It celebrates the resurrection of Christ. The ceremonies, as at Christmas, begin at midnight."

While the impoverished masses crowded the city's churches, the imperial family comfortably attended a private midnight service at the palace chapel.

"Everyone of the people has a right to kiss the emperor's hand on this sacred day. It is a privilege, however, mostly claimed by the [men of the] court, which sometimes keeps him up until a very late hour of the night," Louisa wrote of the contradiction, while noting that women were not allowed.

⌇

Visiting these rugged Russian places in the season of Easter forced John to come face-to-face with one of his most deeply held principles. He must decide what to do about the holiday's preponderance of gift giving. All Russians, from the poorest paupers to the princesses at the palace, gave eggs at Easter. The mujiks boiled eggs, painted them red, and expected rubles in return. Members of the diplomatic corps left cards, paid visits, and of course, exchanged glamorous eggs.

"Persons of higher standing," John observed, "present eggs of sugar, glass, gilt wood, porcelain, marble and almost every other substance. . . . Some of these eggs are made to cost a hundred rubles or upwards."

He could not ignore the expense and practice. Everyone was giving and receiving eggs. What was a principled republican to do? Was accepting an egg the same as receiving a bribe? He fretted at the possibility. Advocating above-board diplomacy, he wanted to avoid any suspicion, not to mention the expense.

"Easter Sunday is a great day at St. Petersburg, and we received presents from some of our friends of painted and cut glass eggs without paying the fee generally asked for the compliment—as a religious ceremony and were obliged to accept them," Louisa wrote of one reason for her husband's sudden compliance.

Why did John accept the eggs? Seeing the factory's hazardous hammocks holding infants and smelling the stench of half-clad beggars prostrating themselves at church altars altered Adams. Sometimes seeing someone in worse circumstances than yours makes your own life seem not so bad. He may have been exiled from his country and family, but he was still free—free to return on the next boat to America once the ice broke. He was not begging on the streets or so poor that the only egg he could give was one he stole from a henhouse.

Easter nudged Adams to budge. After all, the occasion celebrated the resurrection of Christ, whose spilled water and blood made him the greatest of equalizers, the atoner of both peasants and kings. Whether rich or poor, everyone in St. Petersburg shared the same fate. All were trapped by both the frozen river in winter and the chains of humanity's sins. Though their customs and languages were different, he shared the faith of these Russians—their core belief in redemption from a God of grace.

John accepted the eggs, his only exception to gift exchanges. Meanwhile Easter gave Louisa something else. Hope. Summer would soon arrive and break nature's shackles, perhaps freeing her from exile for good.

⤙⤚

John was not a betting man, but many mujiks in St. Petersburg were. The date of summer's arrival was the most talked-about topic and the main object of gambling. "It is a subject of so much interest here. . . . It furnishes a continual fund of conversation and innumerable wagers."

While some probably guessed the date—May 10, 1810—no one guessed the hour. Though usually breaking in daylight, winter escaped that year under the dark of night.

"The ice on the river at length broke up at two or three o'clock this morning. This circumstance is said to be unusual. The most ordinary time of the day when this event occurs is between two and six in the afternoon."

Louisa described the thrill this way: "A handsome sight but perfectly delightful to us poor exotics."

John was so excited that he rushed to see it with his own eyes. He spent two hours walking along the river's stone quay. He made it all the way to the factory. It was as if Mother Nature had taken an ice pick and chiseled along the edges of both sides of the river. The result was a giant floating mass of ice that melted as it drifted away from town toward the gulf.

"The river was entirely open, nearly to where the bridge had been. Below that, although in motion, it [the ice] was slowly passing, and in solid mass, extending from bank to bank," Louisa observed.

By 3:00 p.m., guns fired from the angel-spired Peter and Paul Fortress.

"When all the ice is gone, the chain bridge of boats is put across the river and the country is free to the Petersburg public," Louisa explained.

The fortress governor stepped into the first boat, crossed the river, and presented Alexander with a glass of river water. The emperor drank it and gave the governor money in response. Though less grand than the religious blessing of the water in January, the annual custom was just as symbolic.

Returning at sunset, John again walked along on the quay. What a difference a few hours made! Instead of one moving, detached, solid block of ice, the river was running completely free. "The whole passage was then clear, and several boats were then crossing the river," he noted.

The entire town of St. Petersburg awakened from winter hibernation. No longer a foe but a friend, water was nature's great equalizer. The Adamses joined in. John ordered their servants to remove their hotel room's double-paned windows and put up single-paned panels for summer.

As excited as he was, he was also worried. American ships, including the *Horace,* would soon depart St. Petersburg's docks. Would they survive the Danish straits? Worse, would US ships trying to reach Russia make it through those waters, or be condemned?

Neither John nor Louisa realized that the river's loosening effect would also radically alter their mission, loosening the behavior of the emperor.

23

Pretense and Propriety

MORE THAN ICE BROKE THE SUMMER OF 1810. PROPRIETY SWIFTLY followed.

"My sister and myself were accustomed to walk out occasionally when the weather was not too cold on the Nevsky Perspective," Louisa explained.

Both John and Louisa believed exercise eased the climate's effects on their health. The stone quay along the river was ideal for walking, as were the garden grounds near the palace. Sometimes they walked together, but often Adams walked alone for as long as two hours. As a result, Louisa and Kitty took shorter jaunts. The ladies soon discovered that they were not the only ones seeking fresh air.

"The emperor would often stop and speak to us very politely."

In a little while, the attention became too great, leading Louisa to stop their walks. "As my sister was a great belle among our young gentlemen, this circumstance though customary with the emperor towards many ladies whom he met, gave umbrage to beaux and occasioned so much teasing and questions that we left off our promenades for some time."

Not long after the *Horace* left Boston the previous summer, Louisa realized that Kitty was the focus of romantic attention by the young men accompanying her husband to St. Petersburg. "Before we had been a fortnight at sea with three young men—Squabbles and jealousies commenced and the future was laid bare to my eyes as clearly as if it had passed," she wrote in her diary in August 1809.

The men serving as aides to John had been vying for Kitty's affection ever since. Primal envy aside, Louisa missed their walks.

"But the weather being now very fine, we resumed our walks." She could not let flirting keep her from exercising. "[We] met his Imperial Majesty who again stopped us and inquired 'why we had left off walking out.'"

Not only had Alexander noticed their recent absence, but he also seemed to know quite a bit more about Louisa than she expected.

"And without waiting for an answer; [he] turned to me and said 'that it was good for my health and that he should expect to meet *us* every day (looking at my sister)' that the weather was fine."

His Royal Flirtiness continued his pursuit. "This was a real imperial command in its tone and manner; and he gracefully touched his hat and walked on."

Well aware that the conversation would incite displeasure from the American men, Kitty repeated the incident that evening to Adams and his attachés.

"When we met at [the] table, the usual question and sour looks greeted us from the young gentlemen and my sister answered 'Yes!' Repeating the order that we had received [from Alexander to walk every day] to vex them."

Except for the reserved Adams, the men were "all in a blaze."

Although she had attended some parties and balls, Kitty had not been officially presented to the imperial family. At palace events the imperial family spoke only to those who had been formally introduced to them and not the other guests. However, in a casual environment, such as strolling the streets, the emperor could talk to anyone he chose.

"Adding nought in malice," Louisa explained, emphasizing no harm was done. "The minister looked very *grave* but said nothing."

Louisa was ready to have a little fun. Too much weighed on her. In addition to suffering a miscarriage, she had received no letters from her children since arriving in St. Petersburg nearly eight months earlier in October. A little flirtation with the czar of Russia was just that: a harmless distraction from her real woes. So she thought.

"The young gentlemen disapproved and hoped that we should not do it [walk again]."

Was Louisa aware of Alexander's womanizing? If she knew, she did not record it in her diary as she had of Caulaincourt's reputation for liaisons.

Seven years before he became emperor in 1793, sixteen-year-old Alexander married fourteen-year-old Princess Louise of Baden, whose Russian name was Elizabeth Alexeyevna. His grandmother Catherine the Great chose the match. After losing two infant daughters to death, Alexander and Elizabeth were childless, leaving no legitimate heir to the throne. Unhappy with his arranged marriage, Alexander took the first of many mistresses in 1803. He was the father of several children outside his marriage.

Regardless of whether she knew about these details, Louisa was cautious. One way to limit whispers of gossip was to bring Charles, who was nearly three years old, with her on walks. The boy became the buffer.

"We continued our walks occasionally taking Charles with us who always had a kind greeting from His Majesty and a shake of the hand."

Children are great equalizers. Their candor can humble the greatest of sovereigns. Although Charles had met Alexander at the palace during his visit with Martha Godfrey weeks earlier, he still shrank at the sight of the imposing friendly man who greeted him on these walks. Not even the emperor's oval face, long sideburns, and cheery apple cheeks could make Charles chat with the czar. The nearby uniformed guards who held foreboding swords at their sides probably didn't help the little lad, either. Perhaps he detected that for some reason adults made a fuss over this man, which intimidated him all the more.

"But the emperor complained that he could not make him [Charles] sociable," Louisa wrote with amusement.

—————

The breaking of the ice also loosened lips that summer, especially Mr. Six's.

"He told me a number of anecdotes respecting the revolution which placed the Emperor Alexander on the throne," Adams wrote of their conversation.

Six insisted that Alexander was innocent of involvement in his father's death. "Not only was the emperor in no manner accessory to the murder of his father, but that he was affected with the deepest horror at the event; that he absolutely refused for a long time to assume the government."

Alexander had been a favorite of his grandmother Catherine the Great, whose heart toward her son Paul grew colder with each passing Russian winter. While she despised Paul's pea-sized view of power, she failed to name Alexander as her heir. When she died, Paul took over. Because they loved Catherine's giant vision and believed Alexander was the best one to continue her ideals, the nobility conspired to take Paul's life. Questioning Emperor

Paul's capabilities became as popular as puffing on cigars among Russia's elite. Plotting his demise over a game of cards soon superseded any strategy to win a hand of poker.

According to Mr. Six, the conspirators had a problem. Unlike some czars before him, Paul continued to share a bed with his wife, Maria. The conspirators found a willing partner to help them. Six months before the plot's murderous climax, Paul's favorite Turkish slave intentionally "bred discord between them." The slave's deception led to a barring of the doors between the emperor's and the empress's bedchambers.

The plot was so poorly "kept that at a dinner party in the presence of a prince, one guest proclaimed: 'The Emperor Paul has not four hours more to live.'"

When the conspirators broke into his room that night, Paul quickly realized their intentions. With the door to his wife's chamber sealed, he could not escape to her room. They easily murdered him.

An officer gave Maria the news. She immediately told him that she was now empress. He replied that Alexander was now his emperor. Her assumption was sensible. Unlike other monarchical dynasties where the king's heir is his oldest living child, Peter the Great failed to establish a clear order of accession. Hence claims to Russia's throne were frequently challenged by wives, sisters, brothers, sons, and others.

Six explained that Alexander and his mother had not gotten along very well since Paul's death. She was also unpopular among those in the Russian court who favored France, especially after she prevented her daughter from marrying Bonaparte.

As winter melted into summer in 1810, it became clear to everyone that the empress mother needn't worry about Napoleon becoming her son-in-law ever again.

⎯⎯✦⎯⎯

"The relations between France and Russia, have . . . been . . . affected by . . . the new alliance between France and Austria, formed by the marriage of the Emperor Napoleon with the Archduchess Maria Louisa, eldest daughter of the emperor of Austria," Adams wrote of the marriage that took place by proxy in April 1810.

Though everyone was talking about this stab at Russia's power base in Europe, the Russian government had not officially acknowledged the news. "There has been no public and formal communication of this marriage, made to the Russian government, either by Austria or France. The negotiation which terminated in this contract of marriage was not only kept a profound secret to the Russian Ambassador at Paris, but he was even led to believe and to communicate to his court the belief that the choice of the Emperor Napoleon had fixed upon a different person."

Now forever a French favorite, Austria had won this latest power play. What was Alexander to do? With no official communication from the French government, he could not publicly acknowledge the alliance, especially knowing that Napoleon once considered his sister for a bride. Because France was officially an ally, he could not openly scoff at the marriage's detrimental influence on Russia's political ties with both countries. Caulincourt solved the problem.

"I am told that there has been a confidential communication of the marriage, made by the French Ambassador here to the Emperor Alexander in person."

In May 1810, Monsieur Caulaincourt held a ball at his residence to celebrate Napoleon's nuptials. He invited Alexander, who, under the circumstances, could not refuse the invitation no matter how much the idea disgusted him.

"Went to a ball at the French ambassador's in honor of the marriage of Napoleon with Maria Louise of Austria," Louisa factually reported.

No matter their opinions on Napoleon, the Adamses had no choice but to attend, either. "Obliged to go as the imperial family were to be there," Louisa added.

The ice from the Neva River may have broken, but some social rules remained firmly in place. Loneliness and splendor had danced at the first ball she attended in the emperor's presence. What would she see at this one? Pretense? Of course. Impropriety? Highly unlikely, as the imperial family usually showed good manners to all. What she didn't know as she pulled on her silver tissue dress—unless she had purchased a new one by that time—was that she would soon dance a polonaise with both pretension and impropriety.

As their carriage pulled up to the ambassador's palace, decorum was on full display. Caulaincourt's residence was elegantly illuminated. Although exterior lighting was necessary, it was a pretense too. After all, St. Petersburg was home to the white nights of summer, where sunset lingers until early morning. Thousands of candles were hardly necessary with the lengthening days of summer.

"We went at nine o'clock, but it was daylight as at noon, so that the illumination made scarcely any show at all," Adams astutely observed, noting that many of the other ministers placed lanterns around their homes in honor of the French. The acts were so much of a show that the Spanish minister joked with John that he hoped his house's illuminations would "expiate some of my sins."

Emperor Alexander quickly stood out to Louisa. Rarely had she attended an event where he was not the host. When he was a guest, he was usually the guest of honor, but not this time. Though a phantom presence and far away from Russia at the time, Napoleon was clearly the man of the hour.

Fully aware of the global politics dancing in front of her, Louisa knew Alexander had every right to be peeved at Napoleon's pick for a bride. Russia had plenty of noblewomen who could have strengthened French-Russian relations through a marriage with the French emperor. By choosing an Austrian, Napoleon struck a blow at the czar.

"The ascendancy of France at this court will without doubt be more firmly secured by the result of her new alliance with Austria," Adams concluded of the influence that Caulaincourt would gain over the czar.

At the ball Alexander hid his disappointment over the global nuptial politics. "The emperor was remarkably gracious," Louisa observed of his unflappability.

The Russian emperor was also as dashing as any Prince Charming that night. He most likely wore a dark silk or velvet suit with a stiff upturned collar that gently brushed his jaw line. He most certainly bore the power of gold, braided epaulets on his shoulders and the silver star of St. Nevsky on the left side of his chest. Free from the trappings of protocol that came with hosting events at the Winter Palace, the czar also seemed surprisingly relaxed.

At this event, unlike her first ball, where she knew not a soul, Louisa found herself comfortably conversing with female friends at the corners of the dance floor. She was so relaxed that she didn't notice when a pair of imperial eyes glanced nervously around, looking for her.

"He inquired of Mr. Harris where I sat," Louisa explained. "[Emperor Alexander] immediately came to me and tapped me on the shoulder as I was talking to a lady next to me."

Stunned, she was. What did His Majesty seek?

"I must walk or dance the next polonaise with him."

She couldn't have been more shocked had Napoleon suddenly appeared in Russia. "I was very much confused as I did not know what to do when a lady of the court came and informed me that as soon as I saw the emperor take his place in the dance I must walk up alone and take my place by him."

Louisa had no time to prepare. No time to practice bowing. No time to buy a new dress or remake her old one. "Naturally timid, this idea almost overcame me."

The czar took his place on the dance floor alone. Louisa swallowed her nerves and walked as composedly as she could toward him. "But I got through awkwardly enough."

Other dance partners followed, and the polonaise began.

"He immediately took my hand and we started off—Fortunately for me the polonaise was very short and I bowed when the music stopped."

Although the concluding cadence signaled the end of the dance, Louisa quickly realized that the emperor was not finished with her.

"[I was] intending to return to my seat when he said 'that the dance had been so short he wished to converse with me!'"

There she stood, alone with the emperor, without a soul to tell her what to do. "Imagine my confusion [when] every lady in the hall was seated but myself."

Protocol may have imprisoned her several times over the past few months, but it also provided immense security. Propriety now seemed broken. The sight of Louisa and Alexander dancing caused many women to reach for their fans and cover their lips. What did it mean? While the ladies whispered, Louisa struggled to converse with the czar.

"He did not hear well." Although everyone else was seated, the flurry of whispering made it difficult for Louisa to hear him. She felt that "the climate could only betray my stupidity without being able to understand a word."

He tried to talk. She tried to reply, mustering what Russian she could, but most likely resorting to her eloquent French.

"Thus we stood for about five minutes when he bowed low and retired."

Louisa returned to her seat.

"The music soon struck when his Imperial Majesty again came up and asked me 'where my sister was'?"

She had no time to be shocked. "I told him I did not know but would go immediately and seek her."

He stopped her.

"No. I must not as he would go and do that himself."

After finding Kitty, Alexander took her out to dance. Though she had attended many events, Kitty did not hold the high position her sister held or know the protocol. Louisa watched with mother-like nervousness as Alexander started the next polonaise with her sister. Her jitters quickly turned to alarm when Kitty behaved as the casual American girl she was. "And she not knowing the etiquettes began laughing and talking to him as she would have done to an American partner."

Louisa continued watching in both horror and amusement. On the one hand she knew that Alexander had started this public display. He had abandoned propriety and the rules of his court. On the other hand her sister could easily embarrass the American legation.

Instead of waiting for Alexander to speak first, Kitty began "the conversation contrary to all usages du monde."

How did the emperor react? Was he horrified at her breach of protocol? Quite the contrary. "He was so charmed with the novelty that he detained Caulaincourt's supper twenty-five minutes to prolong the polonaise." He didn't care that the other guests waited for dinner. After all, this was the man who wouldn't allow anyone to leave his balls until he finished his last glass of wine. The delay, however, ignited a fire of whispers around the hall. Female fans flared again. The emperor's breach of propriety became the talk of the ball, not only that night but in the days to come.

"She [Kitty] had never been presented at court so that this extraordinary distinction produced a buzz of astonishment."

The emperor's attention to both Louisa and Kitty loosened more than the lips of his guests. His lack of protocol was about to cause an earthquake reaching all the way to Bavaria.

"Poor Madame de Bray being the only lady beside myself of the diplomatic [corps] was in a 'state of astonishment.'"

Madame de Bray was the only other woman who held the same social rank as Louisa. The emperor's failure to dance with Madame de Bray was an insult to the woman and her country. She was "so distressed at not being noticed" that Louisa called on Caulaincourt, who came to the rescue. He informed the emperor of Madame de Bray's presence. The czar responded with propriety and "took the lady out."

"And thus appeased the jealousies."

Louisa noted that they "got home at two o'clock in the morning and it was broad daylight."

She later concluded that the czar's attention was merely pretense: "The truth was the emperor wished to become acquainted with my sister and the honor conferred on me was only a passport to the act."

Was John jealous? Hardly. On the surface, he responded with understatement. "The emperor was gracious to everybody, even beyond his usual custom, which is remarkable for affability," he wrote in his diary of the event.

Louisa was not the only one who received Alexander's favor that evening. John got a little something out of him too. "He enquired of me whether I had taken a walk this day, and on answering that I had; he observed that he had not met me," Adams said of their conversation at the ball. The czar thought he saw John walking earlier in the day but wasn't sure if the wigless gentleman was him.

"He said that the difference of my looks on the street, without a wig, from that in which he had usually seen me, had been the cause that . . . he did not recognize me." How John longed to permanently abandon his wig!

Something else stood out at the ball. No one seemed genuinely happy to celebrate Napoleon's marriage—including the host. Caulaincourt didn't want to give a party honoring Napoleon's marriage to an Austrian princess. A poor actor, the French diplomat said and did all the right things, but lacked the passion of a good performer.

"I heard the ambassador himself say to someone that he gave this ball because he was obliged to do it—it gave him no pleasure," John noted.

Caulaincourt's lavishness was also more apparent than the eighteen hours of daylight that night. With sixty-five servants and fifty-six horses, the French legation was six times larger than the American embassy. Something, however, was stealing his sparkle.

"There is a becoming gravity, too, and something in his countenance and eye which indicates hardness as well as polish," John later noticed.

That night the Adamses didn't know the emperor's true motives for dancing with Louisa and Kitty. The long-term repercussions would influence not only John's future as a diplomat but ultimately the success of US trade in Europe and thus practical acceptance of America's sovereignty.

24

Plato's Beard

JOHN HAD HEARD ABOUT RUSSIA'S BEARDED LADIES. HE ONCE SAW a painting proving their purported existence. But in the summer of 1810, he witnessed a bearded beauty with his own eyes. What the expatriate also discovered that night revealed more about the French than he ever expected to uncover in St. Petersburg.

———

This patriotic diplomat began the hot summer with a cold determination against the French government. The latest reason? Despite Alexander's request to free the sequestered Americans the previous year, the Danish government merely changed its tactics. The Danes issued a new ordinance encouraging *private* Danish ships to capture American ships. John couldn't help believing that the French government was behind this piratical decision.

"The conduct of France towards the United States has been, and continues to be, such that I have not thought it advisable . . . to cultivate the acquaintance of the French ambassador here," he unabashedly confessed in a letter to the American consul to Hamburg.

In similar correspondence to his father, he poured out his true worries, something diplomat Adams hid in public. Admiration for Napoleon seemed eerily apocalyptic.

"I can only hope that among the mysterious dispensations of Providence is not . . . permitting a fifth part of the human race to prostrate themselves in adoration before the god Bonaparte." Idol worship of Napoleon continued to surpass logic. For example, how could the people of the Netherlands truly believe that they could keep their national independence with Napoleon's brother as their king? Those not enamored were deceived. Many Europeans were convinced that Bonaparte's conquering ways would end at the altar.

As Adams wrote his father, nothing could be farther from the truth: "The nuptial torch is not formed to extinguish the fires of conquest."

Gone was the idea of preserving humanity's God-given rights. Replacing it was order—tyranny disguised as reform. "The transition from infidelity to fanaticism is as easy and as natural as that from unbounded democracy to despotism, a transition of which France is exhibiting so glorious a demonstration."

John's experiences reinforced his father's prediction about France's failed Revolution. "I believe nobody will now deny, that the time has come which you foretold, when nobody would believe you, that the very name of republicanism is more detested in France than that of monarchy ever was at the moment of its destruction," John Quincy continued.

Topping his mind were US trade and independence. If America went to war with England and lost, those ideals might be extinguished forever. Adams believed that Napoleon's disdain for America's form of government was a major reason for his decision to underhandedly encourage nations like Denmark to seize US trade ships.

"This hatred of republics is not without its influence in producing the treatment which we experience from France, which will continue as long as we suffer the same sort of treatment from England."

No, he could not risk cultivating a friendship with Caulaincourt.

⌒

After the ball honoring Napoleon's marriage in May, Adams detected a change in the French legation's behavior. They suddenly seemed friendlier to him. Though the swinging social season was officially over, summer's eighteen-hour days of sunlight brought opportunities for more intimate casual gatherings. To John's surprise, Monsieur de Laval, the French consul, issued him an open invitation. Adams and Louisa were welcome to attend any of the small dinner parties he hosted every Monday evening at his country estate.

So far Adams had spent most of his summer evenings either attending lectures or pursuing his new hobby—comparing the weights and measurements of the Russian pound to the English pound. "I wrote something this day but still gave an undue proportion of the time to my inquiries concerning weights, measures, and coins. My precise object is to ascertain those of Russia, with their relative proportions to those used in America. But I find it extremely difficult," he recorded in late June.

Were Russian weights, particularly minted coins, the same as the published standards? To find out, he bought a set of Russian brass weights and scales and compared them with the medicine chest scales he brought from Boston. "My apothecary's balance was much more accurate, and much more sensible to small weights," he noted.

Adams measured the Russian pound as equal to 6316.596 grains of the English weight. Published trade standards stated the Russian pound was 6292.098, a significant discrepancy. The standards were wrong and disadvantageous to American trade as result. He spent so many of his summer evenings exploring his new hobby until two in the morning that he left his wife lonely.

"Mr. Adams too often passed it [the evening] alone studying weights and measures *practically* that he might write a work on them: no article however minute escaped his observation and to this object he devoted all his time."

She was right. He once spent an entire day visiting the Russian mint to watch the smelting process for silver.

With the obligation to attend at least one of Laval's Monday night dinners weighing on him, he broke away from his measurements obsession one July evening and rode out to Laval's country home. Louisa stayed home.

Adams was one of twenty guests dining on French cuisine that night. One Russian woman, however, arrived late. Her face immediately captured Adams's attention.

"After dinner came some additional company, among whom [was] Princess Woldemar Galitzin, venerable by the length and thickness of her beard." For the first time in his life, he saw the phenomenon of a bearded lady with his own eyes. "This is no uncommon thing among the ladies of this Slavonian breed. There is now at the Academy of Sciences the portrait of a woman now dead, but with a beard equal to that of Plato," he wryly observed.

"But of all the living subjects, the Princess Woldemar Galitzin, is in this respect, of all the females I have seen, the one who most resembles a Greek philosopher," he later joked in his diary.

An avid reader, Adams knew Plato's work quite well. Plato's beard does not refer to the Greek philosopher's literal goatee. Because Plato did not wear a beard, Plato's beard is the philosophy of understanding something based on what *doesn't* exist. The Russian woman's beard was clearly a novelty. She could be best understood by what doesn't normally exist—full beards on women.

Another example of a Plato's beard from that era was the common newspaper practice of deriding Dolley Madison as the queen of America. Some editors concluded that the president's wife dressed like a queen and carried too much influence over the ways of Washington City. Their opinion was interpreted as an insult because it was based on something that doesn't exist—an American queen.

Though not as obvious as the Russian woman's beard, John made another new discovery that evening. He shared something in common with Laval. After dinner he toured the gardens with some of the other guests. They stopped at a gazebo, where they relaxed and conversed freely.

There he learned more about his host. The Laval family property was confiscated during the French Revolution, and they were banned from France. Losing everything, an exiled Laval made his way to Russia, where he later married a Russian princess. His story was also a Plato's beard. Adams could best understand his situation based on something that did not exist—individual liberty in France.

As much as he detested the French, suddenly he felt compassion for Laval. St. Petersburg was his exile too. Napoleon had given Laval a chance to redeem his loyalty by naming him the French consul in St. Petersburg. Though their nation's principles were different, Laval and Adams shared a similar situation, a need to escape their distinct forms of exile and return home to an honorable position.

Adams also conversed with the Austrian minister, whose attention from the French legation had also increased. Summer—and Napoleon's marriage to the Austrian princess—loosened Julien's lips. The Austrian's degrading chatter about the bearded lady and other women that night was as obvious to Adams as the diplomat's accent.

"Licentiousness with regard to women was peculiarly the fashion of high life in that age. Perhaps it is inseparably the vice of high life of all ages," he concluded.

Once again John realized that his principles clashed with those around him. He was living in a place that lacked both the moral compass of congregations from Boston's steeples and the ideals espoused by legislators at Beacon Hill's State House.

Had Louisa accompanied her husband to that garden dinner party at the Lavals, she, too, would have been astonished to see the bearded lady.

"Mrs. Adams did not go with me; being confined to her bed, and this evening very unwell," John wrote.

Her condition could best be explained by what didn't exist, either.

25

Moving On

As the summer of 1810 wore on, everyone seemed to be moving on or moving home—everyone, that is, except Mrs. Adams. The freeing of the river had given her hope for three things: letters from home and moving, first to a new hotel and then home to Boston.

"At last there is a prospect of our getting out of this horrid hotel where I cannot sing at my work or be accompanied on the piano by my sister," she wrote. Whenever she and Kitty tried to practice their singing, they would hear "loud clapping of hands and bravas from the neighboring apartments."

Their hotel walls were so thin that she could also hear their neighbors as they moved about, resulting in too much information about their habits, such as "the directions of a gentleman for the finishing touches of the toilet which always terminates with rouge."

Worse than that, she also needed a more secluded suitable space for Kitty: "Russian houses have no bed chambers according to our ideas for lady accommodation."

Though Louisa would have preferred to board a boat for Boston, she was in no condition to do so at the time. Neither was her husband in a suitable situation for going home. He had yet to receive his US government salary check, which was needed, among other things, for paying for a return voyage home. Instead John solved their privacy problem by relocating the American legation a few doors down to a corner house partly facing the Moika Canal.

"We have moved into a very handsome house for which Mr. A pays $1,500 a year. It is the cheapest we could get being partly furnished and we have everything about us that can be desired, but I do not like the place nor the people," she confessed in a new letter to Abigail.

Her burden over income had also weighed anchor-like in her heart for years. When John asked for her hand in marriage, she assumed that she would bring a decent-sized dowry to their marriage. When her father fled London for America after her wedding, which left his creditors clamoring at the newly-weds' threshold, John couldn't help wondering whether she had deceived him into marriage. She had not and married him for love, but the damage was done. Money conflicts had bred discord between them ever since. Sometimes she felt guilty over the smallest purchases, such as a simple straw leghorn hat, which cost a whopping four and a half guineas in St. Petersburg.

John's salary—as well as other letters from home—were stuck on a ship somewhere across the Atlantic or Baltic. They were living off their savings until his exchange check arrived. How could they return to Boston now? If they were not in Russia when his paycheck arrived, they would fall into an even deeper financial ditch. They had to wait in St. Petersburg for his salary; otherwise it might take another year of transcontinental crossings to access the funds. Their dilemma became so well-known that one of Adams's new acquaintances, Mr. Montréal, offered him a loan.

"Under the circumstances in which I find myself here, it is difficult to resist the opportunities thus presented for anticipating upon my regular income," John confessed. Never before had he faced such temptations to spend excessively. "I declined with thanks Mr. Montréal's kind offer, as I had that of Mr. Harris."

He was determined to live within his means without dependence on others. They soon discovered that they weren't the only Americans looking for better circumstances.

"The emperor wants to have Nelson for his own servant. He has fourteen blacks, who on entering the service take an oath never to leave him—They wait upon the imperial family alone, wear Turkish dresses very rich and expensive, and take their turns of service," Louisa reported.

The perks for Nelson were great. He would receive his own handsome carriage with four horses. He could eat the remains of desserts from the imperial table. As a free black, his life was another Plato's beard. The Adamses had frequently defended his status as a free man. Nelson was also best understood by something he wasn't—a slave. Now Louisa feared he was committed for life: "But he had tasted of freedom and the golden pill of this new slavery."

As Nelson left, she also said good-bye that summer to her female colleague. The de Brays took advantage of the good weather and returned to their homeland. "We are all very sorry to lose them as they are a charming family and I am the only lady left—a sad substitute even if our salary permitted the expense," Louisa noted with jealousy over the de Brays' escape from exile. How she longed to do the same.

More than all this, welling up in Mrs. Adams was homesickness. No housing arrangement would fill the huge hole in her heart.

"Adieu my dear madam, of my beloved boys I think night and day, and this cruel separation becomes almost too painful. Nothing but the firm [con]viction that they can never be in better hands would [enable?] me to endure it, for this is an exile which I fear will not shortly be terminated," she mourned in a letter to Abigail. Wax on the paper later obscured some of her words.

The truth was as clear to her as the newly free-flowing river. By moving to a new residence, they weren't moving where she most wanted to go: home. They were staying in exile, at least for the summer. Perhaps they could make a late escape in October, especially if John's salary arrived.

Louisa had not seen her family in nearly a year. Worse, she hadn't heard a word from them. Nothing. It was as if they were dead. Had she moved from Massachusetts to Georgia, she could have kept in touch at least every few weeks through correspondence. Had she been in London and left her sons in Boston, she would have heard from them about every six weeks. In 1810, living as an expatriate to St. Petersburg was extreme. She might as well have been living in hell. She didn't know anything about the health or lives of her children. She had good reason to worry about curiousity getting them into trouble. At age two John nearly drowned once when he fell into a rain barrel at Quincy.

With the river's breakup, her balm became the arrival of ships. Maybe, just maybe, one of the American captains would warp his boat into the mole and bring her letters from George and John. The hope kept her heart alive.

In contrast John doubted that few US merchant ships would survive the Danish straits. "I wish they may all arrive safe at the places of their destination, but they are all exposed to the danger at least of Danish privateers," he wrote to a friend.

He had every right to be fearful. Napoleon had recently retaliated against Congress's Non-Intercourse Act of 1809, which limited the previous embargo and prohibited American trade with only France and England while opening it to other countries. In March 1810 Bonaparte issued the Rambouillet Decree, which ordered authorities at French Empire ports, colonies, or countries occupied by French troops to seize "US ships that entered French ports or ports of cities occupied by the French." This act also prevented American ships from repairing into any port in France or its territories. This applied to any US ship that had already entered a port after May 1809. Though Denmark was not a French territory or directly under the Rambouillet Decree, the Danish government was being squeezed by Bonaparte nonetheless.

Each summer day seemed worse than the day before, bringing yet another new report of the Danes sequestering an American merchant ship. The news continually heightened their fears of receiving no correspondence from their families and of the disastrous consequences for US commercial sailors and their cargo. Somewhere between Boston and St. Petersburg was a vessel carrying correspondence addressed to John Quincy and Louisa. Those letters were more valuable to the Adams family than three boatfuls of cotton were to the exchange market.

Finally one ship slipped past the Kattegat and into St. Petersburg.

"Thank God we now receive letters from our children and friends in America," Louisa cried with joy.

The letters were dated from late December 1809 to mid-January 1810. John immediately wrote his mother that "after several months of expectation [your letters] gave me new reason for rejoicing at the final release of these regions from the chains of winter."

The correspondence also gave Louisa the relief she most needed to hear. Her boys were alive and "All well."

"Your very kind welcome arrived yesterday and—reanimated my frame, which was almost congealed by the intense cold of these frozen regions," she replied.

The letters were "an electric shock" that cheered "our painful exile from almost all we have loved." Had she not received the letters, "we should have sunk into a state of apathy and have lost even the blessing of hope."

The good news continued.

"Tell John how delighted I was with his affectionate letter and George that I hope to receive one soon from him in his own writing, that I am sure they will take all possible pains to learn what is taught them to show grandpapa and grandmama how much they love them. God bless you my sweet boys."

Louisa understandably hoped more letters would arrive soon. That burst of news was followed by weeks of silence. Danish privateers continued to seize American ships.

"Newspapers from Baltimore and no letters—What severe trials!!" she complained on July 4.

Then her health took a dive. "Taken very ill and confined to my bed—could not see anyone," she wrote on July 15 of her frailty.

"I am just recovering from another severe indiscretion which has deprived me of the pleasure of presenting you with another little relation," she explained in a letter to Abigail.

Louisa had miscarried the same day John attended Laval's dinner party. "It is only four days since and I am so weak I can scarcely guide my pen[;] you will therefore my dear mother excuse the shortness of this letter and present me most affectionately to all the family and to my dear boys."

How she longed to kiss her older boys "a hundred times" in the lonely days that followed. She had now suffered two miscarriages since arriving in St. Petersburg.

Today, modern science publishes statistics for multiple miscarriages. One miscarriage isn't uncommon. Fifty percent of early miscarriages are the result of chromosomal abnormalities in the pregnancy, something unrelated to the parents. Three or more miscarriages are much rarer. Only 1 to 2 percent of women have three or more miscarriages. Sometimes the woman suffers from a blood clotting disorder. In extreme cases, the mother develops an immune response to the baby, attacking the implantation site as an invader. Another explanation is that the parents' blood types are incompatible. Although it is impossible to know what caused her multiple miscarriages, modern medicine suggests that Louisa was in a rare category.

Within a week she recovered her strength. "Resumed my seat in the drawing room and my usual occupations."

Adams most likely cheered his wife by telling her all about the bearded Russian lady at Laval's party. He also probably told her of St. Julien's crude chatter about women, warning her to avoid the Austrian. Louisa, too, was worried about the looser lifestyles of those around her. Despite their opposite personalities, opposing viewpoints on finances, and the angst between them over leaving John and George, their mutual morals and shared losses drew them closer together.

"The licentious manners of this place; and the familiar habits of my countrymen are not easily controlled," Louisa observed, worried about her sister's flirtatious ways, particularly with her husband's nephew, William. In their new lodgings, Kitty had her own room. "God help me," Louisa wrote in her diary of the arrangement.

Pressing on her mind, too, was her husband's reputation. "All eyes are on a foreign minister[,] more especially on one such as my husband."

People were taking notice, which was why she had been concerned about Kitty's behavior with Alexander at the ball honoring Napoleon's marriage earlier in the summer.

"[John was] a marked man everywhere for great ability and statesmanship and already so distinguished by the emperor and his [foreign] minister."

Louisa also detected more friendliness from the French. As much as she longed to go home, she knew her husband was gaining respect, something he didn't have in Boston.

———

The delay of mail had one advantage. Considering it her duty to inform her son of the latest opinions of his political enemies back home, Abigail wrote John and quoted critiques from English newspapers.

"'The American minister is the meddling advocate for the exclusion of American vessels from the Russian ports, under pretence of preventing the frauds practiced under the American flag; but in reality in prosecution of the Jeffersonian anti-commercial system,'" Abigail irately copied of the falsehood in a letter dated in late May 1810 and addressed to John Quincy. "And this sensible paragraph is copied into the federal papers, without any comment and to pass where it will for truth. The British party wish to render the mission to Russia as unpopular as possible."

Fortunately John had no knowledge of this false report that summer of 1810 and would not receive his mother's letter for months. If he had, he might have moved on from his attempts to develop some rapport with the French. Instead he changed his mind about avoiding Caulaincourt and Laval. He was now determined to keep a closer eye on both of them, especially after several countries had suddenly closed their ports to American cargo.

It was time for Adams to fight.

26

Fencing Pirates

Pirates. That was how Louisa described the Danes in August 1810.

"I have written by every opportunity but we have heard of the capture of almost every vessel which contained our letters," Louisa wrote in a letter to Mrs. Cranch, Abigail's sister, who was housing John and George. "It is shocking to think of the immense property which these pirates have taken from the Americans."

Louisa was referring to reports that John had received of Danish privateers capturing at least eleven US ships along the Danish straits. Because of this she realized that her letters might not reach her boys. How would they believe that she longed to give them a thousand kisses if they did not receive her letters? The global circumstances facing US trade affected her personal world.

Danish privateers were not the only obstacles facing US vessels leaving St. Petersburg. Other nations under Bonaparte's thumb plagued American ships with increasing pirate-like cruelty.

⟶

Up first was Portugal. Even though Portugal hosted a US minister, as an ally of Great Britain, Portugal was a potential fencing partner against America.

Local officials at the faraway Russian port of Archangel recently kept two US ships from unloading their cargo because they had first docked in Portugal. In May the Russian government issued a new ordinance prohibiting ships with licenses from Portuguese ports to sell their goods in Russia. The unfairness to American ships was sheer madness to John.

Like children vying for their father's attention, diplomats swarmed Chancellor Romanzoff's house, coming in and out with regularity. Adams would not be outdone. Suspecting France was behind Russia's new Portuguese prohibition, he took the matter to Romanzoff on August 8, 1810.

"These vessels sailed from Lisbon at a time when this ordinance could not have been known there," John reasoned.

Rather than directly accusing Romanzoff of French influence, this skilled attorney stuck to the obvious issue and launched his best argument: fairness. The timing alone made it impossible for the American captains to have known about Russia's new ordinance banning ships that first docked in Portugal. The count responded predictably. The measure arose from Russia's conflict with Portugal and alliance with England. His government could not allow for unfortunate consequences.

Suspecting that Caulaincourt had convinced Romanzoff otherwise, John pleaded by appealing to benefits to the Russian economy. Allowing these American ships to unload their cargo would fill the pocketbooks of many Russian merchants and shop owners.

"They have cargoes which would sell at very high prices if admitted, and which in part, must perish if sent away."

The count fired back with cool inflexibility. No exceptions. Individual hardships unfortunately resulted from such necessary policies. "There was no way to prevent them," Romanzoff countered.

"I then stated the particular circumstances of the *Three Sisters,* one of the two vessels, which sprung a leak, and must be repaired before she can go away," John said, trying sympathy.

At the very least, the captains should be able to sell enough cargo to pay for the repairs. Softened but not relenting, Romanzoff asked John to put the problem in writing. The count quickly changed the conversation. He asked John if he could set aside his official character and talk freely as an individual, not as a Russian government official.

Delighted, Adams agreed to do the same. The gesture was as comforting as it was freeing. Because he competed with his diplomatic colleagues for Romanzoff's good favor, John seized any opportunity to share an off-the-record conversation with the count.

What did Adams think of Prussia's sudden decision to close its ports to American vessels? Romanzoff wanted to know. Was it Napoleon's attempt to keep his brother Louis, who had been miserable as Holland's king, from fleeing from Prussia to America?

Adams believed the decision was more sinister that that. Prussia had also suddenly stalled US trade in its ports. French tax collectors relished the bribes that they were receiving from ship captains in Prussia. "As long as American vessels were openly admitted they could not be laid under this contribution."

Napoleon had turned Prussia against America. When he learned that English ships were falsely raising American flags at Prussia's ports, he encouraged Prussia to ban the red, white, and blue too. He falsely assumed that their cargo was British even if the sailors were US citizens. Americans had no way to fight forgeries of their commerce. The problems with piratical Prussia increased Adams's fear that the French would end American commerce in Russia.

The next pirate was Holland, whose authorities had recently seized all US cargo at their ports. This really worried Adams. Seeing Romanzoff at ease, he took the opportunity to request that Russia would not be next in closing its doors to US trade.

"I added that I hoped that we had nothing of the same kind to apprehend here."

The count assured his American friend. "They [the Russians] should be glad to give every possible facility to *direct* commerce between the United States and this country," Romanzoff promised.

"It was the direct trade alone for which I was solicitous, a trade, I flattered myself, as useful and advantageous to Russia as to the United States." Adams paused. Should he dare ask the count about the rumors he had heard concerning Denmark's attempt to influence Russia's ports? Yes, he decided the time was now or never.

"I had heard that the Danes," Adams proposed, ". . . were endeavoring to obtain the exclusion of our vessels here [St. Petersburg]."

Once again the count reassured John. He had not heard those rumors. Adams clarified. Had any diplomat tried to convince him to close Russia's ports to US trade?

Romanzoff denied any diplomatic influence to cut off US trade ships from selling cargo to Russian merchants. Adams left relieved. At least the count agreed to consider the Archangel problem in writing. More important, he denied rumors of other nations trying to convince him to close Russia's ports to American ships. By denying any diplomatic pressure whatsoever, he was also refuting direct French influence to prohibit US trade there. That pleased Adams more than a hundred days of good weather ever could.

Almost immediately, however, he had every reason to doubt the count's assurances.

———

The next day Harris came to him with new intelligence. He had recently spoken with another count, who chattered as freely as a gossiping gypsy. The emperor's council, a group of elite influential Russians, wanted the emperor to do everything he could to maintain good relations with France, "at all events." The news did not end there.

"The French ambassador transacts business personally with the emperor, of which neither the council nor Count Romanzoff himself are informed," Adams recorded of Harris's intelligence report.

Ah! John should have known that Caulaincourt did not directly conduct his business with Romanzoff. He should have guessed that the French ambassador would discuss matters only with the emperor. How foolish to think otherwise. Although he was the top foreign affairs minister, Romanzoff was not privy to the conversations between the czar and the French ambassador. What was Caulaincourt whispering in Alexander's ear? Was he suggesting that Russia close its ports to US ships? Is that why the Archangel authorities refused to let the American captains sell their cargo, even to cover the cost of repairs?

With this equation, how could Adams possibly strengthen US relations in Europe? The factors for failure multiplied with each fencing pirate, whether Danish, Dutch, Prussian, Portuguese, or French.

———

In the midst of his anguish over the vessels held hostage at Archangel, John received correspondence from home. Mail arrives so regularly in the modern world that it is hard to fathom a time when the arrival of letters *interrupted* one's daily routine. One particular package unleashed John's insecurity, forcing him to think about his reputation back home and the conditions that sent him abroad in the first place.

After resigning his Senate seat in 1808, John took refuge at Harvard as a professor. There he buried his disappointment by giving weekly lectures on the subject of rhetoric. Before he left, he organized his speeches for publication. Mr. Gray had received several packages from a ship captain who had recently arrived in St. Petersburg. Among the newspapers and correspondence was a bound copy of John's lectures—the first time he saw them in print. He was now a published author.

"I was from dinner-time until past two in the morning absorbed in the perusal of my own lectures without a conception of the lapse of time," he wrote after poring over the first volume. The title of his book was long: *Lectures on Rhetoric and Oratory, Delivered to the Classes of Senior and Junior Sophisters in Harvard University.*

Would his words have the same effect on someone else? Were his lectures engrossing enough to keep someone else up until two in the morning? So he doubted but hoped: "What a portion of my life would I give if they could occasion the same accident to one other human being!"

Writing is a solitary practice. Publication is a public product. Seeing a bound volume of his work forced him to face the fact that others would be reading—and critiquing—his ideas. "But they are now in their trial upon the world. I pray that I may be duly prepared for resignation to their fate; whether of total neglect; malicious persecution or of deserved condemnation."

More than neglect, he feared condemnation from his political opponents, which would "mortify his vanity." John still had enemies in the US Senate and back home in Boston. Those who rejoiced in his expatriated status would most certainly not praise his publication. He must let his writings go. He could not control how they were received. Because he was in Russia, he could not defend himself quickly among the newspapers of Boston, Washington City, or New York. If the reviews were bad, he would allow them to teach him humility, "a lesson which I sorely want, and which I pray to God to give me the grace to learn."

He had done his best then. He must do his best now to advocate for his country in St. Petersburg. It was time to move on to what was ahead.

Mr. Six stopped by John's hotel on August 17 to share important news. He was moving to France, at Caulaincourt's request. Napoleon's feud with his brother Louis had prompted the change, paving the way for Bonaparte to incorporate all of Holland into the French Empire. Hence, Six was needed in Paris.

"He could now say with certainty what he had before hinted to me," Adams recorded of the man's loose lips, which flapped more freely than ever before. Six decided to share his opinion on the source of the US government's problems in France.

"Probably most of the difficulty of our situation with France arose from the dislike, which our minister [General Armstrong] there had incurred, of the French government."

Adams had pegged many names as the root of America's conflicts with France: King George III, his son the prince regent, and Napoleon. It never occurred to him that the French government blamed the American minister to France for its problems with the US government.

Adams was familiar with the biography of his counterpart to France. John Armstrong was a self-confident Pennsylvanian. Though he had bravely served in the Continental Army and had risen in the ranks as a top aide to a general, many suspected he was the anonymous writer of publications challenging George Washington's authority and inciting an insurrection by the army against the Continental Congress. After the Revolutionary War, Armstrong served in Pennsylvania's state government, where he honed his political skills. He later represented New York in the US Senate. When President Jefferson nominated the well-connected Armstrong to France in 1804 as the American minister, Senator Adams voted against him. John believed Armstrong was too aloof and cocky to be a diplomat. Nevertheless, he certainly could not confess his true opinion of Armstrong to the Dutchman.

Six then gave John a huge surprise. Caulaincourt wanted Adams to represent the United States in France instead of Armstrong. Six explained that Caulaincourt was willing to "freely converse" with Adams about the Armstrong matter and John's relocation to Paris.

"He [Caulaincourt] was persuaded if *I* was there, the difference between the two countries would soon be arranged to our satisfaction," John recorded with emphasis.

The suggestion shocked the reserved Adams while intriguing him to learn more.

27

French Choice

M R. S IX WAS SO CONVINCED THAT J OHN WAS THE ONLY ONE WHO
could fill Armstrong's seat in Paris that he begged Adams to immediately write
the US secretary of state and request a transfer.

John's stoic nature kept him from doing what he probably wanted to do
in that moment: laugh heartily out loud. How his father would be amused
to know that both Holland's Mr. Six and France's Marquis de Caulaincourt
thought an *Adams* could fit into French society and heal America's wounds
with the antirepublican Bonaparte. "I told him I was much obliged to the
ambassador's good opinion of me."

The idea of transferring to Paris to escape to his "honorable exile" to
Russia had never crossed his mind. The proposition had extraordinary bene-
fits. His sons George and John could voyage with an escort and join them in
Paris. There they could, as he had done years earlier, receive a good education.

The deeper question was more complicated. Could he succeed in France as
America's top diplomat to Napoleon? He doubted it. Could any American succeed there? Perhaps, if that gentleman embraced the free-flowing French high
society as Ben Franklin had done years earlier. The science lover in John loved
to tinker with weights and measurements, but he knew one thing for sure: he
was no Ben Franklin.

"There was certainly no person in the United States that to whom a failure
of such a negotiation would be personally so injurious as to me," he explained,
remembering his political enemies back home. Though he didn't tell Six
explicitly, becoming America's minister to France was akin to political suicide
for an Adams. The move would play into the Federalists' opinion that he was
pro-French. They were pro-British. John was merely pro-American.

"I had reason besides to suppose that the American government would
prefer keeping me here for some time longer, and sending some other minister

in case General Armstrong should go home," he explained with great diplomacy and understatement.

The Dutch minister pressed the matter, noting that while Armstrong had integrity, the French considered him to be "morose, captious, and petulant."

Another question plagued John. Was asking for Armstrong's recall honorable? No, not unless Armstrong was guilty of dereliction of duty. John could not take a man down without a just cause: "I did not even know what General Armstrong's offense had been."

He could not seek to expel Armstrong, even if doing so meant an escape from his own exile to Russia. "I stood with General Armstrong, I could not in delicacy transmit to the American government any intimation that he was obnoxious to that of France."

Adams didn't fault Six or even Caulaincourt for their opinions of Armstrong. Instead of drawing people to him, the man's cranky temperament pushed them away. Yet John also knew that if the French government truly understood how much he despised their methods and ideology, they wouldn't like him very much, either.

After recording his conversation with Six in his diary, he made a resolution about the Armstrong matter: "My own course upon this occasion is plain—to be silent."

His silence lasted only five days. On August 22, John received a summons to a Te Deum at the Winter Palace. The requirement forced him to break from his routine of attending worship services at the English Factory Church. Because the Te Deum celebrated Russia's recent victory over the Turks, he had no choice but to go.

He arrived late, but the service had not started. No sooner had he stepped into the long hallway than Caulaincourt cornered him, making him wish that he had left his home even later. Caulaincourt "hoped the differences between his country and mine would be settled."

The French ambassador's tone was unusually reassuring. He told Adams that "it was the desire of the emperor of France and of his ministers to come on the best of terms with the United States; that they knew our interests were the same."

Would Adams write the US government and convey France's sentiments? Caulaincourt pressed as if fencing with a saber.

If free trade was France's true interest, then yes, John could agree that their interests were the same. Before he could elaborate, the Frenchman thrust a much more pointed request. Slippery as the snake in the garden of Eden, Caulaincourt dangled an apple of opportunity in front of Adams.

He was "persuaded that if any other person than General Armstrong was there our business might be settled entirely to our satisfaction."

"I told him that as I was very desirous of that, we should come to a good understanding," John replied diplomatically, avoiding taking a bite. "I regretted very much that anything personal to General Armstrong should be considered by his government as offensive."

Although he did not want to defame the general's character, the question of what Armstrong did to insult the French intrigued him. Even if he wanted the job, he couldn't risk injuring Armstrong's character to the US secretary of state without good reason. How could he possibly do something like that, especially remembering how the voting men of Boston treated him after the embargo? He didn't dare accuse Armstrong of misconduct unless the evidence was overwhelming. What had he done?

"He [Armstrong] never shows himself," Caulaincourt bluntly complained of Armstrong's failure to attend French social diplomatic functions. "Upon every little occasion, when by a verbal explanation with the minister he might obtain anything, he presents little peevish notes."

Instead of building relationships at social occasions or speaking off the record by meeting with France's foreign affairs minister, Armstrong stayed home, hiding behind written communication with the French government.

Though the hallway in which they stood was long, John felt cornered by the Frenchman's quick jabs, as if in a fencing match. If they had been at a ball, he could have made an excuse to slip into the next room to check on Louisa or get something to drink. The talk about Armstrong was worse than scoring in a duel. It was an intriguing maneuver to trap him into making promises "of which I might be easily made the dupe."

He couldn't escape. He must stand firm and play the game of non-commitment. Before he could practice the art of evasion, Alexander ended their match. The imperial family arrived in the chapel. The service was about to begin. "Just as we were at this stage, however, of the conversation, we were summoned to the Te Deum."

A relieved John entered the palace chapel. Why was Caulaincourt telling him so much about Armstrong? Were his motives to strengthen US-French relations, or was there something more devious about it? Did he truly believe that Adams had the talent to succeed in the French court, or did he somehow feel threatened by him in Russia? Putting all that aside, what was in the best interest of the United States? To serve in Russia or France?

Thousands of thoughts must have crossed his mind as he listened to the unison chanting of hymns and watched the emperor kiss the crucifix. Ceremony rescued him from confrontation.

—◦—

As August 1810 came to a close, John sensed the winds of autumn cooling his arctic post. He knew the clock was ticking for the American vessels that could not sell their cargo in Archangel. Though he had given Romanzoff a written explanation, the chancellor had not made a decision. Once again John visited the count to confront the problem.

Romanzoff, in contrast, wanted to discuss other business. The matter involved territory occupied by the Aleutian people on Alakshak, "the great land." Shortening the Aleutian name, the Russians called the peninsula *Alaska*.

Russia had long traded exclusively with China from posts in that expansive territory. Members of the Russian government wanted to open the route to American trade. They had only one prerequisite. The US government must prevent the sale of weapons from its Northwest Territory to the region's native tribes, who used the guns against Russian traders.

Adams's reserved nature probably kept his eyes from opening wide in disbelief. He couldn't believe what he was hearing. The United States held no more control over its western territories than it did over Great Britain. Explorers Lewis and Clark had only recently achieved their western explorations. The US government could barely manage Indiana, much less posts along the Pacific Northwest. Romanzoff might as well have asked Adams to wrestle a grizzly bear. Opening trade on these routes was plausible, but restricting weapon sales to tribes? Impossible. Holding back his opinion, Adams deftly agreed to write the US government about the count's proposition.

John then brought up the worrisome issue anchored in his mind. "I now recurred to the cases of the American vessels which have arrived at Archangel and at Kronstadt to whose admission so many difficulties and days have been opposed."

Because Archangel was even farther north than St. Petersburg, the waters there would be sealed within a month, by September's end. The ship captains needed time to unload their cargo and purchase new loads for their return voyage before the season closed. "I urged the necessity of a very speedy decision concerning them."

The count did not budge. Adams tried sweet talk, noting the "peculiar favor which his Imperial Majesty had been pleased to manifest to the United States."

Adams noted, "I flattered myself that I was promoting the interests of His Majesty's empire as much as those of my own country; that the number of American vessels which had come here, and the quantity of Russian productions which they would take in return, were highly favorable to the agriculture and manufactures of this country."

Though noncommittal, Romanzoff allowed Adams to present additional evidence, which included statements from American merchants that he had collected from letters, newspapers, and personal conversations.

The Russian government claimed to want free trade with America, but obstacle after obstacle hindered it. The emperor's proclaimed policy conflicted with the practices of his bureaucracy. Was the czar professing trade while doing something else? The possibility of pretense was highly likely and concerning.

Holding back his true feelings, Adams put on a diplomatic front. He explained that he was willing to take up the matter with Baron Campenhausen, the new Russian minister of commerce, but that he had yet to be introduced to him: "I hoped Baron Campenhausen would be made sensible of these circumstances."

Saying he was "fully sensible of the weight and justice" of the problem, Romanzoff agreed to write him an introduction to Campenhausen.

"But he was extremely apt to entertain suspicions," Romanzoff warned about Campenhausen. "And possibly some delays might arise from the circumstances."

"My countrymen felt an extraordinary anxiety at these unusual detentions," Adams explained, reminding the count that Portugal, Denmark, and Prussia also closed their ports to American cargo.

"The emperor's sentiments and intentions with regard to the United States remained unaltered," Romanzoff promised, assuring him that the emperor's position had not changed.

John then fired off his frustration against the French. Each time he received favorable assurances from the French minister, the French government covertly closed another nation's port to American trade.

"In the midst of all these violent ill offices which France was doing to us, her government was making . . . the most friendly sentiments toward us."

He then explained how Caulaincourt had reached out to him, offering him assurances even in the past week of wanting to strengthen France's relationship with America. At the same time, he had just learned that the French government told its consuls based in the United States to stop issuing licenses to US ships leaving Boston, New York, Philadelphia, and other ports. French consuls everywhere were to consider all French licenses given to American ships in the United States as forgeries. Just as offensive, French officials were spreading the idea in Prussia that America did not produce colonial goods, such as cotton or sugar cane.

"This was sporting with the common sense of mankind," he fumed.

Romanzoff listened. The pair then bantered like two old pals about politics. Adams left more hopeful than he came. Perhaps he had caught a fair wind. Maybe Romanzoff's note to Campenhausen would free the American vessels trapped at Archangel. But if those ships didn't unload their cargo soon, they would lose everything and be stuck, broke in Russia for the winter without enough coins to bet on the date when the frozen river would break up.

"Several very recent and rich captures have however occurred," Adams wrote to the US secretary of state in a letter in late August 1810.

He updated his superior on his conversation with Romanzoff. Since the opening of St. Petersburg's ports, he had ceased using the czar's land courier to take his letters to Paris. He had no assurance that this correspondence would reach Washington City, but he had important news to attempt to share nonetheless.

The Danish government had taken a convoy of fifty ships into Kristiansand. Among them were at least eight American ships that sailed from Kronstadt in June. "Some of them had dispatches on board from me to your department," he added woefully, wondering whether the letter he was currently composing would share the same fate.

Just as he saw the threat of impressment with his own eyes while aboard the *Horace* last summer, so America's latest problems also affected him personally. Both his official and his personal correspondence were aboard one of the newly confiscated ships.

Would his sons ever receive the gifts he sent them? He had purchased three packs of cards for George. The cards were in French and featured the ancient histories of Rome, Greece, and France. He also bought a picture book for John.

"I write to you both together, to assure you that although far distant from you, I always bear you both in my thoughts with tender affection," he wrote to his sons.

In a letter to his brother Thomas, Adams asked him to be a father to his sons and make sure that George learned French, improved his handwriting, and developed athletic skills in skating and horseback riding. He also wanted him to learn the proper way to handle a musket. That was not the only sport on Adams's mind. Perhaps his recent conversations with Caulaincourt, a battle of wits, revived a memory from his youth.

"I wish, indeed, he could have an opportunity to take lessons of drawing and of fencing, of both of which I learnt a little at his age, or soon after, and of which I always regret that I did not learn more."

Drawing developed coordination skills, but fencing was even better, a lesson in how to overcome an opponent. He had learned fencing from a French instructor at the boarding school at Passy.

"The second [fencing] is a very good exercise, and besides its tendency to invigorate the constitution, contributes to quicken the operations of the eye, and to give firmness and pliancy to those of the hand."

Louisa, too, was worried about the obstacles facing American ships. She feared that the letter she had recently written to Aunt Cranch might not reach Boston.

Would the Danish pirates keep John and George from learning of her request to "Kiss my sweet boys for me"? Very possibly. They were too young to realize that Napoleon's practices had turned all of Europe into pirates. Bonaparte and the British blockades were the very reasons they had not received fresh reminders of their mother's and father's love for them.

What was really going on with France? Adams didn't know. How closely connected was Caulaincourt to Napoleon? He wasn't entirely sure what to believe about the news he recently heard about the French ambassador. Before coming to St. Petersburg, was Caulaincourt an accomplice in the murder of a French nobleman?

28

French Accomplice

ON THE MORNING OF SEPTEMBER 12, 1810, JOHN QUINCY SHARED A conversation with his friend Mr. Montréal. The pair often exchanged books and discussed current events. On this day Montréal decided to tell Adams the truth behind Caulaincourt's "honorable" exile to Russia.

Six years earlier as an aide-de-camp general to Napoleon, Caulaincourt led a corps of French troops. In March 1804, he received an order to go to Strasbourg, a French border town with Prussia. There on the square, Strasbourg's mayor handed him a sealed envelope, which contained the most shocking requirement of his military career. Napoleon ordered him to use his troops to capture and imprison the Duke d'Enghien, a member of the Bourbons, the family behind the French monarchy overthrown years earlier during the French Revolution.

The mission was odd because the duke's whereabouts were known for years. With the full consent of Napoleon, the Duke d'Enghien lived in exile in Prussia. His banishment from France was strange because it was so loose. On several occasions Bonaparte allowed the duke to cross the border to attend plays in Strasbourg. What no one knew was just how paranoid the French emperor had become. Napoleon suspected the duke was conspiring to create a new coalition against his government.

Always a faithful soldier, Caulaincourt obeyed Napoleon's orders. He arrested the duke on March 15, 1804.

"The duke had notice of the approach of French troops, and was advised to make his escape, as it was supposed they had no other object but to take him; but . . . refused on the idea that there could be any design to seize him," John recorded of Montréal's account.

Caulaincourt's troops captured the duke and took him to prison that night. After a quick tribunal, the duke was shot at 2:00 a.m. the next day.

In the days that followed, newspapers published witnesses' statements presented at the tribunal. Many of these witnesses cried foul, claiming their statements were fabrications. The trial proved a sham. The duke's death reminded many in France of the French Revolution, when members of the nobility were mercilessly executed. Napoleon seemed no better than the murderous generation before him.

"[Caulaincourt] was very much distressed having such a commission entrusted to him but he executed it," John relayed of Montréal's explanation.

Bonaparte rewarded Caulaincourt by giving him the ambassadorship to Russia along with other honors and titles. When the Russian nobility heard that he was an accomplice in the duke's death, they were outraged. Caulaincourt's appointment became so controversial that he was forced to defend his role in the incident to Alexander. Readily accepting Caulaincourt's explanation, and perhaps mindful of the accusations against his involvement in his father's death, he vindicated Caulaincourt.

The Russian czar was so convinced that the French ambassador was unaware of the sham and merely following his commanding officer's orders that he issued an exoneration letter to the Russian elite. Caulaincourt's high style and lavish parties later made him a favorite among these same nobles in St. Petersburg.

Enlightened by this revelation, Adams was more determined than ever to stand up for his country against the French.

—•—

No doubt a part of Adams was jealous of Caulaincourt's access to Alexander. The Frenchman's favor seemed unrivaled. In contrast John feared he had just made a fool of himself. The incident was his most embarrassing moment since arriving in St. Petersburg.

"It is the anniversary festival of St. Alexander Nevsky, a Prince of Novogorad, who reigned about the year 1250," Adams recorded in his diary on September 11, 1810. "And is also what they call the name day of the emperor."

Hearing that the annual ceremony was highly popular, John and

William left in the morning and rode in their carriage down the crowded Nevsky Prospective to the monastery at the end of the road.

The number of people filling the street grew greater with each passing block. The crowds were so large, their numbers confirmed to Adams what he suspected: the feast day of St. Alexander Nevsky was one of the most important events on the Russian calendar. "[T]he concourse of the people, from the perspective to the church, on both sides of the street, was excessive."

The crush of the crowd filling the square outside the church rivaled the scene he had seen the previous Easter. As they entered the Holy Trinity Cathedral, the earthy smell of the paupers stood out to the two Americans as much as the impressive classical architecture.

"When we got to the church, we found it difficult to ascertain a proper place to stand." The cathedral's spacious dome hovered high above, fulfilling its purpose of pointing them heavenward. In contrast, the floor surrounding them was packed with people. Adams's full court dress stood out among the tattered, sacklike cloaks of the Russian common men squeezing next to them. Finding a place to fit comfortably in the crowd was not his biggest challenge. The American diplomat quickly wondered whether he was supposed to be there at all.

"None of the other foreign ministers were there," the reserved Adams observed. No one from his rank, not even Ambassador Caulaincourt, was in view.

Wasn't this St. Petersburg's most important celebration? Shouldn't the envoys attend such an event? After all, the emperor was named after Alexander Nevsky, who drove out the Swedes from the Neva River in 1240 and became a powerful prince. Before his death Prince Nevsky took monastic vows, which earned him sainthood status. Peter the Great built the monastery on the exact spot where Nevsky defeated the Swedes. The feast day marks the day in 1724 when Nevsky's remains were moved to the monastery and enshrined in a silver sarcophagus, displayed at the church's altar in front of them.

Soon Count Schenk, the minister from Würtemberg, arrived, pushing his way through the crowds. Schenk was "as much embarrassed as myself." With no place designated for diplomats, he stood next to Adams.

Seeing their plight, Romanzoff rescued the red-faced foreign representatives. "Count Romanzoff, at length seeing me, came to me and stood next to me during the whole ceremony, and explained to me many parts of the performances."

Watching the proceedings surrounding the silver shrine immediately turned into a sterling opportunity for Adams, enabling him to show genuine interest in one of Russia's most sacred customs. Romanzoff explained his church's traditions as they unraveled before them. His easy manner soon erased John's embarrassment at being one of only two diplomats in attendance.

What stood out most about the church was the red carpet lining the cold, stone floor in front of the silver shrine. With his empress to his left, Alexander took his place of prominence. The rest of the imperial family fanned out across the carpet while crown attendants lined the steps leading to the shrine.

Unlike the cathedral with its simple classical architecture, this shrine was old-style baroque featuring intricate engravings. The sarcophagus was unusual. While its canopy resembled a coffin lid, it hovered three feet above the base. Thin silver rods, carved like ropes, connected the canopy to the coffin at each of the four corners. The paneled partition behind the coffin depicted scenes of ancient Russia. Near the top of the partition was a framed painting of St. Nevsky, flanked by angels.

As Romanzoff explained, the archbishop lit three candles to represent the Trinity and two candles to symbolize the dual nature of Christ as both man and God.

"After the mass was finished, the emperor went up to the shrine of the saint, knelt, and kissed the silver coffin three times—twice on the side and once on the top." The rest of the imperial family imitated him, and the ceremony ended.

"On going out of the church, the crowd was so great that the passage out to my carriage by the way at which we had entered was totally barred."

John made one final blunder. With William at his side, he decided that following the guards was the best way to exit the monastery and avoid the crush of the peasants.

"I followed the crowd of imperial officers through the only passage-way that was open, supposing it led to another issue [exit], until I found myself unexpectedly in the archbishop's apartments, where the emperor and his suite had been invited to breakfast."

Showing up to the monastery when he wasn't expected was embarrassing enough. Barging in on the emperor and archbishop's dining table couldn't have been more awkward had he found himself in the empress's dressing room. A monklike messenger approached the bewildered Americans.

"The attendance of strangers there was not usual," the man explained, ushering them away.

The attendee's words increased Adams's turtle-like mortification.

"I at length found the way out to my carriage," he wrote of taking refuge in his coach's shell. The crowds along the Nevsky were so great that they did not arrive home until three in the afternoon.

Though Romanzoff's warmth cooled his initial mortification, Adams wondered whether he had blundered. Caulaincourt and most of the other diplomats weren't there. If he were General Armstrong, he wouldn't have dared journey to the monastery that day. In contrast Adams was curious about his host country's culture. He would take a sincere misstep for Armstrong's apathy any day.

A few days later, Adams faced Caulaincourt. "About four o'clock I went out to the French ambassador's country-house, on the Peterhof Road, and dined with him."

This was the most intimate dinner he had ever partaken with the French ambassador. The only other guests were the ambassador's family, Mr. Lesseps of the French legation, and four Russian officers.

Before him sat a gentleman who had been used by Napoleon and rewarded handsomely for fulfilling his duty to murder a nobleman. More than ever, John was convinced that Bonaparte tightly controlled Caulaincourt. Undaunted, John got right to the point, launching his duel of words.

"Before dinner I expressed to him my surprise at the measures of France towards the United States," Adams said, referring to recent newspaper articles proclaiming that French consuls in America no longer granted licenses to US ships traveling to Europe.

Portrait by Edward Savage in 1801 of Louisa Catherine Adams at age twenty-six, four years after her marriage to John Quincy Adams.

Horace

THE *HORACE*, COURTESY OF THE PORTSMOUTH ATHENAEUM.

"Our voyage was very tedious—All but Mr. Adams and Mr. Smith very sick," Louisa wrote on August 5, 1809, the day they left Boston aboard the *Horace*. At one perilous point, John Quincy wrote, "I had objects on board more precious to me than my own life."

"The captain became alarmed and declared he would not put [in] anywhere," Louisa wrote of Beckford's courage when a Danish officer threatened him and ordered the *Horace* to anchor at the nearest port.

PORTRAITS OF THE PRESIDENTS

JAMES MADISON.

4ᵗ PRESIDENT OF THE UNITED STATES.

PHILADELPHIA.

Published by C. S. WILLIAMS, N.E. corner of Market & 7ᵗ St.

Senator Rufus King, one of Madison's top political opponents, wrote in January 1814, "I think the President is also mistaken in supposing that Russia is the greatest power in Europe, and especially that she will exercise her greatness in our favor." King was wrong. Thanks to Adams's influence and success, Emperor Alexander favored America, leading the British prime minister to complain: "I fear the Emperor of Russia is half an American."

"VIEW OF THE WINTER PALACE FROM THE NEVA RIVER" BY JOSEPH IVANOVICH CHARLEMAGNE, WATERCOLOR. THE STATE HERMITAGE MUSEUM, ST. PETERSBURG, AND PHOTOGRAPH © THE STATE HERMITAGE MUSEUM/PHOTO BY VLADIMIR TEREBENIN, LEONARD KHEIFETS, YURI MOLODKOVETS.

While standing at a window overlooking the Neva River from the Winter Palace, Emperor Alexander I told John Quincy Adams during their first meeting that "the system of the United States was wise and just."

"And so it is," Emperor Alexander told Adams upon meeting him on a walk in the spring of 1812. "After all, that war is coming, which I have done so much to avoid—everything. I have done everything to prevent the struggle, but thus it ends." Alexander predicted that Napoleon would attack first.

Alexander I
Emperor of Russia

M. le Comte N. Romanzoff,
Chancelier de l'Empire, &c. &c.

The first diplomatic dinner that Adams attended took place at Chancellor Romanzoff's mansion. Romanzoff showed off his collection of porcelain vases and a book of poems given to him by Napoleon. "The rest of the company were strangers to me," Adams wrote. "But they were all covered in stars and ribbons—beyond anything that I had ever seen."

"Went to a ball at the French ambassador's in honor of the marriage of Napoleon with Maria Louise of Austria," Louisa wrote on May 23, 1810. In a public display of preferential treatment, Emperor Alexander danced with Louisa at this ball. "Imagine my confusion, every lady in the hall was seated but myself."

"The ambassador told me I was too serious for a pretty woman; and that when 'we were at Rome, we must do as Rome,'" Louisa recorded of a conversation that she had with Caulaincourt, Napoleon's ambassador to Russia. "If I should go to Rome perhaps I might," Louisa politely but playfully replied.

PORTRAIT OF LOUISA ADAMS, 1816, BY CHARLES ROBERT LESLIE. COURTESY OF THE DIPLOMATIC RECEPTION ROOMS, U.S. DEPARTMENT OF STATE, WASHINGTON, DC.

"I am fully sensible of the difficulty of your situation and should most sincerely rejoice to hear that any hope of a settlement could be entertained," Louisa wrote John in September 1814 during his negotiations to end the War of 1812. "The situation of our country is dreadful, but we must hope that it will mend, and trust in that great power, to whom all is easy, and who could preserve us from the dangers which so heavily threaten."

PORTRAIT OF JOHN QUINCY ADAMS, 1816, BY CHARLES ROBERT LESLIE. COURTESY OF THE DIPLOMATIC RECEPTION ROOMS, U.S. DEPARTMENT OF STATE, WASHINGTON, DC.

"You will now, my dearest friend, receive in the most exclusive confidence whatever I shall write to you on the subject—say not a word of it to any human being until the result shall be publically known," John wrote to Louisa in August 1814 of the negotiations to end the War of 1812.

"On Saturday last, the twenty-fourth of December, the Emperor Alexander's birthday, a treaty of peace and amity was signed by the British and American plenipotentiaries in this city," John wrote Louisa about the Treaty of Ghent. "I consider the day on which I signed it as the happiest of my life; because it was the day on which I had my share in restoring peace to the world."

"These were subjects upon which his government said nothing to him," Caulaincourt replied tersely, his small lips pursing under his long, slender nose.

The French government had discussed only the Armstrong matter with him and nothing else related to the United States. As if taking up a fencing saber, Caulaincourt told John to write the US government of France's displeasure with Armstrong.

"I told him that I should certainly write to my government whatever I could think would have a tendency to reconcile the interests and policy of the two countries," he jabbed with the utmost politeness.

"My situation in relation to General Armstrong rendered me the last person who in delicacy or propriety ought to be the medium of indefinite complaints against him to his own government."

John proposed an idea. If the French government deemed it proper, they could make "any informal and unofficial observations" about Armstrong and relay them to Caulaincourt. John would pass them along to his government despite the "inconveniences of communication."

Adams made it clear. He would not write his government requesting Armstrong's removal without any evidence of wrongdoing. However, he would pass along France's concerns through informal letters written by the Frenchman in his own hand.

"I should take great pleasure in giving every aid in my power to every purpose calculated to restore harmony and good understanding between the parties," he said. Although his mission was to represent the US interests to the czar of Russia, John was fed up with this French game. He was ready to firmly but unofficially state the position and interests of the United States to France.

"I told him the French Government appeared to me still too much addicted to that repulsive policy," Adams proclaimed, boldly observing that France had lost all the influence and goodwill it had garnered years earlier with the United States during the American Revolution.

"The influence of France might be great if she pleased, but that as England by her conduct seemed determined to reconcile us with France, so France by hers was rendering the same service to England," Adams continued, scoring a jab in their phantom fencing match.

Claiming to understand John's viewpoint, the French ambassador agreed to write his government about the port closures in Prussia. He admitted that Armstrong wasn't guilty of misconduct. The man hadn't broken any laws; he'd merely broken the rules of custom. Custom was the law. By not participating in French court events, Armstrong was insulting his host government.

Caulaincourt said that "[Armstrong] scarcely ever saw the minister [of foreign affairs for France]; that he never went to court; and that whenever anything was to be done, he was presenting testy notes."

Adams took one last jab, telling the French ambassador how much trouble his government was causing US merchant ships carrying licenses from French consuls in America. While France now claimed these licenses were forgeries, Adams knew they were legitimate. Once again this was another indication that France's policies and practices were askew when it came to America.

Putting aside their proverbial swords, the men then enjoyed dinner. They agreed to share the newspapers that they recently received, the French *Moniteur* to Adams and English newspapers to Caulaincourt.

"So now I see the whole front of Armstrong's offense is omitting to go to court, and presenting notes too full of truth and energy for the taste of Emperor Napoleon," he wrote in his diary after returning home in his carriage.

Compared to Armstrong, maybe John was making some progress. Perhaps participating in the customs and social outings of the Russian court was important after all. No matter his lean purse, he could find other ways to earn success—as long as kissing the culture didn't violate his moral principles.

⤙

John's diplomatic dinner duel with Caulaincourt led him to change one of his habits.

"I have made it a practice for several years to read the Bible through in the course of every year. I usually devote to this reading the first hour after I rise every morning," he noted in his diary.

He often turned to commentators, mostly English ones, to further understand many passages. "Imperfect as my method is, I regret none of the time thus bestowed."

Many people who attempt to read the Bible through in a year do not finish the feat by New Year's Eve, much less before the end of September. "During the present year, having lost very few days, I have finished the perusal earlier than usual."

What to do? He began again, starting with Genesis but with a twist. He chose to read the Bible in another language—French. "I have begun this time with Ostervald's French translation, which has the advantage of a few short reflections before upon each chapter."

Choosing to read the Bible in French had another benefit: he could improve his ability to speak the French language in the process. Perhaps he could also better duel in diplomacy against the Cain-like Caulaincourt.

29

Obstinate

THE SUMMER HAD BEEN QUIET FOR MRS. ADAMS. WHEN THE emperor retired to his Kamenny Ostrov Palace, not far from Caulaincourt's estate, Louisa no longer ran into His Royal Flirtiness on walks. The change relieved her of worrying about the emperor's intentions toward her and her sister.

The official social season ended with the start of summer, except for one big ball. Each year the imperial family held a mammoth outdoor garden party at one of the grandest palaces in Russia, the Peterhof Palace on the mainland not far from Kronstadt. Thousands flocked to see the fountains, feast on the fresh fruit, and frolic under the fireworks.

"Once a year, usually in the summer season, the emperor gives a great ball at this palace, to which the public in general are admitted. The gardens are all illuminated, and the water works all played by the light of the illuminations," John described of the ritual in his diary.

However, no uniformed messenger arrived at their hotel with imperial invitations to the party. Had Louisa lost favor with the empress again? No. They didn't receive invitations that year—but neither did anyone else. The czar unexpectedly canceled his annual soirée. John asked if his family and attachés could privately tour Peterhof instead. He had fond memories of visiting the palace decades earlier when he served as Dana's translator.

With fall fast approaching, he decided that his family needed a late-summer getaway. Though Louisa had spent many nights entertaining US merchant captains at their hotel and attending the theater, she had not left town. John recognized that after all she had suffered since arriving in St. Petersburg—two miscarriages and scant letters from home—his wife needed a recreational break.

Once again he paid homage to his host country's culture by visiting an ancient architectural relic. He anticipated marveling at the palace's gilded statues, but the excursion would show him something that he never expected to see in Russia.

"The distance is between nineteen and twenty miles, which we went without stopping once, either to rest or water the horses," John observed of their nonstop two-hour ride. "Such is the common practice here; and their small, mean-looking horses appear not to suffer from it at all."

The Adams party spent three hours exploring the early eighteenth-century palace, which Peter the Great envisioned as rivaling France's grand Versailles Palace. Facing the Gulf of Finland, Peterhof's centerpiece was a grand cascade of fountains featuring three dozen gilded bronze statues, canals, and neat geometric green parks. The result was a terraced masterpiece.

"But the principal curiosities of the place were the water works; all of which were set to playing for us to see." Water poured from the mouths of bronze fish, dragons, lions, and mythological figures. From the showcase sculpture of Samson to the statues depicting Adam and Eve, the Adamses marveled at their host country's finest outdoor attraction. What made the fountains and canals unique was the elaborately engineered plumbing system. Fed by nearby natural springs, hundreds of jets transported water with precision.

"The waters are carried to the tops of some of the buildings, made to spout from the summit of their domes and roll down, streaming from their roofs," John observed.

A scene of a dog chasing three ducks, however, was embarrassingly rudimentary. The fountains attempted to mimic barking and quacking sounds, but failed miserably. "The imitation [of sound], besides its being ridiculous, is very bad." The genius of Walt Disney had yet to be born.

Though the grounds were gorgeous, when they entered the three-story palace, they made a startling discovery. "The palace is in a state of decay and looks forlorn," Louisa observed sadly. Considered a baroque masterpiece, Peterhof's interior featured white paneled walls richly gilded with gold trim, intricate carvings, sculptures, paintings, and lacy black iron staircase railings. The gilded paint that once brilliantly ornamented the wainscoting had faded into a graveyard of chipped, stripped paneling.

"The palace is an image of magnificence, in a late, almost the last stage of decay," John noticed, remembering the splendor he saw decades earlier.

Why was this imperial treasure in such bad repair? Weren't rubles and rubies endless commodities flowing from royal coffers? Lack of funds was the real reason for canceling the event. Adams didn't know it at the time, but Russia's exports had fallen by 40 percent. The country's membership in Napoleon's Continental System was taking a toll, forcing an inflation of currency. Times were changing. Something dark hovered on the horizon. What it was, Adams did not yet know.

—↢—

The ceremonial monk summoned John and his nephew-secretary William to the Winter Palace on September 27 for a gathering of the diplomatic court. When they arrived in the long hallway outside the throne room, they learned that the court was canceled. The moment brought an unexpected opportunity for another diplomatic fencing match. "I had some conversation with the French Ambassador," John recorded.

Perhaps they sat on a bench under one of the hallway's grand paintings. Or maybe they walked, conversing as they strolled past the painted panels. Above them was an arched domed ceiling with a sky window. Natural light may have shone softly on their faces as they talked. The conversation began cordially, as if between friends.

"I mentioned to him that I had observed with pleasure the attendance of General Armstrong at Court [in Paris] on the occasion of Napoleon's birthday," John boasted.

Since reading in the newspaper about Armstrong's appearance at this important French function, he was eager to share the news with Caulaincourt. The gesture was a sign that US relations were improving in Paris, and Armstrong was finally showing some diplomatic sophistication.

Caulaincourt concurred. He had recently received assurances that the "dispositions of his government were entirely friendly towards the United States."

With such goodwill on his side, Adams pressed forward on the core problem between France and America: US sovereignty. British ships had long hoisted the US flag and presented forged paperwork to thwart port authorities. In fact he had recently uncovered the scheme of a London man named

Van Sander, who had forged many licenses. Once Adams and Harris figured out that Van Sander was the source of the forged papers, they began rejecting ships carrying licenses from him. As a result, ship captains stopped going to Van Sander for American papers, and the forgeries ended.

If Caulaincourt was not willing to trust Adams or Harris on forgeries, then he needed to develop a new skill.

"[France] should make a clear and strong distinction between the English and the Americans," Adams said.

It was time for the French government to learn how to tell the difference between Americans and Britons. Doing so was easier than detecting wine from water. Suddenly their cordial conversation halted, as if both men threw aside their gentlemen's coats and grabbed fencing sabers from opposite corners of the hallway.

"That in relation to commerce was very difficult," Caulaincourt rebutted, referring to colonial trade, the goods of sugar, cotton, and others carried by both British and American ships.

To encourage French industry and promote a commercial war with England, France's pre-Napoleon legislators decreed years earlier in 1796 that any ship carrying British goods could be seized in French ports. This act also designated many products, such as cotton, wool, refined sugar, tanned leather, and others, as distinctly "English." Thus many people in France, including Caulaincourt, didn't know or believe that America grew its own cotton.

"I assured him the only difficulty was in the inclination," John replied pointedly, that "nothing was more easy." American trade with Russia proved it. If the Russians could tell the difference between British and American ships, sailors, and cargo, why couldn't France and the rest of Europe?

John knew what the Frenchman was thinking.

"Two days ago the minister of police had sent me two sailors who pretended to be Americans, but whom upon five minutes of conversation, I found not to be such," Adams told Caulaincourt.

He explained that he and Harris had easily caught others pretending to be Americans. As he had done with previous impersonators, he sent them to the police.

"The different pronunciation of the language," he explained, was the primary way to differentiate between the English and the Americans.

Not only that, but official US paperwork was different. "The personal acquaintance we have with many of the merchants who trade here and the secret marks of the papers," he said, referring to the emblems on the licenses, were other ways to tell the difference.

The question was quite simple. Who or what was France at war with? The British people or merchandise?

"There was a pretty strong sentiment against the colonial trade in Paris, because they considered it as all English," a peeved Caulaincourt replied.

Adams immediately sensed French snobbery against colonial goods. Caulaincourt's attitude shone more brightly than the early afternoon sun through the skylight above them.

"You for instance, you raise no sugar," the French ambassador accused.

"A great deal of sugar was raised in the United States, and particularly in the country ceded to us by France—Louisiana," Adams boastfully refuted. Though without access to the latest census at the time, he was correct. The United States produced nearly 8 million pounds of refined sugar valued at nearly $1.5 million.

"But cotton—indigo—we were perhaps the greatest raisers of these articles in the world," John continued.

These statistics would have aided John's argument. The Orleans Territory annually harvested more than forty-five housand pounds of indigo, valued at a dollar per pound in 1810.

The French ambassador didn't deny Adams's assertions but disagreed on one particular matter. He was convinced that the certificates of origin presented by American ship captains were false. The French consuls in the United States no longer issued such licenses.

"I assured him in the most earnest terms that this was a mistake; that to my certain knowledge, vessels which had sailed from the United States as late as the month of June had brought genuine certificates of origin from French consuls."

Newspapers had recently reported claims from the French government that French consuls in Boston, New York, and other ports had stopped issuing licenses to outward-bound American ships. After talking with recently arrived US ship captains and reviewing their paperwork, Adams concluded that those newspaper reports were false. The news was propaganda intended to deceive port authorities throughout Europe.

Adams suddenly spoke boldly. France's present policy was foolish and highly injurious. America produced good products cultivated in the United States, not the British Isles or Bermuda. The French were missing great opportunities to enrich their fledgling factories and aid their people by rejecting all colonial merchandise because it was English.

"However strong the friendly dispositions toward the United States might be said to be," Adams said, unleashing his fury, "the course of policy pursued must be injurious to them in the highest degree."

With his voice boomeranging through that long palace hallway, he spoke more frankly than ever to the French ambassador.

"You will do us immense injury." Then he made a daring prediction.

"You will oppress the continent of Europe and yourselves with it; but take my word for it, and I pray you three years hence to remember what I say, you will do England more good than harm, you will not cut off her communication with the continent, you will not essentially distress her commerce, but you will lay the world under the most grievous contributions for her benefit and advantage."

If the halls of that palace had been made of straw, John would have blown them away with the force of his accurate political prophecy. Caulaincourt disagreed. Napoleon's trade policies were bankrupting England.

"Her [England's] bank paper money is depreciating, her merchants and great manufacturers are becoming bankrupts, the course of exchange is draining her of metallic specie," Caulaincourt replied. "And therefore perseverance in this system must eventually compel her to come to terms of peace."

"Why then did she not snatch at the offer which you have just made her, of giving up the whole system?" John retorted, referring to Napoleon's recent suggestion through an emissary to repeal the Berlin and Milan decrees if England removed her blockades. "No, she wishes you to adhere to your system because she knows and feels that it turns to her advantage."

Adams had arrived at the heart of the matter. As much as France wanted to claim that English merchandise was spoiling because of a surplus, the truth was that France's goods were rotting among wooden crates because of Napoleon's trade policies. The English blockade and backhanded tactics were circumventing France's coffers, the opposite of what Napoleon wanted.

"You speak of the accumulation of colonial articles in her warehouses. What is the accumulation of your wines and brandies, and what was the accumulation of your grain upon your hands?" he jousted.

John Quincy Adams may have been the US minister to Russia, but in that moment he exceeded his instructions from President Madison. Instead he represented America's interests to France in the clearest and most certain terms.

No matter how frank he was with the French ambassador, Adams had another battle to fight. As October began, the American ships that had arrived from Portugal were still bedeviled at Archangel. Nothing had changed except the weather. John received a summons on October 9 to visit Count Romanzoff. Snow had just begun falling. The practical Bostonian responded by ordering double windows to be installed on their house. Winter was fast approaching.

More than anxiety over the ships at Archangel weighed on Adams as he rode over to the count's house that day. He feared the news he carried would not please Romanzoff. John had recently received instructions from the US government regarding trade with Russia's Alaska territory. The Russian envoy to America had also raised the matter with the US secretary of state, who sent John a reply.

It was the "sincere and earnest desire of the President of the United States to concur in any measure which might be useful to the Russian dominions and agreeable to His Imperial Majesty," Adams told the count.

The crux of the matter, however, was territorial limits or jurisdiction. The US government could not restrain its citizens from trading guns with the region's native people.

"The people of the United States were so extensively engaged in commercial navigation to all parts of the world, that the traffic with the Indians on the northwest coast could not be prevented by special prohibitions of law."

The problem was also about practicality. America didn't have custom-houses and trading posts established on the northwest coast. Americans were only beginning to explore the West.

"And although nothing could be easier than to draw upon an article of a convention to prohibit the trade, it would indicate a want of frankness and candor in the United States to contract engagements and then find them not executed," John noted.

Congress could easily pass a law preventing gun trade with tribes in Alaska. Enforcing the law was impossible. Passing such a law would be dishonest without enforcement. He waited for Romanzoff's response. Was the chancellor angry that the US government had refused the request? Or did he understand?

The count responded cautiously, saying that it was not a matter of great concern and he would pass the news along to the emperor.

Relieved, John then raised another question. Where did Russia draw the boundary between their lands?

"As to the fixing a boundary, it would be most advisable to defer that to some future time," Romanzoff replied, not wanting to "strike a new spark" of dispute. Given the lack of peace in Europe, the Alaska question would have to wait until another era.

Adams reassured him. His government believed that Russia had never been friendlier toward America. Romanzoff paused, taking in the information before making a careful reply.

"Our attachment to the United States is *obstinate—more obstinate than you are aware of,*" Romanzoff stated as firmly and emphatically as he possibly could.

While the meaning was a bit vague, the intensity and inflection on the word *obstinate* were strong. With no elaboration, Romanzoff continued their conversation, drifting into their usual banter about Napoleon.

"I understood the force of the term which he had used," Adams later recorded in his diary. What did the count mean by "more obstinate than you are aware"?

Adams had not forgotten his first substantial meeting with Romanzoff, who personally wanted America to rival Britain in trade but said at the time that the czar had not yet reached the same conclusion. Did the count's latest words, "Our attachment to the United States is *obstinate*," mean the emperor now agreed? Was he fully embracing free trade with America? If so, what a victory it would be, indeed!

30

American Cinderellas

FRESH EVIDENCE OF THE EMPEROR'S "OBSTINATE" FAVOR TOWARD the United States burst like fireworks the next day.

"Invited to the theatre at the Hermitage," Louisa wrote excitedly.

They received three tickets to attend the theater followed by fireworks: one with John's name, one with Louisa's, and in great surprise, one with Kitty's name. The invitation came with special instructions from the czar himself. Though not formally introduced to the imperial family, Kitty received an invitation too.

"The emperor has given orders as I am the only *lady* of the corps diplomatique that my sister should be invited also," Louisa emphasized in her diary. "And this is considered one of the greatest honors ever conferred upon a foreign young lady; as well as the invitation to minister of the second degree."

The emperor's favor—and obstinacy—toward the United States couldn't have been more obvious.

"This privilege is only assigned to ambassadors, and we owed this distinction to my sister's dance with His Imperial Majesty as also to the great partiality of the emperor for my husband—It is very kind."

John noted that the czar himself had written Miss Johnson's name on the ticket, "a very extraordinary mark of distinction." The gesture was highly unusual.

Suddenly America was equal to France in social status in the emperor's eyes.

"In the evening we went to the palace at half past six; at seven we were ushered into the Hermitage Theatre," Louisa explained.

Their horses led their carriage over the arched stone bridge, the distinctive architectural feature of the theater's exterior. In 1783 Catherine the Great ordered an Italian architect to design the Hermitage in the Palladian or Greek temple style, a contrast to the baroque-inspired Winter Palace. Shaped in a semicircle, the Hermitage's theater seated 250 guests on church-style pews in concentric semicircles.

"The emperor and the imperial family came in at eight and took their seats in a row of chairs in front—immediately behind the orchestra," Louisa noted.

Their seats directly faced the stage.

"The French ambassador in the same line with His Majesty took the seat next the Grand Duke Michael [the emperor's brother]."

From any seat in the house, guests could enjoy the performances on the stage. They could also marvel at the colored marble pillars, which were topped with white Corinthian-style crowns. White painted niches held statues of Apollo and the Muses. Behind the imperial family sat "all the great officers of the crown and their ladies for there are no boxes."

John joined the other foreign diplomats. Louisa and Kitty took their special seats. "The corps diplomatique sat on the right hand second row; and the hall was filled up by the noblesse, the men on one side and the women on the other."

The performance selection could not have been more appropriate. "The piece was Cinderella—The music magnificent, the acting excellent, and the ballets beautiful."

Following the play, the emperor's guests crossed to the river side of the palace, where they watched fireworks bursting over the Neva. For the Adams family, the real fireworks came in the form of the emperor's invitation to Kitty. This was a highly visible sign to the rest of the diplomatic corps that Alexander was showing his preference for the United States. America was not only officially recognized but now highly favored by the largest nation in Europe.

"The distinction to Miss Johnson was a matter of wonder to all the world," Louisa exclaimed at the success. Indeed. It was a triumph for John Quincy Adams, a sign of his emerging success as a diplomat and the rising status of the United States abroad. With Russia as a true political and commercial ally, the US government might soon be able to pressure Parliament into disbanding its oppressive trade policies against America.

Suddenly the czar's decision to dance with Louisa and Kitty at the ball at the French ambassador's party celebrating Napoleon's marriage made sense.

What seemed like a near breach of protocol then was, in fact, the first grand display of power. By dancing with the *American* women at a ball hosted by the *French* ambassador, Alexander was sending a signal to Caulaincourt. He used the moment to show his favor, implying that the United States was important to him. Watch out. The United States is a player, an emerging rival to you and England.

The French legation took notice and got the message, which was why Adams almost immediately began receiving invitations to smaller, more intimate French gatherings, such as Laval's party where he saw the bearded lady, a Plato's beard.

John realized that much had gone on in Russia behind the scenes on behalf of the United States. The Archangel problem had not been fully resolved. Baron Campenhausen had sent the matter to Archangel's local port authority, who had not yet cleared the vessels. Nonetheless Campehausen assured Adams that he would soon reorganize the system to overcome the port of Archangel's inefficiencies.

Had Adams taken the same approach in St. Petersburg as Armstrong had in Paris by refusing to attend court functions, he would have alienated his hosts. Even his embarrassing moment at the monastery showed the count—and the czar—that his efforts to build friendship between the United States and Russia were sincere.

Caulaincourt had noticed, too, which motivated him to convince Adams to transfer to Paris—and get out of his way with the open-minded Alexander.

Years before his reign, the Russian emperor began to favor Western ideas. His childhood Swiss tutor, La Harpe, was a republican who cultivated in Alexander a belief in the rule of law. He encouraged him to hate despotism. The principles of the United States intrigued him as a result.

The tickets to the theater combined with Romanzoff's assurances of the emperor's obstinate intentions toward America underscored what Adams now concluded. He perhaps expressed it best in a letter he wrote to a former Senate colleague, William Plumer of New Hampshire. As in Adams's case, Plumer's support of Jefferson's embargo had cost him his Senate seat. Adams had recently received a letter from Plumer, who told him that the newspapers continued to abuse both of their names over the embargo.

"You tell me, that I am often much reviled in certain newspapers, and that the clumsy animals who still earn their sop by howling at me have not yet instinct enough to forbear coupling your name with mine in their yell of slander," Adams fumed in his reply to Plumer.

Then he shared his good news: "The object of my mission has, I believe, hitherto been completely accomplished."

He could not contain his joy: "If you will compare the conduct of Russia toward American commerce with that of all her neighbors, not even excepting Sweden, you will easily perceive the object of my mission, and thus far its success."

———

Such sentiment from her husband naturally cemented in Louisa another conclusion: no matter that her husband's salary had not arrived. With the mission a success, it was time to go home.

In contrast, to Adams, wasn't his *obstinate* opportunity just beginning?

31

Christening

"I HAVE FREQUENTLY PRESSED MY DESIRE TO RETURN HOME, BUT HE says unless the government recalls him, he will not return for three years," a heartbroken Louisa reported to her mother-in-law in a letter dated October 23, 1810.

Snow was falling daily, a sure sign that St. Petersburg's sea would soon be sealed. Both John and Louisa knew they did not have many—if any—more opportunities to send letters home or receive them through US merchant vessels. Once the Neva River froze, they would have to depend on haphazard chances via the czar's land courier or hire their own—another burdensome expense.

As she reminded Abigail, Louisa had agreed to accompany her husband to Russia because he had lived in such a "state of cruel anxiety and uneasiness" in Boston after resigning the Senate in 1808. She saw firsthand the angst he felt when most of his friends deserted him back then. Only William Plumer, Ezekiel Bacon, William Gray, and a few other colleagues seemed to understand his principled but unpopular stand on the embargo.

Now Louisa, not her husband, was the one living in cruel anxiety. That autumn she realized she would be separated from her sons longer than her original fears. This along with St. Petersburg's diplomatic demands of dissipation and the upcoming isolating winter left her depressed. No wonder bitterness flowed from her pen faster than the ink.

"I did not need my second trip to a splendid court to convince me of the incompetence of such a life to afford happiness or real pleasure and had never been so weak as to have admired it," she told Abigail.

Rank and splendor were insufficient substitutes for cuddling close to George and John by the fireplace or watching them smile triumphantly after learning how to bridle a horse for the first time. No matter how clean the champagne tasted at the czar's Cinderella balls or how enchanting the palace's theater performances, nothing could compensate for the loss of her children.

"Rely on it dear mother that no station, however high, can ever atone for the sacrifices I have made."

John's renewed resolution to stay in Russia crushed his wife's latest hopes for reunion. She mistakenly thought "one year would have been the extent of my stay." Had she known she would not see George and John for years, not merely a few months, she would not have left them. John had already concluded that his mission was a success. Why, then, didn't they board the last vessel departing for Boston in the fall of 1810? The answer was complicated.

Adams had recently received a letter from his mother, who enclosed a critique of his newly published Harvard lectures. Overall the reviewer praised his work. However, the critic also ranted against John's politics.

"The author may say what he will about his political antipathy to me, I take him to have had, even while he was disclaiming my friendship, a SNEAKING kindness for me," John replied with emphasis in a letter to Abigail.

The scorching review reminded him of the turncoats he left behind: "I had great numbers of these secret friends among my dear fellow townsmen of Boston, who in defiance of their own consciences were joining in the hue and cry, and making themselves the tools of my real enemies."

Human nature was weak. Men were fickle. "That a man should be deserted by his friends in the time of trial is so uniform an experience in the history of mankind, that I never had the folly to suppose that my case would prove an exception to it."

With the topic fresh on his mind, he confided in the like-minded William Plumer. "By adhering to my principles I had been deserted and sacrificed by my friends."

The criticism was only getting worse. Detractors back home were now complaining about the high financial cost of sending him to Russia. They considered his mission a waste of time and money. At the same time he wrote Abigail, he expressed his angst over these recent newspaper reports in an emotional letter to his brother Thomas. "There is no escaping one's destiny, and I have been abused in the newspapers, both for putting the nation to the enormous expense of a frigate to transport my precious carcass across the ocean," he wrote bitterly and emphatically, "and for landing at Kronstadt from a merchant vessel loaded with *sugar and coffee.*"

Adams described these snakelike sentiments "as venomous." Then he said, "Perhaps one half the ministers of the United States, who have come to Europe since the Declaration of Independence, have come in frigates, and never a syllable was lisped at the expense."

He compared his feeble salary of $9,000, which he still had not received from the US government, with Caulaincourt's $300,000. Even the ministers of "petty principalities whose names are scarcely known" earned $20,000 a year. Referring to himself in third person, his tirade to Thomas continued unabashed: "He therefore limits his expenditures to his allowance from his country, shines as much as he can in those circles of society with whose splendor he cannot vie, and lives almost entirely retired within the bosom of his own family."

These vicious newspaper critiques and accusations combined with the delay in receiving his salary weighed heavily on him. Such fresh reminders of his failures and foes reinforced his decision to stay in St. Petersburg. What would he do if he resigned and returned to Boston? Had anything truly changed? No. He needed an honorable way home, a place to go and position to hold. Although General Armstrong had recently resigned as US minister to France, Adams did not want to replace him in Paris. John was too sly to play fox to the hunter Napoleon.

Though outwardly reserved, he was not cold or indifferent to a longer separation from his oldest boys. He wrote a letter to George that clearly expressed love and fatherly concern.

"We are, my dear child, indeed very far distant from each other; but we love you and your brother John as much we could if we were all together—We hope that your brother Charles and you will still grow up together enough to love one another with the tenderest brotherly affection. He enjoys, we thank God, very good health, and grows very fast."

The realization that he was succeeding in Russia gave him hope and induced him to stay.

"Ever since the 4th of July, 1809, I have had upon file a letter from you of the preceding 29th of June," he began in a letter to his former colleague Ezekiel Bacon. "It was one of the earliest notices which I received of my exile, as you termed it, to this place."

Though France was a thorn, trade was starting to thrive: "Notwithstanding all the vexations and depredations to which our commerce during the present year has been exposed, I presume it will upon the whole prove profitable, even to our merchants."

He might not have been able to compete financially with his counterparts, but he was winning their respect, especially Alexander's. Trade with Russia was still open, as he explained to his mother: "From that day to this the emperor has treated me with the same kindness and attentions, and, what is much more important, he still gives a welcome reception to my countrymen, while all his neighbors have excluded them from their ports."

Adams's appointment to Russia was giving him a rebirth, a new start to make a difference for his beloved country. He was not quite ready to let go of his strengthening relationship with the czar. Only to Thomas did he hint at his greatest fear for America's future trade success: Napoleon.

"But at this moment you may be assured that the only object of my concern is, that circumstances which I cannot control may occasion us to lose some of the favor in which we now stand. This may be unavoidable."

As both John and Louisa wrote these last letters home before the ports froze, he expressed delight over the emperor's favor while she confessed anguish at staying in Russia. Whereas his Eve had everything to gain by returning home—reuniting with her oldest boys, mother, and other sisters—Adams had little else in Boston besides his immediate family and a few fair-minded friends.

———

By November 7, 1810, the Neva River was completely frozen. Their fate was sealed. On that day the emperor's master of ceremonies sent John and Louisa an invitation to visit the Anichkov Palace, which Alexander renovated in grand style for his sister. Louisa sadly declined.

"I was too unwell to go," she wrote succinctly in her diary. While not recording what ailed her, a temporary ailment, such as a female condition too delicate to put in writing, likely kept her from seeing the palace that day.

Three days later a second invitation to visit Anichkov arrived. Louisa felt better and eagerly embraced the opportunity to tour the palace. Together she and John paid homage to their host country's culture by visiting the newly decorated and expanded imperial mansion. Completed in 1754, this baroque building faces the river and takes its name from the adjacent Anichkov Bridge near the Fontanka Canal. After ordering the construction of a new neoclassical addition along the Nevsky Prospective side of the mansion, the emperor gave the palace to his sister, the Grand Duchess Elena Pavlovna.

"It contains every luxury that can be conceived with a refined delicacy under the immediate inspection of Alexander himself," Louisa noted of his intimate involvement.

She admired the estate's rose-colored décor and impressive collection of Chinese vases and Russian bronze works. Her keen sense could not help noticing one flaw, a crack in the otherwise perfect palace plaster. The chapel was so new that its most intimate worship area was not yet sanctified, which was to Louisa's advantage the day she visited it. Otherwise she could not have seen the inner sanctuary for one simple reason. She was a woman.

"As the chapel was not consecrated, we ladies were permitted to go into the sanctuary—A place forbidden to women we were told by the priest in a very coarse mode of speech."

She knew her mother-in-law would have taken as much offense to the cleric as she did. Years earlier, in March 1776, Abigail had asked her husband to remember the ladies as he contemplated the idea of declaring independence at the Continental Congress. Louisa also favored fairness for the female sex.

"On our return home found letters announcing the birth of another son to Mrs. T. B. Adams," Louisa wrote in her journal after visiting Anichkov. They received letters from one of the last ships to arrive from America.

For a woman longing for a baby, the news was likely joyful and wistful at the same time. Life in Boston had moved on without them. She could not nuzzle her nephew's tiny nose to her face or smell his soft skin as she kissed his forehead. How happy she would have been just to hear the heartiness of one of her nephew's burps. Had they been living in America, they might have witnessed his christening service, stood as godparents, and rejoiced with the rest of the Adams clan as they listened to the reverent, prayerful tones of the clergy's blessing over this new life.

No matter their joy in discovering "new beauties in every direction" at the Anichkov Palace, nothing could erase the truth. They had arrived in St. Petersburg a little more than a year ago. Nothing could bring back the lost time with her sons. The news of her nephew's birth delighted her, but she felt anguish too. She could not go home, but neither could she add to her family there. Had she not miscarried in February and again in July, she, too, would be welcoming a child soon. Louisa longed to find a key to unlock her prison so she could freely run and embrace George and John again. At the same time she also wanted to welcome another wee one.

"In fact we all pined for home and I could scarcely endure a longer separation from my loved children," she later wrote mournfully in her diary.

Diversions took her mind off such depressing thoughts, but only for a short time. She soon attended an opera at the French ambassador's and enjoyed the ballet at the theater, "an amusement in which I delight." One invitation, though, put her face-to-face with the sight of an infant. Their butler delivered his good news. His wife had recently given birth. Would the Adamses host a christening service in their residence? And would they do the honor of standing as sponsors for his child?

No matter her personal heartache, she could not say no. Louisa immediately stepped into the dual role of both hostess and godmother to her butler's child. Believing this new baby deserved a full audience for his baptism, she arranged for all her husband's aides to attend.

The event took place on November 15 under the practices of the Lutheran Church, which were less familiar to the Adamses. As soon as the priest arrived at their home, he explained that a husband and a wife could not serve as dual sponsors. Only one of them could be a godparent. Feeling anxious over holding another baby while longing for one of her own, Louisa was relieved to pass her sponsorship to Kitty.

"We all met in the drawing room at two o clock. . . . Catherine was substituted for me," she explained. "Mr. Adams held the child as he was a boy."

The ceremony was short. The priest repeated the Lord's Prayer, recited the

Apostles' Creed, and baptized the infant's forehead with water. "Mr. Adams gave fifty rubles to the father and five to the nurse." Such a moment couldn't help reviving emotions and memories. George, their oldest son, was christened in the English Church; their two younger boys at their Congregational Church in Boston. The evidence that followed suggests that the christening— or something else about this time—stirred John and Louisa quite a bit.

32

The Snub

Two weeks after the christening service, Louisa and Kitty walked along the quay by the frozen Neva River to get some fresh air. Snow in St. Petersburg was now falling daily, though not heavily, and settling into a cakey substance. Predicted to rise to four feet by March, the "snow cake" was about a foot above ground by the end of November.

For some reason walking over this snow soufflé was extra tiring to Louisa that day. Soon another problem quickly overtook her physical exhaustion. As she glanced behind, she saw Emperor Alexander walking in the distance. His gait seemed to quicken with each step as if he was trying to catch up with them. Maternal alarm immediately took over.

"Being quite fatigued, I saw the emperor behind us hastening on with great strides; and not intending to do anything rude, and far from supposing that His Majesty would notice it, I beckoned to my servants to drive up and with my sister got into the carriage and drove on."

Louisa feared that the sight of her sister publicly conversing with the emperor would further loosen the lips of Russia's nobility. Smoky fireworks might have concluded their Cinderella-like visit to the Hermitage theater in October, but the haze of gossip had lingered ever since. She couldn't let Kitty become a king's conquest.

"The great distinction shown to my sister, at the invitation to the Hermitage had occasioned so much talk, I thought it was injudicious to encourage it."

Seeing them board their coach, Alexander responded with coolness when they turned around and passed him.

"On returning up the street, we met the emperor but His Majesty turned his head away and looked at the river and took no notice of us at all."

Louisa had just snubbed the czar. Worse, he'd had noticed it, as she emphasized in her diary: "I was very sorry but had no idea that *he* would be offended."

How great was the rupture? She did not know but feared the imperial glare nonetheless. Nearly a year earlier, the empress mother had threatened to remove Louisa's name from future guest lists after she missed the emperor's birthday ball. Now she had committed another social sin of omission, this time to prevent one of commission.

Would this slight affect her husband's rising success? With the Neva now frozen, they were stuck in St. Petersburg until May, when the river broke. Though a Russian winter brought the "dissipation" of parties as John derisively called them, a social season snubbed by the imperial family was a fatal freeze. If their names were dropped from the palace invitation list, they might as well move to Siberia. Direct contact with Romanzoff alone was not enough to strengthen America's trade relationship with Russia. They needed to woo Alexander more than ever.

As her carriage returned to her hotel, all Louisa could do was hope that the incident would blow over and the emperor would not hold it against her or her husband.

—◆—

John, however, was worried about a different rupture. Once again the practices of Russian customs officials and the French government's anti-English antics threatened US trade.

When he visited Romanzoff on November 30, he succinctly presented the latest problem. Sixty-seven American ships arrived with a large convoy at Russian ports just as they closed for winter. At first Russian customs officials freely admitted several of these ships. Then suddenly they forbade the captains from unloading their goods to sell at market. Next they refused to admit the remaining US ships in the convoy. All these vessels were now stalled in Russia for the winter. The American captains appealed to Adams for assistance. If they were unable to sell their cargo, they would lose an entire year's earnings. Their plight was perilous, similar to the stalled merchant ships that John had seen in Denmark the previous year on his voyage to Russia. His reaction was just as passionate; his plea just as bold.

"The persons interested in these vessels and cargoes were alarmed and uneasy under these difficulties, and some of them had applied to me for my interposition in their favor," he explained to Romanzoff.

The count countered. Suspicion arose because these ships "belonged to the great convoy of 600 sail, which had been so long signalized by the Emperor Napoleon, and which it was said had entered the Baltic, coming from Göteborg [Sweden]."

John acknowledged that the sixty-seven US ships came from Sweden and probably belonged to the convoy of mostly English ships, which were officially forbidden in Russia's ports because of Alexander's alliance with Napoleon. However, Adams was confident that the ships on his list were American, not British vessels disguising themselves by hoisting US flags and presenting fraudulent paperwork.

"But I trusted he would not suspect me of attempting to shelter under the American name any traffic or property prohibited by the laws of this country," he responded, relying on his honor and reputation to make his case.

Though evasive, the count reassured John of his good standing.

"[Romanzoff] said he could hardly express to my face what he thought upon this subject; but it was certainly nothing distrustful of me."

Confident these ships "were bona fide American," Adams gave the foreign minister his list documenting the sixty-seven US vessels. "The owners of almost all were personally known to me as citizens of the United States."

The count promised to present the matter to the emperor. The pair then agreed to put aside their official roles so they could discuss French and British politics as easily as two old friends. They spoke off the record.

Adams openly shared his opinion about Napoleon's recent offer to repeal his Berlin and Milan decrees. Instead of declaring victory over the suggestion, the British should have revoked their policies or issued a major gesture toward peace. An insulted Napoleon instead flew into a rage and released the Fontainebleau Decrees in October 1810. These new ordinances authorized officials to burn all English merchandise found in warehouses in French Empire states and territories, such as Italy, Holland, and Spain. The measure increased unofficial pressure on allies, such as Russia, to show hostility to England by destroying English cargo.

Napoleon's offer to repeal his decrees was a response to changes in US government policy, as the French emperor's emissary had hinted to General Armstrong in Paris in August, before Armstrong's departure. Months earlier, in May 1810, the US Congress had revoked the 1809 Non-Intercourse Act and implemented a new law, Macon's Bill No. 2. This measure officially restored trade with England and France. However, if either England or France revoked its trade policies and the other failed to do the same within three months, then President Madison had the power to reinstate the embargo against the remaining uncooperative nation. Though he knew the bill was flawed, Madison hoped the new law would motivate Napoleon to rescind his Berlin and Milan decrees. His goal was also to pressure Britain to revoke its Orders in Council and cease its piratical policies against America.

Napoleon's latest overture appeared to be "new modifications of the system of French decrees, favorable to the commerce of the United States," but John doubted Napoleon's sincerity. He was correct. By merely *offering* to rescind his Berlin and Milan decrees, Napoleon believed he was committing himself to nothing, no change at all. He put forward the suggestion without implementation. His public proclamation did not match the latest practices of his customs officials. French courts continued to confiscate US ships.

As Adams wrote: "[W]hile France is holding to us now the language of friendship and conciliation, she is playing us all the sly tricks in her power elsewhere."

What neither John nor Romanzoff knew at the time was the latest news: a month earlier President Madison had reinstated the US embargo against Britain, which is exactly what Napoleon hoped would happen through his offer. By suggesting one practice and continuing another, Bonaparte deceived Madison and got what he wanted out of the US government: an embargo against England but not France. Had Madison waited a week, he would have received communication from Armstrong that French officials were refusing to release captured American vessels and that Napoleon intended to continue restricting US trade through his Continental System's licensing practices.

However, it was too late for an embarrassed Madison to revoke the new embargo against England. At least Napoleon's offer gave Madison an official reason to cross France off America's potential war list. England was the worse foe. While Napoleon hated America's government because it was a living repudiation of his, the English hated America more because they believed the United States stole their prosperity when it declared independence. Revenge, not jealousy, was a greater threat to American sovereignty.

———

On December 5, Louisa longed to breathe fresh air again. Because it was too cold to walk, she decided to ride in her carriage. However, as soon as the horses began shuffling over the snow-packed road, she became ill. "I could not bear the fatigue of the motion of a carriage and four over the stone pavements."

Within a few days she found a solution to her motion sickness: a sleigh, which slid over St. Petersburg's snow-souffléd streets as easily as a baker frosts a cake.

"The winter being bitter to very mild I rode in a sleigh with my sister and child or with Mr. Adams," she recorded with renewed joy. "We rode every day wrapped in furs and this exercise was smooth and delightful."

Though Louisa suspected the source of her sickness, she embraced the fresh air as often as she could and spent time socializing with friends she loved and trusted.

The next day Mrs. Krehmer visited her. "In the course of conversation, she told me that the emperor had seen all our letters to our family."

The news was as shocking as it was disturbing. The emperor had been spying on them. No wonder Romanzoff had offered to send their letters through a special courier, who, after the czar read their letters, carried their correspondence to Paris, where someone in the US legation forwarded them to America from France.

Mrs. Krehmer explained that some of John and Louisa's correspondence had raised royal eyebrows. Louisa tried to recall what she had written about Emperor Alexander to her family. Had her pen offended His Majesty? Probably not, she concluded. If anything, she was effusive about him—embarrassingly so.

Mrs. Krehmer explained that Martha Godfrey, Louisa's chambermaid, was the target of imperial ire. Martha's letters had been "abusive" of the czar. She had written about her fear of being mugged and assaulted by Russia's lower class. As shocking as the news was, the revelation also explained why the imperial family had invited Charles to the palace months earlier and specifically requested Martha to accompany him instead of Louisa.

"[The emperor] did not think her [Martha] at all handsome."

Mrs. Krehmer then relieved Louisa's worry. "[The emperor] was much pleased with the description and remarks which I had written of him to my friends."

Despite his approval, she felt violated.

"I observed that it was very ungenerous of His Majesty after offering to send our dispatches by a private and especial courier to use the opportunity against *us*," she tersely replied, not caring if the fissure between her and Alexander grew worse.

"For it was perfectly natural that with the idea of perfect safety attached to the conveyance of our letters that we should describe our first impressions without disguise to our friends to whom they must certainly be very interesting."

Though political shrewdness kept her from writing anything compromising, she chided herself. Of course he would have been suspicious of the new US minister and his delegation. With Napoleon as an official friend, whom could Alexander really trust?

Louisa did not hide her displeasure: "I knew that she [Mrs. Krehmer] would repeat this to the emperor."

Indeed, Alexander learned of Louisa's fury.

33

New Year's Bang

NO MATTER HOW ANGRY SHE FELT AT THE EMPEROR, LOUISA KEPT
to her routine in December 1810. The possibility of running into His Coldness
did not stop her from riding in her sleigh. Only her health or the weather prevented her from enjoying the outdoors. Her next outing led to a royal test. Had
the imperial chill set in? Or had it thawed?

"As usual we met the emperor but he turned his head away and did not
look at us. I could not help laughing but was sorry when I found that he had
taken offence," she wrote.

She wasn't as concerned about the emperor's feelings as much as how his
displeasure could affect her husband's success and standing with his fellow
diplomats. "For I knew that Mr. Adams would feel unpleasantly about it: as
the subject would become very disagreeable if the court as customary adopted
the same tone."

Physical illness soon superseded Louisa's insecurity over the emperor's
favor. Her health abruptly ended her outings.

"Taken suddenly and severely ill—and continued so all night," she wrote
of vomiting and fatigue on December 13. Such sickness is difficult no matter
the season, but winter's woes worsened the effect.

Meanwhile John saw the climate as a culprit of their physical ills. He
observed that the sun was visible only about once a week in St. Petersburg's
arctic climate. When it did shine, the sun hugged the horizon, hardly hovering over the streets. The Adamses didn't need scientific advances to tell them
about the health benefits of sunshine, vitamin D, or serotonin. Both John
and Louisa instinctively knew that they felt better on sunny days. The sun's
presence, no matter how infrequent, made the winter blues better for these red-
blooded, homesick Americans.

"[T]he first fine day my sister and I resumed our walks—we met the
emperor on the Fontanka," an improved Louisa recorded on December 16.

One advantage of a St. Petersburg winter is the opportunity to walk on the frozen river itself or other waterways, such as the Fontanka, the widest and most remote of the city's three canals at the time. The sunny hues of the Summer Palace, Peter the Great's Dutch-style home facing the Fontanka, may have also lifted her spirits on a cold winter's day. Unlike the nearby Winter Palace—a grand, green giant with hundreds of windows—the yellow Summer Palace is small for an emperor, only two stories tall holding a mere fourteen rooms. Although she didn't say so, the Summer Palace's size and scale—though not its sunny color—may have reminded her of the cool-toned Peacefield, the Adamses' family home in Massachusetts. Like Peacefield, the Summer Palace was a large box with two neat rows of windows on each side. The structure was so simple, it looked as though it belonged on a Boston farm, not among St. Petersburg's intricate baroque buildings.

While walking on the Fontanka that day, Louisa suddenly saw him. Alexander was coming toward them. She may have elbowed Kitty with schoolgirl discreetness at the sight of him or nervously tightened a scarf around her neck. How would His Majesty respond? Would he turn his head away and pretend he didn't see them again? Or would his sunny side make an appearance on this winter day?

"He immediately stopped us and looked and spoke a little coldly addressing my sister; but at parting [he] turned to me and said that it was essential to my health that I should take such exercise and desired that *we* should walk every fine day when he should hope to meet *us*," Louisa reflected with emphasis.

She couldn't have been more relieved unless she'd read a letter from President Madison requesting John's return to the United States. Though a tad reserved, Alexander's favor had returned. By emphasizing his desire to see both Kitty and the married Louisa, he showed that his intentions were honorable. His comments about Mrs. Adams's health were highly intimate, however. Did he know of her illness? Did he suspect the reason behind it? Surely not. No matter how many may have worshipped him, Alexander was merely an emperor, not God omniscient.

One observation about the incident lingered, leading Louisa to laugh whenever she thought of it. Months earlier, when the emperor had first begun talking with Kitty and Louisa on their walks, his flirting had unleashed jealousy among William and the delegation's other aides, Mr. Gray and Mr. Everett. The czar's sudden lack of attention to Kitty aroused their passions even more. Their jealousy grew with each slight. "The gentlemen had all been as angry at the want of notice as they had been at His Majesty's attentions. . . . The minister took no notice."

For all her worry over the emperor's coldness affecting her husband's success, Adams appeared quite uninterested in the whole affair.

When she had first learned of her husband's and father-in-law's decision to send Kitty to Russia with her, Louisa had been upset. No matter the era, such a lack of control often leads to anger. The Adams men didn't understand the strain of chaperoning a young woman in a foreign land. Now with the greatest threat—flirtatious Alexander—subdued, Louisa relaxed and saw the benefits that Kitty's presence brought her.

"I thank my stars that my sister is with me as things have turned out," she concluded. "What should I have done with all these young men? A young lady in the family is quite an acquisition—She is a companion to me and to them, and their squabbles among themselves are quite amusing as I have nothing to do with them—They help to pass the time quite pleasantly."

⁓

Inaction from the Russian government was more absent than the winter sun. Nearly a month had passed since John first asked Romanzoff to admit the cargoes of the sixty-seven American ships confiscated at Russian ports for the winter. Persistence was in order. He took the matter to Baron Campenhausen, who was minister of commerce, a role previously held by Romanzoff.

They met at 11:00 a.m., breakfast time after a 9:00 a.m. winter sunrise. The problem was urgent. John needed to send a report to his government about the problem.

"I was now about to dispatch a courier to Göteborg, to embark there for the United States," Adams explained. "I was desirous of informing the [US] government what the ultimate decision of these vessels and their cargo would be."

Campenhausen explained that the emperor ordered his council to conduct a special investigation of the six hundred ships. "They belonged to a convoy,

about which *a great deal had been said*," the baron said with strong emphasis. Newspapers recently revealed that Napoleon was as hysterical as he was
emphatic. He believed that all the convoy ships were English. No matter the
evidence, Russia should admit none of them.

"I supposed the only paper required by law, of which these vessels would
be destitute," attorney Adams observed to Campenhausen, "would be certificates of origin from the *Russian* consuls."

The bottom line was simple. These US vessels came to Russia because
the ports in Denmark and Prussia were suddenly closed to them earlier in the
summer, thanks to Napoleon's underhanded intimidation tactics. When they
departed Boston, New York, and Philadelphia, these captains could not have
possibly known about the closures or the need to obtain a Russian permission
slip from a Russian consul from their ports of origin. John reminded the baron
that only two months earlier both he and Romanzoff admitted two American
vessels under similar circumstances.

"In those cases the decision was by the special order of the emperor himself," Campenhausen replied, noting that the season of the year made dozens of
exceptions problematic. "It was very hard upon Russia to have such immense
mass of foreign merchandise thus thrown upon her."

Russia's ports were open when the previous two ships were admitted, a
time when merchants could easily sell American colonial cargo. With the ports
now closed, St. Petersburg's merchants could not afford to buy an abundance
of raw materials such as cotton and sugar.

The lawyer in John emerged with patriotic strength. He must do something, especially if Caulaincourt was whispering in the emperor's ear against
these latest ships. If Adams could convince the baron that this cargo benefited
Russia, even when the ports were closed, then maybe he would admit the ships.

"That of the trade carried on by the Americans here, the balance was in
favor of Russia," John pressed, releasing his most flattering argument.

Campenhausen could not conceive "how the balance should be in favor of
Russia when the ships came almost all laden with colonial articles."

The man's snobbery against colonial items was as obvious—and
unflattering—as the wig on his head. By Campenhausen's calculation, one
cargo of colonial articles from America equaled three cargoes of Russian

merchandise in return. The assessment surprised John because he knew Romanzoff used a different standard.

"From the very nature of the trade between the United States and this country, it must be in the interest of the Americans who carried it on to load their vessels with the richest cargoes of Russia's manufacturers that they could carry," John praised.

The baron then prodded Adams's political savvy. Why were the ports in Prussia and Denmark closed to American ships?

"France had undertaken to levy a duty of 50 percent upon most of the articles brought by American vessels," John explained of the latest oppressive tax.

"Was there not a great abuse," Campenhausen countered, "of the American flag made by the English? Did they not counterfeit their papers?"

"There were undoubtedly cases of that kind," Adams replied, noting they were fewer in number this year and more easily detected, especially by him.

In most cases the English forged American licenses and certificates, not the other way around. He reminded the baron that these delays made it harder for the sixty-seven ship captains to sell their cargo.

"They could do nothing while the question about their admission was in suspense," Adams stated in the most forceful but polite tone he could muster.

After two hours of bantering, the baron finally said that the council should decide the matter by the beginning of the next week. Everything on his part was ready; he was waiting on the emperor's council, which was debating new measures regarding imports. Once those issues were settled, they would consider the American ships.

"As to the greater part of the cargoes, those would certainly be admitted; and as to the rest, we will try and find some expedient to let them in, too," the baron promised.

While agreeing to put off his couriered messenger a few days more, John was grateful that Campenhausen politely received him and spent so much time discussing the issue. Nonetheless, as Adams knew full well, politeness in Russia rarely translated to progress. He was still waiting for the US ship captains in Archangel to receive their clearance papers. Each day of delay was more and more disastrous to the pocketbooks of his countrymen. What was Caulaincourt whispering to Campenhausen, the emperor, or his council?

Politics, politeness, and pretension pressured John and Louisa as the year came to a close. Then another worry emerged. While she continued to battle her fatigue and illness, Charles suddenly began wheezing and coughing. "Charles was threatened with the croup and I was in an agony of alarm."

Drawing the three-year-old close to her, Louisa became his steadfast nurse, scouring their medicine chest for help. "I took him into my own chamber and Mr. Adams was obliged to occupy the study."

The tonics in her medicine box were not sufficient for relieving Charles's hoarse, brassy cough. She called for an English-speaking physician. "Dr. Galloway stayed and dined with us. I was quite sick myself."

Their quarantine worsened into a quandary on December 22, when the palace messenger arrived at their hotel with another invitation. "There came a notification from the master of the ceremonies inviting Mr. Adams, Miss Johnson, and myself to a ball."

The ball was scheduled for December 24, a mere two days away. Louisa was too sick and too worried about Charles to attend. That left Kitty and John.

"Mr. Adams informed him [the master of ceremonies] that my child and myself were both sick and that Miss Johnson according to etiquette could not go alone," she noted, worried that the decision would rankle royal sensibilities again.

"[The master of ceremonies] replied that he was ordered by the imperial family to say that Miss Johnson would be [considered] as already presented and be privileged to attend on all occasions when notified." The palace offered "that if Miss Johnson wished to be presented it would only be necessary for her to call on Countess Litta."

Such a presentation meant money. Kitty would have to visit a dressmaker along the silver arcade and buy a long train and other expensive accessories. John opted against a formal presentation.

"I have formed my domestic establishment in a very exact proportion to my means," John had recently ranted in his diary. In November he finally received a check for four thousand dollars, about half his salary, sent to him by the US Treasury back in April. The money had been stalled on a ship stuck between America and Russia. John was determined to live within his means. Kitty would not be presented and would not attend without Louisa.

As she nursed Charles, Louisa worried about her absence from the ball, the same event that she had missed the year before. Back then she had been fatigued from the early stages of pregnancy and had spent a quiet evening with a friend. Would the empress mother threaten to take her name off the list again? Would Alexander feel snubbed once more?

Charles was too sick, and Louisa was not much better. Unwilling to jeopardize their family's health, they risked royal wrath instead. John would go *solus*. The morning of the ball, he attended court at the palace.

"The empress mother told Mr. Adams she hoped to see me at the ball in the evening—He said he feared that the state of my health must deprive me of the honor—when Her Majesty kindly said she should much regret it," Louisa recorded with some relief. At least the woman's response was polite.

The ball was unremarkable in John's mind. Without his wife and sister-in-law, he felt lonely. "Great part of the time I stood gazing, and doing nothing." He missed Louisa.

⁓

The Adamses could not have ended 1810 more depressed. Once again they were stuck, sick, and saddened by the problems suppressing US trade. "I have pursued no object steadily, and the year has left no advantageous trace of itself in the annals of my life," John reflectively fretted in his diary.

Such sentiment was a stark contrast to his conclusions in October that his mission was a success. Although he had dispatched a courier telling his government about Campenhausen's assurances that the ships would be admitted, he felt uneasy because the officials had yet to issue the paperwork. In Russia it was easier to obtain a decision than a signature. Adams's countrymen were anxious. They could not legally sell their cargoes until they received permission papers.

⁓

"We end this year in bad health and in worse spirits than ever—God help us these are honors dearly bought," Louisa similarly observed in her diary.

Charles recovered, but Louisa's exhaustion increased. Attending a small dinner party was as fatiguing as a large ball. While avoiding socializing as much as she could, she knew she couldn't easily miss the upcoming Russian New Year's ball on January 13.

Though the lights of thousands of candles against the beautiful murals frescoed on the Hermitage's ceilings were brilliant, the crush of a crowd of thirteen thousand made walking from room to room an ordeal. The aroma of lamb or other decadent meats at the diplomatic dinner might make her nauseous.

While Louisa and John welcomed the first day of 1811 depressed and worried, French soldiers began the New Year with jubilant symbolism. Unknown to Emperor Alexander at the time, French soldiers had raised French flags in the newly annexed Hanseatic cities. For the first time Napoleon's empire stretched to the Baltic Sea, the czar's backyard.

The annexation adversely affected the Duke of Oldenberg, the father-in-law of the Grand Duchess Catherine, Alexander's sister who had refused to marry Napoleon. The duke was under Alexander's special protection. Worse, the annexation violated the Treaties of Tilsit, one of the prized agreements that had previously turned France and Russia into allies. Thus the New Year of 1811 began with a bang, a French volley across the Russian bow of the Baltic.

34

Exit Strategy

"I hear that you are leaving," Emperor Alexander said, implying a question as he addressed John during the diplomatic circle the afternoon of January 13, 1811.

As usual the czar began the Russian New Year with a noon liturgy at the Winter Palace and a ball for the masses that night. In between he held a meeting of his diplomatic court. Alexander did not want to wait until evening to find out the truth behind his American friend's plans. Was John leaving Russia to return to the United States?

"I hope, Sir, that woe will not yet come," Adams replied with reserve over the weighty question. With Caulaincourt listening, he chose his words carefully.

"I hope that this will not be soon," the emperor replied.

President Madison's October 16, 1810, letter arrived January 4, 1811, a surprisingly fast delivery because the Baltic froze in November. Most likely Madison sent the correspondence on a ship to Paris. From there a land courier brought it to Russia. After discovering John's financial hardships, Madison proposed an exit strategy.

"I received a letter from Mrs. Adams, your highly respectable mother, communicating your anxiety to leave a situation rendered insupportable by the ruinous expenses found to be inseparable from it," Madison began, noting that if the information was true, then he assumed Adams would have asked the secretary of state for a recall. Writing that it was not "the intention of the executive to expose you to unreasonable sacrifices," Madison gave him permission to leave.

"As no communication of your wishes, however, has yet been received from yourself, I cannot but hope that the peculiar urgency manifested in the letter of Mrs. Adams was rather hers, than yours; or that you have found the means of reconciling yourself to a continuance in your station."

The president assured Adams that he appreciated his service abroad. He then shared his fears. If John decided to return home, he must "spare no pains" to make sure that the emperor did not misinterpret his departure as a sign of American discontent toward Russia. Alexander must know that the US government valued their new relationship and wanted it to continue.

Madison also issued a warning. If Adams departed, many months would pass before a replacement could arrive. The gap alone might destroy the fragile friendship and with it, America's free trade prospects. Madison concluded his letter, "I am entirely persuaded that your patriotism will cheerfully make the sacrifice."

How embarrassed John felt. While his mother's motives were well-meaning, she had meddled nonetheless, emasculating him. Fortunately Madison saw it for what it was. However, rather than offer a salary increase, the president gave him permission to resign whenever the time was right without offering him a position back home—hardly the honorable exit Adams wanted.

A sacrifice to stay it would be. Though John was the second highest-paid US government official, only to Madison himself, the cost of living in Russia was so extreme that he was the lowest paid of the other foreign ministers. He would have to rely once again on his lawyerly logic and compliments on the culture, not lavish entertaining, to succeed.

Adams made one other interesting observation at that New Year's Day diplomatic circle. Absent was Mr. Wiggers, who represented the Hanseatic cities newly annexed by France. He was out, no longer a part of the czar's court.

Before John and the other diplomats left that afternoon, the chief of protocol distributed tickets to the New Year's ball. Would the American ladies be attending?

Yes. Louisa and Kitty would attend.

The protocol chief then gave Adams private instructions. The American party should enter the Hermitage from the petite entrance used only by the imperial family.

"This is considered as a very extraordinary distinction," a pleased Adams observed in his diary.

———

As she stepped into her ball gown that night, Louisa was just as shocked by the czar's special instructions. Only a month earlier at the Fontanka, he had turned his head away from her. Not only had the emperor's favor returned, but he was also treating them better than before, almost like family. She did her best to make her outward appearance as beautiful as possible. However, the true glow on her cheeks came not from entering the Cinderella ball through a secret entrance but from the secret she carried within.

That night they rode through St. Petersburg's streets, which were packed with more than thirteen thousand partygoers. Though the line of carriages leading to the public entrance looked longer than the land route to Paris, they turned and made their way to the private entrance. In contrast to the imperial family's golden-wheeled carriages, their coach was plain and simple. The Adamses did not ride in the luxury of a red velvet interior. They had only two footmen and four horses, not six. No matter, they disembarked and walked through the white pillars of the Hermitage's private entrance.

"We were shown into the receiving room of the emperor. . . . We were informed that this was a most extraordinary distinction ever granted to a foreign minister at that court and that it was the express order of the emperor himself."

The only other guests were the French and Austrian ambassadors.

As she glanced about the room, perhaps admiring the ornate gilded designs dimpled into the white ceiling, Louisa was not sure what to expect next. Would they be greeted by the emperor or escorted to another location? Before she could admire the Hermitage's mythological Greek figures, the French ambassador suddenly made a move more fitting for the palace's theater than an ornate holding room.

"Caulaincourt was seized with a swimming in the head and left the hall immediately," Louisa observed.

Was he truly ill? Or was the Frenchman aghast at the Americans receiving the same privilege as the French? His antics were amusing because they were pretentious.

"The imperial family soon came in and spoke very kindly to my sister and myself."

By special order, the Adams party and the others processed behind the emperor to the main hall. The first time Louisa saw the emperor was at her introduction, when Alexander walked through throne room doors accompanied by nobles. Now she and John were part of the delegation following him and passing through golden doors held open by Turkish-turbaned servants. As she crossed the floor, she may have smiled. Alexander had clearly forgiven her snubs. His politeness and grace returned in greater measure than she had ever expected. He was treating Adams as an ambassador, not a mere minister.

The Hall of St. George was the emperor's throne room, distinguished by a red-and-gold chair elevated on red carpeted steps. The throne room's long floor enabled hundreds of guests to stand at once. That night, the emperor was far less concerned about his special seat and more focused on his guest's special needs.

"On entering the hall [of St. George] the emperor called for the grand master of the ceremonies [and] order'd a chair to be set [for me]," Louisa wrote of the unexpected attention.

After giving Louisa a unique seat for the ball, Alexander's next direction soared louder in her heart than a hundred string quartets could sound in her ears.

"And turning to *me*; told him that he [a palace escort] was to take me under his protection to sit or walk as most agreeable; and not to suffer the crowd to press on me for turning to me 'un malheureux coude vous feroit un grand tort' [needlessly elbow her during the ball] and he was not to quit me during the evening until he had seen me safe into my carriage."

The imperial attention soon reached a crescendo.

About an hour later "we met the emperor when he again accosted me." Alexander suggested that Louisa should go over to "the empress who sat on an elevated seat, attended by her ladies."

She couldn't have been more shocked had the centaurs and other fanciful man-beasts painted on the Hermitage's tile floors suddenly come to life. This was too much for her American sensibilities.

"I thankfully declined the honor—when he insisted and said 'don't you know that no one says nay to the emperor'—I laughed and replied but *I* am a republican—He smiled and went on his way."

After supper the emperor returned and spoke politely to them. "He came round and spoke to my sister in English—He always spoke to me in French—I scarcely saw Mr. Adams the whole evening or any of our party."

John, Louisa, and Kitty departed as they came, through the czar's special entrance. There their carriage awaited them.

The preferential entrance, chair, escort, and offer to sit with the empresses revealed a quality of Emperor Alexander that Louisa had not noticed before. He was a skilled observer.

"My astonishment and embarrassment [were] painful for I had no idea that my delicate situation had been observed by anyone and it put me sadly to the blush."

Blush Louisa did. Her cheeks matched the throne room's red carpet. The emperor knew that she was expecting a baby. Yet she was only two months into this pregnancy. Perhaps he noticed that her face was pale as he talked with her along the Fontanka. Maybe after reading her correspondence the previous year, he knew pregnancy had kept her from previous balls. Perhaps Louisa had told Mrs. Krehmer, the court banker's wife, and she had spread the news. Somehow Alexander knew. The politics behind the politeness was not lost on the savvy Louisa.

"The motive of all this I presume is political and owing to the flattering partiality of the emperor for my husband."

—◦—

John and Louisa returned home from the ball to the news that their footman, Paul, was a new father. Earlier in the day his wife had given birth to a daughter. Would they hold a christening service for him as they did their butler in November? Because his child was a daughter, would Louisa and her chambermaid, Martha, stand in as godmothers?

This time a pregnant Louisa did not hide her enthusiasm over hosting a christening service. She embraced the role of godmother with gusto, finding "a piece of showy calico to wrap the babe in." Unlike the previous service, which followed Lutheran Church practices, this service upheld the Orthodox Church's traditions.

"A table was set covered with a handsome white damask napkin with candles and a camel's [hair] pencil," Louisa described.

The ceremony started with a procession. The head priest—or pope, as Louisa called him—led the godparents, nurse, and babe to the table. The priest consecrated the bathing tub, a small silver-plated bowl filled halfway with cold water. He placed the nurse and godparents in a circle around the tub.

"The child was presented to me to hold quite undressed," she explained. "The pope took the child from me, made a prayer in a sort of chant and dipped it three times into the tub."

In between each dip, the priest swiped the camel's hair brush across the babe's forehead in a blessing. With a wet sponge, traditionally dipped in oil, he made the sign of the cross on the infant's breast, shoulders, and feet. The priest gave the babe to Louisa, who held her while Martha dressed the child with the cap, shirt, and calico wrap.

Then they did something Louisa never thought she would do. With their backs toward the tub, they marched three times around the basin. Each time, the priest ordered them to spit "out the devil and all his works." Louisa never imagined spitting on the floor of her parlor. The tradition fit Orthodox customs but was far from orthodox to her Anglican and Congregational propriety.

The priest ended the service by cutting three locks of the babe's hair, rolling them into a little ball, and throwing it into the baptismal water. Louisa had reason to hope that soon she could host her own baby's christening service.

~⁃~

Two days later, her health dove into uncertainty. "I was taken very ill this day and Dr. Galloway was sent for."

She didn't say what her symptoms were, perhaps vomiting and dizziness. Worse, she may have felt a lightning-bolt jolt of pain across her back—a sign of miscarriage.

"In fact we all pined for home and I scarcely endured a longer separation from my loved children," she wrote. "This was burthensome to all, surely a man loses more than he gains by exacting such a sacrifice."

Just months earlier, Louisa had begged her husband to leave Russia. They had quarreled so much that she wrote Abigail about her sorrow over their continued sojourn. Now Madison's letter of recall had come, and she was pregnant.

"How could we be happy under such circumstances—To give birth to another child in a strange land after all I had suffered was a cause of incessant fear and anxiety," she wrote in her diary, adding that staying longer would deprive Kitty of suitable prospects for matrimony.

Would having another child keep Louisa from being reunited with her other sons? The irony hovered darkly over their horizon. Hope suddenly was as infrequent as the sun.

About the same time, John met with Count Romanzoff. A month had passed. The neutral navigation commission had yet to receive orders allowing the sixty-seven stalled American ships to sell their cargo. Because Campenhausen blamed the count for the delay, Adams had no choice but to return to Romanzoff, who promised that "he would see what he could do in the case." The papers were in front of the emperor and depended upon his "personal pleasure" for signature.

Adams suspected Caulaincourt was behind the delay. France was unhappy with the imperial council's new trade policy, which restricted imports on wines, silks, velvets, lace, and other similar items. Because these were mostly French products, Caulaincourt and the local French merchants were furious. Delaying the American cargo paperwork was likely a way to appease the French.

Napoleon was not the only ruler whose words did not match his policies. Pretension permeated the Winter Palace too. Alexander's inaction did not match the attention he had given the American delegation at the New Year's ball. More than party favors, John wanted action for those sixty-seven American merchant ships. No matter his frustration, he had to live within the pretension. He pushed back with polite persistence.

As usual Romanzoff changed the subject and asked for John's opinion on world affairs. Then he made an unusual move. He confronted Adams. Was the rumor true?

"I mentioned to the count that the president of the United States, in consideration of circumstances relating to my private affairs, had given me permission to return to the United States."

Adams did not intend to leave, not yet.

"And he could assure me, when I should go, I should be much regretted here; that he had a very great and sincere esteem for me, and would be happy that my stay should be prolonged," he recorded of Romanzoff's reply.

John responded with gratefulness, promising to remain as long as possible.

What he could not tell Romanzoff was how worried he was about Louisa. Could she endure a voyage? Land travel to Paris was the only option this time of year. With all she had suffered, would it be fair to ask her to do so?

"At any rate, I could not take my leave until the approach of summer and perhaps I might stay until the appointment of a successor," John concluded.

Had his wife not been expecting, would John have resigned? Was financial strain an honorable exit to diplomatic exile? The questions played like a funeral dirge in his mind. Although leaving under such circumstances was not dishonorable, it certainly was not the answer he longed for. Accepting another position was the most respectful way to leave a diplomatic post. Leaving under Madison's current terms would not merely hint at failure but reinforce John's fear that he had not accomplished anything worthwhile in his life. The matter was tough for anyone, especially someone named John Adams. Resigning at that moment was not what he wanted, not on those terms. Not yet.

35

French Cooling

GENERAL HITROFF WAS AN AIDE-DE-CAMP TO ALEXANDER. MORE than once he had pulled silk stockings over his aging Russian feet, tightened his shoe buckles, and stepped into fur-lined outer boots to depart for a formal event. As was the custom, he threw a shoop, a fur outer garment worn only when riding in a carriage, on top of his formal military coat. Like everyone else, when he arrived at the Winter Palace for a ball, he would remove his shoop and outer boots and toss them to his footman.

Caulaincourt entertained in a similar style, providing a Swiss porter dressed in gold lace and embroidery to greet guests after they disembarked from their carriages. The Swiss porter opened the folding doors leading to the stairs, where Hitroff and other guests would pass twenty more footmen, who lined the steps like statues, until reaching the top to enter the upper level for the formal ball. Such was the ritual. Hitroff knew the routine well. After all, he had attended many events at the French ambassador's mansion. He had become good friends with the French legation—particularly good.

One winter night in 1811, as Hitroff headed to a party, the uniformed Russian police hailed his carriage. Did they know the truth? Yes. And they arrested him for it.

What was his crime? Treason. Hitroff had furnished the French with information about Russia's military forces. As John understatedly relayed to the US secretary of state in a letter, the material Hitroff had conveyed was too detailed to be considered "consistent with his duty."

Hitroff was lucky. Alexander was mild compared to the madness of previous czars. He banished the traitor to a Siberian prison, not to a gallows or a firing squad. John observed that the incident excited "an extraordinary degree of attention." Indeed it did.

Treason was not the only news lingering on whispering lips. In response to

France's New Year's annexation of the Hanseatic towns, the Russian government moved 120,000 additional troops to the Polish border.

———✦———

February 3, 1811, began as usual for John. He read a few chapters in the French translation of his Bible and ate breakfast. A messenger from Caulaincourt soon arrived with an inquiry. Was Monsieur Adams at home today? Yes. Could the French ambassador come by for a visit? Of course.

Caulaincourt wasted no time when he arrived. He talked in general terms about trade and then observed that an increased number of US merchants had entered Russian ports the previous trading season.

"I told him that it had been very considerable, greater than any former year," John stated clearly, noting that they also faced more interruptions along the Baltic than ever before.

"And then, your vessels have done a great deal of business here on English account," Caulaincourt accused in a fencing-match tone of voice.

"That was a mistake; that the American vessels which came here were directly from America and returned directly to thither," Adams defended with equal force.

"But how happens it, then," he said, "that several of them have been sequestered, or a least that their admission has been suspended?"

"Why," Adams accused, "the credit of that is attributed to you." It was the most direct accusation he had ever made toward the French ambassador.

"That is to say, that we are supposed to have required that a strict examination should be had," Caulaincourt said, spinning John's charge.

Adams was sure his opponent had tried every maneuver to push the czar into excluding all American commerce from the convoy. Though the Russian government promised to admit the US vessels, the paperwork was absent, a sign that Caulaincourt had so far succeeded. He had to make his case, allowing justice to provide the fair wind.

"I had sent to the government here a list of the vessels which I knew to be American, and the cargoes which I had no doubt were American property,"

John explained, adding that he personally knew some of the captains and had received reference letters for the others.

"Where [could] the American vessels get such large quantities of sugar as these had brought?" the Frenchman accused, implying that only the British could supply such great amounts.

"Our own country produced sugar, particularly Louisiana and the state of Georgia," Adams replied, reminding him of the territory that Napoleon had sold to the United States.

"The desire of the French government manifestly was to harmonize," he assured before abruptly changing the subject and inviting John and Louisa to a children's ball. With his diplomatic sword withdrawn, Caulaincourt departed. The debate abated, for now.

⟶

"Sick as usual after these fatigues which I cannot learn to support à la Rousse— And now I am more delicate than ever," Louisa wrote on February 8.

The next day was no better: "I still confined to my chamber—I must have been a strong woman or I could not have borne such climates and so much anxiety and suffering."

While her husband traded jabs with Caulaincourt, Louisa battled the physical stresses of pregnancy against the social demands placed upon her as the only minister plenipotentiary's wife residing in St. Petersburg. Unlike the previous February when she was ill and could not attend social obligations, she had a new resource. The imperial family's implicit acceptance of her sister into their court now allowed Kitty to attend dinners in her place. Rest was a commodity she tapped as willingly as chocolate to alleviate her cravings.

By February 11, Louisa decided she was strong enough to go out in public again. She attended a party hosted by a prominent Frenchwoman. The best evidence of her improved health was her Abigail Adams–like propriety, which poured from her pen after she returned home.

"Madame Lesseps is a very sensible woman—Sensible women [are] not always the most agreeable though the most valuable—The maxim of men 'that pretty is better than good' is almost universally adopted by them where money does not bias the taste," she wrote with Jane Austen–like astuteness.

Louisa's pregnancy seemed to be bringing out a suppressed side of her personality. While her belly expanded, she also grew more outspoken about female virtues and more conscious of social changes.

"The French were a little down," she detected after one event. Another recent party "was so cold and heartless that it was different altogether from anything that we had seen before."

"Rumors of war between Russia and France—a new anxiety."

The winds from Paris to St. Petersburg were blowing a cold gust.

Adams called on Caulaincourt by appointment at noon on February 15. The pair resumed their diplomatic duel. John brought up a crucial point: the French government refused to acknowledge licenses that French consuls legitimately gave to ship captains at US ports before their departure.

"Some of our American vessels, though not of this last list, had met with objections for having been provided with certificates of origin given by the French consuls in America," he asserted.

"The French consuls in the United States gave no such certificates," Caulaincourt replied just as sharply, saying that the measure was not mere newspaper speculation. His government had sent him a formal declaration of the change.

"This was certainly a mistake," John declared, revealing a new weapon—tangible evidence. He handed the ambassador a copy of a certificate signed by the French consul in Boston only a few months earlier on October 31, 1810—long after the announcement by France's government-run newspaper in July 1810.

Adams prodded him further. The French government "when informed of its mistake" should take measures to correct it and protect the honor of its public officers.

"But, supposing our consuls have given these certificates in disobedience of their orders?" Caulaincourt countered.

"It [was] more probable," John replied, ". . . that if such orders had been dispatched to them, they had not been received."

The slowness of ship travel was most likely the cause. Even if the French consuls had directly disobeyed their government, it "became a question between the officer and his government." The matter certainly should not "affect the rights, reputation or property of persons who had received their certificates."

Caulaincourt listened silently while Adams continued his monologue.

"If they had violated their duty, their government might say so to the world—might recall and punish them—might disavow their acts and discredit them after due notice," John said with polite but clear force.

"But this was a very different thing from declaring their real signatures to be forgeries. It was merely a question of fact: Did they or did they not give the certificates?" he continued.

Then he used his best logic against the ambassador. "If they did, and you declare they did not, it is precisely the case that an individual should deny his own handwriting to a promissory note."

Caulaincourt agreed with the comparison.

"The dishonor of such a procedure must fall ultimately upon the officer himself whose government falsified his acts or upon the government which thus gratuitously discredits the officers," Adams said, adding a forceful blow: "I could not suppose such an intention in the government of France."

The Frenchman studied the paper. Clearly the son of John Adams knew how to fight honorably—how to accuse a man's government of dishonesty in a way that did not dishonor the man himself. Though he fenced him into a corner, by suggesting noble motives, Adams also gave the French ambassador a way to retain personal dignity.

"To be sure, there could not be two opinions upon a case so clear, considered as a question of *law* or of *morality*," Caulaincourt responded.

John had not forgotten how much honor mattered to his counterpart. When the Russian nobility questioned his role in the killing of the Duke d'Enghien, whom Napoleon had ordered Caulaincourt to capture, the ambassador had worked tirelessly to clear his name with Alexander. Despite the French government's recent orders, one value still mattered to Caulaincourt.

"Consider it, Monsieur l'Ambassadeur, as a question of *honor*—as a question between men of *honor*—what would be the answer then?" John posed with emphasis.

"Precisely the same," he agreed, as if resting his saber. "By the late measures in France, it appeared that the government was inclined to come upon good terms with the United States."

Adams raised another crucial point. If the French government knew that one of its officers had falsified a signature, then France would disdain such an act of injustice because it reflected dishonor on the government. Caulaincourt agreed with the theory, but couldn't say anything further. The French government would willingly avert its eyes away from legitimate licenses if it meant that other governments would confiscate American cargo.

"But, it seems, you are great favorites here. You have found powerful protection, for most of your vessels have been admitted," the ambassador jabbed.

"They had, but after a delay of three months, and after their papers had been taken from the commission of neutral navigation and had undergone a very strict examination before the imperial council," John responded, not knowing the final outcome of the US ships belonging to the convoy. He was hopeful Campenhausen would bring him good news soon.

John told Caulaincourt that in his first meeting with the emperor, Alexander had professed a strong desire to trade with the United States while also declaring a strong alliance with France. The two were not mutually exclusive.

Caulaincourt disagreed. From Napoleon's perspective, Russia could not be an ally to both America and France. "I hope they will be more reconcilable still as France and the United States will come to a better understanding with each other. But, after all, you have had a very advantageous commerce this last year," Caulaincourt replied. "I am told you have had more than a hundred vessels at Archangel."

John fired back: "But, you are to consider, that, thanks to you, we have had scarcely any part of the continent of Europe open to us. We have had only the ports of Spain and Portugal, where you are not the masters, and Russia. For you made Denmark and Prussia shut their doors against us, without a shadow of a reason for it."

"You could not, however, have much commerce with Denmark."

"It was considerable."

Cornered, Caulaincourt put down his proverbial sword and ended the conversation. What neither realized at the time was that this would be their last duel of words. Soon everything would change.

36

Recall and Relocation

"It is confidently reported that Mr. Adams is shortly to be removed to France," Louisa wrote on February 14, 1811. While John battled Caulaincourt, Louisa confided in Abigail. "I however put no faith in it and it is far from my wish, as it [is] universally said to be the most unpleasant and expensive residence for a foreign minister in Europe."

Although she did not want to relocate to Paris, she assured Abigail that she would "cheerfully acquiesce" to plans her husband considered "advantageous."

What bothered her more than newspaper speculation was Abigail's silence. They had not heard a word from her since July. Knowing how suddenly a fatal disease can sweep through a town, Louisa trembled in fear of receiving bad news from home.

"Our solicitude and anxiety to hear from you adds terribly to the tediousness of our banishment and renders my residence here almost insupportable."

Though she thanked Abigail in her letter for caring for George and John and begged her to give them kisses on her behalf, she did not reveal that she was pregnant. The risk of a miscarriage was too great. Why share the news if disappointment could soon follow?

⤙

The wife of the American minister knew she could not refuse one social engagement, no matter how tired the event might make her: the examination ceremony of the noble girls' school. The reason she could not decline? The empress mother had issued the invitations.

"Most of the members of the corps diplomatic attended with their legations and we were obliged to appear in full court dresses—All the ministers of state and the imperial family with the haute noblesse of the empire."

While Louisa admired the number of girls graduating, eighty-one, and their ability to master a variety of dances, what stood out to her was their ghastly appearance. "None of them are handsome—The performance of their religious duties is strictly attended to and their long fasts reduce them so much that they look like skeletons—Of course their complexions suffer."

The outing fatigued her so much that all she wanted to do when she came home was crawl into bed, but she couldn't. Romanzoff was hosting a ball for a Russian prince and princess. The Adamses had already promised to attend. Because the count invited the entire diplomatic corps and she had seen most of them at the examination ceremony earlier in the day, she felt additional pressure. How could she explain attending one event and then declining another or sending Kitty in her place on the same day? She could not risk offending the chancellor.

"At ten o-clock went to a ball at Count Romanzoff's." The Adamses dashed away in their coach pulled by four horses. As usual, they threw off their coats and outer boots and handed them to their footman before entering Romanzoff's home. The count greeted them formally in the receiving line, and they admired the glittering diamonds, embroidery of the women's silk dresses, and the pristine ribbons decorating the gentlemen's uniforms.

These upper-class guests very likely wore any strong scent available to them. She had smelled these aromas many times before. However, perfumes and oils can often become repugnant to the nose of a pregnant woman.

After such a long day, she likely was hungry and could hardly wait for dinner, which was usually a meal of six or seven different salty meats. Fish was served with pastries and vegetables. The dancing and festivities droned on for five hours before dinner was served. Whatever she craved or smelled, Louisa soon discovered that her dinner partners were the greatest aversion, not the perfumes or food.

"The invitation was to a supper and I sat between Count Markoff and the Duke of Serra Capriola."

The count was eighty years old. A pregnant Louisa found herself squeezed between two old men who could no more relate to her condition and cravings than teenage boys.

As was the custom, carafes of red and white wine dotted the table, alternating every two people. Each guest had a wine glass. In between sipping the wine, the men began boasting like boys of their previous lives. Realizing that an American woman sat between them, they decided to talk about what else? The savage United States.

"The conversation turned upon America and Count Markoff mentioned many things that Talleyrand had told him of his travels in the United States."

Louisa was familiar with Prince Charles-Maurice de Talleyrand-Périgord, the Frenchman who had come to the United States years earlier in a temporary exile. He had visited England as an unofficial French diplomat. When the British government issued a warrant for his arrest in 1794, he'd fled to the United States, where he'd lived as a house guest of then US Senator Aaron Burr of New York. For two years the Frenchman worked to rebuild his fortune as a bank agent in commodity trading and real estate investments. Talleyrand's tales of the United States did not reflect the America that Louisa knew.

In the coarsest terms, Count Markoff relayed what he'd heard about American men and women.

"Particularly of the beauty of the women and the easy morality of the husbands," Louisa noted.

The dirtier his jokes, the more Louisa's blood pressure rose. Perhaps the fatigue of such a long day got to her. Maybe the men's colognes were too strong. Or perhaps she was suddenly in need of sugar and couldn't wait to pick up her silver dessert spoon and dive into ice cream or liquid jellies, common desserts.

"I was perfectly enragé which was very foolish," she reflected.

Regardless, she could no longer politely sit silently and listen to insults about American women. The lioness protecting her homeland emerged.

"I told him that it was very well known that Talleyrand never spoke truth—that therefore everyone would estimate his assertions according to their worth," she roared, speaking her mind with the greatest clarity.

"My situation was becoming so disagreeable that had not the chancellor [Count Romanzoff] risen to return to the ball room, I was so disgusted that I should certainly have made an esclandre [caused a scene] to the horror of Mr. Adams," she wrote.

"What on earth is so disgusting as two old men chuckling over their past follies and vices!!!"

The incident and Talleyrand's influence were hardly calling cards luring her to Paris. More than ever she needed Madison to appoint a different man to represent the United States in France and bring her husband home to Boston.

These insults may have led her to break with pretension and speak her mind, but Louisa was also wrestling with the suffocation she felt as a woman living in European society in 1811. How far she would take her views, she did not know.

An exhausted and insulted Louisa declined the next party. Kitty and William attended the "Masquerade for foreigners—It is the last of the season," she wrote gratefully.

"Lent begins this day—Now for a little rest."

"Caulaincourt," Adams wrote in a letter to his mother on March 19, 1811, "has received his recall." Acknowledging him as "one of the greatest enoblemen of the Napoleon creation," Adams regretted the French ambassador's departure. He admired his "easy unassuming simplicity of manners." Despite their quarreling, they were now friends. Caulaincourt would remain in St. Petersburg several more weeks until his successor arrived.

Would Adams soon follow the ambassador to France? No, Madison had appointed someone else to replace Armstrong as minister to France, which ended the speculation of the Adamses' relocating to Paris. Both John and Louisa felt relief.

An even more satisfying piece of news soon arrived. At a diplomatic dinner hosted by the soon-to-depart Caulaincourt, Baron Campenhausen approached John as soon as he saw him.

"He was happy now to say that the cases of all the American vessels . . . were definitively decided; that the cargoes and parts of cargoes which had not the necessary certificates should be admitted."

Because these sixty-seven ships belonging to the convoy and the others in Archangel did not have certificates issued by Russian consuls from their ports of origin, the Russian government decided to require bonds from the captains, who promised to acquire the certificates and forward them to the customhouse. This was a way for the Russian government to save face, maintain a sense of public honor, and exert its authority while doing the right thing by freeing the ships.

Campenhausen noted that everything recognized as American would be cleared. He apologized for the delay.

The news was the best that John could have received. Russia had not caved in to France's pressure after all. Had the sea been free of ice, John could have voyaged to Boston and back in the time it took for the Russian government to complete the paperwork, but the results were a victory for American trade nonetheless. Campenhausen also strongly suggested that the US government make a public statement against France's refusal to accept its own consul's certificates.

John took up the baron's suggestion and wrote US Secretary of State Smith: "At least it may be important for the protection both of the property and reputation of many of our citizens, to demonstrate that they are unjustly charged with having produced forged papers."

He also gave his boss a warning: "If . . . according to the expectation now generally entertained here," he wrote partly in the US government's secret code, "a war between France and Russia should very speedily ensue, it may be of some importance to consider what its effects upon our commercial relations may probably be."

John doubted that war would come soon "unless it be the deliberate and irrevocable determination of France to come to a rupture with Russia."

Soon he had a good reason to reconsider his optimism.

———⚬———

No doubt Count Czernicheff had grown as tired of wearing his shoop and loose outer boots on his journey back to St. Petersburg as he had of drinking wine with Napoleon in Paris. Czernicheff had been around Napoleon so many times that he knew the man's worst habits. He wasn't sure which afflicted the French ruler more: insomnia or arrogance. Alexander's special envoy to the French emperor traveled as fast as six horses could pull his coach from post to post from Paris to St. Petersburg. The letter from Napoleon to Alexander was the most important message he had ever carried.

Twenty-six-year-old Czernicheff, whom Louisa had described as the most handsome man she had ever seen when she met him the year before at a dinner, knew Alexander well. Unlike General Hitroff, he honorably served his Russian sovereign.

Czernicheff arrived in St. Petersburg on March 17, 1811. He immediately rode to the Winter Palace to personally deliver Napoleon's letter to Alexander. The czar wasted no time. No sooner had he read the correspondence than he demanded a meeting with Caulaincourt. No matter that Napoleon had recalled him; until his replacement arrived, he was still the French emperor's ambassador. The two talked until 10:00 p.m. Caulaincourt spent the next day writing letters. He refused to meet with anyone.

John heard the news from another diplomat, who whispered while the pair walked the streets of St. Petersburg. As the weather began to warm in Russia, the relationship with France was growing chillier.

"The coolness or misunderstanding between the cabinets of St. Petersburg and of Paris . . . has become a subject of very general notoriety," Adams wrote to the secretary of state.

How would a Russian-French war affect America? The possibility was horrific.

———

"In constant expectation of letters from my children," Louisa wrote with worry.

The Neva River broke on April 24, 1811. Ships were docking again. Adams would no longer rely on a Russian courier to send his letters to the United States by way of Paris. Perhaps they would finally receive correspondence from home. Louisa was more desperate than ever to learn about the well-being of her children. Maybe she would get relief soon.

The breakup of the river also enticed these prisoners of winter to get out and about. The day was May 6. Adams longed to see the long blocks of ice sweeping down the Neva. To do so, he changed his routine and took an afternoon walk along the Fontanka.

As he approached the canal, he met Alexander, who was walking toward him and away from the water. The emperor stopped and signaled for Adams to stand next to him at an iron railing along the canal. They spoke while the imperial guards stood with their arms turned outward, facing the Fontanka.

"The weather was warmer and finer," Alexander proclaimed, noting it was more pleasant than he remembered from previous springs.

"It was very long," Alexander remarked of the time he'd last seen his American friend walking.

John explained that he had not abandoned his habit but his timing.

"I believed it was the hour at which I usually walked that had deprived me of the happiness of meeting His Majesty."

The emperor had often "of late been so engaged in business that he could not take his usual walks."

Suddenly Alexander stepped away, as if signaling an end to their conversation. Just as John started to bow and turn away, the emperor faced him again, leaning intently on the canal's iron railing. He waved his hand to dismiss the guards. His face was earnest. In a whispery voice, he asked a question. Did Adams have "any late accounts from home?"

"I had letters up to the 20th of February."

Did they contain "information of any particular importance?"

"They did not."

Alexander was not immune to winter's prison. Just as Louisa and John longed for an encouraging letter from home, so the emperor was anxious for news about America. He continued to fish.

"What was the state of our affairs with England?"

Though surprised by the Russian ruler's frank discussion of politics when previous conversations on such walks concerned trivial matters, a curious Adams answered forthrightly about the US relationship with Britain.

"They remained in an unsettled state; . . . our minister there had taken leave and was gone, but he had left the chargé d'affaires there."

The emperor frowned. "And I hear you have lately made in acquisition?" Alexander asked, abruptly changing the subject.

John understood the reference to America's latest territorial controversy: Florida. The emperor was intrigued by the process. When Russia acquired land, it was the result of war or diplomatic arm-twisting—not the will of the people.

"But it appears to have been a spontaneous movement of the people themselves, who were desirous of joining themselves to the United States," Alexander astutely observed.

John agreed, detailing the controversy behind it. The Florida territory was ceded by France to the United States in the Louisiana Purchase. Spain objected, especially claiming West Florida and Baton Rouge. France's latest attempt to annex Spain changed the dynamics. On September 23, 1810, many inhabitants rebelled against Spanish rule and created the West Florida Republic. Three months later, the United States annexed the territory.

"Since then the people of that country had been left in a sort of abandonment by Spain, and must naturally be very desirous of being annexed to [the] United States. Under these circumstances the US government have taken possession of the country."

"*On s'agrandit toujours un peu, dans ce monde,*" the emperor replied with a sparkle of understanding, saying in French that "annexation grows a little bit in the world."

The czar's reference to Napoleon's takeover of the Hanseatic territories was unmistakable.

Alexander bowed. Adams replied in kind and left. He had been so focused on the emperor that he'd failed to notice the large crowd that had gathered between the two bridges to watch them. As John walked away, he passed many who had witnessed their conversation. They stared at him and moved out of his way as if he were "a very important personage." He wryly concluded, "Such is the magic of an emperor's countenance."

Once he was out of view of the czar, he noticed a change in the people he passed. They ignored him. These peasants had not seen him speaking to the emperor. "And every new mujik brushed by me with little notice as if passing one of his fellows."

John understood the reason behind Alexander's questions about America's relationship with England. His advisors were pushing him to make peace with Britain and go to war with France. If Russia officially renewed trade with England, then American ships would be at even greater risk of French cannon fire and caught in the crosshairs of war. Adams was grateful that Alexander had declined the advice of his council. The czar was determined not to be the aggressor. If France wanted war, Napoleon must strike first.

Adams wrote to the secretary of state that the times were no longer notorious but disastrous. "The catastrophe is near at hand."

37

Correspondence and Contractions

"I IMMEDIATELY SAW BY THEIR DISTRESSED COUNTENANCES THAT bad news had come to us."

By the third week of May 1811, Louisa was growing more and more uncomfortable with the woes that come with the last trimester of pregnancy—such as fatigue, backaches, and the occasional fleeting contraction. After enduring the coarseness of the two old codgers at Count Romanzoff's party, she avoided the social swirl by spending time among supportive intimate friends. With sisterly admiration, she praised the Spanish diplomat's wife: "Went to visit Madame Colombi—She is so gay; so sensible; and so attractive it is impossible to know her without loving her."

Though she found comfort in her small sorority of diplomatic sisters and satisfaction in championing female virtues, her heart continued to sail as a ship through rough waters. Any day a vessel carrying letters from home could arrive in St. Petersburg. While such correspondence might bring the greatest joy—such as the handwriting of her Boston birches—she was oh too fearful that some letters might carry words of woe. Her greatest anxiety was receiving tragic news. Now that day had come.

As soon as she walked into the study the morning of May 23, 1811, she knew something awful had happened. Her husband's ashen face and her sister's tears along with the limp, soiled papers they held in their hands spoke louder than any words. Fear gripped her so intensely that she could hardly breathe as she asked what was wrong. Their hesitation only made her heart beat faster.

"They could not conceal it from me."

Yes, they had received correspondence from home. Yes, the news was bad. Abigail was the messenger. After learning of an opportunity to send mail to

John and Louisa by way of an outward-bound ship, she had written three letters in January 1811. In the first two she dished enticing political news, particularly pointing out the appointment of Massachusetts's Lieutenant Governor Levi Lincoln to the US Supreme Court. She joyfully noted that Lincoln "accepted only to keep the place warm for JQ Adams whenever he returns."

Abigail sought to fortify the possibility through her own prediction: "I would fain believe, what has long been impressed upon my mind, that you are destined to serve your country in her most essential and important interest for years yet to come."

Then suddenly, tragic news had arrived in Boston from Washington City. Abigail had no choice but to write another letter. With great heaviness of heart she'd picked up her pen on January 24, 1811.

"I thought it best to communicate to you the sudden death of Mrs. Hellen, who was at church on Christmas day and buried on the New Year," Abigail had written of the death of Louisa's sister Nancy and her infant. "She died in childbirth."

Nancy was two years older than Louisa. They were as close as two sisters could be. John and Louisa had lived with Nancy and her husband, Walter, at their home on K Street, while John was a US senator. As Adams labored on Capitol Hill, Nancy and Louisa had spent hours swapping ideas about mother-hood, playing the piano, and riding horseback. Often Nancy and Louisa had listened to Adams as he read aloud from the classics in the evening. Nancy was the one who'd convinced John to accompany her to President Madison's inaugural ball so he could show his support in case Madison wanted to appoint him to a position in his administration. Now her flashing smile and zest for life were gone. She left behind three children.

"Say to your wife that I enter her grief and most tenderly sympathize with her, and Kitty; however we may live, there is not any religion by which we can die, but the Christian which gives us the glorious prospect of life," Abigail had written with as much tenderness, understanding, faith, and hope as she could muster.

Though Louisa's greatest fear—the death of her son George or John—had not come, the news and its timing with her own delicate condition caused her great alarm.

"My heart collapsed with agony at the sudden shock in a dead fainting fit."

John and Kitty immediately helped Louisa into bed, so she could cry and grieve freely without embarrassment. There she could soak her sheets with a torrent of tears. Adams, however, quickly detected that his wife needed more than a comfortable bed. Though she was more than two months from her expected delivery, she appeared to be in labor and needed a physician. He sent for Dr. Galloway.

Sometime after she began sobbing, Louisa felt her belly tighten and quickly loosen again. A stronger surge suddenly wrenched her womb, and then just as abruptly, it subsided. She felt another pain that ripped like a lightning bolt. Then another. And another. Each time the intensity grew worse and seemed to last longer than the one before.

When contractions come close together, a woman cannot easily discern when one ends and the other begins. The result is a continuous stream of intense, scream-producing pain. Occasional contractions are not abnormal thirty or so weeks into a pregnancy. However, these jolts were forceful enough to cause grave concern. Thinking of Nancy, who had felt similar sensations just before her death in childbirth months earlier, was enough to launch a thunderstorm of tears once again.

"The fright produced alarming consequences and a premature birth was threatened with dangerous symptoms for some hours."

Louisa most likely suffered from what modern medicine describes as preterm contractions. Emotional stress alone cannot induce the physical symptoms of labor. Very likely her sobbing—combined with a lack of eating and drinking—left her dehydrated, which is the most common cause of *preterm contractions*. Today, physicians prescribe medication to stop such contractions in a woman who has not reached full term. Louisa had no pills to pop to make the contractions stop. Intravenous medications were not available to intervene. All she had was supportive care and intuition.

"My physician remained with me for many hours of intense suffering." Dr. Galloway encouraged her to drink water and eat. She rested, perhaps lying on her side, hugging her womb, and praying that her child would not come too soon or that she would not suffer the same fate as her sister.

Though she had miscarried many times in the early weeks of pregnancy, Louisa had also experienced one traumatic full-term birth. Occasionally a woman would go days or weeks past her due date without going into labor. The child would grow, becoming too big, and then die inside the womb, resulting in a stillborn death. The risk of dying from an infection from the decaying infant was high. In June 1806 Louisa spent twenty-four hours in labor before giving birth to a son, who died shortly afterward. The experience broke her heart. However, the successful birth of Charles the following year on July 4 became her balm. Modern medicine induces labor to prevent such tragedies. Back then, stillborn deaths, infant death shortly after birth, and maternal mortality were all-too-frequent realities.

Louisa lived before municipal and state governments carefully counted the deaths of its residents and the causes behind them. The documentation that does exist from the early 1800s suggests that the maternal mortality rates and infant death rates were high. For every ten thousand births, sixty or more mothers would die, usually within two weeks of the birth.

The infant death rate was substantially higher than the maternal death rate. For every thousand births, four to five mothers might die, but one hundred infants would die. Although the death of a child was far more frequent than the death of the mother, maternal mortality was common enough to make it highly feared among families.

Just as people today know someone who has died from cancer or a heart attack, most everyone in the 1800s knew of a woman who had died in childbirth. What should have been one of nature's most joyous occasions turned into its greatest crimes, stealing a mother from her child; a wife from her husband. Though Louisa feared the death of the child she was carrying, especially after experiencing so many miscarriages and the loss of a son at birth, she didn't need statistics to know that losing a child was very common. Abigail had lost a daughter at a young age.

Knowledge about obstetrics was in its infancy in 1811. Doctors and midwives did not understand the benefits of washing their hands before delivering a child. Why wash beforehand if your hands were going to get dirty anyway? So the thinking went. Postpartum infections, such as the notorious puerperal fever, and hemorrhage were the most common killers of mothers in childbirth. This tragedy would not improve until 1865, when Joseph Listerine made his discoveries about the benefits of washing one's hands with antiseptic solutions.

Nancy likely either bled to death after giving birth or died from an infection she'd received following the delivery. Because Nancy's child also died, it is more likely that she died from an infection than a hemorrhage.

The rise of antiseptics, penicillin, and improved obstetric standards has radically changed mortality rates. The infant death rate in the United States in 2010 was 6.14 infant deaths for every 1,000 births. According to the Center for Disease Control: "The maternal mortality rate in 2007 (latest available data) was 12.7 deaths per 100,000 live births." These reductions are among medicine's greatest triumphs.

In this case Dr. Galloway's supportive care, however, helped Louisa. "A favorable change took place and perfect quiet was relied on for recovery."

With the contractions easing, Louisa would have been able to sense the baby's movements again. The pleasure of feeling the baby stretch his or her arms or legs or turn over would have given Mrs. Adams great comfort that her child was alive.

With his private world in turmoil, John received news about his public world that shook his normally reserved nature. "Mr. Krehmer sent me the *London Courier* from the 19th to the 26th of April," John wrote in his diary on May 24, "where I found articles which give me great concern upon the account of my country. They [the British] threaten war in the most unequivocal terms."

Diplomatic attempts to resolve America's conflict with Britain had failed, with little hope from new attempts. Though British envoy Augustus Foster would soon arrive in Washington City, he carried instructions from his government refusing to change its trade policies or make reparations for the 1807 *Leopard-Chesapeake* incident. The US government insisted that the British government make amends for the HMS *Leopard*'s attack on the US frigate, the *Chesapeake*, off Virginia's coast. The British overplayed their hand by firing several broadsides when the *Chesapeake* fired only one and surrendered. Americans were still angry that the British had killed three sailors, injured eighteen, and captured four when the nations were at peace.

"I fear the British ministry have made it unavoidable. They menace us with an 'Illiad of woes,' and already deny us every particle of compassion for our sufferings under them," John ranted.

America was such a young nation. Though George Washington had died more than ten years earlier, few had forgotten the American Revolution that shaped John's childhood. Had the United States grown into adulthood by 1811? The problems with Britain revealed the glaring truth. The United States was still an infant in the eyes of the world. Each time a British ship hoisted the red, white, and blue to avoid Napoleon's trade restrictions, the British spit at American sovereignty. Every time a British admiral impressed an American merchant into service in the British navy, a piece of American independence was kidnapped too.

Adams understood the gravity of the situation better than most. If the Brits coaxed President Madison into war and won, the English lion would dominate the American eagle. Independence would be lost. America would be annexed by Great Britain. Those who had lived loudly for liberty during the Revolution would have died in vain.

"Non nobis Domine!" Adams wrote in Latin, which means, "not to us, O Lord." He added, "If our trial is now to come, God of justice and mercy! Give us your spirit to bear with fortitude and to derive ultimate power and virtue from all the evils that they can inflict, and spare us from that woe of woes—*the compassion* of Britons!"

38

Supreme Recall

"After appearing better for the whole day of yesterday, I was again seized with violent illness and hope was nearly crushed both for my life and that of my child."

Louisa relapsed. A worried John called Dr. Galloway again. He resorted to one of the strongest sedatives available, a mixture of opium and alcohol. To prevent labor, physicians used alcohol, albeit intravenously, until the 1970s. The bitter balm, which tasted like licorice, had a sweet effect, as did John holding her hand.

"Laudanum was freely resorted to by my physician but it at first aggravated my illness, but a second dose judiciously applied produced sleep."

Her contractions relaxed. "On awaking I was quite composed, the crisis had passed and hope—blessed hope was renewed."

Opium and alcohol provided medicinal comfort while faith gave her spiritual support. She clung to the truth of her heart, the promises that "lie dormant" in the everyday. She took comfort in her belief that Nancy was dancing in heaven—perhaps even a polonaise. Such peace "rush[ed] forth uncontroul'd." Her faith and hope were her "best sympathies."

Soon she received a tangible comfort, one tailor-made for her.

"Slowly recovering God in his mercy has spared me—received letters from our children—This was the best cordial in my weak state—They allayed my fears and assisted my recovery."

Another of Abigail's letters arrived. "I have the great pleasure to say to you, that your sons are well, that they grow in stature, and increase in knowledge."

Cheered by her mother-in-law's words and letters from John and George, Louisa felt much better by the week's end. Her crying eased; her contractions subsided. One statement from her mother-in-law, stood above the rest.

"Your mama wrote me that she expected quite a crop of little ones this winter. No less than four. May they live and prosper," Abigail wrote about Mrs. Johnson's expectation for grandchildren from her other children. Neither grandmother knew of Louisa's advanced pregnancy. "The Russian climate is too cold to produce an American," Abigail added.

How Louisa longed to prove her mother-in-law wrong.

—————

"Was able to sit in the parlor, the adjoining room to my chamber and Mr. Harris kindly called to see me—He is very attentive."

About the time Louisa regained her strength, the Russian consul general to France arrived in St. Petersburg from Paris. Although he delivered papers of importance to the Winter Palace, he also brought Adams the most important correspondence he ever received from the US secretary of state.

"I have the satisfaction to inform you that the president had thought it proper to avail the public of your services at home, and has accordingly appointed you, by and with the advice and consent of the Senate to the seat on the bench of the Supreme Court of the United States vacated by the death of Judge Cushing," Smith had written to John four months earlier on February 25, 1811.

Adams could hardly believe it. Though his mother had suggested that Lieutenant Governor Lincoln had assumed the post to keep it warm for him, her information was wrong. Lincoln had declined the offer. John must have read the lines a hundred times as the news sank into his mind and tormented his heart. President Madison had appointed an *Adams* as a Supreme Court justice.

The response from the other end of Pennsylvania Avenue was just as unexpected. Not only had the US Senate confirmed his appointment, but the senators also had done so *unanimously*. Even his political enemies voted for him. Adams was shocked and more pleased than his reserved nature could outwardly express.

"This appointment will make it proper that you should return to the United States as soon as the public interest and your own convenience will permit. You are accordingly herewith furnished with a letter of leave to the emperor," Smith ordered.

As he had previously made clear, Madison did not want Alexander to misconstrue Adams's recall as evidence that America wanted to distance itself from Russia. Smith instructed John to assure Alexander of the continued friendship of the United States.

A thousand thoughts must have crisscrossed John's mind at once, contracting and tightening as he considered the greatest public service offer of his life. In his gut he knew what he wanted to do. Nevertheless, he needed a multitude of walks along St. Petersburg's quay to think through the options and implications of his decision. He had many factors to consider: his wife, Charles, their unborn child, George and John, their finances, the honor of the position—not to mention his mother's prophecies of his future and his father's boundless expectations.

He would need to make a decision soon. Because the Russian consul to France had delivered the correspondence, Count Romanzoff probably knew of the appointment before Adams did. If he didn't know already, Alexander would soon find out.

⚬⟶

On May 31, Adams took a walk along the Fontanka. By that time the canal was as iceless as the sun. Though the day was unseasonably cold, the water flowed briskly. A crisp wind kissed his face as he walked and thought. Sure enough, the emperor also embraced the fresh air. They met near the bridge where the canal joins the river.

"Monsieur Adams, *il y a cent ans que je ne vous ai vu*," Alexander hailed, suggesting that he had not seen him in a hundred years, though it was less than a month since they had last spoken. They shook hands with great cordiality.

Did Adams intend "to take a house in the country this summer?" Alexander inquired.

"No, I had for some time had such an ambition, then had given it up."

"Why?"

John hesitated. How could he possibly afford to take a country home?

Alexander relieved him from embarrassment. *"Fort bien vous avez raison. Il faut toujours proportionner la dépense à la recette,"* he replied in French, suggesting that it is better to live within your means.

Have you "received any late news from America?"

"I had," John replied coyly.

If Alexander was aware of John's appointment, he gave no hint. Instead, he came right to his point. What was the status of America's affairs with England?

"They had a very hostile appearance, and . . . the English journals were threatening us," John replied, referring to the *London Courier* reports that had earlier caused him such heartburn. Instead of showing his true feelings or relying on the propaganda of English newspapers, John spoke only of what he knew from his official correspondence. He told Alexander that the letters he had received from the US government did not seek a war with Great Britain.

"It has, however, very much that appearance—at least if we believe the French journal," the emperor replied, referring to the prediction of war between the United States and Britain in the French government newspaper. "But we know how much the *Moniteur* is to be believed and certain deductions are to be made from whatever that contains."

"To be sure, people were very apt to publish as fact what they had an interest and a wish to believe," John said to him.

The emperor raised his hand and gave John a military salute. The pair parted, each continuing his separate walk. Both had much to mull over. The appointment to the Supreme Court and America's woes with England weighed on John's conscience, while a possible war with France tormented the czar.

⚊⚊

Two days later on June 2, John put his decision in writing to the secretary of state: "Deeply sensible of the honor done me by the President and Senate in the appointment to the bench of the Supreme Court, I lamented that circumstances beyond my control have prescribed declining it."

Though the president had offered him the most honorable exit possible from St. Petersburg: the bench, and not just any bench—the supreme one—he could not accept the honor.

39

Summer Solstice

LOUISA PICKED UP HER PEN AFTER HER HUSBAND'S DECISION.

"With the mind sorely depressed by the late appalling intelligence from America and the many additional circumstances which are hourly occurring to increase the difficulties of my present situation," she began her letter to Abigail, "I feel almost incapacitated from writing even a few lines."

She thanked her mother-in-law for the tender way "you broke to us the melancholy tidings of our poor Nancy's dreadful death." After explaining how the shock had sent her into a premature confinement, she assured her that her health was better.

When Louisa had first heard about the possibility of returning home, the news had soared like a symphony in her heart. Her husband had finally received what he longed for—an honorable position, respect from his peers, and an exit from St. Petersburg. She could finally be reunited with her darling boys. How she longed to hold them again, kiss their foreheads a thousand times, and run her fingers through their hair. She hadn't seen them in nearly two years. They had probably grown so much that she would not recognize them if they unexpectedly stepped onto St. Petersburg's wharf and chased each other around Peter the Great's statue.

But the pleasure of feeling her baby roll over in her womb was the best evidence of her situation.

"I am restored to health with every prospect of going through my full time, but even this circumstance adds to the present uneasiness of our family here, as it renders a removal impossible," she explained of her husband's decision to decline the nomination.

Louisa and John discussed returning. They debated leaving as late as October, after the baby's birth. Yet the nights were so long by then and the seas so shallow that Adams did not think it wise.

"At least Mr. Adams will not hear of it and the season of the year when I shall be released will render a passage very dangerous . . . for all of us but particularly for myself and so young an infant."

She, however, was so desperate to return home that she made another suggestion. What about hiring a carriage?

"Mr. A. does not like the idea of rushing a journey by land which would be attended with almost equal difficulties before we will reach a port from when we could sail with less danger."

The irony was as obvious as St. Petersburg's daily eighteen hours of summer sunlight. Giving birth to another child would keep her from being reunited with her sons. Shakespeare himself could not have created a more ironic plot point. Timing was their foil. Like a heroine acting in a play, she covered her anguish with a mask of pretense.

John wrote to the secretary of state and explained his reasons for declining the nomination:

> One of them, itself decisive to dictate my determination, is the impossibility of my return to the United States during the present year, arising from the peculiar situation of my family, the length of time necessary to accomplish a voyage from the extremity of the Gulf of Finland to the coast of North America, and the short portion of the year during which such as voyage can be commenced.

John also wrote a private letter to President Madison and expressed his gratitude over "the new mark of confidence, which you have been pleased to show me in the nomination to an office so highly honorable."

Keeping within the austere manners of the day, he diplomatically explained his situation without explicitly stating that Louisa was pregnant: "My expectation is to be detained here until the next winter, by ties which the affections of a husband and a parent can neither dissolve nor sever."

Her brush with labor after receiving notice of Nancy's death worried him deeply. How could he possibly ask Louisa to make the journey? With her sister's death so fresh on their minds, how could they dare take the risk? Ambition two years earlier had led him to leave his sons behind. Though outwardly reserved, he knew his wife's heartache. He felt it too. He could not let ambition—no matter if it came from him or his parents—endanger the love of his life or their unborn child. Adams had softened. He had changed.

Recent newspaper articles gave Louisa new cause to worry, as she wrote Abigail: "[T]his circumstance places us in a most uncomfortable situation as we are beset by reports that keep us in a state of perpetual agitation."

They had received more newspapers, likely from London. President Madison had appointed an old but respected Republican rival, James Monroe, as the new US secretary of state. The accounts suggested that outgoing secretary Robert Smith was en route to St. Petersburg to take John's place. How they hoped the news was a mistake or miscommunication!

As politically astute as her mother-in-law, Louisa could hardly imagine that Madison would send a replacement without waiting for her husband's answer. Yet she did not have all the facts. Had she been in Washington City, she would have heard the whispers of Smith's backstabbing and misrepresentation of Madison's policies to foreign diplomats. Though Smith saw his appointment to Russia as an exile to Siberia, a slap in the face, neither he nor Madison realized what an awkward predicament the Adamses now faced. If Smith arrived in St. Petersburg soon, as the newspapers predicted, they would find themselves jobless and without income—stuck in Russia until the water broke free in the spring of 1812.

Such uncertainty about John's employment status understandably bothered Louisa and kept her mind "in such a state of trouble, agitation, and suspense that I hardly know what I write and I am sure you will feel and accept my excuse," she concluded, begging Abigail to "kiss my sweet boys for me."

Adams knew one person would be extremely disappointed over his decision to decline the president's Supreme Court nomination. "The commission, inasmuch as it offered me an honorable station, and a pittance (a miserable one indeed) for the maintenance of my family during the remainder of my days, was all that my ambition could wish, or that my estimate of the value of money could expect," he explained in a letter to his father.

Though he could not accept it, he wanted to show his father that he appreciated the appointment and its importance: "Yet I am deeply sensible to the personal kindness, as well as to the honor, shown me by the president in the nomination, and to the more surprising, though not more unexpected, unanimity of the Senate in approving it."

The appointment renewed his hope in returning home with honor. He assured his father that he longed to be restored to the bosom of his country and resume the superintendence of the education of his "darling boys." He also dreamed of a more southern climate. And compared to St. Petersburg, Boston was a hot spot.

"From this dilemma the blessing of Providence (for so I fervently pray that I may ultimately have cause to consider it) had, by a simple and very natural circumstance in the condition of my family, graciously pleased to relieve me. . . . In this state of things I cannot embark for a voyage to America."

No serpent's apple could tempt this Adams to expose his Eve and infant to the dangers of an ocean journey. His decision was as firm as the core of the earth itself. If Madison had already sent Smith to replace him, then John would stay in Russia as a private citizen until his tender family could withstand a rough ocean voyage.

Why didn't he ask Madison to hold the seat open until he could return the following year? The possibility squeezed his principles as tightly as Louisa's preterm contractions wrenched her womb. Wouldn't such a request seem selfish? Was it honorable to ask for a delay? Judge Cushing had died in September 1810. By the time Adams could return in the summer of 1812, the seat would have been vacant for nearly two years. What would happen to the cases pending before the Supreme Court in the meantime? Adams did not believe it was right to ask the public to wait such a long time to fill such an important position.

Honesty was the very reason the president had chosen Adams. In a letter to Jefferson, Madison explained the sentiments of New England Republicans on the Supreme Court vacancy: "They wish for J. Q. Adams, as honest, able, independent, and untainted . . ."

Hypothetical questions can never be authentically answered—even under oath—but a few questions lingered. Had Louisa not been pregnant, would John Quincy Adams have accepted the 1811 nomination to the US Supreme Court? If an appointment to the US Supreme Court had been the pinnacle of Adams's ambitions, would he have stretched the public's trust and asked the president to hold the seat for him? Likely, yes, but he also had his doubts about his ability to weigh justice's scales.

"I have long entertained a deep and serious distrust of my qualifications for a seat on the bench," he confessed in his letter to Madison. Before learning of the nomination, he had written his brother Thomas that he did not long for a judicial post, suggesting that other men were better at banging the gavel of justice than he would be.

Though anguished at rejecting such an honorable position and returning home, he didn't regret the decision. In his gut he knew he was not a man suited to wear a judicial robe any more than he should wear a clerical one. Though as knowledgeable about the law as he was religion, Adams's mind was better suited for the plain suit of republican politics. Regardless, his choice had consequences.

"I am sorry, very sorry, to disappoint the expectations of my country, by withholding myself from that judgment seat," he admitted to his father, "but happier for me than it would be to disappoint their expectations upon the seat itself."

⌁

By then Adams had informed Romanzoff of the appointment and explained his decision to decline. He wanted to assure his host government of the continued friendship of the United States. He also brought up a new subject. Among the packets of letters that he had received were a set of specific, confidential instructions. The secretary of state had given him permission to enter into negotiations with the Russian government for a commerce treaty with the United States. Just as Adams expected, Romanzoff replied the time was not right. The political seas in Europe were too turbulent. Not now, not yet.

"It has been painful to me to be brought to this test of my principles," he confessed to his father.

John would have to wait for another honorable exit to his honorable exile.

———

That summer Louisa also struggled to juggle her delicate health against the tugging obligations she held as the wife of the most senior foreign minister living in St. Petersburg. Because Madame de Bray had returned to Bavaria in 1810, Louisa remained the only woman married to a diplomat of the official high rank of minister and a de facto ambassador in Alexander's court. As a result, she was the unofficial leader of the women in the diplomatic corps, which placed burdensome social expectations upon her.

"Mr. Navarro brought Madame de Bezzara and introduced her to me."

She was the lady of the Chevalier de Bezzara, the newly appointed Portuguese minister. Navarro had long served as the lower-ranking chargé d'affaires for Portugal. Now he had a new boss, thanks to Russia's recent elevation of Portugal as an ally—an in-your-face move against France. Just as Mr. Harris had introduced Louisa to Madame de Bray, the only other minister's wife at the time the Adamses arrived in St. Petersburg, so Navarro had asked Louisa to advise Madame de Bezzara on her introduction ceremony to the czar. Such pressure came at the most inopportune time. Nevertheless, culture remained the law. Though she felt imprisoned by the expectation, she graciously met Madame de Bezzara.

———

John also turned to other matters to keep him occupied. The peculiarities of St. Petersburg provided just that.

"In the evening I went to the top of the round tower at the corner of the house in which we dwell," he wrote on June 19. The summer solstice was fast upon them. He observed "the redness of the sun as evening and morning twilight at the same time."

He had witnessed the unusual effect of living so close to the Arctic Circle in summer, when the hours of daylight almost never end. The lingering colored effects of sunrise and the approach of sunset mingled together in a strange, mystical phenomenon. The white nights danced above him, capturing his amazement as if he were a ten-year-old child.

"I returned again to the tower a little after midnight and observed a second time the same phenomenon. I read without candle at midnight."

John did not know it at the time, but this was the last time he would see the wonder of the summer solstice—at least from that round tower in his corner house.

40

The Removal

"Mr. Plinky came to inform us that our house was sold and that we must move out of it as soon as possible: that is in thirteen days as the emperor had purchased it," Louisa wrote of their landlord's surprising notification in July 1811.

No wonder Alexander had asked John if he was planning on taking up a country residence for the summer. He had so admired the American legation's rented corner house by the Moika Canal that he'd decided to buy it, no matter how inconvenient it was to a family expecting a baby in August. The Adamses had not planned to move again, but now they had no choice.

"This was rather severe: To look for a house: to find a suitable one and to move by the first of August, which we thought to be absolutely necessary under the circumstances, [were] both trying and distressing to me, who had never entirely recovered from my illness and was not very well able to bear the fatigue and anxiety of a removal," Louisa wrote.

John had no more time to admire mingling sunsets and sunrises or take long walks in the summer garden near the Winter Palace. Instead he needed to spring into action, lest his wife be without a residence for her impending confinement.

When they'd first arrived in St. Petersburg, John had looked for houses without Louisa. Perhaps her complaints about the places they lived induced him to share the responsibility with her this time. Or maybe Louisa had recently spoken so passionately on the capabilities of women, as she had written in her diary, that he sought her opinion on the location of their next home. Regardless, the choice to involve her was a sign of change in him, a deepening confidence in his wife's judgment and capabilities. Involving her was something Louisa had long needed from John, particularly when he chose to leave their sons behind in Boston without asking her. The change was encouraging, though the process of finding a home was challenging.

"I accompanied Mr. Adams in the search for houses and we went to see one which was recommended to us opposite to the palace at Kamenny Ostrov—It is very pretty but too far out of town being eight miles from St. Petersburg—returned to town much fatigued to look farther."

They faced what many house hunters encounter. No matter the generation, real estate has long been about location, space, size, and cost. Next they investigated a home recently vacated by an Italian duke, a man who generously invited them to use his theater box on many occasions. Though closer to town, this home was a budget buster.

"It is very large; very expensive; and very cold—We can procure nothing within our means," she worried. "The rents are so high that we must submit to necessity and take the only house that offers, although it must occasion another removal in October."

With no other options, they chose a house next to the surgery school on Apothecaries' Island, across the river from Kamenny Ostrov. Because the home was not suitable for winter habitation, they could rent it only a few months. Moving again in the fall seemed a better solution than submitting to the distance of the first house or the expense of the second.

With only thirteen days to move, they wasted no time packing. Louisa not only took an interest in the preparations but also was intimately involved in the details.

"Went out to Kamenny Ostrov to make arrangements for the disposal of the furniture of my chamber, got ready immediately—Every hour is of consequence to me. It is a trial both for body and mind: but God in his mercy gives me strength in my need."

No matter how much she might have longed to crawl in bed in the afternoons to rest her aching back, she persevered while also finding some humor in her husband's penchant for distraction: "Again at the house with Mr. Adams to arrange books and papers—Slow work for he reads a page in every book that passes through his hands."

John's literary collection was what one would expect for a man nominated to the US Supreme Court. Adams was among the most well-read men in America and Russia. More than likely, he was *the* most well-read. The slower pace and long summer days of St. Petersburg gave him the opportunity to collect additional books on law, philosophy, religion, science, and literature. He traded volumes with his colleagues and spent many hours debating with them the finer points of Plato's philosophy and sermons by respected theologians. He also spent many hours teaching Charles, an occupation that delighted him.

Within two weeks, they moved into their new place, which was near the summer homes of the French ambassador, the Danish minister, and the czar. They were so close to the czar's Kamenny Ostrov Palace that they could hear the imperial band, which played on a pavilion jutting into the water.

"[W]ith the open doors and windows of warm weather, we heard it as if it had been before our own door," John observed.

They enjoyed concerts each afternoon at four o'clock, when the emperor took his dinner. Yet the close proximity had one disadvantage.

"The situation is very pleasant—but from the windows of the palace they can see into the house and grounds all the time," Louisa noted.

Despite the ability of palace occupants to watch them—or spy on them—she could take comfort in one fact. They had a home. If she went into labor now, at least she had a very large bedchamber to accommodate her and her newborn. Unlike many women of her social stature who hired a wet nurse, Louisa personally nursed her infants.

In this paradise of botanical plants and pleasant waters, they now had access to something they did not have before: a flagstaff. The house boasted a lush garden and a pier that extended into the river. At the pier's end was a flagstaff, an important feature for a diplomatic legation.

"[O]n the days when we receive company [we] hoist the flag of the United States," John proudly noted.

Another change came to their household. After living in St. Petersburg for two years, Mr. Everett returned to America. His departure removed some competition for Kitty's attention, which for a time was focused on Mr. Gray, who would also soon depart. William Smith continued as Adams's secretary.

No sooner had Louisa unpacked her clothing trunks than she faced another Eve-like dilemma in her garden of Eden. As a pregnant woman, she lacked proper fig leaves for another formal occasion.

"Madame de Bezzara and Monsieur Navarro were here in the evening—much exhausted," Louisa wrote. No matter her urgent need to unpack, Louisa's duty as the only foreign minister's wife diverted her time. "She seems much interested in my troubles and is very kind in her manners."

Though not insensitive to Louisa, the madame peppered her with multiple questions about her upcoming introduction to the czar. She needed encouragement about what to wear, how to bow, and what to expect.

"She is a remarkably sensible woman: full of that worldly knowledge which adapts a lady for a political station—Shrewd, observant, and practiced without any excess of sensitive delicacy," Louisa commented.

As she had throughout her pregnancy, Louisa praised female virtues when she saw them and put a good spin on those qualities, such as Bezzara's busybody nature, that were less appealing: "Every way she is full of anecdote, knows everything that passes and is ready to offer advice wherever it is needed."

The madame, however, placed Louisa in a most awkward position: "She requests me to go and introduce her to Madame Litta."

Though she expressed sympathy for Louisa's advanced stage of pregnancy, her request was burdensome. Louisa's extreme fatigue alone motivated her to say no. Yet she remembered the day of her own introduction. John had been obliged to go to the Winter Palace earlier for a liturgy, which had left her to go through the fright alone. She had longed for a sisterly type who could have whispered which of the palace murals to admire because they were the empress's favorite or which side of the staircase was the easiest to ascend while wearing a full-length train. However, Louisa was unfamiliar with the czar's Kamenny Ostrov Palace and could not advise the madame on which garden sculpture the czar preferred or other attempts at flattery.

Another glaring issue was her wardrobe. Once again, she lacked sufficient dress for her pregnant condition. As long as she felt as big and full as the moon, the idea of wearing a full court dress in her advanced stage of pregnancy was as far from her desire as the moon was. On top of that she was in mourning for her sister, which required her to wear black crape, such as a shawl or armband. "I cannot refuse but I am ashamed to go."

By this time she was close enough to her expected confinement that other questions haunted her situation. What if she went into labor at the czar's

Kamenny Ostrov Palace? Nothing could hide her shame if the unthinkable happened right on the palace floors.

———

John also had social obligations to fulfill, namely, Chancellor Romanzoff's diplomatic dinner. Because it was summer, the count encouraged his guests to wear their lighter frock coats instead of their heavier full court uniforms. Adams made a new discovery at this dinner. Like John, the new French ambassador appeared a bit disheveled no matter how nice his clothing.

John and Louisa had met Jacques Alexandre Bernard Law, the marquis de Lauriston, earlier in the summer, before their move. Caulaincourt came to their home to say good-bye and introduce Count Lauriston. Louisa thought the new ambassador was handsome but rough and unpolished, "not comparable in any way" to Caulaincourt "either in mind, person, or manners."

Indeed Caulaincourt looked as distinguished as ever that day. He came "to take leave of us in full costume." His uniform glittered with the usual golden braided epaulets and broad ribbon crossing his chest from right to left. He also wore "diamonds presented to him by the emperor as a mark of his personal regard."

Much had changed since their earlier encounters, when Caulaincourt had told Louisa that she was too pretty to be so serious. She had proved her poise and grace when she danced the polonaise with the emperor at the ball hosted by Caulaincourt.

As it turned out, John's success—and America's rising stature—contributed to Caulaincourt's downfall. When Alexander refused to fully bow to French pressure to reject US trade, the French ambassador lost the battle of wits and became ineffective. For these and other reasons, Napoleon recalled him. To Caulaincourt, all was politics. Nothing was personal. Adams had treated him with honor despite their differences.

Referring to Napoleon, Caulaincourt explained to John of his recall, "The emperor governs so much by himself, that a minister is nothing more than the pen, and not the hand that guides it."

Napoleon offered him a good position for his return, which allowed Caulaincourt to leave honorably. The Adamses would miss his refined elegance.

Diplomacy is based on relationships. With Caulaincourt gone, Adams found himself with the unpleasant task of having to start over with Lauriston. Because they were just a year apart in age, perhaps they could find something to build upon, beyond the fact that both were disheveled gentlemen disdaining expensive clothes.

At Romanzoff's dinner that July night in 1811, Lauriston engaged John in conversation. Though he was no less decorated than his predecessor, with a messy mane of dark curly hair, Lauriston was less distinguished looking. His tear-shaped, droopy eyes resembled those of a basset hound. Putting aside pretense, Lauriston got straight to the point. What was the state of America's relationship with England?

"I thought it probable that his government would make our peace with England," John answered.

"How?"

"By not keeping [your] word," Adams replied, referring to the French government's failure "to repeal the Berlin and Milan decrees" as promised, which angered Parliament.

Lauriston understood the ways of war. As a cadet, he had been on friendly terms with Napoleon, which allowed him to rise in the ranks to a general and command the French division that conquered Pamplona, Spain. He knew the power of exerting even a touch of military force.

"Oh! But you must seize two or three English vessels, and then I will promise you that you may come freely to France," he half-teased. The hound stuck to his scent. "And will never be troubled with the Berlin and Milan decrees. Only you must not bring English merchandise to us."

Adams saw through the bluster and deceit: "Americans will not bring you any English merchandise except when you insist upon having it."

Then the conversation turned to good-humored goading.

"Ah! Ah! my spies," the Frenchman exclaimed, joking that his informants had told him that the Adamses had moved into his neighborhood. "My spies give me quite different information. Well, if we get English merchandise, it is only to burn it."

"Yes, and you have burnt so much that now you are obliged to send for more for your own use."

John reflected in his diary that "all this was said on both sides in a good sort of banter; half jest, half earnest."

He must build trust with Lauriston. Diplomacy would take time, but at least they were off to a jovial start. Humor eased the tension of the ominous threat. Though the Russian government seemed deeply worried about a war between England and America, France seemed to be goading the very possibility.

———✦———

"Mr. & Mrs. Bezzara came according to appointment and I was obliged to accompany in full dress mourning to introduce [them] to Madame Litta at the palace which was more than a mile round from us as we had to cross the river."

Although she expected to give birth in early August, Louisa fulfilled her commitment to the Bezzaras on July 25, despite the risk of going into labor. Traveling over a bumpy road and crossing the river at such an advanced stage of pregnancy left her exhausted before her swollen feet ever stepped an inch into the Kamenny Ostrov Palace.

"Countess Litta received us very kindly but begged that I would go home directly and not wait for Madame Bezzara's presentation to the empress."

How she longed to take Litta's kind advice. "As however she [Madame de Bezzara] had no carriage but mine, I was obliged to remain nearly an hour before I could get home."

In this way she waited at the palace while the imperial family formally received Madame de Bezzara. Except for the palace's exterior's pale orange color, the entrance was similar in shape to the President's House in Washington City. Both boasted a triangle pediment supported by a handful of white columns. With plenty of time to gaze at the views of the park and the water, what would happen if Louisa's water broke? Though a rare occurrence, women have long feared going into labor in public. As she waited, she could not afford for her delicate condition to lead to a delicate embarrassment.

"And when the countess came back from the empress, she took my hand

and sent me off saying, while she laughed, that she had never taken leave of anybody with so much pleasure in her life."

Litta was relieved, and so was Louisa as she said good-bye and passed through the palace's iron gate toward her new country estate.

"We reached home in safety and they stayed to pass the evening," she wrote, adding that "this was a killing life."

⤙⤙⤙

The day after his wife jaunted to the palace, like Mary to Bethlehem, John did something he rarely did. He wrote about his love for her. His diary often reflected his work, a method for documenting conversations so he could copy them into letters to the US government. Rarely did he reveal his deeper feelings about his private life. Most of his statements about family were mere facts, such as "went with Mrs. Adams" to the ball.

Perhaps observing how well his wife had made arrangements for their move led him to pick up his pen. Or maybe it was her willingness to reach out to Madame de Bezzara in spite of how she felt. Regardless of what motivated him, he was inspired.

"I have this day been married 14 years, during which I have to bless God for the enjoyment of a portion of felicity, resulting from this relation in society, greater than falls to the generality of mankind, and far beyond anything that I have been conscious of deserving," he began his entry on July 26. "Its greatest alloy has risen from the delicacy of my wife's constitution, the ill health which has afflicted her much of the time, and the misfortunes she has suffered from it."

Their union had not been without dissension. She could be irascible; he, harsh. "But she has always been a faithful and affectionate wife, and a careful, tender, indulgent, and watchful mother to our children, all of whom she nursed herself. I have found in this connection from decisive experience the superior happiness of the marriage state over that of celibacy, and a full conviction that my lot in marriage has been highly favored."

About this time, Louisa was also more reflective and appreciative: "At last for a few days we have obtained a little quiet—I go down to the end of the garden; have a chair on the bank of the river with Charles; and we catch fish

300

not worth eating—It is an indolent sort of an amusement that just suits me for I *do not think*." The countryside brought pleasure and quietude.

"When I look forward I tremble," she wrote, reminded of her sister's death in childbirth. "But I bow down with trust in him who has mercifully saved me through a life of trouble and granted to me so many blessings."

As if gently draping her Turkish shawl around her shoulders, Louisa wrapped herself in faith and fortitude as she anticipated the birth of her child.

41

The Confinement

WHAT JOHN MOST NEEDED THAT SUMMER WAS THE YET-TO-BE-invented telephone. As August 1811 began, he had one last major social obligation to attend before the season's end. Because the emperor had canceled the Peterhof party the previous year, attendance was even more expected this year. Indeed only one diplomat, Mr. Navarro, declined.

At 11:00 a.m. on August 3, John reluctantly left his very pregnant wife behind to travel some twenty miles to Peterhof. While riding, he tried to pass the time by reading recently arrived reports of Congress's winter session, but his mind was distracted even more than usual. Though the horses didn't stop, the distance seemed farther than he remembered. The time lasted three hours instead of two. "The road was crowded with carriages of all kinds from the city gate to the palace at Peterhof."

Despite the packed path, he arrived early enough to spend an hour walking in the gardens before returning to his room and donning his finest clothing for the festivities. As distinguished guests, the emperor's diplomats wore their lighter-weight full court suits for this summer event. They received privileges not available to the throngs who would flock the lawn that night. Adams's invitation included the masked ball, fireworks, dinner, and overnight lodging at Peterhof's outer buildings.

He joined the other diplomats inside the palace. The protocol officer assembled them in a line where they would be presented after the emperor spoke from a balcony to the crowd of fifty thousand gathered on the grounds. The most obvious changes were the diplomatic corps's newest additions: the recently arrived French ambassador and the Bezzaras from Portugal. Not only were both newcomers, but they also received the prestige of serving as line leaders. The gala brought out some mischief from the protocol officer, who purposefully paired them to lead the others in the parade before the people. As an ally of Britain, Portugal was an enemy of France.

"A Portuguese minister's lady escorted by the French ambassador was, in the present state of the world, a singular curiosity," Adams observed wryly, noting that the other diplomats were also amused at the sight of Count Lauriston taking Madame de Bezzara's arm at the front of the line. Louisa would have appreciated the irony.

The diplomats, however, had every reason to be relaxed. Napoleon had recently given a speech suggesting pacific intentions toward Russia. Adams wondered whether Caulaincourt "had administered a cooling and quiet potion" to the French emperor after returning to Paris because Napoleon suddenly seemed satisfied with Russia's compliance to his Continental System. John doubted the appeasement would last.

However cunning the Russian protocol, the fête brought out the best of summer produce. Silver serving trays abounded with appetizers of "cherries, strawberries, raspberries, apricots, plums, peaches, oranges, grapes, and pineapples." Louisa's sweet tooth would have found much satisfaction had she been there. Though he had attended other events without her, John felt especially uneasy and lonesome this night.

After enjoying the fruit, the diplomats rode around the gardens in court carriages to wait for the fireworks, which began at nine o'clock. The illuminations delighted all.

"Countess Litta said that the whole garden was lighted in ten minutes; there were three hundred thousand lamps and sixteen hundred persons employed to light them."

The diplomats then returned to the palace to play cards and dance. Soon the imperial family arrived, circling the room to speak to each envoy.

"They asked the same questions—whether my wife was there? Why was she not there? Where we now resided? Whether we had a comfortable house?" Adams recorded of the empress mother's inquiry. While wearing a tiara entirely covered by diamonds, she asked the most unbelievable question of all: "Whether Mrs. Adams would be conveniently situated for her confinement!"

Had the emperor not bought their house, the empress would not have asked these questions. Such was the trouble with royalty. With thousands of servants to take care of their every need—including lighting lamps for fireworks—the imperial family could not possibly understand that John's greatest fear at Peterhof that night was the lightning bolts back home—that Louisa had gone into labor.

As was the custom, Adams could not leave the party until the czar retired. Miss Gourieff, a Russian noblewoman, noticed Louisa's absence. He then confessed his desire to return to St. Petersburg as soon as the emperor retired rather than stay to enjoy the overnight accommodations as the other diplomats preferred.

"Miss Gourieff told me that if I returned home this night I should find the bridges raised but I thought she was joking."

Though keeping his reserve, Adams was surprised that the Russian government would keep the bridges upright on the night of the Peterhof party. He hoped she was mistaken.

Very often dinner is the last event at an imperial evening. Because the diplomats were expected to spend the night, they were invited to tour the gardens again. For nearly two hours Adams found himself obliged to ride around the garden in a court carriage. Finally, at a quarter past one in the morning, the emperor released them.

"The daylight was already beginning to return," John observed, noting that many lamps were already extinguished.

Within fifteen minutes of arriving at his overnight lodgings, he had packed his trunk and was ready to depart. He boarded his carriage and ordered his postilions to drive straight home. He quickly understood why the imperial family provided overnight lodging for the diplomatic corps. Partygoers packed the route back to St. Petersburg.

"The lines of carriages on the road were almost uninterrupted from Peterhof to the city gate, and they were often two or three in front. I passed upwards of two thousand, as I presume on the road, and during the first half of the way great multitudes of persons returning on foot."

Finally, by a quarter of four in the morning, he saw the river.

"On arriving at the lower bridge, I found, as Miss Gourieff had told me, that it was raised."

By this time he had been away from Louisa for more than eighteen hours. Once again he needed the out-of-time invention of the telephone. Had he a telephone or access to a telegraph, he could have stayed in reasonable contact with his wife throughout the day. He rode over to the upper drawbridge, which was also impassable.

"I now learnt, and not without concern, that they raise both bridges every morning at two o'clock, to let the vessels pass through, and that they are kept raised for two to three hours."

All he could do was wait and worry about his near-term pregnant wife at home without him.

⤙⤚

"If we have a war with England, I may perhaps find it difficult to get home, but I suppose a passport for myself and family would be obtainable," he'd earlier strategized in a letter to Thomas dated July 31, 1811.

Though he'd heard about the horror from an English newspaper, the outcome was the same regardless of who fired the first shot. The USS *President*, a fifty-four-gun American frigate, and the *Little Belt*, a smaller, twenty-two-gun British sloop of war, had engaged in battle off the North Carolina coast on May 16, 1811.

After accepting Napoleon's pretense of revoking the Berlin and Milan decrees, Madison had reinstated the embargo against Britain in November 1810. The English responded by sending more warships to America's coast and increasing the practice of impressment. On May 1, 1811, British sailors from the HMS *Guerriere* took captive an American sailor from a US brig sailing near New York and impressed him into the British navy.

Outraged about the latest *Guerriere* incident, the secretary of the navy had ordered the USS *President* to patrol the coast and prevent more kidnappings. The *President*'s captain had kept a close watch on *Little Belt* when it came within its view in the waters near North Carolina. Claiming the *Little Belt* fired the first shot and initially thinking it was the *Guerriere*, he ordered the *President*'s crew to fire. Nine British *Little Belt* sailors were killed and more than twenty were injured, while only one American was injured. The battle had escalated tensions between the two governments.

"A war appears to be inevitable, and I lament it, with the deepest affliction of heart and the most painful anticipation of consequences," John continued in his letter to Thomas, observing that a war between the United States and Great Britain would do great political and financial damage. It would divide the states along party lines and strike a blow to the already depressed economy.

Jefferson's embargo had merely delayed war, not prevented it. Not since the Revolution had the American people been tested so much. The English hated the French because they considered France a superior power. They hated America merely because the United States had beaten them years earlier. Yet more than jealousy consumed the passions of Parliament, King George III, and his son, the prince regent. England loathed America more than France because of its commercial potential, which was as vast as the western frontier and likely to surpass Britain's trade capabilities in the future.

In response to this latest incident, a squadron of five British ships of the line carrying a regiment sailed for America to "humble" the Yankees.

"Whether it be of mere menace or direct hostility, I trust the spirit of my country will prove true to itself. But it opens in either case a prospect before [us], at least as formidable as that of 1775 and 1776 was to our fathers," John said.

He confessed to Thomas that their time had come. They must follow their father's example from the American Revolution. They must stand firm for freedom and live loudly for liberty: "The school of affliction is, however, as necessary to form the moral character of nations as of individuals. I hope that ours will be purified by it."

Adams also urgently needed a telephone to be able to quickly communicate with Secretary of State James Monroe, his new boss. He desperately needed some questions answered. What should he do if Russia officially resumed trade with England? The possibility seemed more likely now that the Portuguese Bezzaras had arrived in Russia on an English ship. Of greater concern was outgoing Secretary of State Robert Smith. Was he coming to take John's place in St. Petersburg as the newspapers reported?

Perhaps more than any correspondence with his brother or boss, he desperately needed to speak to his father. Since his first diplomatic assignment to the Netherlands in 1794, Adams had written appropriate but stifled official correspondence. In contrast his letters to his father were far more frank, flowing with a high tide of emotion and details. Even when his father was president and his boss's boss, Adams gave blunt assessments on the extremists in the Federalist Party and other topics but hid them from his superior, the secretary of state. Now, not even the yet-to-be invented telegraph would fix the miscommunication between Adams and his father over the Supreme Court nomination. They needed to talk.

John continued to receive correspondence from his family and friends, begging him to accept the high-shelf Supreme Court appointment. Even though he knew his father wrote his letters before receiving his son's initial explanation, his father's pleas and expectations bothered him.

Years earlier, on April 23, 1794, about a month before President Washington officially appointed John Quincy to his first diplomatic post, Vice President Adams had given his son a warning against settling for mediocrity: "You come into life with advantages which will disgrace you, if your success is médiocre." His letter continued more sternly: "And if you do not rise to the head not only of your profession, but of your country it will be owing to your own laziness, slovenliness, and obstinacy."

No wonder John Quincy continued to fret in his diary year after year that he had accomplished nothing worthwhile with his life. No wonder he could not fully embrace his successes. No wonder he pushed harder. Such painful past admonitions combined with fresh correspondence from his father drove John to write another letter in late July 1811 to free his conscience over declining the Supreme Court nomination.

"When I came to Russia my motive doubtless in the opinion of many was ambition," he explained to his father, noting that "more than one of my friends wrote and spoke to me of it as of an exile."

Adams confessed that he viewed the Russian mission with disadvantage: "I knew equally well that it was going straight away from the high road of ambition, and, so far as related to political prospects, retiring into obscurity."

He had accepted his St. Petersburg post out of duty: "My real motive was perfectly simple. The constitutional organ of my country had assigned this to me as my proper post. I saw no reason sufficient to induce me to refuse it."

Now the same constitutional organ called him home to the US Supreme Court, but a different kind of duty led him to decline. How he longed to have a long talk with his father from the porches of Peacefield. The best technology available to him was a pen and paper. And he used it with fervor.

"How does it appear to you?" he continued about the Supreme Court post with unveiled emotion: "You welcome it as the means to procure my return, and because it would remove me from the tourbillon of politics. But yet you specially wish me to accept, because parties are splitting up, because one secretary is out and another in; because the governor and senate of Massachusetts are Republican; because all was uncertainty from Europe and a special session of Congress was expected."

Something else crashed over John's mind like ocean waves, growing taller each time the idea hit him. The more he thought about it, the less he wanted to be on the Supreme Court. He candidly confessed that he did not believe the appointment would protect him from political commotion. Instead his opinions might cause the very tidal wave his father thought he could avoid with a lifetime judicial appointment. John then made one of the most astonishing declarations for an American attorney. He admitted that he opposed the idea of common law.

"I entertain some very heretical opinions upon the merits of that common law, so idolized by all the English common lawyers and by all the parrots who repeat their words in America." His doubts about common law were so strong that he knew he could not possibly serve on the US Supreme Court without ruffling the robes of judges up and down the thirteen original colonies and beyond.

Though John didn't think it was dishonorable to pursue public office, he believed that he should wait until called by the voice of his country. With war on the horizon and his wife about to go through the agony and danger of childbirth, he had no idea what his next calling would be. If his country did call again, he assured his father that he would "repair without hesitation to the post assigned me."

He had one consolation in his need for quick resolution with his father. As many as two hundred US ships had arrived in Russia that summer. One from Delaware came in fewer than forty days, a record time.

"For seven months of the year my great embarrassment was to devise means of sending my letters for America to places from which they could be dispatched, but now the opportunities of the direct conveyance are so numerous, that it is impossible to write by them all," Adams explained of the effects of Russia's more open trade policy toward American ships. Gone were the restrictions of previous seasons. Not only that, but Danish privateers no longer menaced US ships passing through the straits.

His father just might receive this letter in six weeks—not six months—such was the definition of instant gratification in 1811.

After the Peterhof party, John waited for the workers to lower the bridge. He waited so long his eyes seemed glued to his pocket watch. Near a quarter to five in the morning, the laborers lowered the bridge. Adams sprinted home, where he found Louisa as he had left her: pregnant and not in labor, not yet.

42

Christening Reprise

LOUISA ALSO COULD HAVE USED A NONEXISTENT TELEPHONE, ESPE-
cially on August 11, when the tightening of her womb began in earnest. The
time arrived. Because they were living in the country, the distance from town
delayed the arrival of help. In an era when messengers on horseback carried
urgent news, Louisa had to wait before hearing the soothing tones from the
voices of an experienced midwife and nurse.

"We were obliged to send to town for my requisite help. Mrs. Heinche
came out and remained through the day—Mrs. Buitzpon here."

Though she probably thought otherwise, she likely had access to better
midwife care than her sister Nancy had received in the nation's capital. In
America—especially in the remote town of Washington City—midwives were
sometimes the closest woman available to help. In contrast most European
midwives were licensed by church, local, or provincial governments after
they received some training. At a minimum midwives were part of a guild.
Midwifery in Europe was a respected trade.

Every woman is different, but the first stage of labor is usually the longest. Mild contractions begin to squeeze the womb while the cervix dilates.
Sometimes the contractions come every fifteen to twenty minutes, and for
some, they quickly become much closer and more intense. Louisa's contractions were slow to mature.

"Continued quite ill," she wrote about the next day, August 12.

Women who have previously given birth often have a shorter labor, but
Louisa's lasted more than twenty-four hours. Her emotions became more
intense as she dealt with contraction pain. Then her mood shifted into out-
right anger. Sometimes gearing up with hostility or getting mad can help a
woman push through the pain. The nurse may have suggested that Louisa

walk around or squat or remain still and focus her energy on the work of labor. Perhaps the ladylike Louisa failed to scream as loudly as the average Russian woman, or maybe the midwife decided that because Mrs. Adams was not quite ready, she had time to visit another woman in labor.

"Mrs. Heinche left me to go and see a lady in the city, taking my carriage horses and servants and did not return until six o'clock in the evening."

The anxiety of losing her midwife in midstream sent Louisa into a panic. Because Mrs. Heinche had taken their carriage, John had no easy means for calling Dr. Galloway for additional help. No sooner had the woman left than Louisa's contractions grew more intense, her back pain piercing with lightning-bolt fierceness.

"This indiscretion nearly cost my life," Louisa wrote of the midwife's abandonment. Perhaps, too, she couldn't shake the knowledge that her sister had died in childbirth.

Louisa could not have imagined having a telephone any more than she could have conceived wearing a beltlike contraption to measure her contractions or watching the baby's heart beat on a digital screen. Hearing the beeps and seeing the screen's magic numbers would have given her the comfort that she most needed in those moments—her baby was alive.

By the time Mrs. Heinche returned, Louisa's delirium had reached a peak. She was not the only one who was worried. "This was a day of great suffering and dreadful anxiety to my dear husband," she wrote.

Louisa entered into the final work of labor. The midwife may have encouraged her to change her position and take deep breaths after each contraction. Ever since Eve, women have been giving birth. Without the aid of drugs, however, Louisa endured intense, indescribable pain. The fear of death was as real to her as the contractions.

"God was very merciful to me for I had been in great danger ever since morning."

Within an hour and a half after Mrs. Heinche's return, Louisa felt the burning ring of fire that comes with the crowning of the head.

"My child, a daughter the first that I was ever blessed with, was born at half past seven o-clock."

A rush of relief came after the last push.

"My sister went and announced her birth to her father, and he soon came into bless and kiss his babe."

Joy. Bliss—all something to write home about.

⎯⎯⤙⤚⎯⎯

Nine months after hosting their butler's baby's christening in their home, John and Louisa felt the joy of beholding their daughter's dark eyes among the beauty of white satin calico or a similar fabric. They held the ceremony in their country house.

"This day my lovely little babe was christened," Louisa wrote on September 9. Reverend Loudon King Pitt, chaplain of the English Factory Chapel in St. Petersburg, performed the service according to the Church of England's traditions.

How they missed Quincy, Massachusetts, in that moment! John and Charles had been baptized in Boston by a family friend in the Congregational tradition. John preferred public baptism rather than a home christening: "Because it is done in church, a place devoted to divine worship, and in the presence of the congregation. It is therefore more solemn and more public than private baptism can be."

He also appreciated the practices of Boston churches for another reason: no godparents: "Because the father of the child is the only sponsor, and solemnly undertakes what it is his duty to perform—that is, to educate the child to virtuous and Christian principles; while the sponsors of an English christening are often strangers, who are never likely to have any control over the child, and therefore rashly enter into solemn engagements, the performance of which will never depend upon themselves."

Louisa noted with some irony the religious differences of the godparents: "The sponsors were strangely selected: Madame de Bezzara, Roman Catholic, Mrs. Krehmer, Episcopalian, and Mr. Harris, Quaker."

They had faced the same dilemma in Berlin when George was born. Though lacking access to their preferred church, christening was so integral to their faith that they dare not postpone it merely to avoid another church's traditions, which was why John insisted on his daughter's baptism without delay. "But the rite itself, the solemn dedication of the child to God, I prize so highly, that I think it ought never to be deferred beyond a time of urgent necessity."

One person who meant a great deal to them was absent from the ceremony. Public politics permeated this private affair. "We dared not ask the emperor to stand as sponsor, least it should not please in America," Louisa explained.

As much as they longed for their own traditions and their neighbor the emperor to serve as a figurehead godfather, they also mourned over George's and John's absence from this happy family celebration.

About a dozen guests attended. The Adams in John emerged. Nothing would move him on one crucial decision. "The child was baptized by the name of *Louisa Catherine*, being that of her mother," he wrote.

"She was named after *me* by her father's special desire contrary to my wish," Louisa described of the awkwardness.

Self-conscious or not to his wife, naming a female after her mother was familiar to John. His sister Nabby was named for their mother, Abigail. John's younger sister, Susanna, who died at thirteen months of age, was named after his father's mother, Susanna Boylston Adams. Louisa's middle name and her sister's formal name, Catherine, came from their mother, Catherine Johnson.

Although the ceremony was a brief fifteen minutes, the celebration lasted several hours. They entertained by playing cards and serving food.

"The company dined with us and I got through the fatigue pretty well," Louisa recorded.

About this time John wrote letters to their sons back home. Earlier in the summer, after declining the Supreme Court, he had told John and George that he and Louisa would not be able to return home until the next year. Had he a telephone, he could have broken the news in real time and answered their anguished questions. Of course, had he a telephone, he would have also had access to a train to expedite a land journey to Paris and then a boat ride home. Within days after his daughter's birth, Adams wrote to his sons about their sister's arrival and that Charles talked about them often. Their mother was doing as well as expected.

What John didn't know as he signed that letter was the significance of the signs in the sky. With them would come the woes of the world.

43

Comets

Comets have a bad reputation. They are known for letting their hair down and growing a brilliant train as they head for earth. Over the years humans have had trouble making heads or tails of these celestial lights. Some welcome these eccentric stars as signs of hope. To the masses, however, these masses of gas and dust are omens of impending disaster. Many would prefer that a comet keep its distance and stay as close to the sun as possible. The reason? Excessive tragedy seems to follow in the wake of these long-haired stars.

With so much woe over one comet, what would happen if two comets suddenly appeared in the sky? That was the question on Alexander's mind as he took a walk on December 9, 1811. When he saw his American friend, he knew he would receive a thoughtful reply.

"Monsieur Adams," the emperor called enthusiastically in a good-humored tone. "I have the honor to pay my respect."

John responded cordially. As usual the pair discussed the weather, which could not help leading to a conversation about the mysterious lights in the sky.

"We have two comets at once," Alexander observed of the twin prediction.

Adams instantly knew what he meant. The comet of 1811 was becoming more and more unmistakable and brilliant. With its tail "warming them" for some months, the latest reports predicted that two comets, not merely one, would streak past St. Petersburg before the year's end. John doubted the newspaper's prediction of double trouble.

"Oh, that is certain," Alexander said playfully.

He offered another cosmic puzzle for Adams to solve. "But, furthermore, I hear that one of the fixed stars—namely, Sirius—has sunk one degree in the firmament," Alexander continued wryly.

Unlike his American friend, the emperor's information came not from a newspaper but a person. In a sarcastic tone, he revealed his source: "But for this I will give you my authority, 'says the ambassador from France.'"

"This was extraordinary news indeed," John responded with equal sarcasm over Count Lauriston's planetary predictions.

"*C'est un bouleversement général du ciel,*" Alexander replied in French of the "general upheaval of the sky."

"But as it is generally understood that one comet portends great disasters," John observed, "it is to be hoped that two must signify some great happiness to the world."

"Or at least that their mischief will operate mutually against each other and by reciprocal counteraction destroy the evil efficacy of both," Alexander suggested.

"I congratulate His Majesty of his happy solution of the portentous knot."

"*Il y a moyen d'expliquer toutes ces choses là,*" he said with a laugh; that is, there are ways to explain all these things. The czar added that the best way to respond to cosmic harbingers of calamity was to let the heavens take their own course without meddling in their management.

Indeed. The czar may have recently brought the Turkish Empire to a truce, freeing thousands of Russian soldiers to fight France if need be, but even with all his power, he could not control a comet.

⎯◦⎯

A Frenchman first discovered the Great Comet in March 1811, when Honoré Flaugergues's telescope detected a very faint light in the evening twilight. A month later another French astronomer tracked its movements. That same night, a German astronomer recorded a streak of light.

The nighttime sky of 1811 was very different from that of the modern world. Today, the naked eye easily sees the blinking lights of satellites and aircrafts. Humans are used to watching jets streak across the nighttime sky. Not so back then. All the lights in the sky above Alexander, Adams, and the astronomers were made by the hand of God. None came from the hammers of man. Because their skies were filled only with stars, a brilliant, blazing comet stood out even more as a result. Astronomers predicted the comet would move northeast across Europe and become extremely bright by year's end. They were right. This brilliance was why newspapers erroneously predicted two comets, not one.

By December 1811 the comet's tail was twenty-five degrees long. What no one could predict was just how big and bright this comet would become the following year. In 1812 its coma would grow, spanning more than a million miles across and becoming 50 percent larger than the sun. What no one could also forecast was the name history would give to this widespread wonder. The comet of 1811 is known as Napoleon's comet.

Indeed Bonaparte's destruction across Europe would soon seem as daunting as the comet hovering above.

—⁓—

"I have got into such a regular and quiet course of life, and have now so little troublesome public business to do, that my time passes smoothly away," Adams confessed in a letter to his father that autumn.

Freezing early, the Neva River was passable on foot by October 31. No boats would be able to dock. If the newspaper reports were accurate, John had great reason to rejoice. Finally he received the confirmation he needed.

Anticipating that Adams would accept the Supreme Court nomination and wanting to rid himself of the troublesome, inept Robert Smith from his cabinet, President Madison offered Smith the St. Petersburg mission. Though at first accepting and telling the newspapers he would go, Smith changed his mind and turned down "the Siberian exile." Instead he turned his attention to spitefully writing a pamphlet to tear down Madison's administration.

"For my own part, I am not displeased that he chose to stay home," John wrote his father. Had Smith arrived at the Russian post, Adams would have found himself in the unenviable position of spending the winter as a private gentleman without income in St. Petersburg. In his letter to his father, John confided that he hoped to see him within the year. His destination still depended, however, on the president's pleasure.

"As respects myself, the interest of my family, and the service of my country, I know not which would be more desirable, for me to remain here or to return home; but the sense of duty prescribing my return is so strong that I still feel myself uneasy until I comply with its commands."

John made an important decision. If Madison did not recall him or give him explicit instructions to leave before summer, John would ask the president for a recall. He was ready to return home and resume the "superintendence" of the education of his older boys. Tutoring four-year-old Charles was one of his favorite activities. The Supreme Court appointment vindicated John's integrity with his political enemies. He could now return home with dignity. That is, if war didn't prevent him from leaving when the Neva River broke in the spring. Though he longed to talk politics with his father, he dared not take the risk: "The political state of affairs on the European continent is equivocal and threatening. But on this head, I can say little."

From Americans in Paris, John had recently learned that the French police were intercepting his letters from any Russian courier they could catch. He could write sensitive passages in cipher or the latest secret code to US government officials, but not to his brother or parents. For now he must give up writing freely about the state of European affairs to his family.

At least he no longer needed to advocate to the Russian government on behalf of American commerce. France was clearly now a foe to Alexander, and US trade flowed much more freely into St. Petersburg ports—as did, unofficially, British ships.

⤙⤚

Overall the autumn of 1811 had been rather quiet for the Adams family. They said good-bye to Mr. Gray, who departed for London not long after baby Louisa's christening. As planned, they also moved again because their country house was not suitable for winter. Although she chose the summer house, Louisa's need to nurse her infant prevented her from house hunting.

"[We] moved into a house in the city selected by Mr. Adams, a miserable place but the only one that would suit our finances. The accommodations were altogether unfit for a family," she wrote in her journal about their new home. "Debt or meanness is the penalty imposed by the salary of an American minister."

Not long after returning to the city in October, John met Alexander during a walk along the quay. After discussing the weather, the czar was full of questions. Among them, where was their new home located?

"In a corner house of the Vosnesensky and Little Officer's Streets," John replied. Without telling Alexander, John knew that Louisa considered the spot "a very vulgar and unpopular part of the city."

After walking St. Petersburg's pathways for more than thirty-five years, the emperor said he knew the place. Then, remembering Louisa's pregnancy, he posed an important question: Had Madame—Mrs. Adams—been confined?

"She had been," John confirmed.

"When?"

"More than two months ago."

"What! In the country?"

"In the country."

"Had her confinement been fortunate?"

"Entirely so."

"What had she got?"

"A daughter."

Alexander shrugged his shoulders and waved his hand. He often used this gesture to imply that he did not know a thing you were telling him. Neither John nor Louisa believed the czar was as unaware of the birth as he pretended to be.

"As he is informed of everything concerning foreigners, he knew all about it before he put these questions," Louisa mused when her husband relayed the conversation. She offered an explanation for His Majesty's pretension: "He felt I suppose what a serious inconvenience he had put me to."

His Flirtiness's interest, however, intrigued her.

"How inquisitive!!!" she recorded.

The czar's attention may have reminded her, too, of the notice she'd received from the Prussian monarchy when she gave birth to George on April 12, 1801, in Berlin. The queen had sent a servant to Louisa's home each day to inquire how the new babe and mother were doing. The Prussian king was so moved that he'd ordered the street where the Adamses lived to be closed to traffic so the family could recover and live in peace during the tender time of caring for a newborn. As she now was in St. Petersburg, Louisa had been a favorite of Prussian court.

Unlike her husband, who had encountered the Russian emperor several times that fall during walks, Louisa had not seen the emperor since the summer. She attributed the reason in part to politics: "Everything is changed since the departure of Caulaincourt."

She didn't expect to miss the fine-styled French ambassador. However, when he left, he also carried away much of the gaiety of St. Petersburg's diplomatic life. Count Lauriston was not a grand host. His lack of entertaining had one positive benefit. It lowered the entertaining expectations—and burdens— of the other diplomats.

Louisa made another keen observation about the new French ambassador. Unlike his initial feelings of inferiority toward Caulaincourt, John did not need to prove himself to Lauriston. In contrast, though equal in age, the new French ambassador looked up to Adams, viewing him as a wise but rivaling elder brother. Perhaps Caulaincourt had told Lauriston that Adams would have been an excellent minister to France. Or maybe he noted that the frugal Adams was an honest man whose best weapon was his ability to show honor to his opponents in a battle of wits. As if pulled by a magnet, Lauriston was, as Louisa explained, "a constant visitor at our house, and on very social terms as he seemed extremely partial to Mr. Adams."

Something else had solidified too. Though he still lacked the financial ability to entertain in splendor, John was the most successful diplomat in the imperial court. "Indeed he was styled the father of diplomacy among the corps, who all live with us upon terms of intimate friendship," she wrote with pride.

Louisa's assessment of her husband was accurate. Though a short man, Adams's integrity was tall, towering above his colleagues. He did not attract people with charisma or flattery, like Alexander or Caulaincourt. Rather, his keen intellect and careful conversations had earned the trust—and respect—of his fellow diplomats.

Except for these musings, Louisa's pen was mostly silent during this time. Baby Louisa captivated her heart and took so much time that she had little left for writing.

"O she grows lovely—Such a pair of eyes!! I fear I love her too well," she doted, noting that they had vaccinated her for smallpox.

The theater occasionally lured Louisa from her home and later to her journal. One particular performance in November 1811 motivated her to record her thoughts about the genre of tragedy—an interesting choice considering the comet casting its spell across the sky at the time. She wrote her opinions on the difference between historical and personal dramas. Historical tragedies were based on real events, such as the French Revolution from the previous generation. Personal dramas were rooted in everyday life. She noticed that the acting in historical plays was often bad; the story itself, contrived. She faulted the playwright, concluding that children who grow up to write historical dramas could not fully understand the manners and customs of their parents' generation. How could someone accurately portray the French Revolution and the beheading of Marie Antoinette if he or she had not lived through it?

Louisa knew her beloved birches of Boston would not understand the American Revolution in the way John or his father did. As a result, she believed that authors of historical tragedies were usually unsuccessful. Their facts may have been accurate, but they were unable to adequately convey the emotion behind the story.

"And this is the reason why the characters in tragedy are always stiff and stately or cold and uninteresting—or overstrained and vulgar." She then hit upon the very point that makes history come alive. The best historical dramas are the ones that tap the subjects and emotions that transcend generations.

"The domestic tragedy is always touching because they are the tragedies of everyday life, which speak to the heart and soul, whether in tatters or in royal robes."

Indeed. Tragedy can affect anyone. Louisa had no idea how prophetic that particular diary entry would later become. Only one comet streaked through the Russian sky, but John and Louisa would soon experience the theatrical pain of double, even multiple, tragedies.

44

Baltic Freeze

"SEIZED WITH A VIOLENT FEVER," LOUISA RECORDED ON DECEMBER 7, 1811.

She was not the only one who was ill. Both Charles and the baby were sick with fevers and chills. Louisa was worse than anyone. Her head boiled with cometlike heat, sending her into danger.

"My fever ran so high and the delirium so violent that the physician announced to Mr. Adams that if a change did not take place towards morning, he must prepare for the worst."

Her condition was so serious that she could no longer nurse her daughter: "My child was taken from me for the time—The children were both very ill, and our complaint was said to be the grippe."

Grippe is another name for influenza. Within two days Louisa's fever diminished, but she was not well enough to ease the doctor's mind. "Still considered in great danger, but the head partially relieved—The children severely ill."

Finally, after ten days, Louisa regained her strength. This lioness remained quite worried about her youngest cub: "Myself out of danger and Charles better, but my babe very ill—All of us much reduced and very suffering."

Nearly two months after becoming sick, the baby regained her health, and Louisa returned to life as usual. Her first outing was, of course, a palace ball.

"After a long protracted confinement by sickness and anxiety, I once again take my station in the world for which I care so little," she wrote sadly on January 28.

She may have wrapped herself in a familiar Russian fur coat or her Turkish shawl, but she almost didn't recognize the social and political world she rejoined. The thickest chill she had ever seen congealed the emperor's court.

The freeze was just as obvious to John. He had noticed it a month earlier when the diplomats gathered at the palace for the emperor's birthday. Though they dressed more magnificently than ever, with stunning diamonds, the members of the imperial family were unusually reserved. Their embroidered silks stitched a pattern of power while their manners reflected steel reserve. Removing the glove of friendliness, they wore aloofness instead.

"The emperor and empresses said very few words to the French ambassador and each of the ministers," John noted.

Why should they? Before the river froze weeks earlier in late October, French privateers had blockaded the Baltic to prevent any ship carrying colonial goods, particularly American or British, from going past Denmark. Then the French threatened to block any ship—not just American or British but also Swedish and Russian—from entering the Baltic. Napoleon issued an order to conscript 120,000 soldiers. Alexander responded with a similar order, conscripting 130,000 serfs from their landowners.

In contrast, one conversation at that cold December meeting of the diplomatic corps gave John reason to smile. While the comet—which means "let the hair grow longer"—expanded its tail with each mile, Alexander commented on John's wigless appearance.

"The emperor noticed that I had at last left off my wig. I said I had considered His Majesty's example as a permission, and accordingly followed it."

Alexander had let his hair down too. He replied by saying, "It was not so showy but it was more convenient to go without it."

The emperor's decision to go wigless was another sign that the times were changing. Seriousness was replacing splendor. The precise, predictable pattern of the emperor's customs now entered a new orbit of significant consequences.

While favor for the French was near absolute zero in arctic Russia, John held a different status in the czar's court of opinion.

"Mr. Adams's position is as high as ever with the imperial family, and . . . [he] is the sun-shine of St. Petersburg," Louisa proudly observed.

At the same time, she stated the obvious: "The aspect of society is greatly changed—The corps diplomatique is no longer so brilliant, and a cloud has risen to veil the future for a time."

Her husband put the change this way in a letter to his friend William Plumer: "In Europe darkness and gloom, blood and desolation yet prevail." They hoped and prayed that "out of this darkness, light will also in due time be made to appear."

While the comet hovered, the likelihood of doom loomed just as ominously.

"A letter full of woe announcing my mother's death," Louisa wrote on January 29, 1812. Before tears could stain her eyes, she learned that the news was even worse: "[And] that of my brother-in-law, Mr. Buchanan [husband of her sister Carolina]." Both died in a fever that swept through Baltimore and Washington City. Her mother was fifty-four years old.

That was not all: "Mr. Adams's Uncle and Aunt Cranch [died] within twenty hours of each other."

The tragic news continued: "And the dangerous and hopeless illness of his only sister—God help us!! Yet we are always praying for letters."

John's sister Nabby had breast cancer. Four members of their family were now dead, and one was seriously ill. Imagine the pain Louisa must have felt at not being able to say good-bye to her mother. One of her greatest fears had come true.

When she left America in 1809, Louisa worried that she would lose a family member in her absence. Now she would never see her mother's face again. Nor could she reminisce with her sisters and brother about their childhood in London, when as wife of the US consul her mother had played hostess to Americans traveling through or living there. Now Louisa was left alone in grief, halfway around the world in a foreign country on the brink of war.

"Full of mortal affliction—My poor mother! After ten years of poverty, dependence, and severe suffering, which at this great distance was so utterly out of my power to mitigate or assuage," she said in her grief.

Her sister Nancy was gone, and now a brother-in-law too. The Cranches were beloved relatives of the Adams family who had boarded George and John.

Though Louisa did not know it at the time, not long after the Cranches died, the boys went to Atkinson, New Hampshire, to study and live with Elizabeth and Stephen Peabody. George had studied there for two years when John Quincy served in the Senate in Washington. By November 1812, George and John changed schools. This time they traveled to Derby Academy in Hingham, Massachusetts, which was about seven miles from Quincy. There they studied with Reverend Daniel Kimball, the academy's master teacher.

Would John and Louisa be able to return to America within a year as they planned? When would these tragedies end? Would his parents, either John or Abigail, die before they could see them again?

"How different will home appear should we live to return—God's will be done!"

One other matter weighed on Louisa. The relationship between Kitty and William Smith had become very close—too close for Adams's sensibilities. Mr. Gray's departure removed the final obstacle to Kitty's affection, clearing the path for William, who took full advantage.

From the day she learned that Kitty was to accompany her to St. Petersburg, Louisa had worried about the young woman's lot in life. She felt that she had failed their now deceased mother as a chaperone to her sister. She worried about her relationship with William, who was younger and showing the same destructive habits for excessive drinking and gambling that had brought down his father, who'd abandoned his family. Perhaps she was thinking of Kitty when Louisa penned these words: "He afflicts us in mercy for here we are placed amid many sore temptations."

More than ever it was time to go home to Boston.

~

Although the year 1812 had just begun, the truth of their official circumstances was becoming more and more ominous. Official US government correspondence had also recently arrived, bringing disappointment. John knew he must tell Count Romanzoff as soon as possible.

The meeting took place on February 4, 1812. When Adams arrived, he thanked Romanzoff for the packets he had received from Paris through the

Russian courier and quickly got to his point. He had recently received a personal letter from the president of the United States and a dispatch from the secretary of state. Madison had nominated another person to the Supreme Court. His new instructions were as firm as the frozen surface of the Baltic. John was to remain in Russia and continue the US mission there until further notice.

"A circumstance which I thought it proper to communicate to this government," he noted.

Romanzoff's long face broke into a wide smile over the news. He had read otherwise. Both English and German newspapers reported that Adams was "to be removed to England." The count confessed that he'd believed those articles so much that he "had mentioned it to the emperor and had thought it probable." His trust came from reports that England appeared to be showing "conciliatory dispositions towards the United States."

Rubbish. Propaganda. John knew better. English newspapers printed predictions as facts. Their motive was to make the news, not merely to report it. "It was much the fashion to announce appointments by anticipation, which never came to be realized; that I had not the slightest insinuation of an intention by the president to remove me to England."

Adams was confident in the position of the president. The reason he had not been appointed as America's top envoy to England was quite simple. Convinced that the British intended to wage war instead of revoking their abusive Orders in Council, Madison saw no need to send anyone else to London to replace US Minister William Pinkney, who returned to America in June 1811 after talks with the British government terminated in London. Instead British envoy Augustus John Foster arrived in Washington City as British minister to the United States about the same time Pinkney returned home. Peace talks with Foster started badly because of the *Little Belt* incident. The British government would not allow Foster to negotiate reparations for the 1801 *Chesapeake* incident until the US government made amends for the *Little Belt*.

After President Madison announced hostile intentions toward Britain in his annual message to Congress in October 1811, Foster quickly concluded negotiations on the *Chesapeake* reparations. He then revealed that Britain had stiffened its terms for ultimate peace with America. Because they did not accept Napoleon's alleged revocation of his Berlin and Milan decrees, the British would not repeal their Orders in Council until the US government required France to admit both British and American cargo.

Given all this, John explained to Romanzoff that his only hope of America avoiding war with England was the widely anticipated death of King George III: The "spirit of delirium and of stubbornness" in the old king "had almost constant rule of the kingdom of Great Britain."

Although King George III's reign was officially over, he was not dead. The English king who had stubbornly refused to give America independence was now insane. His son the prince regent took the throne in February 1811. But as long as his father was alive, he competed for power with Parliament. Adams hoped the prince's judgment was better than his father's, whose death might free the prince to treat for peace.

John also prayed that his country would be wise. If Congress chose war, the US government's preparations must be substantial. In a letter he had recently written to his mother, he hoped "that Congress will have the wisdom still to preserve our country from war in which we could gain nothing and could not fail to lose something of what is worth more than all other possessions to a nation, our independence."

Though all this weighed on his mind, Adams took his cues from the count in their February 1812 meeting. Romanzoff wanted to change the subject, noting "that in France a better understanding with America was intended and even professed."

Double rubbish.

"With regard to American vessels which should arrive in France there would be little or no difficulty made as to whence they came or as to the nature of their cargoes."

While Napoleon hoisted a flag of hope through front-facing official policy, he held a pirate's flag behind his back. French privateers continued to seize American ships. Reports of French hostilities reached President Madison on January 1, 1812, leading to a heated exchange with the French minister at a New Year's reception at the President's House. French privateers were so successful that the English decided to abandon their blockade of the port of Elsinore in Denmark. Why harass the Americans if the French would do their dirty work for them? When it came to Napoleon's commerce policy, nothing was permanent. Every decision was a momentary impulse.

"Today the impression [of Napoleon's character] was of one sort, and the measure corresponded with it; tomorrow the impression would be of an opposite nature and the measure would follow that too," Romanzoff told Adams.

Caprice crowned Napoleon's character. He was more chameleon than king. "To make them consistent was not in the nature of the man."

Napoleon failed to see that commerce concerned all humanity. Trade didn't affect just the merchant class; it affected everyone regardless of rank and position. He was a crafty cupid, romantically luring his allies into a setup or trap.

"But in truth, commerce is the concern of us all," the count continued. "It is the very chain of human association."

Exports and imports were the foundation of peaceful relationships between nations. Gone was the isolation of previous centuries. The modern world of 1812 depended on free trade.

"The Emperor Napoleon will never see it in this light, and so his commercial regulations and promises will never be systematic or consistent—you can place little dependence upon them," Romanzoff huffed.

John gave his opinion on France's supposed better understanding with the United States. Napoleon was merely taking advantage of the situation. Officially reaching out to America was a pretense as long as French privateers continued to arrest American ships.

"Tranquility is not in his [Napoleon's] nature," the count continued. "I can tell you, in confidence, that he once told me so himself."

Romanzoff then relayed a conversation he once had with Napoleon: "I was speaking to him [Napoleon] about Spain and Portugal, and he said to me, 'I must always be *going*. After the Peace of Tilsit, where could I go but to Spain? I went to Spain because I could not go anywhere else.'"

Bonaparte's motives were based on nothing more than wanderlust—the idea that he had to be going somewhere, he had to be conquering some place.

"And now as perhaps there [Spain], he is not quite satisfied with his going, he may intend to turn against us, from the same want of any other place to go."

While he favored France over England in Russia's foreign policy, the count distrusted Bonaparte. Like the comet overhead, Napoleon followed his own eccentric whimsical orbit. The farther he moved from his power source, his sun—Paris—the wider his trail of destruction. Both John and Romanzoff knew that Napoleon's erratic star longed to move over Russia's borders.

45

Interference

"MY LOVELY BEAUTIFUL BABE IS VERY, VERY ILL," LOUISA WROTE IN mid-February 1812.

While war threatened Europe and the United States, John and Louisa faced a more intimate battle at home. Their six-month-old was suffering from something mysterious.

"Ah! The fountain of her precious existence is sapped by these constant shocks, and I look at her with fear and trembling."

The convulsions were perhaps febrile seizures or epilepsy. Baby Louisa's condition was evident to all who saw her tiny arms and legs tremble. The episodes came on suddenly and violently.

"Everyone who sees her stops her in the street, and they all say that she is born for heaven."

Imagine hearing such dire predictions from total strangers. What audacity! What insensitivity! And what good did these statements do? Did they give Louisa hope? Hardly. They incited fear, which was already very real.

The comet, the talk of war between France and Russia, the possibility of war between England and America, the loss of dear family members back home, and now the sight of her daughter's tiny body suffering from shocks—all were too much.

"The Russians are very superstitious, and I fear that with the impressions already made upon my weak mind during my four years residence in Berlin, I am too ready to fall into this error," she worried.

She had listened to the gypsy-like predictions of the Prussians. Would she now do the same of the Russian ladies?

"Toward evening my babe was better—I am not naturally melancholy but my trials are heavy."

Russia was always cold in winter, but this year it was worse, likely a result of the comet's atmospheric interference. The freeze exceeded all calculations, dipping as low as forty degrees below zero. No matter. Arctic Alexander was as comfortable as a polar bear.

"The emperor said he had not seen me for a long time and he supposed we walked at different hours," Adams wrote on March 3 of his recent walk on the quay where he met the czar. "I told him that I had adopted the practice of walking in the morning early, and sometimes saw His Majesty's window open in very cold weather."

Alexander replied that he "always made it a rule to rise in the morning and dress with his window open."

John asked if he did "not suffer from the cold."

"On the contrary," he said, explaining that the practice adjusted or "inured him better than anything to the cold."

Alexander recalled the heating habits of his grandmother Empress Catherine. She shut up the palace, which made the apartments so warm that they might as well have been growing flowers. Alexander did not find the confinement cozy. Just as a sea lion dives into arctic water with abandon, so the czar preferred the refreshing freezing chill on his bare skin in the morning, which made the cold more bearable when he took to the outdoors. So he thought.

He then confessed another intimate personal habit to Adams. Years earlier the emperor had discovered he could not do as other men did in St. Petersburg. He could not wear flannel to keep warm. His skin was too sensitive.

"He had then worn a flannel waistcoat, but he found it irritated and fretted the skin so much, and made him so delicate, that he could not endure it."

The royal doctor offered a remedy. Go without flannel. "A physician therefore advised him to leave it off, and told him that either he would die under the operation of the change, or would have his health much better."

The emperor joked that he left off the flannel, did not die from the cold, and his skin felt much better—no more blotchy red patches, hives, or itching.

"You are not of my opinion about flannel?" Alexander teased John.

No matter how harsh Russian or Boston winters, Adams could not do as the emperor did. He could not get dressed with the windows wide open, and he could not go outside without wearing his flannel vest, especially when taking a walk.

"I had so long been in the custom of wearing it in winter that I believed if I should leave it off, I should die under the operation," John joked.

"But there are now many physicians here who think flannel is a bad thing for wear," Alexander replied with a smile.

⟶

Two weeks later, on March 19, 1812, the pair met again on a walk. This time Alexander turned their usual banter about the cold into a more significant revelation. He had recently seen an American businessman at the weekly review of Russian troops and wondered why the man would have come out to watch drills under such extreme weather conditions. Though the czar usually canceled the weekly troop review when the temperature dipped below freezing, times had changed. The troops marched under extreme cold conditions, and the US businessman had attended despite the frozen temperature.

Knowing the American in question, John immediately tried to allay the emperor's fears of spying. The man was a friend of one of the officers and nothing more. Alexander paused ominously.

"And so it is," revealed His Majesty, "after all, that war is coming, which I have done so much to avoid—everything. I have done everything to prevent the struggle, but thus it ends."

"But are all hopes vanished of still preserving the peace?" Adams asked.

"At all events we shall not begin the war; my will is yet to prevent it; but we expect to be attacked."

"Then as Your Majesty has determined not to commence, I would fain hope it may still pass over without a war."

"I wish it may. But all indications are war," he said.

As many as eight regiments had already marched from St. Petersburg to the Polish border, with others following two or three times a week. Adams appreciated the czar's candor. In that moment Alexander confided in him as if he were a close friend or a member of his cabinet.

Three weeks later, on April 9, John again encountered Alexander. "In my walk before dinner I met the emperor, who spoke to me of nothing but the weather—said we should have a very late spring."

Snow lingered in St. Petersburg, sprinkling spring with a frosty dust, another atmospheric interference by the comet. Alexander worried that natural disasters would follow. "That the floods would be extraordinarily high when the rivers would break up, the late snows having been so considerable. It had been snowing all morning," John recorded.

Unlike their recent exchanges, John noticed a change in the czar's ruddy face that April day. Gone were humor and candor. Replacing them were brevity and solemnity.

"The emperor is to leave his capital in two days to join his army. His manner today was graver and less cheerful than I have usually seen him."

Adams picked up his pen many times as April ended and May began in 1812. The Neva River was now open, which enabled him to again send letters by boat. Pressing on his mind were two matters: his responsibility to update his government and his urgent need to write his mother about his plans for his oldest boys.

"Two days before His Majesty's departure, Count Romanzoff sent me a note requesting me to call upon him the next morning, which I accordingly did," he explained to Secretary of State Monroe in a letter dated April 28.

Romanzoff confirmed Alexander's departure to review the troops. The count was also going to the frontier. Some of the upcoming discussions at the emperor's headquarters would involve America.

"What was the precise state of the relations between the United States and France or England or both?" an urgent Romanzoff asked, adding that John should reveal only information that he had officially received from his government. The Russians had heard rumors of a treaty between the United States and France.

Adams explained that no definitive arrangement had been agreed to with France. As far as England was concerned, Mr. Foster was in negotiations with Secretary Monroe.

"I was perfectly sure it [a treaty] could not [happen], unless the revocation of the British Orders in Council should be one of its explicit conditions. If Mr. Foster is authorized to stipulate for the revocation of the orders, a treaty is possible," John doubtfully explained.

With a right to protect its commercial interests, the United States deserved free trade and actual acceptance as a sovereign nation.

"And unless restored by the revocation of those Orders in Council I had no doubt that the United States would vindicate it by war. But I did not anticipate a declaration of war by the United States at present."

The Senate had begun preparations, passing a bill to raise twenty-five thousand men, though the enlistments were voluntary and not enforceable. John hoped that Britain's prince regent would bring fresh perspective and perhaps some wisdom to the situation. After all, England and the rest of Europe were experiencing a famine. The United States was a great source of grain. The emerging power source was the prime minister. As long as one man lorded over the rest in England, John doubted the Orders in Council would be revoked, no matter how many Britons were starving.

"I thought their existence now depended solely on that of Mr. Perceval, as prime minister of England."

"Did I think Mr. Perceval would remain prime minister?"

"I believed he would."

"But as it is the nature of the serpent to sting, it is the duty of man to bruise his head for self protection," he wrote his mother not long after relaying his conversation with Romanzoff in a letter to Monroe.

With war looming, he needed to revoke the request he made of her: "In that case we shall have no access to or from the Baltic the present year, and I must at all events be disappointed in the wish of having my sons come to me."

After learning that Madison wanted him to stay in St. Petersburg, John had devised another plan. Because American ships so freely entered the Baltic the previous summer, his sons could travel to Russia in safety. Perhaps reunion was meant to happen in St. Petersburg. The politics of the pending wars now dashed his hopes.

"I expressly requested in my former letters to you and to Mr. Gray that they [George and John] might not be sent, if we should have war with England."

The political drama was drawing toward its catastrophe. Under the circumstances, he could not possibly subject his sons to the terror of sailing through Europe on an American ship with a world at war. He didn't need a sailor's spy glass to study the horizon. John was now stuck in St. Petersburg and his sons stuck in Boston.

"But as far as I can make up my mind, I am satisfied that my duties both to my country and to my family beckon me homeward."

How he longed to take over his sons' education! He wanted his parents to meet their granddaughter and see how much Charles had grown. Baby Louisa was his most "precious engagement." Nonetheless, from going home to bringing his sons to Russia, the prospect of war interfered with all his plans, hopes, and dreams.

46

Tomorrow

JOHN VISITED COUNT LAURISTON ON JUNE 19. THE TWO HAD BANtered several times the past few months. With each new conversation, Lauriston increasingly carped. Why wouldn't Alexander negotiate? What was the reason for war?

On this occasion, Adams found Lauriston as he had never seen him: physically unwell. His headaches were the size of Russia. Lauriston complained of both tremors in his head and the diplomatic dueling that precedes war.

He was "soured and exasperated, principally by the refusal to allow him passports to go to Vilna."

Vilna was one of many ancient names for an East Prussian city, which is present-day Vilnius, Lithuania. The Russian government continued to deny the French ambassador's request to leave Russia. Back then a passport was required to leave a country, a leftover practice from the French Revolution.

John discovered even more interesting news from Lauriston. The French government had also denied Prince Kurakin, the Russian ambassador to France, a passport to leave Paris. Though the prince was highly esteemed by many, politics was behind the pretense. Adams fished for more news.

"I asked him where Emperor Napoleon was."

Lauriston did not know.

"Perhaps at Warsaw. He heard the Russians had concentrated their forces [there], because they said the Emperor Napoleon always attacks the center."

Lauriston then let his vehemence flow: "They think because he has done so before, he will do so again." He chastised the Russians for thinking Napoleon would follow previous strategies: "But with such a man as that, they will find their calculations fail them. He will do something that they do not expect. He does not copy himself nor any other. He does something new."

All Adams could do was let Lauriston vent. Later he wrote his own assessment: "The facts show at once the extreme jealousy, suspicion, and distrust existing between the parties, and the reluctance they have to begin the war, with the anxiety on each side to throw the first act of aggression upon the other one."

⌒

During this time John did what he often did in the summer. He took advantage of the long hours of sunlight to read. He opened a collection of sermons by an English preacher. One on the topic of anxiety caught his attention.

"My own disposition has in it too much anxiety," he reflected. "And the experience of life has a great tendency to increase that propensity."

The sermon addressed the scriptural concept of "take no thought for tomorrow" and "do not worry about what he shall eat or drink." These were tough principles for Adams.

"A father of a family in this world must take thought of tomorrow—not for what he himself shall eat or drink, or wherewithal he shall be clothed, but for his wife and children." Since becoming a husband and father, he had encountered "perpetual temptations and stimulations to waste the means of provision bestowed upon me by the goodness of that Heavenly Father, who feeds the fowls of the air and who clothes the lilies of the field."

Focusing on the future—tomorrow—drove him to provide for his family. His fear of poverty outweighed his lust for lavishness. Just as Atlas held the world on his back, so Adams bore the responsibility to care for his family's temporal needs. No matter how much he worried, life was beyond the power of his pen and purse.

Never before were so many circumstances beyond his control at once, not at least since he had formed a family of his own. He understood what his mother and father had experienced during the American Revolution when chaos reigned. They couldn't stop King George III from sending troops to Boston any more than John Quincy could stop Napoleon from threatening Russia or convince Britain's prime minister to revoke the Orders in Council.

Most intimately of all, he couldn't stop his daughter's convulsions or his wife's sobbing or find a way to return to America. He was now living in a so-called exile that was no longer practical or productive. The feeling of a wasted life glared brighter than the comet's tail overhead. He felt more useless than ever.

"What with all the thought that I do bestow, and all the precautions that I can take . . . frequent untoward events and unforeseen accidents disconcert all my prudence, and require new sacrifices of feeling, of pleasure, and even of indulgence, to [the] thought of tomorrow."

The sermon gnawed on his conscience and tugged on his sense of spiritual truth. He concluded that this passage did not suggest that man should abandon his responsibility to himself or his family. Quite the contrary. Instead these verses warned humans against excessive worry and promoted trust in Providence. Faith was all he had.

The immediate morrow, the next day, brought more conflict and raised the stakes. Adams learned that once again the Russian government had denied Lauriston's latest request for a passport to leave. He had applied three times. Likewise Kurakin had applied three times in France to return to Russia. The French government gave passports to everyone in Kurakin's family except the prince himself. Both diplomats were being held hostage, tormented exiles to countries that had turned from ally to enemy.

Lauriston may have believed that Alexander let the dogs of war loose, but it was Napoleon who crossed the Rubicon. Just as Caesar had made his decision and crossed the Rubicon River in Italy centuries earlier, so Napoleon invaded Russia by crossing a river, the Memel, and invading Russia. Also called the Neman, the Memel separated Russia from Prussia in what is present-day Lithuania. Some historians mark the day as "June 22, 1812." Others say "June 23," and still others note "June 24, 1812" as the day of Napoleon's Rubicon into Russia. The sheer size of his force and the time it would take for such a large army to cross the Neman make the discrepancies in dates understandable.

Napoleon's Grande Armée of 600,000 was the largest allied military force in history to date. More than 400,000 soldiers advanced in three armies while 200,000 initially stayed behind in Prussia as reserves. Half were French. The rest were Germans, Austrians, Prussians, Poles, Italians, and others. Napoleon's marriage to an Austrian princess required Austria to be an ally.

His fast-paced plan was designed to split the Russian front line into two and encircle them. He expected to achieve victory without going any farther than fifty miles. Surely a force of more than half a million soldiers against Russia's forces of fewer than two hundred thousand would intimidate Alexander into capitulation. So Napoleon thought.

Adams first heard the news of the invasion on June 28, when the secretary of the French embassy called on him to let him know he was leaving Russia, though Lauriston remained passport-less. Another sign that the hostilities had begun was a change at the palace. The empress and the empress mother usually spent their summers at palaces in the countryside. They had returned to the Winter Palace, as was the custom during wartime.

Two days later the *St. Petersburg Gazette* provided more information. Alexander responded to the invasion by issuing a resolution. No matter that he was outnumbered. He had time, space, and most important, climate on his side. He declared that he would not make peace as long as the enemy remained under arms on his turf—hardly the response Napoleon wanted.

47

Heaven

NOT ONLY COULD ADAMS HAVE USED A TELEPHONE, BUT HE AND the rest of America and England desperately could have used the nonexistent television in the summer of 1812. Had the technology existed, it just might have prevented war.

"We have lived in eventful times, but in the course of my life I have no recollection of a moment so full of portent as the present," John wrote ominously to his father the day after he learned of Napoleon's invasion.

Weighing on him more than Bonaparte was shocking news from England. Through recently arrived British newspapers, which were increasingly warlike and threatening against America, he learned of the prime minister's assassination.

"The most powerful patron and supporter of the Orders in Council, Mr. Perceval . . . was murdered within the walls of the House of Commons on the 11th of last month by an individual of [a] disordered mind."

The prime minister, the man in England who most supported the Orders in Council, was now dead. Though tragic, this news gave John a glimmer of hope that a new prime minister might revoke the British Orders in Council, which would avoid war. How he longed to take a walk with his father in the gardens of Peacefield and discuss the possibility.

His pen was his only substitute: "I had flattered myself when the survivors of the Perceval administration resigned, that their successors would immediately remove the great stumbling block, the Orders in Council, and that we should be saved thereby from the impending war."

But there was a problem. The members of Parliament were quibbling among themselves. This internal battle delayed the out-of-power party's ability to change the troublesome policy. The House of Commons asked the prince regent to form a new administration, with a friendly hint on how it was to be formed. The Perceval opposition began mining and countermining to launch one of their own into power to overthrow the Orders in Council.

"The Perceval policy appears likely to maintain its ascendancy yet a little longer, long enough I fear to produce that catastrophe from which we have so long endeavored to preserve ourselves, but in which it seems the will of Heaven that we should be involved."

All he could do was wait for letters from home, newspapers from England, or word from the Russian front. With France blockading the Baltic and invading Russia, the postal system was mostly shut down.

―

"I am 45 years old," John recorded in his diary on his birthday, July 11, 1812. "Two thirds of a long life are past, and I have done nothing to distinguish it by usefulness to my country or to mankind. I have always lived with, I hope, a suitable sense of my duties in society, and with a sincere desire to perform them."

He blamed laziness for his inability to do anything worthwhile for his country. How wrong he was.

―

Two days earlier, on July 9, John called upon Count Lauriston at his new quarters, a hotel. Because the Russian government no longer recognized France as an ally, Lauriston was no longer an ambassador. They evicted him from the French embassy, the mansion owned by Alexander.

Lauriston longed to hear from the front. He applied for a passport again and wanted to know the truth. Was he a "hostage or a prisoner?" No one knew. St. Petersburg's officials had not received directions from Alexander about Lauriston. They did not know what to do with him, whether to send him home or to keep him there.

The Frenchman complained that peddlers had begun selling fusees, or illuminations, on St. Petersburg's streets. The masses needed to be ready to light the skies for a victory celebration more widespread than the comet.

"Ah," said Lauriston. "They prepare for illumination beforehand. I know they will illuminate; let the event be what it will. But I shall look, the next day after, upon the map to see where the headquarters are."

The next day Lauriston's fate was clear. He and the remaining members of the French legation received passports. The outgoing envoys were ordered to stay at Oranienbaum, a palace west of St. Petersburg. From there they could stage their departure at the palace's sea channel on boats provided by the Russian government.

Lauriston wanted to leave by land, but the Russians wisely denied his request. Because he was a French officer, they couldn't afford for him to travel through the very frontier where they had placed soldiers. They couldn't take the risk that he would gather intelligence and use it against them. The diplomats from France, Bavaria, and Westphalia were required to leave by water for their voyage to Memel, where Napoleon had crossed into Russia.

In contrast the Prussians, Austrians, and Spanish received passports allowing them to return home by land. The Russian officials told them exactly where they could go and required them to ride in government carriages. By giving them better treatment than the French, Russia was sending a signal. Alexander wanted to court these nations as allies and perhaps turn them against Napoleon.

Despite John's birthday feelings of inferiority and lack of contribution to his country, evidence of his success on behalf of America and his revered status by his colleagues began arriving on his doorstep. Dozens of crates came to his residence. He received numerous wooden chests holding the archives and papers of the French embassy as well as the Dutch, Bavarian, Würtemberg, and Westphalian legations. He was one of the few diplomats left, and his colleagues trusted him so much that they left their nation's paperwork with him. They could have sent their papers to a bank, but they chose Adams instead. If he left, they asked him to deliver the crates to the court banker, Mr. Krehmer.

John wished he could join the departing diplomats. Yet he could not risk his daughter's life by putting her on a boat or subjecting her to an extensive land voyage somewhere in Europe. She was too fragile. He had seen her body writhe unexpectedly and uncontrollably. The sight was heart wrenching. Just as her birth had prevented them from leaving Russia the previous year, so her illness and war now chained them there. As long as the French did not directly threaten Moscow or St. Petersburg, they would stay.

While the diplomats fled, good news arrived from England. This time, Adams chose his mother to share the optimistic report. "On the 16th of June, the death blow was given in the British House of Commons to the political pestilence, which has been raging nearly five years under the denomination of the Orders in Council," he wrote with hope on July 13.

He called the revocation an exhortation. Finally Parliament had listened to the cries of its own starving people and revoked the Orders in Council. As jubilant as he was over the news, one serious fear plagued him: "My principal anxiety, therefore, now is for what may have been done in America."

He knew that the US government had been preparing for war. Treasury Secretary Albert Gallatin proposed doubling the tariff on certain imports while increasing license fees and taxes on liquor, salt, sugar, and carriages. Gallatin also sought a loan of $10 million. With much debate and reluctance, Congress passed these tax increases and expanded government powers in case of war against a European nation. This was the strongest proof that they were preparing for battle. John's worst fear was that Congress and the president had declared war before they learned of Perceval's murder and the revocation of the Orders in Council, which along with impressment was the root cause of the conflict between the United States and Britain.

"I am uneasy lest in the moment of hurry to show the seriousness of our intention to vindicate our right [to free trade] we may have lost the benefit of their tardy repentance, and put the weapon of defense from our own hands into theirs."

"My coachman this morning was taken for a soldier. In the evening he was released again upon payment of 25 rubles by his master," Adams recorded in his diary.

Because St. Petersburg was only a three-day journey from the war front, the city quickly moved into a military mind-set. Calls continued for money, men, and grain. The government required the nobility to give up one peasant for every ten they owned. These restrictions came faster than the comet-sprung spring floods. Alexander issued strict orders forbidding movement of foreigners, particularly the French. These declarations sparked confusion, which resulted in the arrest of Adams's coachman.

Cables were as absent from the ocean floor as satellites from the sky in 1812. In a world where carriages, boats, and horseback riders were the only channels of communication, no one could have imagined the instantaneous nature of telegraphs or television. Word from the war front came sporadically. What did come smacked of propaganda. Because the Russian government shut down its postal service, the officials could more easily control the messages that did arrive.

"The official news from the armies is all favorable, and according to the hand-bills, they have had nothing but a series of successes from the first day of the campaign," reported John.

Official orders arrived in St. Petersburg. This time the police directed all inhabitants to be ready to post lanterns and other victorious illuminations on their houses when Alexander returned. He was expected any day.

"I walked before breakfast in the Summer Gardens, and in turning around the boulevard, I perceived the imperial flag flying over the palace, which first gave me notice of the emperor's return," John observed on August 3.

The sight brought relief but not good news. The czar and his army had been completely separated from the second army commanded by a Russian prince. Worse, they were retreating. Rather than engage Napoleon's army, they chose the scorched earth policy of burning land—along with the precious commodities of grass and grain—as they traveled. The Russians failed to push back the French army at the borders. Napoleon was inching closer to Moscow.

John received additional information about America three days later, on August 6. Soon newspaper accounts confirmed the news. After regaining his composure, he picked up his pen and wrote his mother a letter on August 10.

"I then flattered myself that the revocation of the British Orders in Council, of which I had just been informed, would be known in the United

States in season to prevent the war, which I knew would otherwise be unavoidable," he began.

Indeed he had ardently wished that the news of Perceval's assassination had reached Washington before Congress declared war.

"In this hope I have been disappointed." An American, who had recently arrived in St. Petersburg, brought Adams a New York newspaper that included President Madison's war proclamation. The newspaper's date was June 22. Madison's proclamation chronicled the correspondence between Secretary Monroe and British Minister Foster. Their failed negotiations left the president with no option but to declare war.

"After reading Mr. Foster's letter to Mr. Monroe of 30 May, I cannot indeed perceive any other course which was left to the American government without self degradation to pursue than that which they did adopt," he wrote.

Unaware of Parliament's June 16 decision to revoke the Orders in Council, the House and Senate approved the war declaration and Madison signed it on June 18. Though the policy was extinguished, war was ignited nonetheless. Such was the irony that only instant communication could have prevented.

"I lament the declaration of war as an event which in the actual state of things when it passed was altogether unnecessary."

The votes were seventy-nine in favor to forty-nine opposed in the House of Representatives, and nineteen to thirteen in the US Senate. Two senators were absent. War had come to America for the second time in its infant history.

Adams concluded that there was "no alternative left but war or the abandonment of our right as an independent nation."

The United States now faced the giant that it had defeated thirty years earlier to gain its independence. Failure to stop the redcoats again could result in re-enslavement to Britain. King George III was mad, but not dead. America could lose its sovereignty. Liberty was thrown upon the chance of events.

"How far the policy of our government will be affected by the revocation of the Orders in Council when they learn that it preceded the declaration of war, I can hardly foresee," Adams moaned. "My own most fervent wishes and prayers are that peace may be restored before any further irritating and aggravating hostilities shall have been committed on either side."

How he longed for a touch of heaven to prevent his country—and his child—from experiencing hell on earth.

In early September John learned of news from the front. After a severe four-day battle, the Russians continued their scorched earth policy. They set fire to the town of Smolensk, which was on the road to Moscow from the western border, and were continuing their retreat. Losses for the French were greater than for the Russians.

Meanwhile baby Louisa was getting worse. Because she was cutting several teeth at once, Louisa decided to wean her from breast milk. The infant's convulsions continued, and she developed dysentery. Her health was as precarious as ever.

On September 6, Adams received an unexpected summons. A woman named Madame de Staël sent him an urgent note requesting him to meet her at the Hôtel de l'Europe. When he arrived at the hotel, standing in front of him was an Englishman named Lord Cathcart. He was no ordinary Brit but an envoy. Cathcart had recently arrived in St. Petersburg to present his credentials as the British ambassador to Russia.

"I had not expected that in a state of declared war between Great Britain and the United States, he would have sent to us; but as he did, I concluded to return the civility in the usual form."

Adams was shocked that Cathcart wanted to meet him. The circumstances were odd indeed. John had enjoyed his status as the father of diplomacy in St. Petersburg. Although he was one of the few diplomats left, at least the others who remained were on friendly terms with America. Now standing before him was an official diplomat from a government at war with the United States.

For once John was able to take advantage of the slow postal system. His knowledge about the war with England had come only through newspapers. He had not received official notification or new instructions from his government, which allowed him to more easily converse with Cathcart. The man seemed cordial enough, a proper Englishman.

"He professed to have a particular attachment to America, with which he felt a strong personal relation (alluding, I suppose, to his having married an American lady) and to cherish a wish that the political differences between that country and England might yet be amicably settled."

"I assured him that my own sentiments in this respect altogether coincided with his. I believed peace and friendship to be easily attainable between them, and highly important to the best interests of both."

So went the diplomatic posturing.

———

Meanwhile baby Louisa's condition worsened. They took her to the country for several days. When the fresh air did not help, they returned to the city. Adams recorded on September 11 that Dr. Gibbs, a surgeon, came to lance one of the seven teeth cutting through the baby's gums. The idea of lancing was to speed the teeth-cutting process and relieve the patient of extended pain. "But the violence of her illness increases," John wrote.

Having just returned from the war front, Count Romanzoff sent Adams an invitation to dine, but he declined because of the rapidly declining health of his child. He was very worried.

"My dear child had a quiet and composed night, but early this morning was seized again with violent convulsions, which continued the whole day, and announce her approaching dissolution," he gravely wrote on September 12.

They bathed her in warm water, administered laudanum, and gave her digitalis, a drug made from the leaves of the foxglove plant. One doctor ordered that they shave her head and administer blisters to encourage bleeding. The practice of bloodletting dated to the Hippocratic medical writings of ancient Greece and ended in the middle of the nineteenth century with the rise of germ theory. Sometimes physicians or nurses would heat a glass, grease the rim, and hold it over a blister or a cut on the skin to "cup" or draw blood. At other times they would place a leech into a glass of wine, cover the top with a piece of paper, turn the glass over, and remove the paper to allow the leech to bite the patient. They would remove the leech after it produced a teaspoon or so of blood. Physicians at the time thought bleeding would eliminate poisons from the body.

"Language cannot express the feelings of a parent, beholding the long continued agonies of the lovely infant, and finding every expedient attempted to administer relief, utterly unavailing," John wrote.

Louisa was just as distraught. Though suffering from the negative physical effects of abruptly ending breast feeding, the emotional distress over her daughter's declining condition was too much for her. Her diary during this time understandingly showed only a few lines. Louisa possibly wrote those later because her dates were out of sync with John's. His account was much more specific and precise.

"Her mother, fond and affectionate by nature, and attached to this child in particular to an only daughter, affected in her own health very seriously . . . was this afternoon forced to quit the side of the cradle, which for three days and nights before she had scarcely left a minute, and remove to another chamber, to be spared witnessing the last struggles of her expiring life," John wrote, noting that Kitty and a nurse kept watch by the baby's cradle. Louisa also "could not keep herself long absent from her." She moved back and forth to the adjoining chamber.

On September 14 the physicians once again applied a blister to the back of baby Louisa's head. "A gleam of voluntary hope was kept alive this day from an apparent relaxation of the extreme rigor of the symptoms," John recorded.

At 8:00 p.m. a change for the worse took place. About this time Kitty fainted, which was an understandable occurrence in the midst of a forty-eight-hour vigil. She resumed her post by the cradle within thirty minutes. John took turns tending to his wife and child, writing, "I was there myself as frequently as I could for a few minutes for my dear wife, who is suffering little less than her child."

They could do no more. Her convulsions continued. "The Lord gave and the Lord hath taken away. Blessed be the name of the Lord. At twenty-five minutes past one this morning, expired my daughter, Louisa Catherine, as lovely an infant as ever breathed the air of heaven," John wrote on September 15.

The baby died in the presence of Kitty. John delivered the news to Louisa: "My dear wife, to whom it was my lot to communicate the bitter knowledge of the event, fainted for a few minutes but received the shock with a resignation and fortitude, which manifested that her strength had been proportioned to her trial."

Thirteen months after giving birth to her precious daughter, Louisa Adams said good-bye. She simply stated in her diary: "My child gone to heaven."

This precious girl, her only daughter, was dead. Louisa's namesake, her pride, her joy, was gone. She would never forget her smile or her tiny nose. She would never be able to raise her into the woman she could have been. She would never have the chance to teach her how to play the harp or pianoforte. Though she would never hear her daughter sing, she would always be the music of Louisa's heart.

John took comfort that his daughter was no longer suffering. "Believing in the existence of another and better world than this . . . and that her transition from the pangs of death to the bliss of heaven was instantaneous, and complete."

He oversaw the funeral arrangements. Two days later, Dr. Pitt, their minister, buried baby Louisa in the graveyard at the English Factory Church. John turned to his faith that day. "I endeavor to collect my scattered spirits and to seek consolation for the heavy calamity that has befallen me by reflecting on the mercies of Divine Providence." Following the service, John took a walk in the Summer Garden with Charles.

"As life is the gift of God, and is obviously given for enjoyment, it becomes us, not to say that the gift is without value," John wrote that day. As he bid adieu, he was determined to be thankful for his daughter's brief life.

In the midst of the wars of 1812, private tragedy struck the Adams household. Domestic tragedy eclipsed the historical drama surrounding them. Without their oldest children, life in St. Petersburg was never what they wanted, but now life in St. Petersburg would never be the same without their baby girl. Their so-called exile had worsened, deepened. Soon the need to escape life there—life anywhere—would overwhelm them, especially Louisa.

48

Enemy Within

NAPOLEON'S GRANDE ARMÉE HAD CAPTURED MOSCOW.

At least that was the rumor swirling through the streets of St. Petersburg the third week of September 1812. Fears of the enemy within Russia's most symbolic city and former capital spread with cometlike speed. Meanwhile the Great Comet itself remained faintly visible in Russia's skies above. The news about Moscow frightened John's proprietor so much that he was afraid to actually speak of it out loud: "My landlord, Mr. Strogofshikoff . . . came to me much alarmed and mortified at the present condition of his country—hinting but afraid expressly to say that Moscow is in the hands of the French."

The man had good reason to fear. Local authorities had recently forced several mujiks to sweep the streets for the crime of merely saying out loud that Napoleon controlled Moscow. Superstition reigned over them more than the czar. If the Russians openly said something, then it might come true. Though Peter the Great had moved the capital from Moscow to St. Petersburg in 1710, Moscow was symbolic, embodying the soul of Russia. If the French had taken Moscow, then they would surely come to St. Petersburg. Government officials had yet to confirm the news. Rumors in war were as unreliable as they were common.

While the Russians fought the French within their borders, John also faced a new enemy within. The realization became evident when he and William Smith attended the funeral of a field marshal's wife. The makeup of the remaining diplomatic corps in the audience was sobering to John. He was one of only three left from the original group.

Two years earlier John had reigned as an equal with the French ambassador, not in actual rank but in favor with Alexander. The presence of the new British ambassador now rattled the dynamics.

"The courtiers were as assiduous to the British Ambassador as eighteen months ago they had been to the Duke of Vicence [the French ambassador]."

Lord Cathcart's presence couldn't have been more awkward for the esteemed American diplomat. John still had not received official word from his government that the United States was at war with Great Britain. Though he could technically speak to Cathcart, without instructions from home he risked making a mistake and misrepresenting his country with a representative of the enemy, a dangerous possibility. How much interaction, if any, with Cathcart was appropriate? How much could he say? What irritated John, however, was the British ambassador's pretense and lavishness. As if he were king, seven attendants accompanied Lord Cathcart to the Russian woman's funeral. Not even Caulaincourt required that much attention at a court function.

Though John's status in St. Petersburg seemed to be fading faster than the comet's tail, he received hope for deliverance. Romanzoff summoned Adams to a meeting. Alexander may have been leading the Cossacks in battle, but he had not forgotten his American friend. The count delivered an imperial message. The emperor expressed his regret over the war between the United States and Great Britain. He was disappointed that the war would interfere with US-Russian trade relations. Adams knew that with English ships now openly admitted at Russian ports—instead of covertly—American merchants would have trouble competing and might lose their cargo. The problem was as bitter as the chests of English tea flowing into the ports. Alexander had an idea to solve the larger problem.

"It had occurred to the emperor that perhaps an amicable arrangement of the differences between the parties might be accomplished easily and speedily by indirect [rather] than by direct negotiation," John recorded of Romanzoff's explanation.

"Was [Adams] aware of any difficulty or obstacle on the part of the government of the United States if he [Alexander] should offer his mediation for the purpose of the effecting a pacification?"

Alexander wanted to mediate peace between the United States and England. What news indeed! A thousand thoughts must have pulsed through John's mind as he processed the opportunity, both for his country and his personal desire to return home.

"I answered that it was obviously impossible for me to speak on this sub-ject," John replied, explaining that his initial response was based on his general knowledge of his government, not on Madison's specific instructions or plans regarding the war and peace.

"I was very sure that whatever determination they might form upon the proposal of the emperor's mediation, they [President Madison and Congress] would receive and consider it as a new evidence of His Majesty's regard and friendship for the United States, and that I was not aware of any obstacle or difficulty which could occasion them to decline accepting it."

He then gave his personal opinion: "For myself, I so deeply lamented the very existence of the war that I should welcome any facility for bringing it to a just and honorable termination."

Romanzoff assured Adams that the czar himself had made the offer. "He thought an indirect negotiation conducted here, and aided by the conciliatory wishes of a friend to both parties, might smooth down difficulties."

Direct discussions might fail. Pretension and game playing could obscure compromise. Indirect negotiations through a third-party mediator would allow each side to more fully express its position. "To a mutual friend each party might exhibit all its complaints and all its claims."

Romanzoff had already suggested the idea to Cathcart, who promised to notify his government. John agreed to do the same. By approaching the new British ambassador first, however, the Russians seemed to be favoring him over their American friend.

⸺

As the days went on, reports of the Grande Armée taking Moscow gained credibility. Muddling the news were suggestions that Napoleon had already lost 150,000 soldiers to death and attrition from the long supply lines and murderous march from Paris to Russia. Then the information grew worse. Not only had the French taken Moscow, but they had also burned it. Capturing a capital—whether literal or symbolic—was common; burning it was barbaric.

By September 29 the Russian government officially reported the occupa-tion of Moscow, which the French had invaded eleven days earlier following the Battle of Borodino, seventy miles west of Moscow. Russian commander in chief Mikhail Kutuzov tried to block the French advance at Borodino. The Russians lost 45,000 casualties to death, wounding, or capture; the French, 30,000. The Grande Armée followed the retreating Cossacks to Moscow. To preserve the Russian Army, Kutuzov abandoned Moscow.

Over the next few days, John had several opportunities to converse with Mr. Laval, the former French consul, who was preparing to depart for Sweden with his wife and children. They spoke privately at a dinner party at Laval's home, where he told John what he knew. Twice the Russians tried to burn the houses adjacent to the Moscow mansion where Napoleon took up headquarters. French troops retaliated by setting several buildings on fire at once. Abandoning Moscow, the Russian army then welcomed the French by releasing inmates from the prison. "It is feared that the whole city may be destroyed."

The French mistakenly thought that Napoleon's capture of Moscow would push Alexander to the peace table and return him to the Continental System. Laval saw it for what it was. The move had the opposite effect. The idea of negotiating peace with Napoleon was now "offensive to the emperor, and so it [the war] would continue, unless his army should be defeated, which it had not yet been."

"His [Alexander] spirit stiffens with adversity. The situation of the French army in the midst of their triumphs is considered as absolutely desperate."

John asked him why the war had begun.

"Women! Women! Women!" Laval proclaimed. "Women had been the cause of all the late disastrous wars against France."

Adams was amused at his friend's rant.

"It was unquestionably the late queen of Prussia who had caused the Prussian war. It was the late empress of Austria who had produced that last Austrian war. And it was Grand Duchess Catherine who had occasioned the present war."

The Russian duchess was responsible for this war because she refused to marry Napoleon. Their union would have ensured a long-term alliance between the two nations. For the moment, Laval was correct. Austria, the home nation of Napoleon's current wife, was allied with France against Russia.

"The time of real danger to the invader is now but just commencing, and it is a species of warfare to which Napoleon is not accustomed, and for which he may not be prepared," Adams wrote in his diary.

Indeed. Alexander's scorched earth policy had just begun.

The personal situation of the Lavals saddened Adams. They were similar in age and family status. Laval had come to Russia to flee the French Revolution. He was leaving his exile in the same spirit—the need to survive.

"They are to go in five or six days. They both appear to be much dejected. They are fugitives from one of the most magnificent establishments in St. Petersburg, a house where splendor and hospitality went hand in hand. They are going with the family of small children, literally they know not where, and to return they know not when," John reflected sadly.

Most of John and Louisa's friends had fled while they remained stuck in St. Petersburg.

"We shall have scarcely any acquaintance left," observed John.

⟶

Louisa's grief led her to many places that autumn—down the avenues of doubt, guilt, denial, depression, and nightmares. Like that of the Russians, her greatest obstacle was the enemy within. Her mind was as dark as an arctic winter's day.

Needing some way to process her thoughts, she began using a new journal on October 22. Bound by boards decorated with marble paper, the book felt firm in her hands. The leather spine was just as sturdy but far more flexible than the board. The paper was handmade and a little coarse, lacking the sophistication of perfectly trimmed pager edges. But what better place was there to pour out raw emotions than on crude sheets of paper? Like its owner, the book's beautiful exterior concealed its rough contents.

"I have procured this book with a view to write my thoughts and if possible to avoid dwelling on the secret and bitter reproaches of my heart for my conduct as it regarded my lost adored child, whose death was surely occasion'd by procrastination."

Procrastination was a surprising choice of words, but it reflected her depression. She had not forgotten the Russian ladies who predicted that her daughter was born for heaven. Their words haunted her. Should her daughter have died sooner? Louisa's thoughts may have been irrational, but they were honest.

The next day she added, "[S]till my mind dwells on the past and nothing can fill the dreadful void in my heart, and my babe's image pursues me wherever I go."

Had she done something wrong? Was her daughter's death a punishment?

"Bitter reflection adds to my pangs and in religion alone do I find consolation." She confessed her sins, throwing herself before the "conviction of the justice and mercy of my God." She believed the Almighty would give her the strength to change and subdue the pride in her heart in "which all my errors spring."

Her journal absorbed her guilt, sins, and depression without passing judgment. The next day her entry was short. She agreed to rejoin society and capture "a little [of] the sameness of my sister's life." With Kitty and William, she visited the theater, where a year earlier she had compared domestic and historical tragedies, never expecting to become an actor and her home the stage.

"I visited the theatre. [W]hile I was there I was amused," she wrote.

The outing was only a temporary balm. As soon as she stepped into the familiar sounds and smells of their apartments, her heart split open once again. "But on my return to my home, how cold, blank and dreadful! [My] first object used to be my child, but alas now I see only the spot on which she died and everything recalls her last agonies."

Louisa's depression also led to dissension in her marriage. The moment started simply enough. As usual she read prayers aloud to Charles.

"It has been my practice for some time to teach Charles his prayers and the commandments. Mr. A expressed himself dissatisfied with my method," she explained.

Louisa couldn't handle her husband's criticism. Her anger led to flight. "And I suffer'd myself to be hurried away by my temper in a very unbecoming manner."

He couldn't see how hard she was trying to be a good mother. Charles was the only child she had left, at least in St. Petersburg. Nothing was working— not going to the theater, not teaching her son. Nothing could alleviate her pain.

"I am peculiarly unfortunate for what I undertake with the best intentions almost always turns out exactly contrary. I read. I work. I endeavor to occupy myself usefully but it is all in vain. My heart is almost broken and my temper, which was never good, suffers in proportion to my grief."

Louisa was determined to correct her faults—perhaps out of fear that something else tragic would happen. She needed to give herself grace, some room to let her hair down instead of nit-picking her shortcomings. She was expecting too much of herself, and perhaps those around her were expecting too much of her as well.

"For those I love, no sacrifice will ever be too great for me to make. All I claim is a little indulgence," she wrote, revealing that she perceived John's rebuke as harsh.

From her perspective, her husband simply did not understand. His patience seemed as thin as the silk stockings he had to wear with his full court suit to the palace.

"I feel what a burden I must be to all around me, and it is this which has made me so solicitous to return home."

The death of her daughter made her heart cry out even louder for her sons. She longed to escape the prison of St. Petersburg. It was time—past time—to leave this so-called honorable exile.

"There is something in an American life more active and varied and the idea of seeing my children was an object on which my mind could rest with real pleasure."

John's reserved emotions and high expectations were not what she needed in this time. His grief led him to increase his attention to Charles's education, particularly mathematics, and take him on long walks. By keeping his emotions to himself, John seemed cold to her heartache. She knew there was someone in their family who would understand her suffering, whose heart had experienced the loneliness and despair marked by the loss of a daughter.

"In Mrs. Adams, I should have found a comforter, a friend who would pity my sufferings, which *she* would have understood," she emphasized.

Susanna, John's younger sister, had died on February 4, 1770, at age thirteen months, the same age as baby Louisa. Oh, how Abigail could have comforted her! For now the board-bound book with its crude handmade paper would have to do.

News from the war between the United States and England understandably came much more slowly than the hurried horseback messengers beating the roads from Moscow. Mr. Harris delivered the latest startling report found in the *English Courier*.

The USS *Constitution* had defeated the HMS *Guerriere* at sea on August 19, 1812. After being chased by a British squadron off the coast of New Jersey, the USS *Constitution* had sailed east of Boston, where it had been commissioned fifteen years earlier. Led by the plucky Isaac Hull, the *Constitution* came across the *Guerriere*. Under fire Hull maneuvered his ship within musket-firing range and launched a successful broadside at the British warship. After thirty minutes of violent and close action, the *Guerriere* was such a wreck that it had to be burned after its defeat.

Because so many of the British shots failed to penetrate the *Constitution's* oak sides, the American sailors gave their vessel the nickname "Old Ironsides." For a US ship to win a battle at sea against the best navy in the world was an astonishing feat. Suddenly Congress's decision in January against building twenty-two more warships, as Madison had requested, now seemed foolish.

The news, however, was not all good, not by a cannon shot. Years earlier President Jefferson had named distinguished Revolutionary War veteran General William Hull—who had adopted his orphaned nephew, Isaac Hull— as governor of the Michigan territory. Madison subsequently looked to General Hull to capture Fort Detroit and launch an assault into Canada. Hull's initial efforts were successful. He captured Fort Detroit on July 5, 1812, and moved into Canada on July 12. "Suffering from the residual effects of a stroke in 1811 and aged 59, Hull cut an unimpressive figure." Then the tired, corpulent general, known for excessive drinking, wasted two weeks preparing for an assault on a nearby puny fort.

Meanwhile British General Isaac Brock had enough time to move a small, elite army to Detroit, where Brock called on Hull to capitulate. Brock scared Hull with threats of an attack and massacre of women and children led by Shawnee Chief Tecumseh and his combined forces. At the same time these tribes swarmed Hull's two-hundred-mile-long supply line, weakening it and validating Brock's scare tactics. Perhaps under the influence of too much liquor, Hull began to break down. His erratic behavior included crouching in corners, trembling as he spoke, and drooling at the corners of his mouth. Without a fight Hull surrendered Fort Detroit to the British on August 16. His defeat completely erased any hope of capturing Upper Canada. Worse, America lost vital territorial gains to the British and Native Americans in Ohio and the entire Northwest Territory.

John knew very little of this at the time, only the outcome, which horrified him: "There are scarcely any details of the affair given. The honor of my country—O God! Suffer it not to go unredeemed."

49

Impressment

WHILE THE RUSSIAN GOVERNMENT POSTED HANDBILLS ASSURING St. Petersburg residents that they were safe from invasion, the loss of Moscow was too serious to ignore. Rest would not come until the enemy within became the enemy expelled.

"About noon this day a report of cannon fire from the fortress announced that important and pleasing intelligence from the armies had been received," Adams recorded on October 27.

Mr. Harris discovered the reason for the victorious salutes and hurried over to the Adams residence to tell his boss the good news. Moscow was back in Russian hands. A corps under the leadership of General Wintzingerode retook the city, though the French captured Wintzingerode. At noon the palace summoned John, the other diplomats, and the Russian nobility to a Te Deum celebration. That night residents lit lanterns on their doorsteps, illuminating the city in celebration. The Moscow victory was sweeter than any French wine but with a far more satisfying aftertaste. Hope for ultimate victory lingered.

"The passions of almost all the politicians whom I now see and hear are concentrated upon the head of one man. It seems almost universally to be considered that the destinies of mankind hang upon his life alone," John wrote after dining at the home of Mr. Krehmer, one of his few friends left in town. Everywhere Adams went, he heard about the desire to kill Napoleon. Everyone had an opinion.

"I know not how it has been with former conquerors during their lives, but I believe there never was a human being who united against himself such a massive execration and abhorrence as this man has done."

John now had little business to occupy him. He occasionally conversed with Count Romanzoff, who had returned from the battlefield. Until he heard from President Madison or Secretary Monroe on the US acceptance or rejection of the czar's offer to mediate the war with England, John did not have much to do. With the Orders in Council repealed, he mulled over what now mattered the most in making peace with England: the practice of impressment, the moral cause behind the war.

He picked up a book on philosophy, whose English author had been a strong advocate for abolishing the slave trade. Though the trade itself had ceased five years earlier, the practice of slavery continued.

"The trade is beyond question an abomination, disgraceful to the human character," John reflected, hoping that slavery would be outlawed one day.

Like his father and mother, Adams abhorred slavery. His family managed their Massachusetts farms with tenants and paid laborers, not slaves. The practice of impressment bothered him just as much as slavery. Impressment was the act of forcibly taking someone into military service. It was one thing for the British to compel lads from the English countryside into wearing the redcoat uniform; it was another to take Americans from US ships and force them to turn their coats from blue to red.

"[F]or the impressment of seamen is to all intents and purposes a practice as unjust, as immoral, as base, as oppressive and as tyrannical as the slave trade."

While he admired the author's abolitionist views, he saw hypocrisy too. Adams wrote:

Yet the same members of the British Parliament, who have been the greatest zealots for abolishing the slave trade, are not only inflexible adherents to the practice of impressments among their own people, but are now waging a rancorous war against the United States to support the practice of their officers in impressing men from American merchant vessels on the high seas. Every particle of argument [that] can bear up against the slave trade bears with equal force against impressment.

He would never forget the forlorn looks of his countrymen trapped in Kristiansand, Norway, on his ocean voyage to St. Petersburg three years earlier. Those merchants had lost their cargo and ships, but they had not lost their identity as American citizens. They had not been captured by the British and impressed into His Majesty's navy. But many sailors had. Likewise he would never forget the fear in the eyes of the lad from Charleston, who was nearly taken from the *Horace* by an English officer.

By 1812 the British had impressed as many as nine thousand American citizens. Now many of these same Americans were being forced to fight against the country of their birth or of their adoption. Such injustice! This crime was the strongest proof that US sovereignty was in name only. The king of England may have lost America during the Revolutionary War, but he had found a way to enslave US independence nonetheless, suppressing it through impressments. If independence depended in part on John Adams in 1776, actual independence now depended in part on John Quincy Adams and the War of 1812.

———

The mind can be a dark place. Louisa's psyche became her worst enemy, plaguing her with ideas she had never entertained. Her depression took a dangerous turn.

"My thoughts have been so very gloomy that I have refrained from writing some time, and I dare not commit to paper all that passes in my mind," she wrote in her journal in early November. Though she tried to "fly from them," her efforts were in vain.

Depression deepened. Nightmares haunted her. Her mind tapped her visual memory of her daughter and other deceased loved ones and twisted them into horrific scenes. As long as her eyelids were closed, these visions seemed as real as her bed: "My babe's image flits forever before my eyes and seems to reproach me with her death."

Louisa blamed herself: "Necessity alone induced me to wean her and in doing it I lost her."

She couldn't help wondering what would have happened had she continued to nurse. Did weaning baby Louisa too early lead to her sickness and dysentery? One dream took Louisa to a house where she'd lived as a child. Her daughter was there, and so were her deceased father and sister Nancy.

"I was playing with my babe, who appeared in full health, when I was suddenly called by my father, who was sitting in the next room with a party of gentlemen to beg that I would go down into the cellar to fetch him some wine."

Feeling afraid, she agreed but asked Nancy to go with her.

"We descended a flight of steps which appeared to lead to a deep vault, and at the bottom of the stairs, I stumbled and fell over a body newly murder'd from which the blood still appear'd to stream. I arose with difficulty and looked for my sister who seem'd to stand as if immovable and as if just risen from the grave not withstanding my terror."

Instead of running up the stairs to tell her father about the murder, Louisa took him some wine. "Methought I got three bottles and carried them to my father, who upon examining them told me that they were bottles of Port which was entirely spoilt."

Nightmares are often strange narratives. "With the usual inconsistency of dreams, I got over all these painful impressions and was as at first playing with my child who was all life and animation."

In another dream, a storm sparked vivid flashes of lightning toward the heavens. "I was left alone in indescribable terror. I fell upon my knees and implored the mercy of heaven."

Then the thunder and lightning suddenly ceased. "And I raised my eyes and beheld as it were a stream of fire which extended completely across the heavens in which was distinctly written 'be of good cheer[;] thy petition is granted'—I fell flat upon my face in a swoon and awoke."

Soon the desire for death left her dream world and became real.

"I struggle in vain against the affliction that consumes me, and I feel that all my wishes center in the grave," she wrote. "I am a useless being in this world . . . surely it is no crime to pray for death. [I]f it is wickedness, I implore thy mercy, O Lord, to cleanse my heart and to teach me to bear my trials with fortitude."

Depression deeply impressed Louisa's mind, overtaking her longtime yearning to be reunited with George and John. "My heart is buried in my Louisa's grave, and my greatest longing is to be laid beside her, even the desire of seeing my beloved boys gives way to this idea [of] cherished hope."

50

Retreat

"[T]HERE WAS A REPORT CIRCULATING IN THE CITY THAT BONAPARTE [he is now nothing more than plain Bonaparte] was killed," John wrote on December 8.

"We afterwards, in the course of the day, heard the same report from two other quarters; and even that his body had been found after a battle."

———

John had first heard of the Battle of Krasnoi nearly two weeks earlier on the morning of November 25, when the master of ceremonies sent a messenger requesting his attendance at an impromptu victory service at the Cathedral of Our Lady of Kazan.

Adams had walked along the Kazan's mosaic tile floor many times. When the emperor opened the Latin-cross-shaped cathedral in 1811, he made sure the diplomats received several opportunities to admire its fifty-six interior pink granite Corinthian columns and massive chandelier. Alexander's father, Paul, envisioned the cathedral as a rival to St. Peter's Basilica in Rome, which is why Kazan's dome soars more than 230 feet above a colonnade of ninety-six columns arranged in an arch. The cathedral's purpose was to pay homage to the Russian church's highest icon, Our Lady of Kazan, whom the Russians credited for ending the Polish occupation of Russia in 1612.

As soon as John stepped into the cathedral that day, he couldn't help noticing the obvious. Standing in front of the bejeweled lady icon were trophies from the Battle of Krasnoi. Chief among them was a truncheon, a spear-shaped club. What made this baton special was not its size or shape but its owner. The club belonged to Louis-Nicolas Davout, one of the French field marshals defeated by the Russians from November 15 to 18 in several skirmishes in and around Krasnoi.

"It is the greatest victory that the Russians have gained since the war commenced, and is perfectly decisive of the fate of the campaign and of the Emperor Napoleon's main army," Adams observed.

During his invasion of Russia, Napoleon had chosen Smolensk as one of several supply depots. When Alexander failed to negotiate after the burning of Moscow, Napoleon abandoned the now useless burnt city and retreated 260 miles to Smolensk, which he planned to make his winter headquarters. Brutal subzero temperatures, starvation, and supply losses had degraded his army so much that he decided to continue his retreat rather than stay in Smolensk.

Thinking the Russian army was as worn down by the weather as his was, Napoleon miscalculated Russian commander in chief Kutuzov's capabilities and location. As a result Bonaparte ordered his dwindling army to march from Smolensk to nearby Krasnoi in waves, leaving at separate times and on separate days. They marched in linear columns, not battle-ready blocks. Napoleon himself led his Imperial Guard.

Though failing to launch an all-out assault, Kutuzov took advantage of the situation. Among the booty they captured was French marshal Louis-Nicolas Davout's personal baggage, which included maps and his beloved truncheon. Fewer than thirty thousand remained of the Grande Armée.

"Joy and triumph were upon every countenance" who entered the church. Each time someone arrived, the person next to him whispered the exciting news about Krasnoi. Each face brightened in succession, as if lighting candles.

"It is now morally impossible that the remnant of them should escape. In every probability they are at this hour all prisoners of war. He is lost without resource," John observed.

Alexander and the imperial family led the congregation and "performed their prostrations to the miraculous image of the Virgin." Religion and government were so intertwined in Russia that it was hard to know where one ended and the other began.

"The emperor, on leaving the church, was greeted with loud shouts of the populace."

The enemy within was close to being without an army. This latest victory launched an earthquake of convulsions that could be felt more than sixteen hundred miles to Paris. The aftershocks were not known. But by early December, the hope of Bonaparte's death was very real.

"The crisis is great and awful beyond all example. Almighty God, grant that it may turn to good! To peace! To the relief of mankind from the dreadful calamities of unbridled ambition."

Meanwhile Louisa continued to face her enemy within. "It is long since I have written. My spirits are still dreadful and nothing but constant occupation prevents me from dwelling with unremitted sorrow for my irreparable loss," she wrote on November 27.

She tried to distract her mind by reading books, including a biography of the mistress of Henry II of France. The woman had lived forty years "of uninterrupted virtue" only to be seduced by the teenage Henry. "How often when we think we have attained to the highest state of perfection, of which human nature is capable, are we dashed from our elevation and degraded to the lowest stations of infamy?"

As she thought about how fragile human virtue can be, no matter how great the talent, her mind naturally turned to Napoleon: "We behold here, the emperor of France, after sixteen years of the most unheard of successes, in the short space of one month, plunged into all the horrors of extreme distress, flying for his life, pursued by barbarians, a revolt in his country, his army totally overthrown, and surrounded by treachery, dashed instantaneously from the summit of splendor, into such a scene of horror, and calamity."

Louisa may have been depressed, but she was not losing her mind. Her analysis of Napoleon was as sharp as a bayonet: "The character of this man produces unceasing astonishment, and we cannot trace his rise and see his fall, without shuddering at the length to which a blind and inexhaustible ambition will lead mankind. And though conscious of the justice of his fall, we shrink with pity and horror from a fate so dreadful, so hopeless."

She did not know whether his downfall included his death.

By December 7, 1812, Adams had received official notification from the US government about the war with England. Although the declaration was six months old, he needed to clarify a few points and update Romanzoff.

"The first was the desire of the United States that this war might be confined to them and Great Britain, that no other power might be involved in it," he told the count.

The US government did not consider itself at war with any of England's allies and wanted to continue its amicable relationship with Russia. Romanzoff told Adams that America's desire for ongoing commercial relations with Russia would be "peculiarly agreeable to the emperor."

Adams, however, couldn't communicate what he most wanted to tell the count. He didn't know whether Madison had accepted Alexander's offer to mediate. Romanzoff also updated Adams. The British government had not accepted the czar's mediation proposal, but neither had they rejected it. Lord Cathcart hinted that Parliament was waiting until the outcome of the 1812 US presidential election with hopes that Madison would lose. Believing the British were stonewalling, John plainly gave his opinion: "I believed the emperor's proposal would be very acceptable, whatever the event of our election might be."

Romanzoff asked if the US government's position had changed since Parliament revoked the Orders in Council.

"It had not, but that although I was satisfied, if that revocation had been known, the declaration of war would not have been made."

Knowing that Russia might mediate, Adams used his best legal argument to persuade the count about the main moral issue behind the war: "Upon the chief of these, the impressment of seamen from our merchant vessels, it appeared the British government would listen to nothing." This practice made it impossible for the United States to have a "sense of independence."

The count challenged attorney Adams. Didn't the British complain that they'd lost great numbers of men, who claimed to be naturalized Americans?

"It was not exactly that. There were very few British sailors who ever were or could be naturalized as Americans." Adams explained the conditions for naturalization outlined by US law and noted that "few foreign seamen can avail themselves of them." The problem was economics, not national loyalty.

"The American sea service, public and private, was more attractive than the British, for our common seamen were better fed, better paid and better treated than English seamen are wont to be in their own service. It was natural therefore for English sailors to prefer our service to their own, and to seize every opportunity they could of entering it."

Rather than improve their system, the English opted to kidnap Americans instead. "And they have no other remedy against it, than that violent and tyrannical practice of their naval officers, of stealing men from our merchant vessels. I did not know that it would be possible ever to come to a compromise with them upon it."

John put forward a bold suggestion. If the Americans could not solve impressment through war, perhaps "he, the count, would furnish us with one [a solution]" through a peace treaty.

Though persuaded by his friend's logical argument, Romanzoff could not promise to advocate against impressment. For now all they could do was wait to hear whether or not the US and British governments would agree to the mediation.

———

In the days that followed, new information emerged. Though defeated, the nucleus of Napoleon's army had slipped past a Russian officer and escaped over the border. For all their successes, the Russians were as much indebted to famine and frost for the French army's demise as their own might. Dead men littered the roads. Those who survived were so sick with dysentery that the route out of Russia toward Courland was a long, continuous latrine. Napoleon miscalculated the severity of Russia's winter, which at thirty degrees below zero was more frigid than usual from the atmospheric changes of the fading comet.

By December 9 a credible report arrived in town.

"The news of the Emperor Napoleon's being killed is not authenticated." Napoleon was not dead. He had escaped.

Louisa continued to immerse her mind in all sorts of books, particularly French biographies. However, dealing with depression is more than just finding distractions. A depressed person often has difficulty facing new problems that arise from everyday life.

"Kitty has been very sick and the doctor kindly told me that if we did not make haste and return home that the climate would kill us both."

Louisa's response revealed the depth of her depression: "To me there is nothing frightful in this idea. I am only desirous of mingling my ashes with those of my lovely babe."

She believed her petition was well thought out, not a crazy whim: "I know myself I never was calmer or easier in mind and body than I am at this moment."

Her wish to die now surpassed her hope for reunion with her sons.

As 1812 came to a close, John discovered the latest news from America while playing cards with Louisa and Kitty. When Mr. Harris brought him a special edition of the *London Gazette*, he learned that the British had defeated US forces as they attempted to cross the Niagara River border into Canada in the Battle of Queenston Heights on October 13, 1812. The casualties were severe, with ninety Americans killed, one hundred wounded, and eight hundred captured.

Adams felt distress and shame for "one who loves his country." He noted, "The reliance of man in all cases can only be upon heaven. God grant that these disasters instead of sinking may rouse the spirit of the nation."

More certain than the war's outcome was the comet's fate. What was first seen in France in March 1811 disappeared from the skies as the year 1812 evaporated. For the Adamses, two wars and personal tragedy were more than enough to say farewell to the worst year of their lives.

At the time, they did not know of a recent coincidence. The last of Napoleon's army had surpassed Russia's borders and reached the Baltic Sea by December 19, the very day that Alexander had made a surprising decision for the leader of an army that had just evicted the enemy. Instead of retiring, the czar chose to continue the war and chase Napoleon toward Paris. Burnt Moscow illuminated his soul. As far as he was concerned, it was either him or Napoleon. They could no longer reign in Europe at the same time.

"The Emperor Alexander is gone to the army, I suppose he intends to become as famous in pursuit as he is in retreat," Louisa observed.

51

Dry Bones

MRS. CABOT WAS SERIOUSLY ILL. IF SHE PASSED AWAY, SHE WOULD be buried next to the infant Adams in St. Petersburg's English graveyard. The possibility was too much. Louisa couldn't let Mrs. Cabot have the spot next to her daughter. In her mind that dirt belonged to only one person—Louisa Catherine Johnson Adams.

"They tell me that Mrs. Cabot is likely to die, and I cannot describe the terror I feel, lest they should usurp the little spot of earth which I have set my heart on that adjoins my Louisa's grave," she wrote in her diary in March 1813.

"In vain I reason with myself, the desire is uncontrollable, and my mind is perpetually dwelling upon some means to procure this desired blessing."

Except to be buried in it, Louisa had no interest in sliding into her silver tissue ball gown or silk threads of any other color the winter of 1813. She also had scant need to wear her fanciest dresses. St. Petersburg's eighteen-hour nights made life gloomy in any winter, but this season was the worst to date for the Adamses. They had little to occupy their minds; no balls or parties to attend. The social scene was as dead as dry bones in a graveyard.

Leading troops on the frontier gave Alexander insight into the plight of the Russian common man in a way he had never known. He heard the wailing and mourning that rattled the shacks throughout his land. People were reduced to beggary. As a result, he banned entertaining at the Winter Palace, especially on his birthday. This great bear of Russia couldn't bear for anyone to taste wine, enjoy stringed melodies, or pleasantly touch a lady's hand during a polonaise while soldiers were dying on the battlefield.

"The emperor's birthday which, for the first time since I had been here, passed over without any celebration and almost without notice," John had observed months earlier at the beginning of the social season.

By the time of Mrs. Cabot's illness, letters from home seemed even more absent than in years past to the Adamses. Louisa had no fresh samples of her boys' handwriting to admire or updates about the subjects they were studying. The two great wars severely restricted the arrival of any kind of mail, whether by ship or by land. They had nothing but books to occupy them. John turned to Plato, Cicero, and other philosophers while she read the writings of a female French author.

Louisa was consumed by the letters of Madame Anne Marguerite Petit du Noyer, a Frenchwoman who had documented the negotiations of a treaty between Great Britain and France a century earlier. By sorting gossip from reality, Noyer had become an early journalist and a female one at that. Then her religious conversion from Catholicism to Calvinism cost her dearly in 1701, when she was banished from France.

Identifying with this woman's exile from her homeland, Louisa was so struck with the beauty of one of Noyer's poems that she copied fifteen lines of it into her diary. The poem spoke of the suffering of Christ for all humanity, explaining that though he possessed the rights of a sovereign, he lowered his head on the cross and chose death instead, like a human. Nature trembled in a fit. The sun faded "as if the world's end would have been close. He took sin from the heart of a stone." This reminder of the resurrection of Christ's dry bones gave Louisa eternal hope.

The prospect of leaving St. Petersburg, however, appeared quite dead. The best evidence came from John's diary on March 17, 1813: "I sent for my landlord, Mr. Strogofshikoff, and paid him a half-year's rent in advance."

In a letter to Secretary James Monroe the previous October, Adams had requested a recall as planned: "It has, indeed, constantly been my wish not to be continued in the mission here beyond the ensuing spring, and I suggested this desire to the president as early as last February [1812]."

His decision had not changed, but the world had. Traveling through the waters of Europe and into the Atlantic would have been difficult and risky in peacetime, much less under the extreme duress of cannon fire. Before he left Boston in 1809, he thought the voyage to St. Petersburg on the *Horace* would escape the whims of war. The dueling Danish and the English blockade proved him wrong. With all of Europe now in upheaval and the United States at war with England, traveling by ship would be more dangerous now.

"I still retain it, subject to the supposition that my return to the United States with my family should be practicable, which in the event of the continuance of our war with Great Britain it would scarcely be."

Adams had also suggested, but did not insist, that Madison appoint someone else to handle the mediation if he accepted Alexander's offer. Without any real business to conduct and the prospect for returning home chained to the outcome of both wars, all they could do was wait for battle updates. Fresh news of Alexander's pursuit of Napoleon brought occasional showers to their dry lives.

"[Strogofshikoff] conversed with me, as he always does, upon politics, and upon the character of the Russian people. He is very well satisfied with the present state and prospect of affairs, and thinks the Emperor Alexander might now come home and take his ease."

After the Cossacks took Warsaw, officials brought back the Polish city's two brass keys and displayed them at the Kazan Church. More thirst-quenching news came via an army courier. The Cossacks would soon be in Berlin. What was even more refreshing was the alliance between Russia and Prussia. The Russians now possessed a key ally.

The reason for Strogofshikoff's hope of Alexander's near return was a simple equation. Now that fifty thousand Prussians had turned against France and joined Russia, perhaps the czar would transfer his field command to a general.

News from the war between the United States and Great Britain was not as hopeful. America's successes at sea—the taking of two British frigates—only mortified the pride of London, which subsequently turned the war of economic jealousy into a fight for revenge. The British navy retaliated by barricading the Chesapeake and Delaware Bays.

John believed it was another illegal blockade with malicious intent against Philadelphia and Baltimore, two of the three largest cities in the United States.

Propaganda fueled rumors. English newspapers propelled the story that the new US minister to France was so attached to Napoleon that he had followed him to Moscow. This was untrue.

Tattoo them. That was the remedy for impressment prescribed by Sir Francis d'Ivernois, the most eccentric knighted Brit now living in St. Petersburg. The English were swarming the city like bees with poison in their pens. Sir Francis was among them. Adams could hardly believe his ears that March day in 1813 when he learned of the man's unusual solution.

"As to the question of impressment, he [Sir Francis] said he did not see how that could be settled unless all the sailors in the British navy would submit to be tattooed with a G. R. in Indian ink upon the arm; but he doubted whether they would consent to that," John recorded.

G. R. meant *Georgius Rex,* a reference to King George imprinted on British coins. Sir Francis was far from flippant. He was not joking.

"This is the strangest expedient, I believe, that was ever devised; but he mentioned it seriously."

The idea of tattooing British sailors to distinguish them from Americans was the most outrageous solution that Adams had heard. Originally from Switzerland, Francis was a naturalized British citizen. On his first day at the Russian court, he asked to be introduced to John. He knew Adams's father in England. Yet each conversation the younger Adams held with the man proved to be as unbelievable as the one before. His exaggeration and over-the-top ideas made him quite a character, which was fitting for the British agent—or spy—that he likely was.

John and the eccentric Brit talked about many subjects, including the American Revolution. Sir Francis believed that the loss of America was the beginning of King George III's madness.

"As Sir Francis is under personal obligations to the King of England, I did not think it suitable to tell him what I thought—that he had mistaken the cause for the effect," Adams wryly wrote.

One of Sir Francis's current claims surprised him nearly as much as the tattoo option: "He very stoutly contends that the British ministers deplore the war with America."

Adams asked why he thought Parliament opposed the war. Amazingly, Francis was one of the last people to speak to Prime Minister Perceval before his assassination. He had left him five minutes before the murder. Francis believed this was Perceval's war, and the current leadership under Lord Liverpool wanted a way to end it.

"Sir Francis appeared to hope that the war between America and England would yet be short."

Adams hoped the same but doubted it.

⁓

Louisa's depression continued. Not even fresh correspondence from home cheered her for very long.

"We have at length received letters from America—which bring favorable accounts of the health of our friends and my dear children," she wrote with relief on April 4.

Her depression was so heavy and her perspective so disjointed that she now seriously doubted she would ever see her older children again: "To hear from them once in six or seven months is all that is left me as my prospect of ever seeing them more is now alas hopeless."

Likely Mrs. Cabot recovered because Louisa continued to claim that dirt: "I scarcely can define my feelings much as I wish to see my children. My heart is torn at the idea of quitting forever the spot where my darling lays and to which my whole soul is linked."

Weighing on her was the realization that her husband had extended their lease for another six months: "My health, the climate, and this dreadful war have added to the improbability of our return this summer."

George's and John's letters provided a positive effect. Her husband's suggestion that she read a book on diseases of the mind may have also nudged her to pick up her pen and open her heart to someone who would understand her.

"I have just closed a letter to Mrs. Adams. It is the first I have written for many months and it has rent my heart afresh."

The letter was stingingly honest. She tried to control the "pang of my bursting heart" and asked for Abigail's compassion, not condemnation: "Had you witnessed the horrid circumstances of my angel's death you would pity and forgive me, my heart is almost broken, my health is gone, and my peace of mind is I fear forever destroy'd, dreadful."

Searching for answers, Louisa continued to blame herself for her baby's death.

⌁

About the same time, John was becoming more restless with each dour report. He learned on April 17 from a newspaper that US General James Winchester and more than one thousand men were taken prisoner in Canada at the Battle of Frenchtown. Only thirty escaped. The victorious British general left many of these imprisoned Americans under the guard of his Native American allies, who killed as many as sixty of the war prisoners. Called the River Raisin Massacre, the slaughter became a rallying cry for later efforts to control Lake Erie. Despite this catastrophe, John received good news. The USS *Constitution* had destroyed another British frigate.

The War of 1812, as it would later be called, defied logic. Americans should have been strong on land and weak at sea. The upside-down reality did not escape the notice of Count Romanzoff, who brought up the issue at a dinner party.

"How happens it that you are constantly beating at sea the English, who beat all the rest of the world, and that on land, where you ought to be the strongest, the English *do what they please?*" Romanzoff asked with emphasis in an inquisitive but good-natured tone.

Adams pleasantly responded with evidence from the Bible's Ecclesiastes. "I knew not how to account for it, unless by supposing that these times were reserved to keep the world in a continued state of wonder, and to prove that there is something new under the sun."

The count replied with his own biblical allusion: "There had once been a confusion of tongues, and now . . . was the time for confusion of mind."

In a separate private meeting about this time, Romanzoff and John also discussed the latest news from France, which was as intriguing as a novel. With Bonaparte being pursued, King Louis XVIII had issued a proclamation to the people of France. He was ready to take his country back. To Adams, the idea of France returning to a monarchy "reminded me of the resurrection of dry bones in the prophet of Ezekiel."

The dry bones of France's royal family were ready to be resurrected in place of Napoleon. Romanzoff agreed that sooner or later the Bourbons would reclaim France: "It was certain that never since the commencement of the French Revolution had there been so many obstacles removed to the return of the Bourbons as there was at present."

Romanzoff did not believe that the French emperor's overthrow would instantly bring peace to Europe. Adams agreed: "Napoleon might be considered as the Don Quixote of monarchy."

Bonaparte had overthrown many monarchs. Through the pretense of liberty and the backing of a puppet constitution, he had become a monarch behind the mask of emperor. People either loved or hated him. Napoleon was on the run but not quite ready to surrender. The Cossacks thought his political and military careers were near death, but his bones weren't quite dry.

———⟶———

Confusing reports continued to come from the ever-changing center of battle. Adams was beckoned to another Te Deum at the Winter Palace on May 13. This service celebrated a victory of Russian troops over the French army near Lutzen, which is twelve miles from Leipzig in Prussia, or present-day Germany.

"We were told that the Emperor Alexander actually commanded—was on the field, and twice rallied his troops—but he chose to have the Te Deum at the chapel and not at the Kazan church to avoid appearance of ostentation."

John was surprised that the palace called for a Te Deum when so few details were known. Early reports suggested that fifteen thousand Frenchmen were killed and sixteen cannon taken. Absent was information about Russian losses. More confusing details came forward days after the Te Deum. Some reports suggested that more than twenty-five thousand Frenchmen were slain and thirty-six cannon were captured. The Russians and Prussians were in full pursuit of the fugitives. Within a week Mr. Harris heard that the battle was not nearly as decisive. The outcome was merely the Russian possession of the battlefield. By the end of May, the news was worse. The Russians and the Prussians were retreating, while the French were threatening Berlin.

"The situation of things is critical in the highest degree," John wrote in his diary.

In the midst of all this, John learned that the *Hornet,* an eighteen-gun US sloop of war, had defeated the eighteen-gun Royal Navy brig *Peacock* on February 24, 1813. America's miracles at sea remained a treasure chest of hope.

The news from Europe continued in a confusing clash of couriers. William Smith first heard the most disastrous report on June 6 that a three-day battle resulted in a total defeat of the Russian and Prussian armies. The French were said to be in possession of Hamburg. A few days later another report repudiated it and gave the truth. The combined armies were not defeated but had merely retreated to distract the French.

"Napoleon and his army are again in the most imminent danger of having their retreat cut off. In these last battles he lost nearly double the number of men that the combined army did, and prisoners and cannon—whereas they lost none."

They also heard that Napoleon sent Caulaincourt to Alexander's headquarters, but the czar refused to see him.

Soon fresh news proved better than any of the previous reports. The Austrians had declared war against Napoleon and turned on the man who had married their princess. The alliance sent the French Grande Armée retreating to Dresden. The allies were ready to chase the French back to Paris. If they succeeded, King Louis XVIII might just reclaim France. Dry bones would indeed be resurrected.

John also received hope for his resurrection. The prospect of breaking up his establishment in St. Petersburg might soon become a reality. He called on Romanzoff on June 15 to give him the news. The chancellor already knew of John's prospects for departing. His broad grin broke the long lines of his face.

"He then showed me a copy of Monroe's answer to the proposals."

Secretary of State Monroe accepted the mediation "in very handsome terms" and promised to send US negotiators to St. Petersburg. The count "was gratified that this measure had been so received by the United States."

"The report of Messrs Gallatin and Bayard being destined to come out as commissioners—of the accuracy of which I had my doubts," Adams told the count.

According to newspapers, US Treasury Secretary Albert Gallatin, a Republican, and US Senator James Bayard, a Federalist, were on a ship bound for St. Petersburg. Adams doubted they were coming for the mediation: "I presumed that a commission would be appointed, but I questioned whether they would be the men. Mr. Gallatin could not easily be spared, and he and Mr. Bayard were so opposed to each other and our politics that I thought it doubtful whether they would be joined in one commission."

Adams knew both of them. No pair could have been more opposite had Madison appointed former presidents Thomas Jefferson and John Adams to the same team. Romanzoff's reply, however, showed his savvy insight into a republic.

The count said, "In a government like [y]ours that might be the very reason for joining them, so that the great opposing interests might all be represented."

What Adams did not say in that moment was his personal political calculation. He suspected that one of the two men would replace him as minister to Russia and that the other would be a special envoy to the mediation.

Months earlier, when he wrote Monroe asking for a recall, he had suggested that the military vessel bringing his replacement should take him and his family home. He had not forgotten the agony of traveling on the merchant ship *Horace* instead of a military frigate or the embarrassment of traveling without a passport. He took great pains to prevent a repeat homeward-bound voyage.

One question remained. Had England accepted the mediation as well? Not yet. But neither were the British tattooing their sailors as Sir Francis suggested.

The count "did not think the mediation would be directly refused by the British government. It would cause some embarrassment to the ministry."

Negotiating for peace would have been one of the most honorable exits to Adams's "honorable exile." No matter. At least the prospect of leaving St. Petersburg was within sight. Though he did not have an honorable position waiting for him at home, his dry bones might be resurrected soon—so he thought.

PART 3

Journey Resurrected

EN ROUTE TO PARIS, FEBRUARY 1815

PORT DE MONTEBELLO, PARIS, PAR VICTOR-JEAN NICOLLE (1754–1826).
THIS IMAGE IS IN THE PUBLIC DOMAIN BECAUSE ITS COPYRIGHT HAS EXPIRED. WIKIMEDIA COMMONS.

52

Escape

DESPITE HER PAST FEELINGS, LOUISA CATHERINE JOHNSON ADAMS was certain about one fact as she heard the river ice crack that late afternoon in February 1815. She did not want to die as her carriage broke through the frozen Vistula River near Poland. More than that, she absolutely did not want to lose Charles.

"It required a violent effort in the horses to prevent the coach from upsetting on the bank," she recorded of the near-death encounter.

Although the ice gave way, her drivers' skill and the horses' determination saved Louisa, seven-year-old Charles, Madame Babet, and her servants from icy deaths. "We got over and reached the other side of the river in safety."

Shaken but relieved, they resumed their journey through this corner of Poland. Though the villages they passed were among the most filthy and beggarly that Louisa had ever seen, she was not fearful but grateful to be alive and en route toward Paris. She would do anything to feel the comfort of her husband's embrace once again. Thankfully they traveled without incident or delay until reaching Poland's border with Prussia.

"Here I had to wait three hours for horses, and the people were so much inclined to be impudent."

Such rudeness was somewhat surprising. After all, the Prussians had abandoned the French army to join Alexander, his Cossacks, the Austrians, and the Swedes in pursuit of Napoleon. After winning the Battle of Nations at Leipzig in October 1813, the allies had pushed the French emperor and his regrouped army five hundred miles back to his Parisian power center. When Alexander marched triumphantly into Paris in March 1814, Bonaparte abdicated. King Louis XVIII reclaimed the throne for the Bourbon family. Napoleon went into exile at the Tuscan island of Elba in April 1814.

The sight of the Russian insignia on Louisa's carriage window alarmed the Prussian border officer in spite of his country's alliance with the czar.

"I was obliged to produce my letter and to inform the master of the house, that I should write immediately to the [Russian] minister of the interior, and complain of his conduct," Louisa later wrote. Her threats to wield influence with Alexander's government worked.

"The man appeared to be much alarmed, made a great many apologies, and said the horses should be ready immediately."

There was a catch, of course. She would have to take two extra horses, six instead of four.

"He thought the carriage very heavy—This is an exaction to which travelers were constantly exposed, and to pay the tax was an absolute necessity if you wished to avoid delay."

What would John have done in that moment? Could he have convinced the border guard that they needed only four horses? Was the agent taking advantage of her because she was a woman traveling without a male protector? She expected to encounter such hardships on this journey, but matters of business and monetary transactions unraveled her insecurity more than other challenges.

"I cannot rely [at] all on my own judgment more especially as I have never before been obliged to rely on *myself*," she had complained with emphasis to John in a letter the previous summer.

She felt the same way now. Why did she have to make such a difficult journey alone? Everyone had abandoned her—her husband, their aides, her now married sister, and her chambermaid, Martha.

This was hardly the way she imagined escaping her so-called exile from Russia. So much in the past year had been beyond her control. Ever since John left her and Charles in April 1814—the same month that Napoleon went into exile—to travel to Göteborg, Sweden, he had promised to return to St. Petersburg as quickly as possible. During his absence, she'd tried to manage their finances by renting the cheapest place she could find. The apartment was too small, but she had done her best.

"Although I do everything in my power to lessen the expense, I am sure you will think me imprudent in the management of the house," she worriedly wrote to John.

Louisa faced what everyone in St. Petersburg confronted: post-Napoleonic war inflation. Horses were three times more expensive. Dresses for formal events now cost sixteen hundred rubles, more than twice the amount she had paid years earlier when they arrived in St. Petersburg.

Much had changed since then. Too much.

<hr />

The year 1813 did not immediately lead to John's escape from exile as he originally told Romanzoff in June when he thought Madison was sending someone to replace him. Instead John waited for months in anticipation that Alexander's offer to mediate a peace treaty between the United States and Britain would soon take place in St. Petersburg.

Madison initially responded by sending a two-man delegation to Russia. When Treasury Secretary Gallatin and Senator Bayard arrived in St. Petersburg in July 1813, John expected that one of them would replace him and that he, Louisa, Charles, Kitty, William, and Martha would return home on the same ship that brought Gallatin, Bayard, their families, and the son of Dolley Madison to Russia. He was wrong. Far from recalling him, President Madison instead named Adams along with Gallatin and Bayard as US negotiators for the mediation. He was wrong, too, about Gallatin's usefulness to Madison at home. Gallatin had grown weary of the job of treasury secretary, especially when former minister to France John Armstrong became war secretary, an appointment Gallatin opposed. Because he was a naturalized American born in Sweden, Gallatin agreed with the president that his knowledge of Europe would make him useful abroad.

Madison also gave John the prestigious job of negotiating a separate trade agreement with Russia. They waited in St. Petersburg for word on whether the British would also accept the czar's mediation and send delegates. For six months they knocked on Romanzoff's door for an answer. The chancellor could give no official word. Then they discovered through informal channels that the British government had scoffed at Alexander's offer but would not officially refuse it. Arrogantly ignoring the mediation option and insulting Alexander, the British foreign minister instead wrote Secretary Monroe and offered to negotiate directly with the United States but demanded that the talks take place on European soil. Nonetheless Russia's pressure had pushed England to the peace table, which was a triumph and a result of John's positive influence on Alexander and Romanzoff.

Madison accepted and appointed John along with Gallatin, Bayard, and two other distinguished Americans to treat for peace in hopes of ending the 1812 war with Britain. John left St. Petersburg, the city of his so-called exile, on April 28, 1814.

"With this prospect of a general peace in Europe I commenced my journey to contribute, if possible, to the restoration of peace to my own country."

He traveled first to Göteborg, Sweden. He waited there for weeks, only to learn that the British government had changed the location and decided to send its representatives instead to Ghent, a city in the newly formed province of Flanders, also known as Belgium.

John and the Americans arrived in Ghent in July 1814, much sooner than their English counterparts, which gave Adams plenty of time to rest, recreate, and write. His correspondence to Louisa was as comforting as it was lengthy, full of flourishes and details. He chronicled what delighted him about art, literature, politics, and other subjects. One of his most poetic lines came after studying some paintings. "Upon the canvas I never look but for two things: beauty for the eye, and sentiment for the soul."

She hoped he still looked at her the same way, but the longer their separation continued, the more her doubts grew. Their need for reunion with their children expanded into a need for reunion with each other.

Nevertheless, the letter he wrote to her on August 9, 1814, gave her the greatest hope yet of his imminent return: "As I have written [to the secretary of state] to ask again to be recalled from the Russian mission, we shall probably be there at all events until next spring."

The joy of finally being reunited with George and John finally seemed on the horizon. The possibility of reunion with him was even closer.

"At present I do not think that the negotiation will be of long continuance," he also wrote.

Although the British commissioners proclaimed to have "liberal and highly pacific" intentions at their first meeting with the US delegates on August 9,

1814, Adams doubted their seriousness about negotiating peace. He freely gave Louisa his reasons.

Over several weeks newspaper editors under the thumb of the British government had predicted there would be no peace as often as they had washed printing press ink from their hands. One gazette described the negotiations as a hopeless farce. Other theatrics also suggested that the British were not serious about the negotiations. In the closing session of Parliament, the prince regent claimed that he wanted peace with America. He also declared that, in the meantime, they would carry on the war "with increased vigor."

As much as Adams wanted to return to his wife and children, he was fearful for his country's future and its ability to maintain independence. The British were stalling, waiting to hear more news from the war on America's shores. They believed that a significant British land victory in the fall of 1814 would bring Adams and his American colleagues to their knees.

"If they choose to play this game of chicanery they may, I know not how long. But if they will take no for an answer, we shall be released in two or three days."

He was so confident that the British would break off negotiations by the first of September and he would return to St. Petersburg in the autumn of 1814 that he asked Louisa to stop writing letters to him.

He miscalculated both assumptions.

———

As she continued her journey into Prussia in February 1815, Louisa pushed her postilions to drive as quickly as they could. They arrived at post houses late at night and left at daybreak the next morning. One day Louisa discovered just how traumatized Charles was from their close call on the Vistula River.

"We came suddenly upon a view of the [Baltic] Sea, and were apparently driving immediately into it, when Charles became dreadfully alarmed, and turning as white as a sheet, asked me if we were going into that great water."

Assuring him that they would not be going into the sea, she mapped out their plan. They would travel inland in as few days as possible to Berlin. There they would rest, restock their supplies, and visit a few old friends. After that they would aggressively push toward Paris. However, as they continued, their servant Baptiste made her fearful.

"Baptiste . . . began to assume a tone not by any means agreeable, and I began to be somewhat uneasy."

Not understanding her urgency, he may have disagreed with her insistence on pushing through the mountains when the roads looked dark and gloomy.

"I intimated to him that he might leave me as soon as he pleased, as I was in a country where I was very well known, as I had lived four years in Berlin, and was acquainted with the king and all the royal family."

Baptiste's "great desire was to return to his own country, and . . . he did not wish to leave me." He wanted to get to France and "understood I had *agreed* to take him the whole way."

She could understand the source of his anxiety. He had marched with Napoleon across the very country where they were traveling. Baptiste was one of thousands of prisoners of war. Traveling toward Paris likely resurrected difficult memories. No matter. He needed to uphold his part of their bargain.

"The performance of this *agreement* depended on his good behavior, and . . . if he was diligent and attentive, I should have no wish to part with him," she emphasized.

Louisa kept a watchful eye on Baptiste the rest of the day. He "was much more respectful; but there was something threatening in his look, that did not please me, but I was afraid to notice it."

Once again she must worry about the thief within.

⌐⌐

Months earlier in St. Petersburg, Louisa had fretted about another problem. After receiving several letters from John in the summer of 1814, she realized that leaving Russia had been good for him. His spirits were lighter. Each letter seemed happier than the one before. Was it the warmer weather? Was it because he was out of Russia? Or, dare she admit, was he happier living apart from her?

Curiosity and insecurity got the best of her. She asked the question, framing it as a jest. He did not take her suggestion as a joke because he had also noticed that Louisa's letters reflected a lighter spirit than their recent time together. He could hear the amusement in her voice when she wrote that Mr. Bailey, a top British diplomat, had asked to dance with her at the annual Peterhof soirée.

"Mr. Bailey said he would astonish the world and show them that the English and Americans had entered into an alliance, by dancing a polonaise with me. We were followed by the emperor, who seemed diverted by it, and spoke to him when the dance ended."

Worse, perhaps the emperor, freshly returned from Paris, had noticed her again and tried to take advantage of John's absence.

"The excursions and entertainments will, I flatter myself, have a favorable affect on your health and spirits," Adams responded in a letter to her. His tone was either sincere, sarcastic, or both.

She confronted the conflict: "Really mon ami I think you cannot complain as you acknowledge that you received pleasure from the information that I was becoming more contented with my situation."

Calling their separation a cruel disappointment, she regretted suggesting that she was happier without him: "I should never even in jest had hinted that I could live happily without you. There are some wounds which are not easy to heal, and forgetfulness is not my best quality."

Though he had promised to return to her in September 1814, the British continued stalling instead of breaking off the negotiations as he had expected. Disappointed, Louisa understood the politics behind it. Her situation was a paradox, a Plato's beard. She could best understand the reason for their separation by what didn't exist—peace. As much as she longed for his return to St. Petersburg, as much as she yearned to embrace him, she hoped he would succeed at Ghent, both for his sake and America's. She didn't want the negotiations to fail. They needed peace, for without it, their beloved country, friends, and family would lose their freedom and way of life.

"I am fully sensible of the difficulty of your situation and should most sincerely rejoice to hear that any hope of a settlement could be entertained," she wrote.

The irony was obvious. The sooner he returned to her in St. Petersburg, the more likely that failure marked the peace process, and the horrible war would continue. Mustering strength, she sought to encourage him. "But when events are totally out of our power, is it wise to suffer ourselves to be so much depressed? This is a lesson which you taught me when I was deeply suffering under the heavy loss I had sustained," she wrote, recalling his role in helping her to accept baby Louisa's death and overcome her depression.

The strength of her soul now emerged, revealing a healed woman who was far less depressed and self-absorbed than the near-suicidal person of 1812 and 1813. Time, truth, and trust had brought healing to her. In time she was able to accept the truth that she was not responsible for her daughter's death. John's decision to ask for a recall and return to Boston allowed her to trust that someday soon she would be reunited with her boys.

John's departure from St. Petersburg in April 1814 gave her a new test, forcing her to stand alone and represent America without him. The responsibility of caring for Charles by herself drew her out of the final stage of depression. Her son depended on her alone, and she could not let him down. Now she must also be strong for John.

"The situation of our country is dreadful, but we must hope that it will mend, and trust in that great power, to whom all is easy, and who could preserve us from the dangers which so heavily threaten," she wrote.

While Adams's spirits were springlike in Ghent, he missed his wife. He longed to tell her about the details of the peace talks, to share his deepest fears with her. He needed her. Taking a risk that spies might read his correspondence, he made a decision to share with her as much as he could about the negotiations.

Though he wanted to, he could not reveal the details of the British demands, such as their insistence on lowering the US-Canadian boundary line with Maine and Minnesota belonging to the British, creating a wide buffer zone for native tribes—such as the Missouri tribes—and prohibiting the US Navy from operating on the Great Lakes. Yet he could at least share with her the process and how he felt about it. He promised to write what he could about the negotiations but asked for her discretion—and pretense—if need be.

"You will now, my dearest friend, receive in the most exclusive confidence whatever I shall write to you on the subject—say not a word of it to any human being until the result shall be publically known."

He could not afford for her to leak any word about the peace talks to any foreign diplomat or government official in Russia. She should not discuss his letters even with Mr. Harris, whom Adams had left as the American chargé d'affaires.

Her husband, the man who had failed to trust her judgment and made the erroneous decision to leave their sons behind in Boston, now believed in her capabilities so much that he was willing to risk telling her secrets about the negotiations. He did so because he loved her, needed her support, and valued her opinions.

Though his trust in her warmed her heart, the colder the weather grew, the more she longed for his presence too. She especially felt his absence when she was sick. Headaches were frequent. She remembered those moments when he would come and kiss her hand while she was ill. Now her palms were empty.

"I most sincerely wish I could find an opportunity to go home," she wrote, referring to America. If circumstances didn't change soon, she was prepared to take matters into her own hands.

Loneliness got the better of her in St. Petersburg, where she also lost her sister's companionship and Martha's service. Kitty and William had married on February 17, 1813. They, along with their infant daughter and Martha Godfrey, later left St. Petersburg and traveled to Western Europe with plans to return to America.

Tired of waiting for John to return to her in St. Petersburg in December 1814, she offered another option: "My troubles never end until you return, and if it does not soon happen, I shall be tempted to decamp from here whether you like it or not."

After traveling a few weeks in the winter of 1815, Louisa concluded that spring would have been a better time to journey through war-torn Russia, Poland, and Prussia:

"The season of the year at which I travelled; when earth was chained in her dazzling, brittle but solid fetters of ice, did not admit of flourishing description, of verdant fields, or paths through flowery glebes."

She could have waited until summer to make her journey. Being in exile with John had been hard enough for five years. Remaining in exile without him had been so unbearable that she risked the woes of winter to reach him.

As she traveled toward Berlin in late February 1815, she often looked out the window of her carriage. In those moments when Charles and Madame Babet were asleep, she had time to think and stare at the dull landscape. "Everything around us looked blank and dreary." Instead of green fields and forests, she beheld "the fearful remnants of men's fiery and vindictive passions; passively witnessing to tales of blood and woes."

Before her were the graphic consequences of war, which silenced the tongues of thousands of men. The people on the road rarely smiled. The dirt on their faces matched their forlorn emotions. Without saying a word, the men and women of Prussia bore the story of devastation and despair.

At one stop she received an invitation to attend the theater. She would have gone if she "had not been unprotected by a gentleman." She dared not take the risk to socialize at night or walk the streets with people desperate enough to steal her money.

Frequent rain now often delayed her. At one town the cold rain became so strong that she had to wait until three in the afternoon before proceeding. She then persevered into the countryside, where they passed "houses half burnt, a very thin population; women unprotected, and that dreary look of forlorn desertion."

The sight of charred walls was common. Fire had destroyed many Prussian properties. Indeed, it was a very distant fire that suddenly changed the fate of the American peace prospects at Ghent—and her husband's success—in the fall of 1814.

53

American Phoenix

He seems to think himself a mere Phoenix.

—John Wesley, 1775

Classical mythology tells the story of a bird who burns on a funeral pyre ignited by the sun before rising again from its own ashes to live a new or resurrected life. The bird, which *The Oxford English Dictionary* describes as "resembling an eagle but with sumptuous red and gold plumage," is known as a *phoenix*.

When the Old Testament prophet Isaiah described the idea of rebirth, he also used the image of an eagle: "They that wait upon the Lord shall renew their strength; they shall mount up with wings as eagles; they shall run, and not be weary; and they shall walk, and not faint."

In the early days of Christianity, Clemens Romanus, revered as Pope Clement I, is said to have used the story of the phoenix to help Romans understand and accept the resurrection of Christ. Centuries later, in 1674, English minister John Flavel had used the two images this way: "Faith is the phoenix grace, as Christ is the phoenix mercy."

Since his failure in the US Senate, Adams had needed a phoenix, a personal rebirth to lift him from the ash heap of failure and launch him to new heights of respect, wisdom, honor, and accomplishments. Succeeding in Russia was the beginning of that resurrection, while treating for peace at Ghent just might seal it.

What he didn't realize in the fall of 1814 was that his country had just experienced a death by fire that would force the American phoenix to rise again as an eagle soaring higher, more independent, and freer than ever before.

The British commissioners were stalling at Ghent in hopes of receiving news of a victorious battle. To be sure, English newspapers reported that thousands of men had recently sailed for America with the intention to "humble the Yankees and reduce them immediately to submission."

John rightfully feared that terrible news would soon arrive. "It is impossible that the summer should pass over without bringing intelligence which will make our hearts ache; though I hope and trust that nothing will or can happen that will break the spirit of our nation," he confided to Louisa in a letter.

She was just as worried. Her thoughts immediately turned to their boys in Boston. "Your fears of bad news from America in the autumn fill me with alarm, and I open all your letters with trembling, lest I should find some horrid circumstance relating to our families or friends."

She, too, had read reports of British threats against US cities. For eighteen months British squadrons burned and terrorized the inhabitants of Chesapeake Bay towns in Maryland and Virginia. "You are hereby required and directed to destroy and lay waste such towns and districts upon the coast as you may find assailable," Supreme Commander British Admiral Alexander Cochrane wrote his officers when he issued a blockade of the entire US coast in July 1814.

"That proclamation of Cochrane's is always present to my imagination and the consequences which may result from it," Louisa wrote to John.

What also worried both Adamses were the attitudes of their countrymen and women. Americans had yet to show the same fighting spirit that their fathers and mothers had demonstrated during the American Revolution. Even a victory, such as the US Army's capture of Fort Erie in Canada in July 1814, revealed laziness and hesitance.

"When our landsmen have struck one lucky blow, they seem to think they have conquered the world, and have nothing left to do but to slumber upon their laurels," John complained in a letter to Louisa.

Their replies on such topics depended on the speed of the postal service, which turned their letters around in about twenty-five days. Louisa responded to her husband's concerns by hoping that a new leader would emerge: "Alas, there are a few Washingtons in the world."

Both knew that the political infighting between the Federalists and the Republicans had strangled the country. Some Federalists wanted New England to secede and become part of England again, sentiments British minister Augustus Foster and others like him fostered. One of the greatest threats to America's success in the War of 1812 was the war within. Infighting between the political parties threatened to destroy America as much as the British army, so it sometimes seemed. Louisa took comfort when she heard that the war had one good effect: the parties were coming together.

"There is a report in town, said to be very late from America, that the feds [Federalists] are all come round and are determined to support this [Madison's] government. I hope this is true, [as] our own internal discord must do a more serious injury than a foreign war as it paralyzes every effort of the government," Louisa astutely observed.

Her patriotism grew with each newspaper account that she read of the US war. "I could almost wish I were a man in these times for I feel that sort of ardor and enthusiasm in the cause, which I think in a man would produce great things."

She looked to an eternal source for hope: "The melancholy situation of our country warrants almost any degree of apprehension, and we have no resources but the mercy of a divine Providence, which is ever ready to support us through great calamities, when our faith is sincere."

⤙⤚

The bad news literally arrived in John's bedchamber, when messenger and brother-in-law George Boyd burst through Adams's Belgium hotel door early in the morning on October 7, 1814. Married to one of Louisa's younger sisters, Boyd was fresh off the boat, having traveled as a government agent across the Atlantic to deliver the urgent—but now six-weeks-old—news to the US commissioners.

Under the leadership of Admiral Cochrane, Admiral George Cockburn, and General Robert Ross, a royal fleet of more than fifty ships had arrived in waves in the Chesapeake Bay in July and August 1814. Though his spies told him that the British had no cavalry and could not attack without one, Madison worried that an invasion was imminent.

What was mysterious, however, was the destination of the redcoats. Would the British launch their attack against Baltimore or Washington City? Boasting America's third-largest population, with more than forty six thousand residents, Baltimore was the more lucrative take for its commercial value. In contrast Washington City had very few buildings. It was a very small town, characterized only by the President's House, the US Capitol, a few taverns, and some townhomes. However, the classical Greek architecture of the two major public buildings symbolized a fledgling new republic.

Secretary of War General Armstrong bet on Baltimore. With a small standing army, dependence on local militias, and a failure by Congress to authorize a draft of soldiers, Armstrong did not have the resources or federal authority to defend both cities. New England judges earlier rebuffed the federal government's attempt to call up state militia from Massachusetts and Connecticut. Knowing the Federalist sentiment for secession, the governors of both states refused to comply with the president's wishes.

On July 1, 1814, Madison told his cabinet that he was requesting the War Department to create a new military district of fifteen thousand men to defend Washington City. In a follow-up memo to Armstrong the next day, he wanted the militia "in the best readiness for actual service in case of emergency." Though Madison had requested that the governors of nearby states Virginia, Maryland, and Pennsylvania call up their militias, Armstrong waited weeks to notify the governors. The secretary of war also told a Washington City leader, who was worried about a British invasion of the capital city, that he doubted the British would come there. "No, no! Baltimore is the place, Sir; that is of so much more consequence."

By delaying the president's orders, Armstrong defied the president's orders.

On that early morning of October 7, 1814, Boyd delivered the bad news to Adams. The British army and Marine Corps had burned Washington City, including the President's House and the US Capitol.

"The newspapers contain a great variety of details respecting the fall of

Washington and the destruction of buildings and of property, public and private, effected by the enemy," Adams gravely wrote to Louisa.

In the years to come, more would be known as historians gathered information from eyewitnesses. Acquiring horses for the officers by stealing them from Maryland farmers, the British marched four thousand marines and soldiers toward Washington City. Admiral Cockburn convinced a wavering General Ross that they could and must invade Washington. Why make it this far without taking their capital? The British approached Bladensburg, Maryland, around noon on August 24, 1814. On the other side of the river was a similar-numbered US force of militia and regulars, far from the fifteen thousand the commander in chief had requested on July 1. President Madison and his cabinet attended the battle in hopes of cheering the men to victory. Madison became the first and only US president to witness a battle from the field.

With cannon, the Americans killed a number of redcoats as a British unit advanced over the bridge separating the forces. Angry at the loss of their men on the bridge, the British easily forded the water and scaled the hill to engage in man-to-man combat. Seeing this, the American commander called for a retreat. Most men took the Georgetown Road, which opened the other road, the one leading directly to Washington City and the US Capitol, to the British. After a brief rest, about two hundred redcoats marched to Washington City with Napoleon-like speed in scorching one-hundred-degree temperatures.

The British were in such a hurry to continue their path of destruction that on their way from Bladensburg to Washington "they left their own dead unburied on the fields, and their own wounded as prisoners at the mercy of the very people whose public edifices and private habitations they had been consuming by fire."

The casualty count was never firm, but historians have guessed that 64 Britons were killed, and 185 were wounded. The American numbers were much lower: 10 to 12 killed; 40 wounded.

The evening of August 24, 1814, the redcoats easily entered the abandoned, defenseless city. Like unbridled buccaneers, they kicked down the doors of the US Capitol, held a mock session of Congress, where Admiral Cockburn plopped into the chair belonging to the Speaker of the House, Henry Clay, who was in Ghent with Adams. Cockburn called out to his men, "Shall this harbor of Yankee democracy be burned? All for it will say aye!" The troops gleefully called out, "Aye!" They piled chairs, desks, and other furniture into mounds, lit torches, thrust them into the piles, and ran out.

Near midnight they approached the President's House. Finding no one there, Admiral Cockburn and some of the men entered the property. They looted Madison's hats and shirts and piled up the furniture, including the Grecian chairs that Dolley Madison had chosen for the red oval room, her piano forte and guitar, and other furnishings. Then they ate dinner in the dining room, where Dolley had prepared a meal for forty guests in hopes of entertaining her husband's cabinet and officers following a victory at Bladensburg. Instead the British feasted on Dolley's food. Seeing an indented seat cushion at the head of the table, Cockburn took it, saying he hoped that little Jemmy wouldn't mind. The token would remind him of Mrs. Madison's "seat."

Then the redcoats surrounded the President's House with men standing in front of the windows. They tied oily rags into balls the size of dinner plates and attached them to the ends of four-foot-long poles. They passed a torch, lit the rags, and in unison thrust their fiery weapons into the President's House, which instantly caught fire.

"The destruction of the capitol, the President's House, the public offices, and many private houses is contrary to all the usages of civilized nations, and is without example even in the wars that have been waged during the French Revolution," John wrote, not knowing all the details until much later. In fact Albert Gallatin, who was also with Adams at Ghent, later learned that his private residence in Washington City was completely destroyed.

"The same British officers who boast in their dispatches of having blown up the legislative hall of Congress and the dwelling house of the president, would have been ashamed of the act instead of glorying in it, had it been done in any European city," Adams declared.

Revenge for the first American war may have been on the minds of the redcoats. To Adams the real tragedy might yet come. The conquerors were heading north. If they succeeded in capturing Baltimore, they could continue to Philadelphia, New York, and finally Boston. All Americans were in danger. The fate of the Union now depended on the success or failure of local communities to defend their own people.

"Boston is still exposed and our property there may share the fate of the capitol. But in the perils of the country I scarcely think it worth a thought what may befall my individual interests. Our children and other relations near Boston are in no danger but that which menaces the whole country."

Maybe, finally, the fall of Washington would be the catalyst to stir the nation to real action. So he hoped: "If it cannot be produced [rousing the people to action] they are not fit to bear the character of an independent nation, and have nothing better to do than to take the oath of allegiance to the maniac [King George III and the prince regent]."

With the nation's capital in ruins, the question lingered, was America now conquered? Or would the spirit of independence, the American eagle, rise as a phoenix? As Louisa had witnessed in St. Petersburg, after hearing of the burning of Washington City, many Europeans concluded that America was now conquered. Gone were these so-called United States. Returning were Britain's prodigal American colonies.

"The news of the destruction of Washington makes much noise here [in St. Petersburg] and they seem to think as you say that all America is destroyed. Everybody looks at me with so much sorrow and compassion that I hate to stir out," she wrote about how the news affected the diplomats and Russian nobility in St. Petersburg. "You would suppose that we had not a chance left of ever again becoming a nation."

For five years she had longed to return home and embrace her boys. Now she didn't have a country to return to. In the days following the news of Washington City's destruction, her exile seemed permanent. "I felt my exile even more than I had ever done before."

For a time she avoided attending St. Petersburg's social events, especially ones where members of the British diplomatic corps were present.

"I trust in God that the day [of] retribution is not far off and that glory which yet awaits us will far, far outweigh the disgrace which has hitherto attended us."

54

Queen of Hearts

In early March of 1815, Louisa's carriage passed very few houses as they traveled on a remote road to Küstrin, a town in the Prussian province of Brandenburg in Germany. Because of heavy rains, the dirt road sometimes became a muddy stream. Suddenly the carriage's front wheel snapped, jolting to a chaotic stop. One of the drivers jumped down and studied the problem. He gave Louisa the bad news. The wheel was unsalvageable, broken into fragments.

"The evening was setting in, and they advised that one of the two should go to a small place that we had passed on the road, and get some conveyance for me; as the road was in such a state, it was impossible to walk."

Seeing no other option, Louisa agreed. They waited and waited for what seemed like a thousand hours before one of the drivers returned with "a miserable common cart, into which we got."

Baptiste led them to the last hut they passed. The shack had two rooms and a blacksmith shop.

"One woman made her appearance: dirty, ugly, and ill natured; and there were two or three very surly, ill-looking men."

The men's tongues were as salty with insults as their fingers were stained with soot from the blacksmith's shop. Just as she had the night they became lost in the forest, Louisa allowed the intimidating Baptiste to take charge. Explaining their broken wheel, he asked for a vehicle to transport Louisa, Charles, and Madame Babet to the nearest town.

"They answered doggedly that they could do no such thing, but that if we chose to stay there, they could make a wheel, so that we could go on in the morning."

What to do? Just as John had consulted with the captain of the *Horace* on their voyage to St. Petersburg years earlier, so Louisa now asked her two servants their opinion. The three of them devised a plan. They would spend the night at the shack, which had one available room. Because both servants were armed, they could split up, with one keeping watch at her chamber door and the other sleeping in the coach.

"According to this plan, I had my little boy's bed brought in [from the carriage], and while he slept soundly, my woman and I sat up, neither of us feeling very secure in the [dis]agreeable nest into which we had fallen."

Baptiste's terse nature now worked in Louisa's favor. No one tried to enter her chamber. Although she lost a night's sleep, she didn't lose any of her valuables—or her life, for that matter. The wheel was ready the next morning, and they left immediately.

"As I always had provisions in the carriage, we made out to eat something before we started, and at the next stage we took our coffee—Our wheel was very clumsy, and not painted, but it answered all the purpose to carry us through the famous road, which had been begun by Bonaparte from Küstrin."

Once again nature became their worst enemy on the road. Mud slowed their progress, but eventually they reached Küstrin's fortress, which was about fifty miles east of Berlin. Napoleon's troops had burned the town on their retreat to Paris. House upon house "bore the mutilating stamp of war."

They found tolerable lodgings, but were not allowed to sightsee at the fortress, which was famous for imprisoning Prussia's king the previous century. Even though the French had torched this town, the local inhabitants held a far different opinion of the Grande Armée than Louisa expected.

"To my utter astonishment, I heard nothing but the praises of the gallantry of Napoleon, and his officers, and great regret at the damage done to this beautiful fortress."

She quickly discovered the reason: economics. In spite of their burnt houses, the people blamed the Cossacks for the terrible road conditions. Napoleon had ordered a new road to be built in Küstrin, but when the Russians drove him away, they sabotaged construction for the grand road.

"The Cossacks! The dire Cossacks! were the perpetual theme, and the cheeks of the women blanched at the very name."

While in Ghent, Adams thought about the destruction that towns across Prussia and other places had experienced. "There is scarcely a metropolis in Europe that has not been taken in the course of the last twenty years. There is not a single instance in all that time of public buildings like those being destroyed," John had written to Louisa in early October 1814.

Because Napoleon had shattered so much of Europe, perhaps the British thought they could get away with burning Washington City. Adams wondered whether Washington's destruction would eventually backfire on the British.

"The army of Napoleon did indeed blow up the Kremlin at Moscow, but that was a fortified castle, and even this act has ever been and ever will be stigmatized as one of the most infamous of his deeds."

Many French newspapers described the burning of Washington as "atrocious." This description forced London newspaper editors to defend their military's actions by recalling "the most execrable barbarities of the French revolutionary fury."

Louisa, too, had detected that the British diplomats in St. Petersburg were having trouble defending the burning of the US Capitol and the President's House. "It is said that the destruction of our little capitol has produced such a sensation here that his little lordship [the British ambassador to Russia] has more than once been under the necessity of retiring from the soirées in which it has formed the topic of conversation."

Adams kept his wife informed of the latest developments as he received them. The British also took the city of Alexandria, Virginia. Armstrong had failed to take the simple action of ordering militia to build earthen works to block the roads to Washington City from invasion. After President Madison confronted him, General Armstrong resigned.

"Armstrong defends himself as much as he defended Washington," Adams wryly wrote.

John made another keen political observation, one that might affect his fortunes. Madison appointed Monroe to replace Armstrong as secretary of war. This meant that the coveted position of secretary of state was likely vacant. Perhaps Adams's request for a recall might result in an honorable opportunity for him after all.

In the meantime his political fortune was directly tied to success in Ghent.

Failure to get a treaty, and a good one, would prevent him from taking any other diplomatic post, much less the role of secretary of state. Worse, the war would continue, and America could be annexed by Britain.

The fall of Washington City initially gave the British the advantage at Ghent. Though much of Europe was appalled by the barbarism, Parliament was blind to their country's falling status. Lord Liverpool, the prime minister, secretly expressed their strategy this way: "The forces under Sir Alexander Cochrane and General Ross were most actively employed upon the coast of the United States, creating the greatest degree of alarm and rendering the government very unpopular."

He was correct. Americans blamed Madison for the destruction of their capital. One female innkeeper was so angry when she learned that Dolley Madison was taking refuge at her hotel, she threw her out and cursed at her.

Dolley had been queen of hearts in America. Her courage that day at the President's House made her a legend. After learning at 3:00 p.m. that US forces had failed to hold back the British at Bladensburg, Dolley fled the President's House. Before she left, however, she made a crucial decision. She asked her servants to remove Gilbert Stuart's full-length portrait of George Washington from the dining room wall before the British arrived. The portrait was a national treasure, a gift from Congress for the opening of the President's House in 1800. She could not bear the idea of redcoats looting the house, taking the portrait, and then later parading Washington's painting through the streets of London to prove their conquest of America. She received credit for saving the portrait.

Sacrificing most of her wardrobe, Dolley packed all the president's cabinet papers, and possibly her husband's notes from the Constitutional Convention, into one of the few remaining wagons in town. Once those were secure at another location, she fled with other Americans to roads leading to the countryside. Taking refuge at several places over the next few days and disguising herself with a farmer's shawl, she waited until a messenger from her husband told her it was safe to return to Washington. A hurricane had driven out the redcoats.

Lord Liverpool, the prime minister, correctly guessed that James Madison immediately became an unpopular president. Though unknown at the time, Dolley's heroism later made her a gem.

The prime minister believed the demise of Washington would be a game changer for the peace negotiations. At worst, the news would force the US commissioners to accept the new, lower boundary line proposed by the British to enlarge Canada and diminish the United States. At best, they would capitulate and hand the entire nation back to England, where they belonged.

"We may hope, therefore, that if the American government should prove themselves so unreasonable as to reject our proposals as they have been now modified," Liverpool wrote, "they will not long be permitted to administer the affairs of the country, particularly as their military efforts have in no way corresponded with the high tone in which they attempt to negotiate."

After news of the burning of Washington reached them in Ghent, the British commissioners issued a fifteen-page reply to their American counterparts.

John shared his frustration in a letter to Louisa: "It must indeed have been for some of my own sins or for those of my country, that I have been placed here to treat with the injustice and insolence of Britain, under a succession of such news as every breeze is wafting from America."

Louisa, too, bewailed the thought of America being conquered: "The nature of our government, and the habits of the people, place us in a situation of such entire dependence on our own individual exertions, our persons, our children, our property are also so completely at stake." She put her faith in patriotism. Just as Alexander showed, she hoped that "we just might hold up our heads and defy the brutality of our enemies."

America needed a fleet of phoenixes to rise from the ashes and save the country.

———

"We left Küstrin to pursue our journey."

As Louisa returned to the road in March 1815, she hoped the remaining fifty miles to Berlin would be uneventful, slowed only by the routine of showing passports at border posts. When they neared a particular spot, the drivers suddenly stopped.

"One of the postilions pointed out to us the small house, where that most lovely and interesting Queen Louisa of Prussia had stayed with her sick baby on their retreat from Berlin, after the French had taken possession of that city."

While the driver told the story of the queen's daring escape from Berlin, Louisa began to cry over the woman's flight. Hearing of the queen's ill infant understandably resurrected memories of Louisa's daughter, whose grave she would never see again.

Queen Louisa had been the most influential woman in Prussia. She had supported, even insisted that her husband, Friederich Wilhelm III, declare war on Napoleon in 1806. When Bonaparte's army decimated the Prussians, it was Queen Louisa who pleaded with the French emperor at the Peace of Tilsit to remember her people. She begged him to have mercy on the Prussians, calling upon her titles of wife and mother, not queen, as the basis for demanding humane treatment.

Saying she was an admirable queen and one of the most interesting women he had ever met, Bonaparte was impressed with her. Just as some Americans thought of Dolley Madison as the queen of hearts, so the Prussians embraced their Louisa as the queen of hearts. Though she died in 1810 at age thirty-four of a pulmonary embolism, she still reigned as the sentimental people's queen of Prussia.

"My heart thrilled with emotion for the sufferings of one, whom I had so dearly loved, and I could not refrain from tears at the recital of her sufferings," Louisa reflected.

As they entered Berlin in March 1815, she thought about Queen Louisa and others she had known as she beheld the city where she had lived fourteen years earlier as a newlywed with John. "Memory; how ineffably beautiful is thy power! Years had elapsed; affliction had assailed the heart, with its keenest pangs of carking grief; disappointment had thrown its mingled hues of fear and care," she noted.

The past flooded her mind as she arrived at the hotel: "The carriage needed repairs, and our clumsy wheel to be painted, and Berlin was attractive to me—my poor and beloved George having been born there."

George was now a teenager. Oh, how she missed seeing him grow into a young man! John had copied a letter from Abigail that reached him in Ghent.

"George's growth has been very rapid in the year past that I believe he will not be more than an inch or two taller, his voice is changing, and John will insist that he is fifteen years old, and must have a razor in another year. John is short and stocky, full of spirit animation and fire, both of them longing to have you return, so does your affectionate mother," Abigail wrote.

An American traveling to Ghent had recently seen their boys and gave John a firsthand report. "[He] said to me of our sons, 'George, Sir, is a fine, tall, stout boy; but as for John, Sir, he is the very picture of you.'"

The update on her sons warmed Louisa's heart. Now she was in the city of George's birth. She and John had been happy together then. Berlin enchanted her because there she had first experienced "the luxuries, the pleasures, and the novelties of a court."

As she settled into her hotel, Louisa confirmed a decision. Gone was the mantra to rest, not recreate, and then resume her journey. Instead she decided to stay in Berlin a week. She didn't need that much time to repair her carriage, but she wanted to visit former friends by reliving her youth and "forgetting in the lapse of time and distance." The hardships of the journey from St. Petersburg had changed Louisa. She needed the rejuvenation that only socializing with old friends could bring.

———

Did he love her as much as he had when they were newlyweds in Berlin? Their separation had brought out her worst insecurities in the fall of 1814. Early on in the negotiations, when John thought he would soon return to St. Petersburg, he confessed to her a secret passion. Adams longed to visit Paris, which he had not seen in nearly thirty years. Accompanying his father to the famous city gave him an education beyond books. Paris was to John what Berlin was to Louisa.

Perhaps aware of his wife's fears, his desire to see his queen of hearts, however, was more paramount than Paris:

> I had had no small temptation to return by the way of Paris, which is only
> thirty-six hours distance from me, but I am not making this tour of Brussels

for my pleasure . . . what has pleasure to show that would compensate me for an obstruction of three days longer from my queen of pleasure? If I lengthen the journey upon my return, it will assuredly not be for amusement, or to gratify my personal curiosity.

But as the months rolled on with more delays in the negotiations, Louisa couldn't help wondering whether she was still truly the queen of his heart. She found herself lured by the practices of Russian fortune-tellers. Superstition was as common in Russian social circles as snow under their slippers. Surely it couldn't hurt to see if a deck of cards could tell her what she needed to know?

"Mr. Charles, who is very well, informed you that I lay the cards out to see when you will return," she confessed to her husband in a letter that winter of 1814.

One card in particular made her worry, leading her to think that another female now attracted his fancy. "Pray tell me what fair lady it is that takes up so much of your attention? As I understand that it is the fashion of the place and as I know how essential it is to the diplomatic reputation to form this sort of intrigue it is impossible for you to lose so fine an opportunity," she both partially teased and fished.

He responded to her that other diplomats often found distractions in a Delilah, but not him.

"Do not fancy I am *jealous* . . . it is pretty certain that we have no pretension to be so against the temptations that the world throws in your way, which I am sure are strong and mighty. God bless and speed you soon to the arms and heart of your faithful wife," she assured him in a late December letter in 1814.

Playing with the cards seemed so harmless, but something about it haunted her too. Within a few weeks of asking John for reassurance, she found herself face-to-face with a real fortune-teller. Two nights before she left St. Petersburg, Louisa said good-bye to one of her best friends, Madame Colombi, the woman she had taken tea with years earlier instead of attending the ball. That incident nearly cost her a place on the empress mother's invitation list. Louisa loved Madame Colombi: "She was a charming woman and was apparently attached both to my sister and myself."

When she arrived at Madame Colombi's house, she discovered that a

Russian woman also joined them, but without an invitation. Colombi was too polite to turn this Russian countess away.

"Countess Apraxin was a fat coarse woman, very talkative, full of scandal, and full of the everlasting amusement so fashionable in Russian society, the bonne aventure."

Countess Apraxin was also a fortune-teller.

"After tea she took the cards, and insisted as I was going a journey, that I should choose a queen, and let her read my destiny."

Louisa had never seen this woman before or heard her name until that night. The woman was as pushy as she was fat. Unlike John's encounter years earlier with the bearded lady at Laval's party, at least this countess didn't have a beard. Louisa consented and chose a queen. Then Countess Apraxin read her fortune. "She said that I was perfectly delighted to quit Petersburg."

That was true. Just days earlier, when she said good-bye to the empresses at the palace, she could not conceal her happiness. She told them that Mr. Adams regretted not being able to take leave of them in person, but he expected to be recalled to America after finishing his business in Ghent. He would forever remember their graciousness during his time in their court. The empresses could tell that Louisa was thrilled to say good-bye.

"I delivered your message to the empress," Louisa wrote to John, "and she said when a man sent so far for his wife, he had no intention to return. I am a poor diplomat for she saw joy, sparkle in my eyes and she had never seen a woman so altered in her life for the better."

Though Countess Apraxin correctly assessed that Louisa was delighted to leave St. Petersburg, she could have easily detected her elation by watching her talk about her impending journey over dinner with Madame Colombi that night. The countess next predicted that Louisa would soon meet those from whom she had long been separated. That, too, was highly probable.

Then the countess added a warning. "That when I had achieved about half of my journey, I should be much alarmed by a great change in the political world, in consequence of some extraordinary movement of a great man which would produce utter consternation, and set all [of] Europe into a fresh commotion."

Her prediction grew worse. "That this circumstance which I should hear of on the road, would oblige me to change all my plans, and render my journey very difficult—but that after all I should find my husband well, and we should have a joyous meeting."

Louisa responded with great pretension. "I laughed and thanked her, and said I had no fear of such a circumstance, as I was so insignificant and the arrangements for my journey so simple, I was quite satisfied that I should accomplish it if I escaped from accidents, without meeting with any obstacles of the kind predicted; more especially as it was a time of peace."

Departing, Louisa politely said good-bye to Madame Colombi and the countess, who hoped Louisa would remember her predictions.

"I responded I was certain I could never forget her—I note this because it is an amusing and undoubted fact, and I was called on to remember it every moment during the latter part of my journey."

What Louisa didn't know was that a king, not a queen, would be the final trump card in her quest for reunion with her husband and oldest sons.

55

King of Spades

By the time Louisa reached Berlin the first week of March 1815, John had been in Paris almost a month. From his observation, the only remaining traces of Alexander's victory in France were the bricklayers who were still reconstructing a bridge that was destroyed when the allies entered the city. Peace had come to Paris.

After his negotiations terminated, John came to the famed city too. There he found what he was looking for: culture and relaxation. He had received Louisa's note about the "fair lady who according to your cards takes up so much of my attention." He chose to banter, not bait her.

"That fair lady is younger still, and unmarried," he assured, telling her of a twelve-year-old girl named Marianne. She and her cousin had entertained the American delegation with songs and couplets as a tribute to the United States. He responded impulsively. A "fancy" overtook him, leading him to write some verses of poetry in response. He arranged to bind his verses at a bookseller's shop and, through Marianne's mother, gave them to her as a gift. Perhaps the girl's sweet, innocent voice reminded him of his lost daughter, the one who would never grow up to sing like her mother. Though much more reserved than his wife, even he grew tender at the sight of a female child.

"You must not be jealous of my muse, and as for all the rest of the fair sex of Ghent, your friend, Mr. Gallatin, used to answer them by the assurance that all my affections absent from home were platonic."

Adams and the other American commissioners came to Paris for a distinct purpose: to wait for instructions to arrive from the US government about their next assignment.

Within three days of his arrival in Paris, John was introduced to King Louis XVIII, who was installed on the throne following Napoleon's exile to Elba in April 1814. Told that the king and other royals rarely spoke to anyone during formal presentations, a contrast to Alexander's charisma, Adams smiled inwardly when King Louis spoke to him.

"The king, however, asked me if 'I was in any way related to the celebrated Mr. Adams?'"

Though John spoke French, the man performing the introductions answered for him and explained the father-son, president-diplomat relationship. Adams believed that the French government was now stable. King Louis's job was not too difficult. Napoleon had ruled in such extremes that Louis merely had to govern with moderation, going a little in the opposite direction, but not too far, lest he incite another revolution.

"Louis has only to discern how far it [Napoleon's policy] may be relaxed, and where he must stop, that it may not degenerate into the opposite vice of weakness. This appears to be precisely the object of his endeavors," John predicted.

"The great difficulty for him [Louis] will be to manage the army, and to check their martial propensity. They have been deeply humiliated without being humbled. They have all the pride of their former successes, with the galling sensation of their late disasters. They look with a longing eye to their former chief, who is now but a shadow."

Other than the seismic changes in France's government, Adams found Paris just the way he remembered it from his teenage adventures: short on labor and long on leisure. The tendency to dissipation, even to a man his age, was still irresistible.

As he waited for a letter from President Madison, he spent hours at the theater and national museum, which proudly displayed the Venus de' Medici and other works of art. He ate lavish dinners, including one with General Lafayette, the famed Frenchman who as a youth had slipped the bonds of France and voyaged to America to fight for the revolutionary cause of liberty.

While indulging in luxuries and growing fat on delicacies, Adams eagerly awaited the arrival of his queen of hearts. He was completely unaware that Louisa had become lost at midnight in a dark forest in Courland, nearly died while crossing the icy Vistula River, and endured the threatening looks of Baptiste only to have to rely on him in emergencies. He didn't know that his princess had lost a wheel in the middle of nowhere, tramped through the mud in a common cart, and spent sleepless nights in creepy hovels. He didn't know, because she had not told him, and what she had written from the road had not arrived.

⤝⟶

No sooner had she stepped through the door of her Berlin hotel than Louisa wrote a letter to John: "After a very troublesome and tedious journey, we have happily arrived at Berlin, where I expected to have found letters from you but I am cruelly disappointed and impatiently waiting for the next post will not arrive until tomorrow evening."

While she hoped to receive correspondence from him during her weeklong rest in Berlin, Louisa was by no means taking her time. She requested that all repairs to the carriage "be dispatched as quick as possible, so as not to delay my journey."

She found that Berlin's sights, palaces, and bridges were much the same. The Athenian columns of the Brandenburg Gate continued to be as elegant as they were formidable. The linden or lime trees lining the Linden Strasse still resembled graceful ballerinas. Their trunks remained just as poised and statuesque as ever, while their armlike branches bowed as if curtseying to the pedestrians below.

"Everything looked much as I had left it in the city, excepting the manners and the dress of the people—All the nationality of costume &cc had disappeared, and French was almost universally spoken."

After seeking the whereabouts of old acquaintances, she arranged an appointment to visit a young, affable princess who, like the former queen, also shared her name.

"The Princess Louisa invited me to pass every evening with her while I stayed in town; and laughingly said that though she could not entertain as she had once done, she would give me two dishes for my supper, and a hearty welcome—No toilet [formal wardrobe] was necessary."

War had vanquished the pretenses of the German court, which had long reveled in a loose confederation of states and kingdoms. Though Louisa did not identify Princess Louisa's principality, she was married to one of the many

German princes or dukes who ruled more than forty cities and kingdoms throughout Prussia.

During one of their visits that week, the princess was so self-conscious that she apologized for wearing a bright rose-colored silk dress. It hardly seemed appropriate for a woman her age in the circumstances that her country faced, but she thought it was pretty and wore it anyway.

"The great people of Berlin had suffered so much from the war, that there was no pretention of style among them, and they were glad to see their friends socially," the princess explained.

She introduced Louisa to her daughter and then apologized that she could not introduce her to the rest of her family.

"Her husband and sons she told me were at Vienna; I expressed my thanks for the flattering kindness shown me by her invitation."

Louisa was not the only woman still separated from her family because of war. Princess Louisa's husband and sons were among the many gathered for the Congress of Vienna in Austria. Like an orchestra's contrasting wind, string, and percussion instruments, these allied leaders brought their unique sounds to Vienna to play a symphony they hoped would be heard throughout Europe. Their song was classical, with four movements. They needed to dismantle the French Empire, redraw the map of Europe, settle the spoils of the exiled Bonaparte, and determine who had what trade rights on the open seas.

Instead of mimicking Mozart's famous tutti outbursts, where all the instruments play the same music simultaneously and harmoniously, the Congress of Vienna had so far been a series of solos, modulations, and dissonance. Indeed the British were so off-key in Vienna months earlier in the fall of 1814 that the disaster was heard all the way to Ghent.

—⊷—

"When we were at Berlin, you remember there was a treaty of commerce concluded between the United States and Prussia," John wrote Louisa in November 1814. "The first thing the Prussian ministers did . . . was to send me the project of a treaty in form. They never hinted at any question of etiquette, and I am very sure this is the first time that such a pretension was ever applied to such an occasion."

Adams was the most experienced diplomat of any of the Ghent commissioners—British or American. Gallatin was a cabinet member; Bayard, a senator from Delaware. Kentuckian Henry Clay was Speaker of the House of Representatives, while Jonathan Russell was recently named the US minister after serving as chargé d'affaires in London in 1811. None had served as a high-ranking diplomat as long as John had.

From his experience years earlier in Berlin, Adams knew that a common negotiation practice was to first draft a treaty, not issue preliminary conditions as the British had done. They used every excuse to prevent any progress toward peace.

John concluded that the Congress of Vienna was another major reason behind their stall tactics. The Brits expected to triumph at Vienna. If they did, their conductor's hand against the US commissioners would have the full weight of Europe applauding for them—a standing ovation at that.

"Should they [the British] succeed in Vienna, we shall have no peace, because they will prefer war with us, to peace upon any terms," John wrote to Louisa.

"The great effort of Lord Castlereagh [the top British representative at Vienna] has been to exclude France totally from all influence in the general distribution of spoils of Europe, and even from all interference in the affairs of Germany."

Likewise Federalists back in America believed that Madison was mistaken over his belief that Russia would back the United States over Britain. One of the most ardent Federalists, Gouverneur Morris, wrote his friend Rufus King, a senator from New York: "I think the President [Madison] is also mistaken in supposing that Russia is the greatest Power in Europe, and especially that she will exercise her Greatness in our Favor." How wrong he was.

At the Vienna Congress in 1814, France's representative, Talleyrand, astonished the delegates when he offered for France to return to its pre-1792 boundaries. But there was a catch. He expected the rest of Europe to modulate with him and do the same—antebellum. Britain did not want to give up any of its acquired territory.

"The great effort of Talleyrand has been to exercise influence without provoking hostility, to counteract the views of the British government without directly confronting them, and finally to dissolve the league against France under which the congress first assembled," Adams summed up the progress at Vienna.

Talleyrand's suggestion allowed the French to quickly gain ground and pick up the tempo against the unpopular British. Alexander concurred and showed disdain for the English too. Lord Liverpool, the British prime minister, secretly confessed to Lord Castlereagh, "I fear the emperor of Russia is half an American." Indeed, in many ways, Alexander was. The credit for his favor toward the US at the Vienna Congress belonged to John Quincy and Louisa Adams.

What the American commissioners needed the most was an interlude, a game changer. Without it they would never be able to secure a peace treaty with Britain. If they couldn't change the tune, they needed a face-saver. Either way all sorts of politics pressed on them, continuing to prevent John from returning to Louisa in St. Petersburg in the final quarter of 1814.

———

"Early in the morning I left the city of Berlin, for the last time with feelings both of gratitude and regret—There I had felt at home; all the sweet sympathies of humanity had been reawakened; and the sterile heartlessness of a Russian residence of icy coldness, was thawed into life and animation."

As Louisa said good-bye to Berlin in March 1815, she reflected on Prussia's Princess Louisa, who "was as little altered as possible, considering that time had not strewed roses in her path; but though the thorns had left some marks of their wounds, they had left traces of a softer shade of character on her face, than that which she possessed in the brilliancy of youth, and the entourage of splendid royalty."

Louisa could have written the same thing about herself. The thorns of grief had given her face a softer shade too.

"I quitted its [St. Petersburg's] gaudy loneliness without a sigh, except that which was wafted to the tomb of my lovely babe—To that spot my heart yet wanders with a chastened grief, that looks to hopes above."

For so long she felt responsible for her infant daughter's death. Louisa wrote Abigail in April 1813 that she had fallen while holding baby Louisa and perhaps that was why she later died. Babies who experienced an accident of that type would have developed a hematoma or internal bleeding in the brain. If that were the case, baby Louisa most likely would have started vomiting or displayed some obvious altered state. The fact that Louisa didn't observe even a bruise on her child or the "slightest injury" significantly diminishes hematoma as a cause for the baby's death.

Why did the child die at thirteen months of age? Although it is impossible to know, Louisa left a few facts about her baby's health that point to some possibilities. The seizures are the strongest clue in this medical mystery.

"My lovely beautiful babe is very, very ill—Ah! the fountain of her precious existence is sapped by these constant shocks and I look at her with fear and trembling!" she recorded in February 1812, not long after both of her children had the grippe, or flu. Baby Louisa was seven months old at the time.

Febrile seizures are convulsions stemming from a fever in babies and small children. About one in twenty-five children will have at least one febrile seizure in childhood. During a febrile convulsion, which usually lasts less than a minute or two, children can lose consciousness, shaking limbs on both sides of the body. Most children outgrow the condition, while fewer than 5 percent go on to develop epilepsy.

Both of Louisa's children contracted the grippe or flu that winter. If the baby had encephalitis instead, which was commonly mistaken for influenza back then, the resulting brain inflammation could have caused tissue damage, leaving her prone to seizures.

The baby's convulsions could also have been congenital, not the result of disease. By this point Louisa had miscarried at least six times in her lifetime. Without modern contraceptives, families were larger in the nineteenth century. With three boys and one daughter, John and Louisa's family was small by comparison. A genetic disorder is a possible explanation for Louisa's multiple miscarriages and her daughter's convulsions.

It is not uncommon for a woman, back then or today, to experience one miscarriage. Two miscarriages are less likely, and three even more so. If Louisa and John were alive today, doctors would possibly advise them to undergo genetic testing. Chromosomal abnormalities are common causes of miscarriages, particularly multiple ones.

Though it is normal for any couple to produce occasional abnormal chromosomes, some couples are much more prone to mismatches than others. As a result their children may also have a higher chance of developing a congenital condition. Baby Louisa could have suffered from a genetic abnormality or disorder that caused seizures.

By August 1812 the baby was cutting multiple teeth at once, which led Louisa to begin weaning her in the days before her death. The baby developed dysentery, which could have been a side effect from drinking animal's milk or water. Or baby Louisa could have had a congenital disorder that manifested itself through seizures when she faced physical stress, such as high temperatures from the flu or dysentery from weaning.

Her diarrhea could have led to hyponatremia, an electrolyte disturbance where the salt levels in the blood decrease while the brain swells. Hyponatremia can cause death, especially if it comes on suddenly.

Medicine was so rudimentary in 1812 that physicians provided supportive, not scientific-based care. The doctors lanced the baby's gums and administered blisters because they mistakenly thought the practice freed poisons from the brain. In reality bleeding made the patient worse.

Louisa blamed herself for her daughter's death. If only she had waited a few more months to wean her or if she hadn't fallen, she thought. She became so depressed that John encouraged her to read his friend Benjamin Rush's new book, *Medical Inquiries and Observations upon Diseases of the Mind*, which was first published in 1812.

Advanced medical knowledge could not have erased the pain of Louisa's loss, but knowing the cause of her daughter's death would have helped her to more quickly understand what happened. Regardless, she did not need to blame herself.

By the time of her homecoming in Berlin in 1815, Louisa had come to terms with her daughter's death. John's departure from St. Petersburg forced her to depend on herself for her everyday needs—the first time in her life, she observed. She was the sole parent of Charles in his absence. She had to make business decisions that were beyond her expertise. Their separation, particularly her fears that he was happier without her, made her consider what really mattered to her in life.

Happy to leave St. Petersburg, Louisa was also no longer a depressed woman. That woman—the one who had once exchanged her desire for reunion with her boys with a quest to die and be buried next to her baby—was now gone. Replacing her was a lady of courage, a phoenix determined to get to Paris at all costs. She had a new purpose in life. Reunion with her paramour was now paramount. If she could be reunited with her husband, then maybe, just maybe, they could sail home to Boston and embrace their boys again.

Though conversations with old friends cheered her, she left Berlin with some sadness. She had yet to receive a letter from John. Was it merely a delay of the post? Or had he not written her? He knew she would stop in Berlin. She had even asked him for advice on the best route from there to Paris. Lacking suggestions from John, Louisa gathered her own intelligence instead.

"My friends in Berlin had advised me to avoid Leipzig, as I should have to cross the battlefield so celebrated a year before, and we went on a different route."

The roads were now sandy, dotted with pleasant pine trees. Green was replacing the gray. Spring was coming out of hibernation, but so was hidden danger.

"In the evening after dark I used to put on my son's military cap and tall feather, and lay his sword across the window of the carriage; as I had been told, that anything that looked military escaped from insult—My two servants rode on the box armed; and I was always careful to put away my insignia before I came to any house."

Charles's military interest became an asset. The previous fall, he had become so excited to receive a gun from his instructor in St. Petersburg that he had gleefully written his father of his best friend's jealousy. He had also used his finest handwriting to tell his father about some cucumbers he'd planted.

John replied instructively. "And if you take up one of them [a cucumber], and keep it over winter, and cut it open next spring you will find seeds in it, and by planting them in a garden they will produce another crop of cucumbers, for next summer salad," Adams told Charles.

The news had stirred the farmer in the father, motivating him to plant a vision for his son for their future together: "But if you take out the seeds now and keep them dry, and we go home to America the next year, you can take them with you and plant them in a garden there and when the cucumbers come I hope we shall have your brothers George and John to share them with us."

As she left Berlin, it was up to Louisa to make sure that the reunion John had promised Charles would happen. Much exhausted, she decided to stop for the night at a post somewhere between Berlin and Hanau. The master of the house was as hospitable as he was gossipy. What he had to say was ghostlike and shocking.

"A rumor had arrived of the return of Napoleon to France." The innkeeper laughed, noting that the rumor had sparked many "jokes, as he was known to be very safe at Elba! But such a rumor was abroad, and in everybody's mouth."

"I started with astonishment—True or false the coincidence was strange; and the bonne aventure of Countess Apraxin forced itself upon my mind in spite of my reason."

If the rumor was true, Napoleon, now the king of spades, seemed ready to play his final card and trump all of Europe once again.

56

"The Star-Spangled Banner"

THE POSSIBILITY OF NAPOLEON'S ESCAPE FROM EXILE IN ELBA zapped what was left of Louisa's energy the night she first heard the rumor. Her exhaustion led to carelessness: "I went to bed very tired, and for the first time left my purse with some gold in it upon the table."

Madame Babet, who had lived for thirty years with Madame Colombi, was trustworthy. She locked the doors. When Louisa awoke the next morning, she noticed that her chamber's lamp was extinguished, along with her money: "My purse was there, but the gold was gone! I ordered the carriage immediately, and again we pursued our route."

Her friends in Berlin advised her to take the route toward Hanau, not Leipzig. She followed their suggestion. As she journeyed farther away from Berlin, John's letter addressed to her in Berlin likely arrived. Their correspondence crossed in the mail. He had suggested a different route from Berlin to France: "Last week . . . I was informed," he wrote to her from Paris, "that the *best* road was by way of Leipzig and Frankfurt."

His final words would have also cheered her insecurities had she been able to read them: "No farewell but a welcome to the arms of your affectionate husband and father."

The reason her friends advised her to avoid Leipzig was simple. Napoleon had suffered his worst defeat there in October 1813. After his armies failed to take Berlin, he retreated. With 300,000 soldiers, the allies approached his regrouped army of 185,000. They surrounded him from all sides, which forced him into a defenseless battle at Leipzig. The losses were great for both, with 38,000 French killed or wounded and another 30,000 captured, and 55,000 allies killed or wounded. Though the losses were among the war's worst, because the Battle of Leipzig broke Napoleon's longtime hold on Germany, it was the strongest victory for the allies.

Regardless of which road Louisa chose, through Leipzig or Hanau, the air was thick with the same rumor in March 1815. "Wherever we stopped to change horses, we heard of the return of Napoleon," she wrote, noting that many doubted the news.

"At about a mile before we entered the town [Hanau], I had observed a number of mounds like graves with crosses at the feet, in the ditches on the sides of the roads—We entered on a wide extended plain, over which was scattered remnants of clothes; old boots in pieces; and an immense quantity of bones, laying in this ploughed field."

They had crossed into a battlefield, the very reason she'd avoided the road to Leipzig. Had she received John's letter in time, she might have been spared this particular sight, but carnage was unavoidable no matter which road she traveled.

"My heart throbbed; and I felt deadly sick at my stomach and faint; guessing where I was, when the postilions pointed out a board on which it was stated, that this was the field of battle where the Bavarians had intercepted the retreat of Napoleon, and that in this plain, ten thousand men had been slain."

The Battle of Hanau had taken place at the end of October 1813, a couple of weeks after Leipzig. Bavarian forces had attempted to block Napoleon's retreat. The Bavarians had lost ten thousand men, and Napoleon's army had successfully occupied Hanau, but only briefly. Just days later, the surviving Frenchmen crossed the border into France. While Napoleon's losses were far fewer at this battle, about ten thousand French stragglers from both Leipzig and Hanau became prisoners of war.

Ever since Louisa's childhood, she had heard about war. The American Revolution was the very reason her Maryland-born father had fled London to Nantes, France, when she was a babe. As an adult she had read newspaper accounts of European and American battles, but she had never seen carnage with her own eyes until now.

"Conceive my horror at the sight of such a butchery! I could with difficulty keep from fainting, as fancy realized the torture, suffering, and anguish, thus brought before my eyes, with all the ghastly relics of the dead, exposed with savage barbarity to the view."

Louisa's carriage hurried away from the battlefield and into town, where they found many armed men at the gates.

"I was much questioned, and with some difficulty procured horses, which however I was obliged to wait for three or four hours."

When she arrived at an inn, she found the people talkative, but speaking mostly French, not German.

"They . . . took great pains to point out to me the wonders that had been performed by Napoleon, and his officers—three times they were beaten back from the bridge, but at last took it against a strong force, and obtained possession of the town."

The innkeepers showed her the very place where three cannonballs had hit the house during the battle. They boasted that they had hosted three French officers. Praise for Napoleon was so great, she might as well have been in Paris.

"It was a very remarkable fact that in the course of my journey, I heard but little praise of the allied armies, and unceasing admiration of the exploits of the French; yet suffering, and devastation, had followed their steps—but the renowned cruelties, and barbarities, of the Cossacks, seemed to have white washed all other crimes from their minds."

As they traveled, they saw soldiers mustering on the town greens and in fields. Suddenly the isolated German roads changed into cluttered places where people were gathering to chatter over the possibility of Napoleon's return.

Louisa was not the only one affected by the awakening. "At this place I observed that my servants began to grow uneasy, and frequently talked about conscripts, and renewal of the wars—for which neither appeared to have any taste." She added, "Feeling very uneasy; I pushed on with all the celerity that tolerable roads, and good horses, six of which were always forced on me, would admit; and should have found many agreeable objects to attract my attention, if my mind had been more at ease."

As much as the skeleton field unnerved Louisa that March day in 1815, a bombardment was the very news that had put her mind at ease a few months earlier.

Reports of the British departure from Washington City and assault on Baltimore arrived in contradictory waves. In late October 1814 Mr. Harris informed her that the residents of Baltimore had surrendered and declared themselves British subjects. If that was true, then America was indeed conquered. Gossip in the parlors of St. Petersburg burst with barbs that Bostonians had also declared, "Long live the king!" Louisa was much more confident of American patriotism—especially in Boston—than she was in the rumors of Russia.

The pace of the British commissioners in Ghent also increased, suddenly snapping from slow adagio into fast-paced allegro. They were more elated than ever about their chances to defeat the US commissioners and lower the boundary line between Canada and the United States. They were hopeful of soon controlling the coveted Mississippi River, especially if their military captured New Orleans as planned.

From his post in Ghent, John heard the opposite about the outcome in Baltimore. Unofficial word arrived that the Americans had won a victory over the English at Fort McHenry, which guarded the city from its lookout location over the river. He heard that four hundred English soldiers were dead, compared to a thousand Americans. The numbers did not add up to a US victory. Hence, Adams was uncertain whether the news was true.

Eventually the official news from Baltimore reached the commissioners in Ghent. Admirals Cochrane and Cockburn along with General Ross arrived in the Chesapeake Bay with a fleet of fifty British ships and nearly six thousand soldiers and sailors. Taking four thousand men on the southeast side of the Patapsco River on September 12, Ross marched within striking distance of Baltimore. He planned to launch a land attack as soon as Fort McHenry raised the white flag of surrender to the Royal Navy.

Admiral Cochrane sent a portion of his fleet through the Patapsco River to the point opposite the star-shaped Fort McHenry. The bombardment began at dawn on September 13. For some twenty-four hours the Royal Navy pounded Fort McHenry with hundreds of Congreve rockets and shells. When it was over, the fort remained. Instead of showcasing the white flag of surrender, the dawn's early light revealed America's Stars and Stripes on September 14.

The sight of that enormous flag, which measured thirty by forty-two feet, was the most beautiful sight that American attorney Francis Scott Key had ever seen. While trying to secure the release of a US prisoner of war, Key became trapped on a ship during the bombardment. The sound of continuous blasts was frightfully loud. The firing was so earsplitting, some say it could be heard ninety miles away in Philadelphia.

Seeing that flag meant one thing: America was still free. "Through the clouds of the war the stars of that banner still shone in my view." The people of Baltimore saved the nation from being conquered and losing its sovereignty.

Key quickly penned the immortal words of a new lyrical poem first called the "Defense of Fort McHenry," which was published anonymously and distributed throughout Baltimore as a broadside. The words were set to an old English tune, "To Anacreon in Heaven"—the same tune for the "Adams and Liberty" song written to honor President Adams years earlier. The poem title was later changed to "The Star-Spangled Banner." America's second quest for independence, not its first, gave it a national anthem. Decades later the US Army and Navy adopted the song as a national hymn, and the US Congress made it official in 1931.

Adams later understood the confusion about the numbers at Fort McHenry. One thousand referred to the number of patriots who defended the fort, not the total number of casualties. The US losses were much lower. Only three men and a woman died, while twenty-four were injured defending the fort.

When British Admiral Cochrane realized that Fort McHenry would not fall, he took his fleet and fled rather than face the fifteen thousand men of the militia who were ready to defend Baltimore. Several factors influenced his decision. Baltimore ship owners sank twenty of their own ships across the channel, which made the water too shallow for the Royal Navy to safely reach Baltimore's wharf.

One other deciding factor had taken place two days earlier. After preparing for a land attack, General Ross and six officers decided to eat breakfast at a local farmhouse outside Baltimore. Ross, nicknamed the baron of Washington for his role in burning the US Capitol, ordered the farmer to fix them breakfast and taste the food as he served them. They could not risk death by poisoning. After his "guests" finished, the farmer asked if they planned to return for supper.

"No," Ross replied tersely. "I shall eat my supper in Baltimore or in Hell!"

No sooner had the words left his mouth than they heard muskets firing in the distance. Galloping over to the scene, they met their own advance guardsmen, who were shooting at a small group of Americans. Sniper fire suddenly struck Ross, who fell from his horse with a rifle ball lodged in his spine. His men took him to cover in the woods. The newspapers reported that he was greatly concerned about his wife and children as he lay dying, within view of the farmhouse where he had made his fateful prediction.

"The noble baron should have thought about the dear wives he had made widows and the children he had made suffer in his savage exploit upon Washington," Adams mercilessly remarked when he read about Ross's death.

The Capitol may have been destroyed, but because of the people of Baltimore, America was not conquered. Soon the news was even better. When word from Plattsburgh, New York, arrived at Ghent, the reserved Adams could not contain his joy.

A British army of ten thousand left Canada to attack Plattsburgh. They stopped at Lake Champlain to wait for their navy to arrive as backup. With only thirty-four hundred men, the Americans surprised the invaders by pushing back the royal fleet. As a result the patriots secured a victory at Lake Champlain on September 11, 1814.

Instead of marching toward Boston or pushing to New York, the British then removed their forces from northern America. They abandoned the East Coast and steered their ships toward New Orleans. Capturing the Mississippi gulf was their last hope of changing the map of North America in their favor. John was elated over the victories in Baltimore and Lake Champlain.

When Louisa learned the glorious truth, [she wrote:] "Heaven has not deserted us, and if we do not desert ourselves we shall yet make our proud and insulting enemies feel that we are and must be a great nation."

The game changer—the great modulation that the US negotiators needed at Ghent—had finally taken place. Adams, Gallatin, Clay, Bayard, and Russell could now take matters into their own hands.

57

Antebellum

AFTER HIDING BEHIND THE PRETENSE OF PRETREATY OBJECTIONS, the British commissioners dared their US counterparts to write their own treaty. With the news of Baltimore and Plattsburgh lifting their spirits, the Americans did just that. They drafted a response to the pretentious preliminary points of the British and then wrote an actual treaty, a proposal for peace.

"We had never before taken so much time to reply; the reason of which delay is that we have been preparing the draft of a treaty to send with the note. This has brought us upon the whole field of this negotiation," Adams wrote Louisa on November 8, 1814.

They labored for days. Though their internal deliberation was sometimes a dissonant quintet, John was hopeful of cordial unanimity, a tutti outburst at the end: "But our deliberations have been cool, moderate, mutually conciliatory, and I think will result in full harmony."

They retained the treaty items they wanted but didn't realistically expect to obtain, such as the abolishment of impressment and a definition of neutral trade rights. With Napoleon out of power, English navy captains would have no more need to impress American sailors. The moral issue of the war was a moot point as long as Bonaparte was locked away in exile.

Without knowing for sure whether President Madison would approve their draft and fearing they could violate Monroe's initial secret instructions to move the US boundary north into Canada, John made a bold move, one that potentially jeopardized his standing with his government. He proposed keeping the boundary line as it was before the war, antebellum. At first Henry Clay and Jonathan Russell objected. Then after more deliberation, which drew out Adams's lawyerly logic, they agreed to take the risk. Defying Madison and Monroe's old, original orders, they embraced a pragmatic course to peace.

Failure could sink them all, especially Adams, sending them back to private life and professions out of public service.

Several times they had asked the British to discuss a treaty, but the English negotiators replied with pretenses about etiquette. Now the Americans gave them a proposal for peace, which sent the English scrambling back to their bosses. In London government leaders held an emergency meeting to discuss the American treaty option. Adams complained that the English commissioners were nothing more than "a post-office between us and the British Privy Council." He was right. That was exactly what the British commissioners were.

While they waited for the lords in London to respond, a ship carrying letters from the US government arrived in France. A messenger rushed the correspondence to Ghent. Included was the most important piece of paper they could have possibly received in their hour of risk and uncertainty. President Madison had issued additional instructions, proposing exactly what Adams had suggested and the commissioners had already proposed to the British. John didn't need a nonexistent telephone to do what was right and obvious. In the analogy of his father, his conscience approved, and America would soon applaud him as well.

"In the instructions that we have now received, dated 19 October, we are expressly authorized to make the same identical [antebellum] offer. The heaviest responsibility therefore, that of having trespassed upon our instructions, is already removed."

John and his colleagues had triumphed. If the British accepted their terms, America would remain an independent nation once and for all. An honorable peace just might give Adams what he had long wanted, an end to the war and an honorable exit from his St. Petersburg post.

"For the first time I now entertain hope that the British government is inclined to conclude the peace," he wrote, also noting that the Congress of Vienna had not given the Brits what they wanted: supreme power in Europe. France through Talleyrand had prevailed, while Alexander stuck to his support for American trade rights.

"We are now in sight of port. Oh! that we may reach it in safety!" John wrote.

As her husband waited in Ghent for acceptance of the secret treaty, Louisa found herself face-to-face with pretense. She had met an Englishman at a party in St. Petersburg. He wanted to know if John was near success.

"[He] asked me, *formally* if you were likely to make peace, and if affairs were not already arranged," Louisa wrote John. "I could not help staring at the man. I have never had such a direct question put to me. I told him you never wrote me upon business."

The moment also underscored how anxious everyone was for peace—Americans, Brits, and Europeans. The rest of the negotiations hung on a hair. A grain of sand was all that remained—so Adams and his wife hoped.

Soon his joy faded. The British were stalling again. Maybe the de facto king of England had been the trump card. Or perhaps Lord Liverpool was willing to wait for the outcome of a battle at New Orleans. John's colleagues, however, were hopeful that the negotiation would end before the New Year began.

"I speak of it as doubtful whether we shall finish here before the spring, because notwithstanding the present complexion of the rumors and prevailing opinions in England, the prospect of peace is very little brighter than it has been at our gloomiest hours," he moaned to Louisa in a letter dated December 9, 1814.

Peace seemed so close. However, with no response from the British, it lingered as a phantom, taunting them.

———✦———

"I'd write you from this place where I arrived last evening and where I have again met with a severe disappointment in not receiving letters more especially as the public news renders my intention is extremely unpleasant," Louisa quickly penned to John from Frankfurt on March 17, 1815.

Her plan was simple, to leave Frankfurt that evening. She promised to travel "night and day" to meet him in Paris. She would journey through Strasbourg. He should expect her very soon. Before the ink on her letter could dry, she realized that getting to the French border town would not be as easy as she thought.

"My two servants requested to speak to me, and informed me that circumstances having totally changed, since their engagement to attend me to

France; in consequence of Napoleon's return, they must quit my service, and preferred to remain at Frankfurt."

Her servants either saw an opportunity to join the military units that were forming in hopes of following Napoleon or were afraid of entering France amid the rumors of Bonaparte's surprise return. Regardless, they wanted to leave her service.

"*Here was a situation*—I could not compel them to stay; no bribe could induce them to go on in their state of panic," she recalled with emphasis.

Louisa asked them to wait until she visited a banker, a man recommended to her by friends. She sent the man a note, and he quickly arrived at her hotel.

"He was very polite; and urged me very strongly to remain a few days in the city, and he would endeavor to make arrangements for me."

The banker was just as her friends had predicted: understanding and wise. "My position was so unpleasant, he thought it required great prudence in my arrangements."

If she could reach John in Paris, then he would be able to protect her through diplomatic immunity in case of a French civil war. "I insisted that it would be better for me to get into France as soon as possible; as I should probably meet my husband on the frontier, and every moment would add to the difficulty, should I delay—At present the panic itself would prove advantageous; as it would require time to ascertain events, before the governments could take decisive measures."

The banker agreed, but the king's troops were likely already assembled and headed for the French frontier, the very region she was about to enter. The disbanded troops who supported Napoleon were reuniting. The bond of brotherhood was as alive as the man himself. Life in France could revert to its antebellum status as well—as dangerous and divisive as the French Revolution. The greatest threat to Louisa would be the soldiers rallying to Bonaparte and the stragglers who followed them.

The fervor for Napoleon was so great that people began painting their houses in the tri-colors of red, white, and blue. It was as if a carrier pigeon was flying, soaring from one village spire to the next to deliver messages. If Bonaparte had his way, even the towers of Notre Dame would fly his colors.

"He [the banker] advised on the whole that it would be best to proceed, but thought I should change my intended route for one more circuitous but safer; and more likely to be quiet; and he would try to find some person to go with me."

The banker left. Within a short time, he returned, escorting a fourteen-year-old boy, who was "the only creature he could find willing to go."

Arranging her financial accounts and helping her into the carriage, the banker told the driver which route to take and gave her one piece of advice. The boy was smart, but a chatterer.

"He had though so young been in the Russian Campaign with a Prussian officer; and told me a great many anecdotes concerning Napoleon during the retreat—Of his sitting among his soldiers to warm himself! Of his partaking of their soup, when they had any! His kindness to them in the midst of their misery &cc &cc."

While he admired Bonaparte, a part of the boy also despised him. "At the same time he expressed great hatred of the man, with all the petulance of boyish passion—It was singular to watch the workings of this young mind, swayed equally by admiration and detestation, uttered in the strong language of natural feeling."

A shocked Louisa rode toward Strasbourg. Had Napoleon truly returned? She was more grateful for the banker's advice than she could possibly express. Though she didn't mourn the loss of Baptiste, the departure of both of her male servants put her, Charles, and Madame Babet in even greater jeopardy.

Once again her business sense and ability to make sound decisions were put to the test. Now she was traveling with a servant whose young face could not have been much different from George's or John's. Many times she had worried that her decisions in St. Petersburg were too costly. The new route proposed by the banker would lengthen her journey, making it more expensive. Nevertheless, perhaps the route would keep her from the clutches of Napoleon and his rowdy supporters. So she hoped.

"From want of judgment or habit of management I have injured my children's property, I must submit to their reproaches as I have for many years submitted to yours," she had bitterly written months earlier in a letter to John at Ghent.

Though she had not willfully mismanaged their finances, she worried about her husband's approval each time she spent money, no matter how small the purchase. Maybe if he was so displeased with her, he would never make the mistake of abandoning her again. Why couldn't she have traveled with him to Ghent? Then he could have avoided her business mistakes. "It will at least be a lesson to you not to leave me with a large establishment in a foreign country another time."

John, however, had needed Louisa to represent America in St. Petersburg. He couldn't trust Mr. Harris, who often gambled too much and maintained friendships with Englishmen that were too chummy in Adams's opinion.

Guilt over money had also consumed Louisa when she found herself needing another gown for a ball. The occasion was the emperor's birthday on December 24, 1814. She wrote John that gowns had been seven hundred rubles in the summer, but when she went shopping for a new dress in December, she was astonished to find that they had more than doubled. Fearing her husband's displeasure over spending too much money, she'd made a few alterations to a dress she already owned, which cost only three hundred rubles.

While she was enjoying Alexander's hospitality, John wrote her a note revealing just how much he trusted her judgment. This letter would change her life forever.

"On Saturday last, the twenty-fourth of December, the Emperor Alexander's birthday, a treaty of peace and amity was signed by the British and American plenipotentiaries in this city."

The US commissioners had finally triumphed. A month of dithering over details led to an honorable peace. What Adams did not know, of course, was Lord Liverpool's secret position. For weeks the prime minister had been wailing at the high cost of the US war and longing for enough harmony in Vienna to satisfy his people's hunger for real progress. Liverpool was so secretly anxious to get the American war behind him that he was willing for the boundary between Canada and the United States to return to its prewar location—the exact offer Adams had initiated at high risk.

"I consider the day on which I signed it as the happiest of my life; because it was the day on which I had my share in restoring peace to the world," John gleefully confessed in another letter to Louisa.

However, he had to change his plans. He could not return to St. Petersburg as he had promised his wife because he and the other commissioners had to get to Paris to wait for news from President Madison and the US government. If the US Congress ratified the treaty, then he and the others would receive new appointments. The rumor was that Madison would either promote Adams to US minister to England or recall him home to Washington or Boston.

"I therefore now write you to break up altogether our establishment at St. Petersburg, to dispose of all the furniture which you do not incline to keep, and have all the rest packed up carefully, and left in the charge of Mr. Harris to be sent next summer either to London or to Boston and to come with Charles to me at Paris, where I shall be impatiently waiting for you."

If the weather was too severe, he offered for Louisa to wait to travel until the spring or summer. Though the choice was hers, he desperately hoped she would take the risk of winter. Then he gave her some business advice and suggested she hire a good man and woman servant to accompany her. Post houses should provide tolerable lodging along the way.

"I hope neither you nor Charles will suffer much on the road. I hope to embrace you in Paris about the 20th of March. The sooner, the happier for me."

His request was one of the most shocking of Louisa's life. The reality of traveling without a male companion and being responsible for decisions along the road was nearly too much for her.

"Consider the astonishment your letter has caused me if you can and still more the treaty which is published in the English papers," she replied in a letter to him.

Peace thrilled her, while the idea of selling their furnishings and making travel arrangements troubled her. Though shocked, she responded with love.

"I fear I shall be much imposed upon; this is a heavy trial but I must get through it at all risks," she confessed, adding, "and if you receive me with the conviction that I have done my best I shall be amply rewarded."

Indeed. The woman who had bitterly left Boston because her husband and father-in-law thought they should leave their boys behind now ardently longed for her husband's love and approval as she stepped forward and made the biggest journey of her life—*solus*.

The trials Louisa faced on her travels from St. Petersburg toward Paris in 1815 were worse than she had imagined when she wrote that letter to John. Now nothing could lessen the reality of her circumstances as she entered the French border town of Strasbourg.

She had one thing in common with Napoleon. Both were escaping their exile. Both would do anything for reunion.

58

Vive!

"Napoleon had been taken," Louisa learned from the post house master at her next stop. "He had been tried immediately and shot."

Before leaving the room, the innkeeper told her that the news of Bonaparte's death was reliable for one surefire reason. The assurance came from the palace.

"I heard an exclamation of horror; and turning round, saw the boy who I had hired, as pale as a ghost, and ready to faint—he looked piteously at me saying 'O that great man! I did not expect that!'"

Louisa was grateful that the innkeeper left the room before the boy's outburst. Otherwise he might have concluded that she was "some violent Bonapartist" and harassed her, or worse. She left the post house as soon as the horses were rested.

"Wagons of every description, full of soldiers, were continually rushing towards the frontier—roaring national songs, and apparently in great glee at the idea of a renewal of hostilities—What a mere animal man may become!"

They reached the Fortress of Kiel, which was on the Rhine River opposite Strasbourg. The border guard demanded to see her papers and thoroughly questioned her. He subjected them to an intense interrogation by searching their bags, which delayed them. After realizing she was a diplomat's wife, he agreed to let her cross into Strasbourg.

"He [the officer] said the country was in a very unsettled state, and that it would require great prudence and caution, in the pursuit of my journey to Paris. . . . The emperor had certainly returned; and was then on his way to the capital."

Napoleon was not dead. The rumor of his being shot was contradicted by another story. When the king's troops—the soldiers of the Fifth—arrived on the outskirts of a sizable town, the leader of the Fifth had confronted

Napoleon's men over Bonaparte's demands for five thousand rations of bread, wine, and meat from the town.

As the Fifth's leader sent a guard toward the men, Napoleon himself had stepped forward, brazenly flipped opened his coat, and called out: "Soldiers of the Fifth, I am your emperor. Know me! If there is one among you who would kill his emperor, here I am."

None of the soldiers could fire. Instead they'd broken ranks and rushed toward him, crying out, "Vive l'Empereur!" while bowing and kissing his feet.

Because so many similar rumors were whisking into towns faster than the wind, Louisa concluded that her situation was dangerous. Her fourteen-year-old servant's impulsiveness confirmed her intuition. She needed additional help to safely reach Paris.

"The public spirit in Paris now is confident and sanguine. It does not appear that Napoleon has advanced from Lyons. He is undoubtedly there, very weak; and formidable forces are marching from all quarters against him," John wrote in his diary about the time Louisa entered Strasbourg.

Adams had heard that Napoleon arrived at Gulf Juan in coastal Cannes the first day of March with a few hundred men and four cannon. What he did not yet know was that at Elba, Napoleon had ordered a vessel to be painted like a British warship. Boarding it with the ease of an innocent girl, he'd escaped exile without the slightest notice. Not even the Royal Navy patrolling Elba had detected his deceit. Napoleon had also lied to Elba's military governor by telling him that Paris was in arms. He needed to go there and rescue his people.

John's information about Napoleon's weakness was wrong. Bonaparte's few hundred men had swelled to a few thousand. Far from being stalled in Lyons, they were marching toward Paris and expanding their numbers with each town that gave them rations and men.

Adams's ability to understand French and speak it fluently gave him many opportunities to "spy" on those around him, especially at the opera. He spent most of his evenings at the theater, where he captured news and gossip from unaware audience members sitting next to him. Many in Paris assumed that as an American, he probably could not speak French very well, if at all. This assumption gave him an advantage.

A baron had recently proclaimed with soaring confidence that King Louis's government was stable. The pillars at the Palais Royale, the handsome palace whose cafés were magnets for Parisians, boasted broadsides calling Frenchmen to arms against Bonaparte. According to the baron, the number of volunteers offering to march against Napoleon was so great that the government could not accept them all.

"It is ascertained that a part of the troops, as well as of the highest officers, are faithful to the king, and Napoleon's soldiers will probably desert him in the end. There is but one sentiment to be heard in Paris," Adams recorded on March 15, 1815.

The best evidence came from the music, which orchestra conductors infused with couplets saluting "the Bourbons." The royal national air, "Henri Quatre," was sung each night, to rapturous applause. Likewise the cries of "Vive le Roi!" were just as loud at the conclusion of these performances.

In contrast John also noticed that not everyone was as confident in the king's ability to prevent Napoleon from retaking the throne: "I saw in various parts of the city a great number of post-horses, apparently going to take travelers leaving Paris."

More than two centuries earlier Shakespeare had wrtitten, "From their ashes shall be reared, a Phoenix that shall make all France afeared." Though he intended the phrase to apply to England's Henry VI, the same could have been said of Bonaparte returning from exile.

When John returned to his hotel the night of March 15, he discovered a letter from Louisa, which was dated March 5 in Berlin. She told him she thought she would be in Paris within ten to fifteen days. Ten had already passed, and she had not arrived. What could be delaying her?

⤙⤚

Louisa spent an entire day at Strasbourg to rest.

"The day at Strasbourg was very tedious—My health was dreadful, and the excessive desire I had to terminate this long journey, absolutely made me sick—I had been a year absent from my husband, and five years and a half from my two sons; and the hope of soon again embracing them, gave me strength to sustain the fatigue and excitement to which I was necessarily exposed."

After dinner she took a leisurely stroll with Charles through the town; its quaint charm reminded her of Massachusetts. When she returned, the master of the hotel introduced her to Dupin. He was someone she could rely on for advice and assistance, especially on the best route to Paris.

"We immediately entered into engagements; I requested him to see that the carriage was in order, and told him that on the next morning but one, I intended to depart for Paris, and to go on with as much rapidity as possible."

Dupin asked the teenage servant if he wanted to go home, but the lad insisted on finding his old master in Paris.

"As he had rendered me good service, I could not refuse this; and a condition was made by Dupin, that he was not to talk at any of the houses where we might stay, and that he was either to be under my eye, or his, at all times—to which he readily agreed," Louisa noted.

They left Strasbourg the next day and persevered until one o'clock in the morning. Louisa would have continued, but her drivers insisted that she stop at a nearby house in an isolated town.

"We drove up to a miserable place in which we found a long room, with a pine table, several very surly looking men, and nothing but common benches to sit on—Here I was obliged to sit, while they procured us a little milk, the only thing we could get."

The men questioned Charles, who became quite frightened.

"Dupin took the opportunity to ask if I could have some chamber where I could put the child to sleep, and a door was opened into an adjoining chamber even more uncomfortable than the one we left."

Once again Louisa and Madame Babet stayed up all night, both unable to sleep.

"[We] heard threatening conversation in the next room, and the boasts of what Napoleon was to do now that he had arrived, to drive out Louis XVIII and his beggarly crew."

The men hated the Russians and loudly cursed them.

"There were many bitter anathemas against the allied powers and the horrible Cossacks—I rejoiced when I found myself once more safely seated in the heavy Russian carriage, and we renewed our journey with fresh spirits."

Dupin was as judicious as he was discreet and tactful. His smooth manner of speaking commanded respect, even from the cursing men at the inn.

They arrived at the town of Nancy, where they stopped only to change horses. Delighted at the return of the emperor, troops crowded the town square, where they were mustering and preparing to join Napoleon.

"Dupin told me that if we made good speed, we should keep in advance all the way; as it would require some hours for their preparation, and that we should reach Paris with ease before they could get half way there."

They drove quickly, stopping at Chateau-Thierry for the night, without incident. The next morning Louisa and Dupin decided to aim for Epernay, where they could stop to eat. She relaxed. The roads were fair, and the weather was even better. Everything seemed quiet. They reached Epernay just as Dupin had predicted, in time for lunch.

"The waiter said that I must have some champagne as this was the fine champagne country, and he doubted if I could find such in Paris. He was so urgent; I at last consented to have a bottle, which certainly was superior to any that I have ever tasted before or since."

The waiter served them so quickly that they were ready to depart in less than an hour. Then he gave them disturbing news. Yes, it was true. Napoleon was marching in the direction of Epernay. He told her not to worry. She was at least a day ahead of his reunited Imperial Guard, an elite force that sometimes personally guarded Napoleon.

"[The waiter] told me that the people of the town did not expect the troops to pass until the next day, and that I need not hurry."

Meanwhile John again recorded his observations, this time about the king's Tuileries Palace. "I went out half an hour before dinner and walked around by the Tuileries and the Place du Carrousel, where a great concourse of people was assembled," John wrote. "The king was going out to review the troops, who are to march out tomorrow morning to meet Napoleon."

Adams wondered whether the army's support for the king was a pretense, a mask of their true love for Napoleon: "No appearance of anything like defection to the royal cause was discernible, but the countenance of the attendants at the Tuileries marked dejection."

He heard a story that confirmed his suspicions. When a few garrison officers ordered the troops in Paris to cry out, "Vive le Roi!" the soldiers replied, "Oh, yes! Vive le Roi!"; then they chuckled as if hearing the latest joke from a court jester.

Adams also noticed that the Palais Royal walls were covered with "the most violent and furious addresses and declamations against Bonaparte." The calls for "Henri Quatre!" and the shouts of "Vive le Roi!" continued as "boisterous as ever" at the opera, but the military's attitudes revealed an opposite sentiment.

"They had not a hope that the soldiers would fight for the king."

The morning of March 20, John awoke to the news. The king and royal family were gone. The palace was as empty as Napoleon's house in Elba. "They left the palace of the Tuileries at one o'clock this morning," he documented. "It was but last Thursday that the king . . . talked with the two legislative chambers of dying in defense of the country."

Adams took to the streets to catch the vibe of the people, which had turned as quickly as a pigeon could fly from one steeple to another.

"There was a great crowd of people upon the Boulevards, but the cries of 'Vive l'Empereur!' had already been substituted for those of 'Vive le Roi!'"

About the same time that loyalties in Paris switched, John received great news from home. An American newspaper reported that a battle had taken place in New Orleans. General Andrew Jackson had defeated the British army there on January 8, 1815—two weeks after John signed the Treaty of Ghent. The news was a double treat. After messengers delivered the Treaty of Ghent to Washington City in February 1815, Congress ratified and President Madison signed it. Peace was official. The War of 1812 was dead.

John soon learned the details of King Louis's proclamation, which he issued upon fleeing Paris. "He says that divine Providence, after restoring him to the throne of his ancestors, now permitted it to be shaken, by the defection of a part of the army who is sworn to defend it."

Adams took comfort in one fact. The king's route was to the north toward Ghent, not to the east, the direction of Louisa's approach. What he didn't realize was that Napoleon's trek toward Paris and his wife's journey could easily intersect.

———

"We had gone about a mile and a half, when we suddenly found ourselves in the midst of the Imperial Guards, who were on their way to meet the emperor," Louisa wrote of the surprise she encountered after leaving Epernay. The waiter was wrong about her being ahead of the troops by at least a day. She was ahead by an hour at best.

"The first notice I had of my danger was hearing the most horrid curses and dreadful language from a number of women, who appeared to be following the troops."

The banker in Frankfurt had warned her that stragglers could be worse than soldiers. His prediction was as accurate as the Baltimore sniper who took out General Ross.

"Presently I heard these wretches cry out, 'tear them out of the carriage; they are Russians' and 'take them out, kill them.'"

Louisa looked at Charles and then Madame Babet, who was as pale as death and trembling uncontrollably. The carriage jolted forward and stopped violently.

"At this moment a party of the soldiers seized hold of the horses, and turned their guns against the drivers."

The curses grew louder and more threatening with each passing minute.

"I sat in agony of apprehension, but had presence of mind enough to take out my passports."

The guards questioned the drivers.

"A general officer with his staff, consisting of four or five, immediately rode up to the carriage and addressed me—I presented my passports."

Madame Babet continued to tremble. Her memories of the French Revolution's head-chopping atrocities drowned her senses, giving way to hysterics.

In contrast Louisa calmly spoke in French to the officer. She explained her situation, identifying who she was and why she was traveling to Paris. He listened. She sat quietly while the officer studied her papers. Charles was absolutely petrified, sitting as still as a marble statue. They were so close to Paris—so close to being reunited with her husband—and now this.

After all that she had been through, would she die at the hands of an out-of-control crowd, hungry for the return of a mad emperor? This was as dangerous as being thrust into the icy Vistula River. Then the worst of nature had teased them; now the nature of man threatened with a more demonic force. In spite of this, she also felt calm. An unexpected peace enveloped her.

"God in his great mercy seemed to give me strength in this trying emergency; for excepting a heightened and glowing color in my cheeks, there was no evidence of fear or trepidation: yet my heart might have been heard to beat, as its convulsive throbbings heaved against my side."

Employing her best French, she learned the officer's name, General Michell.

"[He] called out, that I was an American lady, going to meet her husband in Paris."

When the soldiers and crowd realized what he said, they suddenly changed their opinion of the travelers inside this Russian carriage. "At which the soldiers shouted 'vive les Americains'—and desired that I should cry 'vive Napoleon!' which I did waving my handkerchief."

The men then repeated the "vive les Americains," adding, "ils sont nos amis" or "they are our friends."

General Michell then ordered a number of soldiers to march in front of Louisa's horses. She was not out of danger yet.

"If we attempted to push on out of a walk, the order was to fire on us directly."

Next he advised Louisa on how to act.

"He told me my situation was a very precarious one; the army was totally undisciplined; that they would not obey a single order; that I must appear perfectly easy, and unconcerned."

He then gave her a suggestion to help soften the pro-Napoleon mobs.

"[W]henever they shouted, I must repeat the Viva's."

Though she hardly loved the man, Louisa willingly agreed to wave her handkerchief and call out, "Long live Napoleon" to help Charles safely reach Paris.

General Michell promised to use his influence to find shelter for her at the next post. He also advised her to delay her departure until all the troops had passed. She should then take a circuitous route to Paris. Agreeing, Louisa thanked him.

"He complimented me on my manner of speaking French, and said that my perfect knowledge of the language would contribute much to my safety, as no one would believe me to be a foreigner."

With great relief Louisa began again but faced an uneasy situation. The officer and his men rode on each side of her carriage.

"In this way we journeyed; the soldiers presenting their bayonets at my people with loud and brutal threats every half hour."

For miles Louisa saw nothing but intoxicated men and women lining the road. All she could hear were loud chants of "Down with King Louis" and "Live Napoleon."

"At twelve o'clock at night we reached the post house—General Michell spoke to the lady, and she refused to take me. At length he awakened her sympathy, and she consented, provided I would consent to stay in a dark room; have my people concealed; and my coach stowed away in some place where it could not be perceived."

Louisa agreed to the conditions. The room was comfortable. Though a fire warmed them, they could hear drunken soldiers rambunctiously and noisily coming and going all night from the crowded house. While Charles fell asleep, her nurse had not recovered from the eventful day.

"Madame Babet really appeared to have lost her senses—She clasped her hands continually; while the tears rolled down her cheeks, crying out, that she was lost! for the Revolution was begun again, and this was only the beginning of its horrors."

Louisa left the next morning, taking her time and remembering the Irish adage that the longest way round was the shortest way home. They arrived at Chatillon that night, where she and Dupin picked up on some interesting intelligence. From one person, Dupin learned that Louisa was the subject of a captivating rumor.

"He told me that in consequence of my being almost the only traveler on the road going towards Paris; that a whisper was abroad, that I was one of Napoleon's sisters going to meet him."

Dupin merely shrugged and smiled at the suggestion, leaving the truth a mystery. At this post they also received stern advice. "I had better not go on to Paris, as there were forty thousand men before the gates; and a battle was expected to take place."

In her heart Louisa knew what she wanted to do: press forward.

"This news startled me very much, but on cool reflection, I thought it best to persevere, as I was traveling at great expense, and I was sure if any such danger existed Mr. Adams would have come to meet me, or by some means have conveyed intelligence to guide my course."

After consulting with Dupin, she relaxed. He agreed with her. The best plan was to push toward Paris. After all, Louisa was now Napoleon's sister.

Not long after Louisa heard of a pending battle at the gates of Paris, John went to the theater. When he came out, he saw a great bonfire burning in the Palais Royal garden. The columns were now covered with Napoleon's proclamations to the French people and the army. Declaring that their complaints had reached him in exile, Napoleon was ready to answer their call for the government of their choice, the only legitimate one. He had crossed the sea to resume his rights, which he fervently believed were theirs.

"The crowd of people in the arches and gardens was considerable, and the cries of 'Vive l'Empereur' frequent," Adams noted. "But although the Palais Royal is not a quarter of a mile distant from the Tuileries, I did not know that Napoleon had actually arrived while I was at the theater."

The next morning he received confirmation of the switch. Without a major battle at the gates of Paris, Napoleon had indeed returned—but quietly. The gate guards accompanied their emperor into the city.

"The front of their helmets and the clasps of their belts were still glowing with the arms of the Bourbons, the three flower de luces. There appeared to be much satisfaction among the soldiers."

That night Adams attended the opera. The change was obvious there too. "The royal arms were removed from the curtain of the royal box, and the imperial eagle had taken their place."

The cries were now 'Vive l'Empereur.'"

John had never heard of such a peaceful coup, much less witnessed one.

Napoleon declared that he would arrive in Paris without firing a shot. He wanted his invasion to appear as a rightful return to power, not larceny.

With Bonaparte resting at the Tuileries, John was anxious more than ever to embrace his wife and son and receive instructions from President Madison.

Louisa and her entourage traveled to Meaux, where she once again heard about the atrocities of the Cossacks. Then they resumed their route.

"I was again on my way to Paris . . . when I observed a man on horse back, who appeared to be making prodigious efforts to overtake us."

The man kept signaling them to stop. Louisa told the drivers to keep driving. "My courage was fast oozing out, when by some accident the postilions slackened their pace."

The man came closer and closer to her carriage. Then he was alongside her. "He came up very politely, and informed me, that for the last half hour he had been apprehensive that the wheel of my carriage would come off, and that he had been fearful I should meet with a bad overset."

They thanked him, and he rode off. Given all they had experienced, the incident was humorously anticlimactic.

"[We] arrived in perfect safety and without molestation at the gates of Paris; and descended at eleven o'clock at the Hotel du Nord Rue de Richelieu—Mr. Adams not returned from the theatre; but he soon came in, and I was once more happy to find myself under the protection of a husband."

Though happy and joyous, the reserved Adams described their reunion with understated relief: "When I returned home I expected to have found my wife's carriage in the yard, and was disappointed—but had scarcely got into my chamber when she arrived."

With a long-awaited warm and rapturous embrace, the fourth act on their Shakespearean drama was finally over.

"[He] was perfectly astonished at my adventures; as everything in Paris was quiet, and it had never occurred to him that it could have been otherwise in any other part of the country."

As sweet as their reunion was, the best—the encore—was yet to come.

Epilogue

The Birches of Boston

The House of Commons was quite full that summer day of June 28, 1815. Whatever the mild temperatures outside, the heat inside was hot. The issue was something that would never be debated by the US House of Representatives. The question before the House of Commons was whether to give a duke six thousand pounds of sterling for his marriage to a princess. From their stiff-backed benches and red-covered cushions, the white-wigged lords debated the pros and cons of the matter.

Unnoticed were the visitors in the gallery above them, which included a man and a fine, tall youth. With the sun reflecting on their faces through Westminster's stained-glass Gothic windows, they sat and watched the debate. The man joyfully pointed out the finer points of rhetoric used by the lords to argue their position. To this pair, the outcome made absolutely no difference. The process—and how different it was from America—was far more important. Greater than that, they were happy just to be together.

John Quincy Adams took his son George with him to the chamber that day. The moment was an education for both. For Adams, watching the debate gave him further insight into the ways of the British Parliament, which would prove invaluable to him as the newly appointed minister from the United States to Great Britain. For George, it was finally a chance to do something he had waited six years to experience: spend one-on-one time with his father.

"If we go to England, I beg you to send my sons George and John there to me," Adams had written his mother on December 24, 1814, no sooner had the ink dried on his Treaty of Ghent signature.

Within ten days of Louisa's arrival in Paris, he received official word of his new assignment. "Mr. Gallatin is appointed minister to France, Mr. Bayard to Russia, and myself to England."

Madison had appointed him to the same position his father had held years earlier. His title was envoy extraordinary and minister plenipotentiary of the United States of America at the Court of His Royal Highness the

Prince Regent of the United Kingdom of Great Britain and Ireland. Adams was pleased with the honorable appointment because it gave him an opportunity to fix many of the unresolved trade problems left over from the Treaty of Ghent negotiations.

In the days after her arrival, Louisa and John enjoyed Paris like a pair of newlyweds. They spent their time taking in the sights and accepting special invitations, such as the annual demonstration of the French Academy and mass at Tuileries chapel.

They went to the theater and watched a performance of *Hector*. Although they didn't see him, Napoleon was in the house that night. The actors paid him homage by leading the audience in cheers of "Vive l'Empereur."

Adams also visited the new minister of foreign affairs for France. He was not surprised that Napoleon appointed Monsieur de Caulaincourt to the position. The pair reminisced like old friends, with Caulaincourt giving John credit for his great triumph in Russia—which in part had been the French ambassador's downfall.

"The emperor of Russia did manifest here at Paris some interest in your favor," Caulaincourt communicated to his American friend of the czar's influence.

That same day Adams saw a crowd gathered under Napoleon's apartment at the palace. While talking with his officers, the French emperor occasionally appeared at the window. That was John's only glimpse of the infamous dictator. "I saw him, but not distinctly enough to recognize his features."

Caulaincourt also provided John with a passport so he could leave France for England when the time came. John, Louisa, and Charles traveled to London in mid-May 1815. They took up residence in a country house outside the city.

Within a month, Napoleon's short return to power, a mere one hundred days, ended. At the Battle of Waterloo on June 18, 1815, Britain's Duke of Wellington deftly defeated Napoleon and his troops by cutting off Bonaparte's famed Imperial Guard. This time the French ruler's exile was permanent. He was sent to an island much farther away than Elba—St. Helena, off the coast of Africa. The admiral responsible for burning the White House, George Cockburn, oversaw napoleon's exile.

George and John arrived in London after traveling on a ship from Boston.

Adams delighted in overseeing their education, which now included visits to sessions of Parliament and Greek texts taken from his own library.

"The forty-eighth year of my life has closed, and I this day enter upon the forty-ninth," Adams added to his diary on July 11, 1815. "It has in relation to public affairs been the most important, and in my private and domestic relations one of the most happy years."

That summer they enjoyed their garden, perhaps ripe with cucumbers and other vegetables. With his brothers and father, Charles likely planted the cucumber seeds that he had saved at his father's suggestion. They were a reunited family. In August they moved to Boston House on Boston Lane in Ealing, a London suburb. The boys attended a nearby boarding and day school. Louisa finally was able to give George and John a thousand kisses and become their mother once again.

Public service was more important to John Quincy Adams than anything else. His purpose in life, his very existence, was to be useful to mankind. His success in Russia and his role in securing the Treaty of Ghent qualified him to become secretary of state in the administration of President James Monroe. He was the mind behind the Monroe Doctrine, which boldly proclaimed the end of Europe's claims to the New World. His weights-and-measurements obsession that had started in Russia became a published book, turning his calculations into US trade standards.

In 1825 he became president of the United States, which made his father proud. Though Abigail died in 1818, his father lived to see his son reach the pinnacle of his career by serving as head of his country. The senior Adams died the following year on July 4, 1826, fifty years after issuing the Declaration of Independence as a member of the Continental Congress.

Among John's finest presidential accomplishments were trade treaties. He was responsible for adding more commerce treaties to the United States than any other president prior to the Civil War. His trade treaties included those with Denmark, Norway, Sweden, the Hanseatic cities, Austria, and Brazil, among other countries.

Adams is the only US president who resurrected a dead political career by way of a diplomatic post to Russia. John's honorable exile, as Ezekiel Bacon termed it, to pre-Soviet Russia is important because his story was a microcosm of the story of the United States at the time. What he needed most in his life were honor, dignity, and the respect of his peers. What the United States needed most in the years leading to the War of 1812 were honor and acceptance by other nations. Everything about America—its government, economy, and people—needed the respect and recognition of other nations. In order to survive as a country, America needed trade to thrive around the world. The United States needed to prove that it was no longer a child of England but a bona fide adult—a separate, independent, and sovereign nation with excellent exports.

The sacrifices John made and his willingness to be a loud advocate for US free trade earned him the honor and respect he so badly needed and deserved back home. His influence—and Louisa's—with Alexander elevated America's status on the world stage, forcing the British to the peace table. Had John accepted Madison's offer to the US Supreme Court, he likely would not have negotiated the Treaty of Ghent, which once and for all secured US sovereignty. The War of 1812 was the second war of American independence with Britain—and thanks to John Quincy and Louisa Adams and others—it was also the final one. The war resurrected the United States from the ashes and turned the Adamses into American phoenixes.

Years later in 1836, Louisa wrote a narrative about her journey to Paris from St. Petersburg. The sacrifices she made for her husband, children, and the United States could never be repaid. Though she kept a diary in St. Petersburg, she regretted not writing in a daily journal while on her journey. She decided there might be some value, particularly to the cause of the female sex, in writing a narrative of her travels through post-Napoleonic Europe in 1815.

"When I retrace my movements through this long, and really arduous journey, I cannot humble myself too much in thankful adoration to the Providence which shielded me from all dangers, and inspired me with that unswerving faith which teaches to seek for protection from above."

Louisa noted that she visited Madame Babet two months after their arrival in Paris. Seized with a brain fever, perhaps a form of post-traumatic stress syndrome, a depressed Madame Babet had not recovered from their perilous travels. Louisa saw the contrast between her and Babet immediately and gave thanks to God for bringing her through her exile and harrowing journey: "I was carried through my trials by the mercy of a protecting Providence; and by the conviction that weakness of either body, or mind, would only render my difficulties greater and make matters worse."

Louisa's desire to champion female virtues and capabilities came alive once again as she wrote her narrative: "A moral is contained in this lesson—If my sex act with persevering discretion, they may from their very weakness be secured from danger, and find friends and protectors: and that under all circumstances, we must never desert ourselves."

Louisa did not think of herself as young or beautiful. She believed that character was more important than both. As a mother she had been willing to make any sacrifice to ensure her son's safe arrival in Paris and to be reunited with John and their oldest sons in England: "I had others under my protection to whom the example of fortitude was essential; and above all the object which drew me on, was the re-union with my beloved husband, and alas, with my now departed children."

Both George and John had died by 1836, the year she chronicled her journey from St. Petersburg to Paris. John Adams II became the first son of a president to marry in a ceremony in the White House. He married his cousin Mary Catherine Hellen, Nancy's daughter, on February 25, 1828. Mary had been previously engaged to George, whose delay of their marriage led her to break off their engagement. By this time George had graduated from Harvard, passed the bar, practiced law, and served in the Massachusetts House of Representatives.

Despite George's accomplishments, Mary married John instead. Fourteen months later, in 1829, George died in a fall from the steamship *Benjamin Franklin* in Long Island Sound. Regardless of whether the incident was an accident or intentional, his death at age twenty-seven was tragic and heartbreaking, especially to his parents and family. Within two weeks they learned of his illegitimate child by a chambermaid who worked for a longtime friend of the family's.

Expelled from Harvard, John made a home for Mary and their family in

Washington. He studied law under his father and served as his private secretary during the first two years of John Quincy's presidency. Afterward he earned a living operating the flour mill owned by his father on Rock Creek in Washington. He struggled with alcoholism and died in 1834 at age thirty-one.

As Louisa reflected on her life when she concluded her narrative, she chose to focus on the blessings, not the immense hurts. "Years have rolled on: but memory recurs with delight to the past!"

Topping the list of those blessings were grandchildren. Mary gave birth to Mary Louisa Adams in December 1828. Lacking a midwife, Louisa helped her daughter-in-law to deliver another daughter in 1830. Mary named her Georgiana Frances after her two uncles. Louisa doted on her two beautiful granddaughters as well as the seven grandchildren that came through Charles.

Unlike his brothers, Charles lived a long life. He married Abigail Brown Brooks in 1829. They honored his parents with the names of their first two children. Abigail gave birth first to a daughter, Louisa Catherine, in 1831, and then a son, John Quincy, in 1833. She also bore Charles, Henry, Arthur, Mary, and Brooks.

Inheriting his father's love of the written word and public service, Charles served three years in the Massachusetts House and two years in the Massachusetts Senate. He moved to the national stage in 1858, where he was a Republican member in the US House of Representatives for three years. In 1861 President Lincoln appointed him as minister to England, the post held by his father and grandfather. Charles served as America's top representative in London until 1868.

He also wrote editorials for the *North American Review* in the 1830s. As part of the antislavery movement, he served as editor and proprietor in the 1840s for the *Boston Daily Whig*. His most extensive literary accomplishment came through his role as editor for his family's voluminous paper trail. Charles compiled, edited, and oversaw publication of multiple volumes, including: *Letters of Mrs. Adams* (1840), *Works of John Adams, Second President of the United States: With a Life of the Author* (1850–1856), and *Memoirs of John Quincy Adams, Comprising Portions of His Diary from 1795 to 1848* (1874–1877), a primary source for *American Phoenix*. Charles had many reasons to be proud of his family, particularly his father's lengthy political and public service career.

Two years after his presidency ended, in 1831, John Quincy Adams was elected to the US House of Representatives, where he served for seventeen years. He is the only US president to also serve in the US Senate, in the House after his presidency, and to decline a nomination for the Supreme Court. Just as he had abhorred impressment, so he was also a strong advocate for abolishing slavery. He successfully argued the *Amistad* case, which freed Africans mistakenly thought to be slaves, before the US Supreme Court in 1841.

John Quincy Adams died on February 23, 1848, two days after suffering a stroke while passionately speaking on the floor of the House of Representatives at the US Capitol. He would have been eighty-one on his next birthday.

Faith fortified Louisa's soul throughout her life. The woman who had wanted to die after the loss of her baby in 1812 overcame dark depression and a harrowing solo journey so that she could live life to the fullest, relying on her Maker to determine her final breath:

> And when it is his will that I lay me down to sleep; that sleep, from which we wake no more in this world; may I die in my Savior Jesus Christ; in the full hope of those divine promises, which lead the purified Soul to heaven for evermore—L. C. Adams, 27th June 1836.

Louisa bid a final adieu in 1852, four years after her husband's death. Her daughter-in-law Mary and her sister Kitty took care of her in her old age. In an unprecedented decision, Congress adjourned so members could pay their respects to the only American First Lady not born on US soil.

Acknowledgments

MANY THANKS TO THE DOZENS OF PEOPLE WHO HELPED MAKE THIS book possible. I am grateful to Judith Graham and Anna Cook with the Massachusetts Historical Society and Caroline Keinath with the National Parks Service for your love of the Adams Family and your professionalism in aiding my research.

Many thanks to Margaret Dorman, Per-Egil Evensen, Jacqueline Nims Phelan, Ashley Profaizer, Scott Szenasi, and Jim E. Whiting for sharing your knowledge to help me better understand the world of historical costumes, Norway, fashion, diplomacy, St. Petersburg, and sailing ships.

I owe tremendous thanks to my favorite physician and OB-GYN, Dr. Glen Silas; the best pediatrician, Dr. Michael Martin; and expert OB nurse and friend Beth Felan for sharing your insights into the medical world and the health issues that may have plagued Louisa and the Adams family.

I am indebted to Jonathan Clements, my beloved agent and founder of Wheelhouse Literary Group, whose tenacity, perseverance, and dedication made this book a blessed reality. I also am grateful for the editing prowess of Victoria Hay and Cari Foulk. This book would not be possible without your direction, guidance, and suggestions. A special thanks belongs to Susan Hotard, my high school English and creative writing teacher. How special it is to keep in touch with the person who first identified my writing aptitude.

Thank you to Joel Miller at Thomas Nelson for his vision and love of history to make this book and so many other great books possible. Much gratitude to the big-picture vision of Kristen Parrish and the keen editorial eyes of Janene MacIvor and Dimples Kellogg, and the sharp cover design by Julie Allen.

Most of all I appreciate my loving husband, Dr. John Kim Cook, for his support of my work, and our sons, Austin and Zachary, who know more about John Quincy and Louisa Adams than any other six- and eight-year-old boys in America.

Notes

ABBREVIATIONS USED

DLA AFP MHS *Louisa Catherine Johnson Adams Diary*, Adams Family Papers, 1639–1889, microfilm edition, 608 reels (Boston: Massachusetts Historical Society, 1954–1959) Reel 264, 269

DJQA John Quincy Adams diary 27, 1 January 1803–4 August 1809, pages 404–410 [electronic ed.] and diary 28, 5 August 1809–31 July 1813, pages 412–413. *The Diaries of John Quincy Adams: A Digital Collection.* Boston: Massachusetts Historical Society, 2005. http://www.masshist.org/jqadiaries

JQA and LA John Quincy Adams and Louisa Adams, Adams Family Papers, 1639–1889, microfilm ed., 608 reels (Boston: Massachusetts Historical Society, 1954–1959) Jan–June 1810 Reel 409, July–Dec. 1810 Reel 410, Aug.–Sep. 1814 Reel 419, Oct.–Nov. 1814 Reel 420, Dec. 1814 Reel 421, Jan.–Mar. 1815 Reel 422

LOC Library of Congress

MJQA *Memoirs of John Quincy Adams: Comprising Portions of His Diary*, edited by Charles Francis Adams, II, Aug. 1809–July 1814; III, Aug. 1814–June 1817

"NRF" AFP MHS Louisa Catherine Johnson Adams "Narrative of a Journey from Russia to France, 1815," Adams Family Papers, 1639–1889, microfilm edition, 608 reels (Boston: Massachusetts Historical Society, 1954–1959) Reel 268

WJQA *Writings of John Quincy Adams*, edited by Worthington Chauncey Ford, III, 1801–10;IV, 1811–13; and, 1814–16

AA   Abigail Adams, mother of John Quincy Adams
JA   John Adams, father of John Quincy Adams
TA   Thomas Adams, brother of John Quincy Adams
CFA Charles Francis Adams, son of John Quincy and Louisa Adams
JM   James Madison, president of the United States
SOS Secretary of state (first Robert Smith and then James Monroe starting April 1811)

AUTHOR'S NOTE: RECALLING THE ONES WHO WERE

Page
xi   *The phoenix riddle:* "Phoenix riddle," John Donne, *Oxford English Dictionary*.
xii *It may perhaps at:* "NRF," Reel 268 AFP MHS, emphasis in original.
xii *If you would not:* Benjamin Franklin, *Poor Richard's Almanac,* 1738.

CHAPTER 1: MURDER OUTSIDE

Page
4   *Here I stopped to:* "NRF," Reel 268 AFP MHS.
5   *an idle boy:* Blanning, *Pursuit of Glory*, 35.
5   *In about an hour:* "NRF," Reel 268 AFP MHS.
6   *Mr. Adams too:* DLA, July 21, 1810, Reel 269 AFP MHS.
6   *I thought it my duty:* Ibid.
6   *I am this instant:* LA to JQA, Feb. 12, 1815, Reel 422 AFP MHS.
7   *I hope that you:* Ibid.
7   *great relaxation of:* MJQA, Oct. 31, 1814, III, 62.
7   *The tendency to dissipation:* Ibid., Feb. 12, 1815, 154.
7   *I am as ill guarded:* Ibid.
7   *The ambassador said:* Diary and Autobiography of John Adams, I, 2.
8   *the same house where I lodged:* MJQA, Feb. 12, 1815, 155.

8   *altogether in decay:* Ibid.
9   *Immediately after my dinner:* "NRF," Reel 268 AFP MHS.
9   *I expressed my thanks:* Ibid.
9   *I, however, assumed:* Ibid.
9   *I told him very coolly:* Ibid.

CHAPTER 2: THIEF INSIDE
Page
10   *After informing:* JQA to LA, Feb. 19, 1815, Reel 422 AFP MHS.
10   *absorb the consideration:* MJQA, Feb. 19, 1815, III, 157.
10   *She has improved:* Ibid.
10   *applauded a little:* Ibid.
11   *I conceived I had nothing:* "NRF," Reel 268 AFP MHS.
11   *He then informed:* Ibid.
11   *Baptiste, I believe:* Ibid.
11   *to baptize:* Oxford English Dictionary.
12   *Here for the:* "NRF," Reel 268 AFP MHS.
13   *At the same time:* Ibid.
13   *I told him:* Ibid.
13   *I promised a:* Ibid.
14   *All this I:* Ibid.

CHAPTER 3: LOST
Page
16   *Finding me determined:* "NRF," Reel 268 AFP MHS.
17   *I was likewise:* Ibid.
17   *After riding about four:* Ibid.
18   *Until eleven o'clock at night:* Ibid.
18   *At twelve o'clock at night:* Ibid.

CHAPTER 4: THE CROSSING
Page
19   *The palpitation of my heart:* "NRF," Reel 268 AFP MHS.
19   *Baptiste rode hastily up:* Ibid.
19   *offered his services:* Ibid.
19   *One of my men mounted:* Ibid.
19   *He [the officer] accepted a handsome:* Ibid.
20   *I therefore expressed:* Ibid.
20   *After thanking most devoutly the Almighty:* Ibid.
20   *[w]here I was presented:* MJQA, Feb. 27, 1815, III, 163.
20   *He asked me:* Ibid.
20   *He saw the resemblance:* Ibid.
20   *I was at that time:* Ibid.
21   *He had a very grateful:* Ibid.
21   *The British will take:* JQA to LA, Jan. 3, 1815, Reel 422 AFP MHS.
21   *Its darkest shade:* Ibid.
21   *My visit here [in Paris] has:* JQA to LA, Feb. 19, 1815, Reel 422 AFP MHS.
21   *But life here:* Ibid.

CHAPTER 5: FIREWORKS
Page
27   *"The Boston Patriotic Song":* Paine, LOC.
28   *distilled spirits:* US Census, 1810, *Series of Tables of American Manufacturers* (by county), 8.

28   *A multitude of little:* DJQA, June, Day, 1809, II7, 408.

29   *After I came home:* Ibid., July 3, 1809, 408.

29   *left me with:* Ibid., 409.

29   *I found in it a paragraph:* Ibid.

30   *the most virulent:* Ibid., July 5, 1809, 410.

30   *sixty consuls:* "Diplomatic and Consular Posts 1781–1997," US State Department, Office of the Historian, http://www.state.gov/www/about_state/history/faq .html#consular.

30   *the vague hope:* Ibid.

31   *While in the church:* Ibid., July 4, 1809, 409.

31   *So far as your public:* WJQA, Ezekiel Bacon to JQA, June 29, 1809, III, 321n.

31   *Though your friends:* Ibid.

32   *A mission to the court:* Ibid.

32   *The procession:* DJQA, July 4, 1809, II7, 409.

32   *But the application:* Ibid.

32   *pay a visit:* Ibid.

32   *We stayed there:* Ibid.

33   *Let fame to:* LOC, http://memory.loc.gov/diglib/ihas/loc.natlib.ihas.100010462 /default.html.

33   *This day the news arrived:* DLA, July 4, 1809, Reel 269 AFP MHS.

34   *I do not:* Ibid.

35   *parties were generally:* Encyclopedia Britannica, s.v. "Federalist Party," www .britannica.com/EBchecked/topic/203519/Federalist-Party.

35   *President George Washington:* Ibid.

35   *I believe you will not:* WJQA, JQA to LA, Mar. 9, 1809, III, 291.

36   *expectation of that or any other:* Ibid.

36   *I had been so grossly deceived:* DLA, July 4, 1809, Reel 269 AFP MHS.

36   *I have determined to go:* WJQA, JQA to William Eustis, July 16, 1809, III, 332.

36   *The public service:* MJQA, JQA to George and John Adams II, Aug. 21, 1809, II, 14.

37   *I had passed the age:* DLA, Aug. 4, 1809, Reel 269 AFP MHS.

38   *They [the fireworks] were principally:* DJQA, July 4, 1809, II7, 409.

38   *No accidents of fire:* Ibid.

CHAPTER 6: GOOD-BYE, BOSTON BIRCHES

Page

39   *Every preparation was made:* DLA, July 4, 1809, Reel 269 AFP MHS.

39   *And even the disposal of my children:* Ibid.

40   *Judge Adams was commissioned:* Ibid.

40   *O it was too hard!:* Ibid.

41   *On the 4 of August:* Ibid., Aug. 5, 1809.

41   *Oh this agony of agonies!:* Ibid., July 4, 1809.

41   *And from that hour:* Ibid.

42   *A man can take care:* Ibid., Aug. 5, 1809.

42   *It is with a deep sense:* DJQA, July 5, 1809, II7, 410.

42   *my personal motives:* Ibid.

42   *welfare of the:* Ibid.

43   *the blessings of Almighty God:* Ibid.

43   *I also enquired of him:* Ibid., July 9, 1809, 412. 57

43   *[T]hey should go altogether:* Ibid., July 6, 1809, 411.

44   *Our voyage was very tedious:* DLA, Aug. 5, 1809, Reel 269 AFP MHS.

44   *I scarcely perceive:* MJQA, Aug. 6, 1809, II, 4.

45   *There is much time:* Ibid., Aug. 31, 1809, 8.

45   *amusement:* Ibid., Aug. 14, 1809, 6.

45   *agreeable companion:* Ibid.

45   *perhaps the most important:* Ibid., Aug. 5, 1809, 4.
45   *Broken hearted miserable:* DLA, Aug. 5, 1809, Reel 269 AFP MHS, emphasis in original.
45   *I had thought:* Ibid., Jan. 26, 1811.
46   *the dangers of war:* MJQA, Aug. 6, 1809, II, 5.
46   *frightful:* DLA, Sept. 17, 1809, Reel 269 AFP MHS.
46   *It was dusk:* Ibid.
46   *If it was to do again:* Ibid., Aug. 5, 1809.
47   *could not live:* Ibid., Sept. 17, 1809.

CHAPTER 7: DANISH PREY

Page

48   *All this time the boat:* DLA, Sept. 17, 1809, Reel 269 AFP MHS.
48   *The Chesapeake-Leopard: Encyclopedia of the War of 1812,* s.v. "Chesapeake-Leopard Affair," 96.
49   *have been severe:* WJQA, JQA to AA, April 20, 1808, II, 232.
49   *I was sworn:* WJQA, JQA to Skeleton Jones, April 17, 1809, II, 303.
50   *to preserve from:* Ibid., JQA to The Honorable Senate and House of Representatives of the Commonwealth of Massachusetts, June 8, 1808, 237.
50   *vindicate the rights essential:* Ibid.
50   *I have been obliged:* Ibid., JQA to AA, April 20, 1808, 232.
50   *the personal liberties:* Ibid., JQA to The Honorable Senate and House of Representatives of the Commonwealth of Massachusetts, June 8, 1808, 238.
50   *I discharged:* Ibid., JQA to Skeleton Jones, April 17, 1809, 303, emphasis in original.
50   *It was not without:* Ibid.
50   *discarded me for:* Ibid.
50   *I was no representative:* Ibid., emphasis in original.
50   *Upon common theaters: Diary of John Adams,* I, 12.
52   *We had a quiet:* DLA, Sept. 18, 1809, Reel 269 AFP MHS.
52   *We were awakened:* Ibid.
52   *I suppose you:* MJQA, Sept. 19, 1809, II, 20.
52   *He said it was:* DLA, Sept. 19, 1809, Reel 269 AFP MHS.
53   *the troops of His Britannic Majesty:* "American Statement," *Salem Gazette,* April 25, 1775.
53   *The boat soon returned:* DLA, Sept. 19, 1809, Reel 269 AFP MHS.
54   *We sent for a pilot:* Ibid.
54   *The captain became:* Ibid.
55   *I was perfectly indignant:* Ibid.
55   *The lieutenant, however:* Ibid.
56   *who the United States:* Nagel, *John Quincy Adams: A Public Life, a Private Life,* 113.

CHAPTER 8: THREE HUNDRED AMERICANS

Page

57   *They found the:* MJQA, Sept. 19, 1809, II, 21.
57   *I went immediately:* Ibid.
58   *Mr. Isaacson, an agent:* Ibid.
59   *The sight of so:* Ibid., Sept. 20, 1809, 23.
59   *The desire of contributing:* Ibid., 23–24.
59   *They request my:* WJQA, JQA to SOS, Sept. 23, 1809, III, 345.
59   *We are ready to:* Ibid.
60   *when the sun crosses:* MJQA, Sept 21, 1809, II, 24.
60   *equinoctial gales:* WJQA, JQA to SOS, Sept. 23, III, 344.
60   *Mr. Isaacson:* DLA, Sept. 19, 1809, Reel 269 AFP MHS.
60   *Mr. Adams obliged:* Ibid.

60   *We saw four:* Ibid.
61   *In the midst:* Ibid., Sept. 25, 1809.
61   *And a lieutenant:* Ibid.
61   *who on examining:* Ibid.

CHAPTER 9: CARICATURE VS. CHARACTER
Page
63   *I have friends:* WJQA, JQA to Skeleton Jones, April 17, 1809, III, 305.
64   *For the instant:* Ibid., July 27, 1824, Adams's appendix to a republished article from JQA's anonymous publication in the June 21, 1808, *Boston Gazette*, 225.
64   *And the delay:* Ibid.
64   *best thing that:* WJQA, Ezekiel Bacon to JQA, June 29, 1809, III, 321n.
65   *The officer not:* DLA, Sept. 25, Reel 269 AFP MHS.
65   *We were left under:* Ibid.
66   *thunder clap news:* Ketcham, *James Madison: A Biography*, 495.
67   *but if I had:* MJQA, Sept. 25, 1809, II, 26.
67   *And you say:* Ibid., 27.
67   *Yes, Sir. My wife:* Ibid.

CHAPTER 10: ALL THE WORLD'S A STAGE
Page
69   *We put down:* DLA, Sept. 25, 1809, Reel 269 AFP MHS.
69   *We had drifted:* Ibid.
69   *I was anxious:* Ibid.
69   *[A] boat from the:* Ibid.
70   *All the morning:* Ibid.
70   *lashed down the:* Ibid.
70   *We were between:* Ibid.
70   *pleasing and not improbable:* WJQA, JQA to AA, Feb. 8, 1810, III, 393.
71   *The light in:* DLA, Sept. 25, 1809, Reel 269 AFP MHS.
71   *To go through:* Ibid.
71   *long voyage:* Ibid., Aug. 5, 1809.
72   *The separation from:* MJQA, Aug. 6, 1809, II, 5.
72   *The age of my:* Ibid., emphasis in original.
73   *All the world's a stage:* William Shakespeare, *As You Like It*, act 2, scene 7, lines 147–50.96.
73   *You should each:* MJQA, JQA to George and John Adams II, Aug. 21, 1809, II, 9, emphasis in original.
73   *some mechanical art:* Ibid., 10.
73   *As a great portion:* Ibid., 9.
74   *justice and fidelity:* Ibid., 11.
74   *The relations of:* Ibid.
74   *There are also:* Ibid., 12.
74   *every individual has:* Ibid.
74   *to the utmost of:* Ibid.
74   *Finally, let the:* Ibid., 17.
75   *to be, or:* Hamlet, William Shakespeare, Act 3, scene 1, line 6399.
75   *and immediately:* MJQA, Sept. 27, 1809, II, 31.
75   *Mr. Adams was prevailed:* DLA, Sept. 28, 1809, Reel 269 AFP MHS.
75   *as they were still:* Ibid.

CHAPTER 11: BALTIC CIRCLE
Page
77   *We all embarked:* DLA, Oct. 2, 1809, Reel 269 AFP MHS.
78   *For three days:* MJQA, Oct. 9, 1809, II, 39.

78   *Thus we went on:* DLA, Oct. 16, 1809, Reel 269 AFP MHS.

78   *The night was moderate:* MJQA, Oct. 9, 1809, II, 39.

79   *Dangers accumulated:* DLA, Oct. 16, 1809, Reel 269 AFP MHS.

79   *The prospect of reaching:* MJQA, Oct. 11,1809, II, 40.

80   *in better hands:* Ibid.

80   *They were no imaginary:* DLA, Oct. 16, 1809, Reel 269 AFP MHS.

80   *Thus we continued:* Ibid., Oct. 14, 1809.

81   *I knew that:* Ibid.

81   *We received an:* Ibid.

81   *I cannot but:* WJQA, JQA to TA, Nov. 1809, III, 358.

82   *But I had objects:* Ibid.

82   *desponding under the:* MJQA, Oct. 17, 1809, II, 43.

83   *Yet, in the pursuit:* Ibid.

84   *At last we reached:* DLA, Oct. 22, 1809, Reel 269 AFP MHS.

84   *My objective was:* MJQA, Oct. 22, 1809, II, 45.

84   *We dressed ourselves:* DLA, Oct. 22, 1809, Reel 269 AFP MHS.

85   *ushered into:* Ibid.

85   *My sister and myself:* Ibid.

85   *was exquisite beyond all:* Ibid.

85   *Not a place could:* Ibid., 112.

85   *warp into the mole:* Ibid., Oct. 23, 1809.

Chapter 12: Fig Leaves

Page

87   *did appear quite:* DLA, Oct. 23, 1809, Reel 269 AFP MHS.

87   *At breakfast Mr. Sparrow:* Ibid.

87   *Here was a position:* Ibid.

88   *A beneficent Providence:* WJQA, JQA to AA, Feb. 8, 1810, III, 394.

90   *[N]o man alive:* Bemis, *John Quincy Adams and the Foundations of American Foreign Policy*, 39.

90   *Immediately after dinner:* DLA, Oct. 23, 1809, Reel 269 AFP MHS.

91   *And the minister was:* Ibid.

91   *Mr. Harris dined with:* Ibid.

91   *[At] seven o clock:* Ibid., Oct. 25, 1809.

91   *[A]ll but the wig:* Ibid.

91   *The count received us:* MJQA, Oct. 25, 1809, II, 48.

92   *He [the count] assured:* Ibid.

92   *Mr. Smith arrived:* DLA, Oct. 26, 1809, Reel 269 AFP MHS.

92   *She entered fully:* Ibid.

92   *[The] whole business:* Ibid.

93   *We this day received:* Ibid.

93   *I was quite ill!:* Ibid., Oct. 27, 1809.

93   *The chamber I lodged:* Ibid.

93   *so full of rats:* Ibid.

93   *My nerves became perfectly:* Ibid.

Chapter 13: Déjà Vu

Page

95   *I had in the:* MJQA, Oct. 28, 1809, II, 48.

95   *the great object:* MHS, www.masshist.org/database/1745use-onview-id, 124.

96   *This was a diplomatic:* MJQA, Oct. 28, 1809, II, 48–49.

96   *The rest of the:* Ibid.

96   *Took our departure:* John Adams, *Works*, Oct. 28, 1774.

97   *The house:* MJQA, Oct. 28, 1809, II, 49.

97   *We heard this day:* Ibid.

98   *But he [Count Romanzoff]:* Ibid.
98   *The formalities of these:* MJQA, Nov. 4, 1809, II, 50.
98   *It is not safe:* Ibid.
99   *The style of expense:* DLA, Nov. 1, 1809, Reel 269 AFP MHS.
99   *The emperor signified:* Ibid.
100 *Sir, I am happy:* MJQA, Nov. 5, 1809, II, 51.
100 *The president of the:* Ibid.
100 *The system of:* Ibid.
100 *to avoid being overheard:* Ibid., 52.
100 *the obstinate adherence:* Ibid., 51.
100 *to reasonable terms:* Ibid.
101 *make her recognize:* Ibid.
101 *everything that:* Ibid.
101 *I had then admired:* Ibid., 53.
101 *handsome and convenient:* Ibid.
101 *Petersburg had the:* Ibid., 54.
101 *Then, we have two:* Ibid.
102 *It was very difficult:* Ibid.
103 *Madame de Bray was:* DLA, Nov. 8, 1809, Reel 269 AFP MHS.

Chapter 14: Eve's Leaves
Page
104 *This morning Monsieur:* DLA, Nov. 8, 1809, Reel 269 AFP MHS.
104 *I had no vanity:* Ibid., Aug. 5, 1809.
105 *Without one sixpence:* Ibid.
105 *fifteen thousand:* Boris Antonov, *Russian Tsars*, 107.
105 *In the evening:* Ibid., Nov. 8, 1809.
106 *Her account of:* Ibid.
106 *Somewhat better but:* Ibid., Nov. 11, 1809.
106 *Very handsome and:* Ibid.
106 *The countess told me:* Ibid.
107 *Of this Mr. Adams:* Ibid., Nov. 12, 1809.
108 *She asked whether:* MJQA, Nov. 12, 1809, II, 58–59.
108 *How so? I thought:* Ibid.
108 *But it is freely:* Ibid.
108 *I hoped we:* Ibid., 59.
110 *And I was obliged:* DLA, Nov. 12, 1809, Reel 269 AFP MHS.
110 *And thus accoutered:* Ibid.
110 *And over all this:* Ibid.
110 *Off I went with:* Ibid.
111 *Arrived at the:* Ibid.
111 *I was received:* Ibid.
111 *She received me:* Ibid.
111 *[She] informed me:* Ibid.
111 *When she came:* Ibid.
111 *take care in raising:* Ibid.
111 *Naturally timid:* Ibid.
111 *a la Turk with:* Ibid.
112 *As their imperial:* Ibid.
112 *The emperor was:* Ibid.
112 *I think the:* Ibid.
112 *Countess Litta who:* Ibid.
112 *We then went to:* Ibid.
112 *She received me very:* Ibid.

113 *I expressed in strong:* Ibid.
113 *Ah mon dieu:* Ibid.
113 *At last I returned:* Ibid.
113 *the savage had been:* Ibid.

CHAPTER 15: LONELINESS AND SPLENDOR
Page
114 *I did not know:* DLA, Nov. 14, 1809, Reel 269 AFP MHS, 149.
114 *I was dressed:* Ibid.
114 *I started in tolerable:* Ibid.
114 *But it resembled in:* MJQA, Nov. 14, 1809, II, 62.
115 *At this, however:* Ibid.
115 *As almost total:* Ibid.
116 *The emperor followed:* DLA, Nov. 14, 1809, Reel 269 AFP MHS.
116 *politely offered us:* Ibid.
116 *He entered into:* Ibid.
116 *won all hearts:* Warnes, *Chronology of the Russian Tsars*, Countess Tiesenhausen, 150.
116 *His forehead was:* Ibid.
116 *Mr. Harris at last:* DLA, Nov. 14, 1809, Reel 269 AFP MHS.
116 *He asked me to:* Ibid.
117 *I was much afraid:* Ibid.
117 *The emperor and empress mother:* MJQA, Nov, 14, 1809, II, 63.
117 *He [the emperor] asked:* Ibid.
117 *must have been:* Ibid.
118 *There were fifteen supper:* DLA, Nov. 14, 1809, Reel 269 AFP MHS.
118 *That of the emperor:* Ibid.
118 *No one was allowed:* Ibid.
118 *I was glad to:* Ibid.
118 *I was seized:* Ibid., Nov. 17, 1809.
118 *[The] voyage: the excitement:* Ibid.
119 *And again I sadly:* Ibid.
119 *The crowd [of four hundred]:* WJQA, JQA to LA, Mar. 5, 1809, III, 289.
120 *He [Jefferson] asked:* Ibid.
120 *When brought together:* Jefferson, *The Jefferson Cyclopedia*, 311.
120 *I was much better:* DLA, Nov. 19, 1809, Reel 269 AFP MHS.
120 *The River Neva has:* MJQA, Nov. 19, 1809, II, 60.

CHAPTER 16: WHEN IN ROME . . .
Page
122 *That some great commercial:* MJQA, Nov. 15, 1809, II, 65.
123 *favored a course:* Ibid., 66.
123 *freedom to their:* Ibid.
123 *unjust and impolitic:* Ibid., 67.
123 *The more liberal:* Ibid.
124 *Tis universal:* Ibid.
125 *My sister was quite:* DLA, Nov. 27, 1809, Reel 269 AFP MHS.
125 *We had much:* Ibid.
125 *Mr. Harris had suffered:* Ibid.
126 *Mr. Adams allowed:* Ibid., emphasis in original.
125 *We took Charles:* Ibid., Dec. 14, 1809.
126 *oceans of champagne:* Ibid.
126 *When supper was finished:* Ibid.
126 *We were struck:* Ibid., Nov. 20, 1809.
127 *The ambassador told:* Ibid.

127   *If I should go to Rome:* Ibid.
127   *The party was small:* Ibid., Nov. 27, 1809.
128   *It is a life of such:* MJQA, Day, II, 73.
128   *extravagance and dissipation:* WJQA, JQA to AA, Feb. 8, 1810, III, 396.
128   *I hope:* Ibid.
128   *But we all, to begin:* Ibid.
128   *Between 3 and 4:* DLA, Dec. 8, 1809, Reel 269 AFP MHS.
129   *overcome or made ill:* Oxford English Dictionary, s.v. "knocked up."
129   *would not answer:* DLA, April 14, 1810, Reel 269 AFP MHS.
129   *Received a notification:* Ibid., Dec. 23, 1809.
129   *Having but one dress:* Ibid.
129   *Not a particle of:* WJQA, JQA to AA, Feb. 8, 1810, III, 395.
129   *The ball was very:* MJQA, Dec. 24, 1809, II, 81.
129   *The empress mother:* Ibid.
130   *Went to take tea:* DLA, Dec. 23, 1809, Reel 269 AFP MHS.

Chapter 17: French Économie
Page
131   *The Emperor Napoleon is:* MJQA, April 16, 1810, II, 117.
131   *This idea:* Ibid.
131   *I do not know whether:* Ibid., 117–18.
131   *better principles:* Ibid., 118.
131   *He [Napoleon] confines his:* Ibid., Nov. 28, 1809, 72.
132   *About nine this:* Ibid., Dec. 10, 1809, 77.
132   *The emperor, accompanied:* Ibid.
133   *The French ambassador took:* Ibid., Dec. 6, 1809, 75.
133   *The empress asked me:* Ibid.
134   *I came at the:* Ibid., Dec. 26, 1809, 81.
134   *unquestionably neutral:* Ibid., 82.
134   *I had flattered:* Ibid.
134   *General peace depended:* Ibid.
134   *rigorous inspections:* Ibid.
135   *not a voluntary act:* Ibid., 83.
135   *Is not the produce:* Ibid.
135   *The United States produced:* Ibid.
136   *If this was a French:* Ibid., 84.
136   *The active commerce:* Ibid., 85.
136   *As this was a measure:* Ibid., 87.
137   *The general impression:* Ibid.

Chapter 18: Ice Hills
Page
138   *We all had invitations:* MJQA, Dec. 29., 1809, II, 88.
138   *Mrs. Adams and Catherine:* Ibid.
138   *Just as I was:* Ibid.
139   *He had ordered him:* Ibid.
139   *proving his friendly:* Ibid.
139   *have the benefit:* Ibid., 89.
139   *already as strong:* Ibid.
139   *We got there about:* Ibid., 90.
139   *The cold, which had:* Ibid.
139   *I saw Baron Blome:* Ibid.
140   *had been goaded by France:* Ibid.
140   *Danes were carrying:* Ibid.
140   *I hoped the day:* Ibid., 91.

141 *It has witnessed*: Ibid., Day, 1810, 92.
141 *It has changed also*: Ibid.
141 *From this new*: Ibid.
141 *These dispatches it appears*: WJQA, JQA to SOS, Jan. 3, 1810, III, 369.
142 *It [the Essex] would undoubtedly*: Ibid., 370.
142 *Went with Mr. Adams*: DLA, Dec. 30, 1809, Reel 269 AFP MHS.
142 *On this day I*: Ibid., Jan. 1, 1810.
142 *I was informed that*: Ibid.
142 *This was charming*: Ibid. 186
143 *shammed sickness*: MJQA, Jan. 9, 1801, II, 94.

Chapter 19: Divorce

Page
144 *Everybody felt*: DLA, Jan. 3, 1810, Reel 269 AFP MHS.
144 *He was one*: Ibid., Jan. 9, 1810.
145 *He has been*: MJQA, Jan. 8, 1810, II, 93.
145 *I asked him*: Ibid.
145 *slept little, waked*: Ibid.
145 *Heard of the Empress Josephine's*: DLA, Jan. 9, 1810, Reel 269 AFP MHS.
145 *I still love you*: Trager, *The Women's Chronology*, 216.
145 *It is certainly not*: MJQA, Jan. 8, 1810, II, 93.
145 *Though the*: Ibid.
145 *The Emperor Napoleon has*: Ibid.
146 *A real plain spoken*: DLA, April 14, 1810, Reel 269 AFP MHS.
146 *Received tickets for*: Ibid., Jan. 10, 1810.
146 *It is a very difficult thing*: Ibid., April 9, 1810.
147 *It is called a*: MJQA, Jan. 13, 1810, II, 96.
147 *All the apartments of*: Ibid.
147 *The gentlemen wearing*: Ibid.
147 *Here is one*: MJQA, Dec. 4, 1809, II, 74.
147 *It is impossible to*: Ibid.
147 *The illuminations exceed*: DLA, Jan. 13, 1810, Reel 269 AFP MHS.
148 *I . . . was gazing*: Ibid.
148 *I immediately walked*: Ibid.
148 *[The empress mother] then presented*: Ibid.
148 *I believe that*: Ibid., emphasis in original.
148 *The other foreign*: MJQA, Jan. 13, 1810, II, 96.
149 *To me he*: DLA, Jan. 13, 1810, Reel 269 AFP MHS.

Chapter 20: Water

Page
150 *On this day was*: MJQA, Jan. 18, 1810, II, 98.
150 *It is a grand ceremony*: DLA, Jan. 18, 1810, Reel 269 AFP MHS.
150 *The foreign ministers*: MJQA, Jan. 18, 1810, II, 98.
150 *We obtained a seat*: DLA, Jan. 18, 1810, Reel 269 AFP MHS.
151 *After the ceremony*: MJQA, Jan. 18, 1810, II, 98.
151 *magnificent furs covered*: DLA, Jan. 18, 1810, Reel 269 AFP MHS.
151 *deviating the breadth*: Ibid.
152 *At supper the 12th cake*: Ibid.
152 *We danced, and it*: Ibid.
152 *I told him the*: MJQA, Jan. 16, 1810, II, 97.
152 *[T]his measure*: Ibid.
154 *My time hitherto*: Ibid., Day, 99.
154 *As usual inquired*: DLA, Jan. 24, 1810, Reel 269 AFP MHS.
155 *We have at length*: MJQA, Jan. 28, 1810, II, 99.

155 *My correspondence:* Ibid.
155 *I have sent:* WJQA, JQA to AA, Feb. 8, 1810, III, 395.
156 *The expectation of an immediate:* WJQA, JQA to SOS, Jan. 31, 1810, III, 391.
156 *This however is not:* Ibid.
156 *On the other it is:* Ibid.
156 *Much of all this:* Ibid.
156 *Mrs. Krehmer sent for:* DLA, Feb. 3, 1810, Reel 269 AFP MHS.
157 *This mode of life:* Ibid.
157 *repetitive miscarriages:* Recurrent Spontaneous Abortion (Miscarriage), NaPro Technology, http://www.naprotechnology.com/abortion.htm.
157 *migraine headaches:* "Increased Frequency of Migraine Among Women with Endometriosis." *Human Reproduction,* December 2004, http://www.ncbi.nlm.nih .gov/pubmed/15513980.
157 *My illness increased very:* DLA, Feb. 3, 1810, Reel 269 AFP MHS.

Chapter 21: Winter Woes
Page
158 *You are acquainted:* WJQA, JQA to AA, Feb. 8, 1810, III, 395.
158 *Here they are greater:* Ibid.
158 *These are burdens:* Ibid.
158 *You will readily:* Ibid., 396.
159 *Count Romanzoff came:* DLA, Feb. 21, 1810, Reel 269 AFP MHS.
159 *Not being aware:* Ibid., 207.
159 *Just getting about:* Ibid.
160 *thick ribbed ice:* WJQA, JQA to TA, Feb. 14, 1810, III, 397.
160 *Unhappily for mankind:* Ibid.
160 *When we were last:* Ibid., 397–98.
160 *There is not a republic:* Ibid., 398.
160 *Princess Amalia, the sister:* DLA, Mar. 3, 1810, Reel 269 AFP MHS.
161 *of the usual line:* Ibid.
161 *I presume these:* Ibid.
162 *Received a notification:* Ibid.
162 *Thus I was obliged:* Ibid.
162 *[His clothes] consisted:* Ibid.
162 *Martha Godfrey attended him:* Ibid.
162 *admiration of Petersburg:* LA to AA, June 2, 1810, Reel 410 AFP MHS.
162 *Mr. Adams . . . was:* DLA, Mar. 7, 1810, Reel 269 AFP MHS.
163 *[John] insisted that I:* Ibid.
163 *But no excuse could:* Ibid.
163 *The imperial family received:* Ibid.
163 *Obliged to go to:* Ibid., Mar. 8, 1810.
163 *brilliant as usual:* Ibid.
164 *I again returned him:* MJQA, Feb. 27, 1810, II, 100.
164 *one of the numerous:* WJQA, JQA to SOS, Jan. 17, 1810, III, 385.
164 *I had also:* MJQA, Feb. 27, 1810, II, 100.
165 *Nothing amused me so:* DLA, Mar. 8, 1810, Reel 269 AFP MHS.
165 *He would favor me:* Ibid.
165 *That a lady must:* Ibid.
165 *lest it should that:* Ibid.
165 *This was quite too:* Ibid.

Chapter 22: Contradictions
Page
166 *The prosperity of:* Supplementary Observations, US Census 1810.
166 *To neglect:* Ibid.

167   *wealth of the United States:* Ibid.
167   *[a]ccording to the recent:* MJQA, April 7, 1810, II, 111.
167   *In two of the family:* Ibid., 112.
167   *It is a very clumsy:* Ibid.
167   *Of the earliest, almost:* Ibid., 110.
167   *looked for the:* Ibid.
168   *I scarcely saw one:* Ibid.
168   *But the confinement:* Ibid., 114–15.
168   *perfection of subserviency:* Ibid., 113.
169   *The multitude of self-crossings:* Ibid., April 15, 1810, 117.
169   *In the meantime:* Ibid., April 27, 1810, 120.
169   *I saw one this day:* Ibid.
169   *But the donors themselves:* Ibid.
169   *Easter Sunday; the greatest holiday:* Ibid., April 29, 1810, 120.
169   *Everyone of the people:* DLA, April 29, 1810, Reel 269 AFP MHS.
170   *Persons of higher standing:* MJQA, April 29, 1810, II, 121.
170   *Easter Sunday is a:* DLA, April 29, 1810, Reel 269 AFP MHS.
171   *It is a subject:* MJQA, May 12, 1810, II, 123.
171   *The ice on the river:* Ibid.
171   *A handsome sight:* DLA, May 12, 1810, Reel 269 AFP MHS.
171   *The river was entirely:* Ibid.
171   *When all the ice is:* Ibid.
172   *The whole passage:* MJQA, May 12, 1810, II, 123.

Chapter 23: Pretense and Propriety

Page
173   *My sister and myself:* DLA, April 29, 1810, Reel 269 AFP MHS.
173   *The emperor would:* Ibid.
173   *As my sister was:* Ibid.
173   *Before we had:* Ibid., Aug. 5, 1809.
173   *But the weather being:* Ibid., April 29, 1810.
173   *We met his Imperial Majesty:* Ibid.
174   *And without waiting:* Ibid., emphasis in original.
174   *This was a real:* Ibid.
174   *When we met at:* Ibid.
174   *Adding nought in:* Ibid.
174   *The minister looked:* Ibid., emphasis in original.
174   *The young gentlemen disapproved:* Ibid.
175   *We continued our walks:* Ibid.
175   *But the emperor:* Ibid.
175   *He told me a number:* MJQA, May 14, 1810, II, 125.
175   *Not only was the:* Ibid.
176   *bred discord between:* Ibid.
176   *The plot was so poorly:* Ibid.
176   *The relations between:* WJQA, JQA to SOS, April 19, 1810, III, 417.
177   *There has been no:* Ibid.
177   *I am told that:* Ibid.
177   *Went to a ball:* DLA, May 23, 1810, Reel 269 AFP MHS.
177   *Obliged to go:* Ibid.
178   *We went at nine o'clock:* MJQA, May 23, 1810, II, 130.
178   *expiate some of my sins:* Ibid.
178   *The ascendancy of:* WJQA, JQA to SOS, April 19, 1810, III, 420.
178   *The emperor was:* DLA, May 23, 1810, Reel 269 AFP MHS.
179   *He inquired of:* Ibid.
179   *I must walk or dance:* Ibid.

179 *I was very much:* Ibid.
179 *Naturally timid this:* Ibid.
179 *But I got through:* Ibid.
179 *He immediately took:* Ibid.
179 *[I was] intending to:* Ibid.
179 *Imagine my confusion:* Ibid.
179 *He did not hear:* Ibid.
179 *the climate could:* Ibid.
180 *Thus we stood for:* Ibid.
180 *The music soon struck:* Ibid.
180 *I told him I did:* Ibid.
180 *no I must not:* Ibid.
180 *And she not knowing:* Ibid.
180 *the conversation contrary:* Ibid.
180 *He was so charmed:* Ibid.
180 *She [Kitty] had never:* Ibid.
181 *Poor Madame de Bray:* Ibid.
181 *so distressed at:* Ibid.
181 *And thus appeased:* Ibid.
181 *got home at two o'clock:* Ibid.
181 *The truth was the:* Ibid.
181 *The emperor was gracious:* Ibid.
181 *He enquired of me:* MJQA, May 23, 1810, II, 130.
181 *He said that the:* Ibid.
181 *I heard the ambassador:* Ibid., 131.
182 *There is a becoming:* Ibid., 141–42.

Chapter 24: Plato's Beard
Page
183 *The conduct of France:* WJQA, JQA to Joseph Pitcairn, May 8, 1810, III, 427.
183 *I can only hope:* Ibid., JQA to JA, April 30, 1810, 426.
184 *The nuptial torch is:* Ibid.
184 *The transition from infidelity:* Ibid.
184 *I believe nobody:* Ibid., 427.
184 *This hatred of republics:* Ibid.
184 *I wrote something:* MJQA, June 30, 1810, II, 137.
185 *My apothecary's:* Ibid.
185 *Mr. Adams too often:* DLA, July 21, 1810, Reel 269 AFP MHS, emphasis in original.
185 *After dinner came:* MJQA, July 16, 1810, II, 141.
185 *This is no uncommon:* Ibid.
185 *But of all the living:* Ibid.
186 *Licentiousness with regard:* Ibid.
187 *Mrs. Adams did not:* Ibid.

Chapter 25: Moving On
Page
188 *At last there is a:* DLA, June 3, 1810, Reel 269 AFP MHS.
188 *the directions of a:* Ibid.
188 *Russian houses have:* Ibid., emphasis in original.
188 *We have moved into:* LA to AA, July 9, 1810, Reel 410 AFP MHS.
189 *Under the circumstances:* MJQA, June 25, 1810, II, 136.
189 *I declined with:* Ibid., 137.
189 *The emperor wants:* DLA, June 3, 1810, Reel 269 AFP MHS.

189 *But he had tasted:* Ibid.
190 *We are all very:* Ibid., June 4, 1810.
190 *Adieu my dear:* LA to AA, May 13, 1810, Reel 409 AFP MHS.
190 *I wish they may:* WJQA, JQA to William Eustis, May 10, 1810, III, 429.
191 *US ships that entered:* Encyclopedia of the War of 1812, s.v. "Rambouillet Decree," 441.
191 *Thank God we now:* DLA, June 6, 1810, Reel 269 AFP MHS.
191 *after several months:* Ibid., JQA to AA, June 6, 1810, 447.
191 *Your very kind welcome:* LA to AA, June 2, 1810, Reel 409 AFP MHS.
191 *an electric shock:* Ibid.
192 *Tell John how delighted:* Ibid.
192 *Newspapers from Baltimore:* DLA, July 4, 1810, Reel 269 AFP MHS.
192 *Taken very ill and confined:* Ibid., July 15, 1810.
192 *I am just recovering:* LA to AA, July 19, 1810, Reel 410 AFP MHS.
192 *It is only four days:* Ibid.
192 *a hundred times:* Ibid.
192 *Resumed my seat:* DLA, July 21, 1810, Reel 269 AFP MHS.
193 *The licentious manners:* Ibid., June 12, 1810.
193 *God help me:* Ibid.
193 *All eyes are on:* Ibid.
193 *[John was] a marked man:* Ibid.
193 *The American minister:* WJQA, AA to JQA, May 28, 1810, III, 415n1.
193 *And this sensible paragraph:* Ibid.

CHAPTER 26: FENCING PIRATES
Page
195 *I have written by:* LA to Aunt Cranch, Aug. 24, 1810, Reel 410 AFP MHS.
196 *These vessels sailed:* MJQA, Aug. 8, 1810, II, 143.
196 *They have cargoes:* Ibid., 143–44.
196 *There was no way:* Ibid., 144.
196 *I then stated the:* Ibid.
197 *As long as American:* Ibid., 146.
197 *I added that I:* Ibid., 147.
197 *They [the Russians] should:* Ibid., emphasis in original.
197 *It was the direct:* Ibid.
197 *I had heard that:* Ibid.
198 *The French ambassador:* Ibid., Aug. 9, 1810, 149.
199 *I was from dinner-time:* Ibid., Aug. 8, 1810, 148.
199 *What a portion of:* Ibid.
199 *But they are now:* Ibid.
199 *mortify his vanity:* Ibid.
199 *a lesson which:* Ibid.
200 *He could now say:* Ibid., Aug. 17, 1810, 149.
200 *Probably most of the:* Ibid.
200 *freely converse:* Ibid.
200 *He [Caulaincourt] was persuaded:* Ibid.

CHAPTER 27: FRENCH CHOICE
Page
202 *I told him I was:* MJQA, Aug. 17, 1810, II, 150.
202 *There was certainly:* Ibid.
202 *I had reason besides:* Ibid.
203 *morose, captious:* Ibid.
203 *I did not even know:* Ibid.

203 *I stood with General Armstrong*: Ibid.
203 *My own course upon*: Ibid., 151.
203 *hoped the differences*: Ibid., Aug. 22, 1810, 151.
203 *it was the desire*: Ibid.
204 *persuaded that if*: Ibid.
204 *I told him that*: Ibid.
204 *He [Armstrong] never shows*: Ibid.
204 *of which I might be*: Ibid.
205 *Just as we were*: Ibid.
206 *I now recurred to*: Ibid., Aug. 28, 1810, 154.
206 *I urged the necessity*: Ibid
206 *peculiar favor*: Ibid .
206 *I flattered myself that*: Ibid., 155.
207 *I hoped Baron Campenhausen*: Ibid.
207 *fully sensible of the*: Ibid., 156.
207 *But he was extremely*: Ibid.
207 *My countrymen felt an*: Ibid.
207 *The emperor's sentiments*: Ibid.
207 *In the midst of*: Ibid., Aug. 28, 1810, 157.
207 *This was sporting*: Ibid.
208 *Several very recent*: WJQA, JQA to SOS, Aug. 19/31, 1810, III, 480.
208 *Some of them had*: Ibid.
208 *I write to you both*: JQA to George and John II, May 1810, Reel 409 AFP MHS.
208 *I wish, indeed, he*: WJQA, JQA to TA, Sept. 8, 1810, III, 497.
209 *The second [fencing] is*: Ibid.
209 *kiss my sweet boys*: LA to Aunt Cranch, Aug. 24, 1810, Reel 410 AFP MHS.

Chapter 28: French Accomplice
Page
210 *The duke had notice*: MJQA, Sept. 12, 1810, II, 164.
211 *[Caulaincourt] was very*: Ibid.
211 *It is the anniversary*: Ibid., Sept. 11, 1810, 162.
212 *[T]he concourse of*: Ibid.
212 *When we got to*: Ibid.
212 *None of the other*: Ibid., 160.
212 *as much embarrassed*: Ibid., 162.
213 *Count Romanzoff, at length*: Ibid.
213 *After the mass was*: Ibid., 163.
213 *On going out of*: Ibid.
213 *I followed the crowd*: Ibid.
214 *The attendance of strangers*: Ibid.
214 *I at length found*: Ibid.
214 *About four o'clock*: Ibid., Sept. 13, 1810, 167.
214 *Before dinner I expressed*: Ibid.
215 *These were subjects*: Ibid.
215 *I told him that*: Ibid.
215 *My situation in*: Ibid.
215 *any informal and unofficial*: Ibid.
215 *I should take great*: Ibid.
215 *I told him the French*: Ibid.
215 *The influence of France*: Ibid., 168.
216 *[Armstrong] scarcely ever saw*: Ibid.
216 *So now I see*: Ibid.
216 *I have made it a*: Ibid., Sept. 26, 1810, 173.

216 *Imperfect as my method:* Ibid., 174.
217 *During the present year:* Ibid., 173.
217 *I have begun this:* Ibid.

CHAPTER 29: OBSTINATE
Page
218 *Once a year, usually:* MJQA, Sept. 24, 1810, II, 172.
219 *The distance is between:* Ibid., 171.
219 *But the principal curiosities:* Ibid., 172.
219 *The waters are carried:* Ibid.
219 *The imitation [of sound]:* Ibid.
219 *The palace is in:* DLA, Sept. 14, 1810, Reel 269 AFP MHS.
219 *The palace is an image:* MJQA, Sept. 24, 1810, II, 171.
220 *I had some conversation:* Ibid., Sept. 27, 1810, 176.
220 *I mentioned to him:* Ibid., 174.
220 *dispositions:* Ibid.
221 *[France] should make:* Ibid., 174–75.
221 *That in relation to:* Ibid., 175.
221 *I assured him the:* Ibid.
221 *Two days ago the:* Ibid.
222 *The different pronunciation:* Ibid.
222 *The personal acquaintance:* Ibid.
222 *There was a pretty:* Ibid.
222 *You for instance:* Ibid.
222 *A great deal of:* Ibid.
222 *But cotton:* Ibid.
222 *I assured him in:* Ibid., 176.
223 *However strong the friendly:* Ibid.
223 *You will do us:* Ibid.
223 *You will oppress:* Ibid.
223 *Her [England's] bank:* Ibid.
223 *Why then did she:* Ibid.
224 *You speak of the:* Ibid.
224 *sincere and earnest desire:* Ibid., Oct. 9, 1810, 178.
224 *The people of the:* Ibid.
225 *And although nothing:* Ibid., 179.
225 *As to the fixing:* Ibid.
225 *more obstinate than you are aware of:* Ibid., 180, emphasis in original.
225 *I understood the force:* Ibid.

CHAPTER 30: AMERICAN CINDERELLAS
Page
227 *Invited to the theatre:* DLA, Oct. 14, 1810 [JQA indicates event on Oct. 24], Reel 269 AFP MHS.
227 *The emperor has given:* Ibid.
227 *This privilege is:* Ibid.
227 *a very extraordinary:* MJQA, Oct. 26, 1810, II, 189.
227 *In the evening we went:* DLA, Oct. 26, 1810, Reel 269 AFP MHS.
228 *The emperor and the:* Ibid.
228 *The French ambassador:* Ibid.
228 *all the great officers:* Ibid.
228 *The corps diplomatique:* Ibid.
228 *The piece was Cinderella:* Ibid.
228 *The distinction to:* Ibid.

230 *You tell me:* WJQA, JQA to William Plumer, Oct. 6, 1810, II, 509.

230 *The object of my mission:* Ibid., 512.

CHAPTER 31: CHRISTENING

Page

231 *I have frequently:* LA to AA, Oct. 23, 1810, Reel 410 AFP MHS.

231 *I did not need:* Ibid.

232 *Rely on it dear mother:* Ibid.

232 *one year would have:* DLA, Jan. 26, 1811, Reel 269 AFP MHS.

232 *The author may say:* WJQA, JQA to AA, Oct. 2/14, 1810, III, 514.

232 *I had great numbers:* Ibid.

232 *That a man should:* Ibid.

232 *By adhering to my:* WJQA, JQA to William Plumer, Oct. 6, 1810, III, 510.

232 *There is no escaping one's:* WJQA, JQA to TA, Oct. 11/23, 1810, III, 521.

233 *Perhaps one half the:* Ibid.

233 *petty principalities whose:* Ibid., 522.

233 *He therefore limits:* Ibid.

233 *We are, my dear:* JQA to George Adams, Sept. 3, 1810, Reel 410 AFP MHS.

233 *Ever since the 4th:* WJQA, JQA to Ezekiel Bacon, Nov. 3, 1810, III, 530.

234 *It was one of the:* Ibid.

234 *Notwithstanding all the:* Ibid., 532.

234 *From that day:* WJQA, JQA to AA, Oct. 2/14, 1810, III, 518.

234 *But at this moment:* WJQA, JQA to TA, Oct. 27, 1810, III, 528.

234 *I was too unwell:* DLA, Nov. 7, 1810, Reel 269 AFP MHS.

235 *It contains every luxury:* Ibid.

235 *As the chapel was:* Ibid., Nov. 10, 1810.

235 *On our return home:* Ibid.

236 *new beauties in every:* Ibid.

236 *In fact we all pined:* Ibid., Jan. 26, 1811.

236 *an amusement in which:* Ibid., Nov. 10, 1810.

236 *We all met in the:* Ibid., Nov. 15, 1810.

236 *Mr. Adams gave fifty:* Ibid.

CHAPTER 32: THE SNUB

Page

238 *Being quite fatigued:* DLA, Nov. 29, 1810, Reel 269 AFP MHS.

238 *The great distinction:* Ibid.

238 *On returning up the:* Ibid.

238 *I was very sorry:* Ibid., emphasis in original.

239 *The persons interested:* MJQA, Nov. 30, 1810, II, 191.

240 *belonged to the great:* Ibid.

240 *But I trusted he:* Ibid.

240 *[Romanzoff] said he could:* Ibid., 191–92.

240 *were bona fide American:* Ibid.

240 *The owners of almost:* Ibid.

241 *New modifications:* WJQA, JQA to AA, Oct. 2/14, 1810, III, 513.

241 *[W]hile France:* Ibid.

242 *I could not bear:* DLA, Dec. 5, 1810, Reel 269 AFP MHS.

242 *The winter being:* Ibid.

242 *In the course of:* Ibid.

242 *abusive:* Ibid.

243 *[The emperor] did not:* Ibid.

243 *[The emperor] was much pleased:* Ibid.

243 *I observed that it:* Ibid., emphasis in original.

243 *I knew that she:* Ibid.

CHAPTER 33: NEW YEAR'S BANG

Page

244 *As usual we met:* DLA, Dec. 16, 1810, Reel 269 AFP MHS.
244 *For I knew that:* Ibid.
244 *Taken suddenly:* Ibid., Dec. 13, 1810.
244 *[T]he first fine day:* Ibid., Dec. 16, 1810.
245 *He immediately stopped:* Ibid.
246 *The gentlemen had:* Ibid.
246 *I thank my stars:* Ibid., Jan. 1, 1811.
246 *I was now about:* MJQA, Dec. 20, 1810, II, 194.
246 *They belonged to a:* Ibid.
247 *I supposed the only:* Ibid., 195.
247 *In those cases the:* Ibid.
247 *It was very hard:* Ibid.
247 *That of the trade:* Ibid., 196.
247 *how the balance:* Ibid.
248 *From the very nature:* Ibid.
248 *France had undertaken:* Ibid., 198.
248 *Was there not great:* Ibid.
248 *There were undoubtedly cases:* Ibid.
248 *They could do nothing:* Ibid., 201.
248 *As to the greater:* Ibid., 202.
249 *Charles was threatened:* DLA, Dec. 22, 1810, Reel 269 AFP MHS.
249 *I took him into:* Ibid.
249 *Dr. Galloway stayed:* Ibid.
249 *There came a notification:* Ibid.
249 *Mr. Adams informed him:* Ibid.
249 *[The master of ceremonies]:* Ibid.
249 *that if Miss Johnson:* Ibid.
249 *I have formed my:* MJQA, Dec. 30, 1810, II, 206.
250 *The empress mother told:* DLA, Dec. 24, 1810, Reel 269 AFP MHS.
250 *Great part of:* MJQA, Dec. 24, 1810, II, 203.
250 *I have pursued no:* Ibid., Dec. 30, 1810, 206.
251 *We end this year:* DLA, Dec. 31, 1810, Reel 269 AFP MHS.

CHAPTER 34: EXIT STRATEGY

Page

252 *I hear that you are:* MJQA, in French, Jan. 13, 1811, II, 212.
252 *I hope, Sir, that:* Ibid.
252 *I hope that this:* Ibid.
252 *I received a letter from:* WJQA, JM to JQA. Oct. 16, 1810, III, 518.
252 *the intention of the executive:* Ibid., 326.
252 *As no communication:* Ibid.
253 *spare no pains:* Ibid., 519.
253 *I am entirely persuaded:* Ibid.
254 *This is considered:* MJQA, Jan. 13, 1811, II, 212.
254 *We were shown into:* DLA, Jan. 13, 1811, Reel 269 AFP MHS.
254 *Caulaincourt was seized:* Ibid.
255 *The imperial family soon:* Ibid.
255 *On entering the hall:* Ibid.
255 *And turning to:* Ibid., emphasis in original.
255 *we met the emperor:* Ibid.
256 *I thankfully declined:* Ibid.
256 *He came round:* Ibid.
256 *My astonishment and:* Ibid.

256 *The motive of all:* Ibid.
256 *a piece of showy calico:* Ibid., Jan. 24, 1811.
257 *A table was set covered:* Ibid.
257 *The child was presented:* Ibid.
257 *out the devil:* Ibid.
257 *I was taken very ill:* Ibid., Jan. 26, 1811.
258 *In fact we all:* Ibid.
258 *This was burthensome:* Ibid.
258 *How could we be:* Ibid.
258 *he would see:* MJQA, Jan. 20, 1811, II, 217.
259 *I mentioned to the:* Ibid., Jan. 23, 1811, 218.
259 *And he could assure me:* Ibid.
259 *At any rate:* Ibid.

CHAPTER 35: FRENCH COOLING
Page
260 *consistent with his duty:* WJQA, JQA to SOS, Feb. 12, 1811, III, 14.
260 *an extraordinary degree:* Ibid.
261 *I told him that it:* MJQA, Feb. 3, 1811, II, 221.
261 *And then, your vessels:* Ibid.
261 *That was a mistake:* Ibid.
261 *But how happens it:* Ibid.
261 *Why . . . the credit of that:* Ibid.
261 *That is to say:* Ibid.
261 *I had sent to:* Ibid.
262 *Where [could] the American:* Ibid., 222.
262 *Our own country produced:* Ibid.
262 *The desire of the:* Ibid.
262 *Sick as usual after:* DLA, Feb. 8, 1811, Reel 269 AFP MHS.
262 *I still confined:* Ibid., Feb. 9, 1811.
262 *Madame Lesseps is a:* Ibid., Feb. 11, 1811.
263 *The French were a:* Ibid.
263 *was so cold and:* Ibid., Feb. 7, 1811.
263 *Rumors of war between:* Ibid., Feb. 6, 1811.
263 *Some of our American:* MJQA, Feb. 15, 1811, II, 224.
263 *The French consuls in:* Ibid.
263 *This was certainly:* Ibid.
263 *when informed:* Ibid., 225.
263 *But, supposing our consuls:* Ibid.
264 *It [was] more probable:* Ibid.
264 *became a question between:* Ibid.
264 *If they had violated:* Ibid.
264 *But this was a:* Ibid.
264 *If they did, and you:* Ibid.
264 *The dishonor of such:* Ibid.
264 *To be sure, there:* Ibid., 225–26, emphasis in original.
265 *Consider it, Monsieur:* Ibid., 226.
265 *Precisely the same:* Ibid.
265 *By the late measures:* Ibid.
265 *But, it seems, you:* Ibid.
265 *They had, but after:* Ibid.
265 *I hope they:* Ibid., 227.
265 *But, you are to:* Ibid.
265 *We have had only:* Ibid.

265 *You could not, however:* Ibid.
266 *It was considerable:* Ibid.

CHAPTER 36: RECALL AND RELOCATION
Page
267 *It is confidently:* LA to AA, Feb. 14, 1811, Reel 411 AFP MHS.
267 *cheerfully acquiesce:* Ibid.
267 *Our solicitude and anxiety:* Ibid.
267 *Most of the members:* DLA, Feb. 21, 1811, Reel 269 AFP MHS.
268 *None of them are handsome:* Ibid.
268 *At ten o-clock went:* Ibid.
268 *The invitation was to:* Ibid.
269 *The conversation turned:* Ibid.
269 *Particularly of the:* Ibid.
269 *I was perfectly enragé:* Ibid.
269 *I told him that:* Ibid.
269 *My situation was becoming:* Ibid.
269 *What on earth is so:* Ibid.
270 *masquerade for:* Ibid., Feb. 26, 1811.
270 *Lent begins this day:* Ibid., Feb. 24, 1811.
270 *Caulaincourt has received his:* WJQA, JQA to AA, Mar. 19, 1811, IV, 26.
270 *one of the greatest enoblemen:* Ibid.
270 *He was happy:* MJQA, Mar. 18, 1811, II, 246.
271 *At least it may be:* WJQA, JQA to SOS, Feb. 19, 1811, IV, 18.
271 *If . . . according to the:* Ibid., 16.
271 *unless it be:* Ibid.
272 *The coolness or misunderstanding:* WJQA, JQA to SOS, Feb. 12, 1811, IV, 13.
272 *In constant expectation:* DLA, May 13, 1811, Reel 269 AFP MHS.
273 *The weather was:* MJQA, May 6, 1810, II, 260.
273 *It was very long:* Ibid.
273 *I believed it was:* Ibid.
273 *of late been:* Ibid.
273 *any late accounts:* Ibid.
273 *I had letters up:* Ibid.
273 *information of any:* Ibid.
273 *They did not:* Ibid.
273 *What was the state:* Ibid.
273 *And I hear you have:* Ibid., 261.
274 *But it appears to:* Ibid.
274 *Since then the people:* Ibid.
274 *On s'agrandit toujours:* Ibid.
274 *a very important personage:* Ibid.
274 *Such is the magic of:* Ibid.
274 *And every new mujik:* Ibid.
275 *The catastrophe is:* WJQA, JQA to SOS, April 29, 1811, IV, 63.

CHAPTER 37: CORRESPONDENCE AND CONTRACTIONS
Page
276 *I immediately saw:* DLA, May 23, 1811, Reel 269 AFP MHS.
276 *Went to visit Madame:* Ibid., Mar. 29, 1811.
276 *They could not conceal:* Ibid., May 23, 1811.
277 *accepted only to keep:* WJQA, AA to JQA, Jan. 20, 1811, Reel 411 AFP MHS.
277 *I would fain believe:* Ibid.
277 *I thought it best:* Ibid., Jan. 24, 1811.

277 *Say to your wife:* Ibid.
278 *My heart collapsed:* DLA, May 23, 1811, Reel 269 AFP MHS.
278 *The fright produced:* Ibid.
278 *My physician remained:* Ibid.
280 *Infant death rate:* Center for Disease Control "Deaths: Preliminary Data 2009." *National Vital Statistics Reports,* 59, No. 4 (Mar. 2011): 6.
280 *The maternal mortality:* Center for Disease Control and Prevention "Deaths: Final Data for 2007." *National Vital Statistics Reports,* 58, No. 19 (May 10, 2007).
280 *A favorable change:* DLA, May 23, 1811, Reel 269 AFP MHS.
280 *Mr. Krehmer sent me:* MJQA, May 24, 1811, II, 267.
280 *I fear the British ministry:* Ibid.
281 *Non nobis Domine!:* Ibid.
281 *Our trial is now:* Ibid., emphasis in original.

CHAPTER 38: SUPREME RECALL

Page

282 *After appearing better:* DLA, May 23, 1811, Reel 269 AFP MHS.
282 *Laudanum was freely:* Ibid., May 25, 1811.
282 *On awaking I was:* Ibid.
282 *rush[ed] forth:* Ibid.
282 *Slowly recovering God:* Ibid., May 27, 1811.
282 *I have the great pleasure:* AA to LA, Jan. 15, 1811, Reel 411 AFP MHS.
282 *Your mama wrote me:* Ibid.
283 *The Russian climate is:* Ibid.
283 *Was able to sit:* DLA, May 31, 1811, Reel 269 AFP MHS.
283 *I have the satisfaction:* MJQA, June 2, 1811, II, 275.
283 *This appointment will:* Ibid., 365.
284 *Monsieur Adams, il:* Ibid., May 31, 1811, 267.
284 *to take a house:* Ibid., 268.
284 *No, I had for some:* Ibid.
284 *Why:* Ibid.
284 *Fort bien vous avez:* Ibid.
285 *received any late news:* Ibid.
285 *I had:* Ibid.
285 *They had a very hostile:* Ibid.
285 *It has, however, very:* Ibid.
285 *To be sure people:* Ibid.
285 *Deeply sensible of the:* WJQA, JQA to SOS, June 2, 1811, IV, 90.

CHAPTER 39: SUMMER SOLSTICE

Page

286 *With the mind sorely:* LA to AA, June 10, 1811, Reel 411 AFP MHS.
286 *you broke to us:* Ibid.
286 *I am restored to:* Ibid.
287 *At least Mr. Adams:* Ibid.
287 *Mr. A. does not:* Ibid.
287 *One of them, itself decisive:* WJQA, JQA to SOS, June 2, 1811, IV, 90.
287 *the new mark of:* Ibid., JQA to JM, June 3, 1811, 93.
287 *My expectation is to:* Ibid., 94.
288 *[T]his circumstance places:* LA to AA, June 10, 1811, Reel 411 AFP MHS.
288 *in such a state:* Ibid.
289 *The commission, inasmuch:* WJQA, JQA to JA, June 7, 1811, IV, 99.
289 *Yet I am deeply:* Ibid.
289 *darling boys:* Ibid., 100.

289 *From this dilemma:* Ibid.
290 *They wish for:* WJQA, footnote to SOS, Feb. 26, 1811, IV, 19, taken from Madison to Jefferson, December 7, 1810. *Writings of Madison* (Hunt), VIII. 111n.
290 *I have long entertained:* Ibid., JQA to JM, June 3, 1811, 95.
290 *I am sorry, very:* Ibid., JQA to JA, June 7, 1811, 102.
291 *It has been painful:* Ibid., 101.
291 *Mr. Navarro brought:* DLA, June 20, 1811, Reel 269 AFP MHS.
291 *In the evening I:* MJQA, June 19, 1811, II, 276.
292 *I returned again:* Ibid.

CHAPTER 40: THE REMOVAL
Page
293 *Mr. Plinky came to:* DLA, July [1]], 1811, Reel 269 AFP MHS.
293 *This was rather severe:* Ibid.
293 *I accompanied Mr. Adams:* Ibid., July 5, 1811.
294 *It is very large:* Ibid., July 7, 1811.
294 *Went out to:* Ibid.
294 *Again at the house:* Ibid., July 10, 1811.
295 *[W]ith the open doors:* WJQA, JQA to AA, Oct. 2, 1811, IV, 230.
295 *The situation is very:* DLA, July 12, 1811, Reel 269 AFP MHS.
295 *[O]n the days when:* WJQA, JQA to AA, Oct. 2, 1811, IV, 230.
296 *Madame de Bezzara and Monsieur Navarro:* DLA, July 8, 1811, Reel 269 AFP MHS.
296 *She is a remarkably:* Ibid., June 20, 1811.
296 *Every way she is full:* Ibid.
296 *She requests me to:* Ibid., July 14, 1811.
296 *I cannot refuse but:* Ibid.
297 *not comparable in:* Ibid., May 14, 1811.
297 *to take leave of us:* Ibid.
297 *The emperor governs so:* MJQA, May 6, 1811, II, 259.
298 *I thought it probable:* Ibid., July 15, 1811, 279.
298 *How?:* Ibid., 280.
298 *By not keeping [your] word:* Ibid.
298 *Oh! But you must:* Ibid.
298 *Americans will not:* Ibid.
298 *Ah! Ah! my spies:* Ibid.
298 *My spies give me:* Ibid.
299 *Yes; and you have:* Ibid.
299 *all this was said:* Ibid.
299 *Mr. & Mrs. Bezzara came:* DLA, July 25, 1811, Reel 269 AFP MHS.
299 *Countess Litta received:* Ibid.
299 *As however she:* Ibid.
299 *And when the countess:* Ibid.
300 *We reached home:* Ibid.
300 *I have this day:* MJQA, July 26, 1811, II, 282.
300 *Its greatest alloy:* Ibid.
300 *But she has always:* Ibid.
300 *At last for a:* Ibid., July 29, 1811.
301 *When I look forward:* Ibid.

CHAPTER 41: THE CONFINEMENT
Page
302 *The road was crowded:* MJQA, Aug. 3, 1811, II, 284.
303 *A Portuguese minister's lady:* Ibid., 285.
303 *had administered a:* WJQA, JQA to George William Erving, Aug. 3, 1811, IV, 176.

303 *cherries, strawberries, raspberries:* MJQA, Aug. 3, 1811, II, 285.
303 *Countess Litta said that:* Ibid., 286.
303 *They asked the:* Ibid.
304 *Miss Gourieff told me:* Ibid.
304 *The daylight was:* Ibid.
304 *The lines of carriages:* Ibid., 287.
304 *On arriving at the:* Ibid., 288.
305 *I now learnt, and:* Ibid.
305 *If we have a war:* WJQA, JQA to TA, July 31, 1811, Reel 411 AFP MHS.
305 *A war appears to:* Ibid.
306 *Whether it be of:* Ibid.
306 *The school of affliction:* Ibid.
307 *You come into life:* Adams Family Correspondence, vol. 10, 150–152.
307 *When I came to:* WJQA, JQA to JA, July 21, 1811, IV, 144.
307 *More than one of:* Ibid.
307 *I knew equally well:* Ibid.
307 *My real motive was:* Ibid.
308 *How does it appear:* Ibid.
308 *I entertain some very:* Ibid., 145.
308 *repair without hesitation:* Ibid.
308 *For seven months of:* Ibid., June 25, 1811, 117.

CHAPTER 42: CHRISTENING REPRISE
Page
310 *We were obliged:* DLA, Aug. 11, 1811, Reel 269 AFP MHS.
310 *Continued quite ill:* Ibid., Aug. 12, 1811.
311 *Mrs. Heinche left me:* DLA, Aug. 12, 1811, Reel 269 AFP MHS.
311 *This indiscretion nearly:* Ibid.
311 *This was a day:* Ibid.
311 *God was very merciful:* Ibid.
311 *My child a daughter:* Ibid.
312 *My sister went and:* Ibid.
312 *This day my lovely:* Ibid., Sept. 9, 1811.
312 *Because it is done:* MJQA, Sept. 9, 1811, II, 305.
312 *Because the father:* Ibid., 401.
312 *The sponsors were strangely:* DLA, Sept. 9, 1811, Reel 269 AFP MHS.
313 *But the rite itself:* MJQA, Sept. 9, 1811, II, 305.
313 *We dared not ask:* DLA, Sept. 9, 1811, Reel 269 AFP MHS.
313 *The child was baptized:* MJQA, Sept. 9, 1811, II, 304.
313 *She was named after:* DLA, Sept. 9, 1811, Reel 269 AFP MHS.
313 *The company dined with:* Ibid.

CHAPTER 43: COMETS
Page
314 *Monsieur Adams:* MJQA, Dec. 9, 1811, II, 329.
314 *We have two comets:* Ibid.
314 *Oh, that is certain:* Ibid.
314 *But, furthermore, I hear:* Ibid.
315 *But for this I:* Ibid.
315 *This was extra:* Ibid.
315 *C'est un bouleversement:* Ibid.
315 *But as it is generally:* Ibid.
315 *Or at least that:* Ibid.
315 *I congratulate His:* Ibid.

315 *Il y a moyen d'expliquer:* Ibid.
316 *I have got into:* WJQA, JQA to JA, Oct. 31, 1811, IV, 267.
316 *For my own part I:* Ibid., Oct. 14, 1811, 244.
316 *As respects myself:* Ibid., Oct. 31, 1811, 267.
317 *The political state of:* Ibid., Oct. 14, 1811, 245.
317 *moved into a house:* DLA, Oct. 10, 1811, Reel 269 AFP MHS.
318 *In a corner house:* MJQA, Oct. 17, 1811, II, 319–20.
318 *She had been:* Ibid., 320.
318 *When:* Ibid.
318 *More than two:* Ibid.
318 *What! In the country:* Ibid.
318 *In the country:* Ibid.
318 *Had her confinement:* Ibid.
318 *Entirely so:* Ibid.
318 *What had she:* Ibid.
318 *A daughter:* Ibid.
318 *As he is informed:* DLA, Oct. 16, 1811, Reel 269 AFP MHS.
318 *How inquisitive!!!:* Ibid.
319 *Everything is changed:* Ibid.
319 *a constant visitor:* Ibid., Nov. 19, 1811.
319 *Indeed he was styled:* Ibid.
319 *O she grows lovely:* Ibid.
320 *And this is the:* Ibid.
320 *The domestic tragedy:* Ibid..

CHAPTER 44: BALTIC FREEZE
Page

321 *Seized with a violent:* DLA, Dec. 7, 1811, Reel 269 AFP MHS.
321 *My fever ran so:* Ibid.
321 *My child was taken:* Ibid.
321 *Still considered in great:* Ibid.
321 *Myself out of danger:* Ibid.
321 *After a long protracted:* Ibid., Jan. 28, 1812.
322 *The emperor and empresses:* MJQA, Dec. 24, 1811, II, 331.
322 *The emperor noticed:* Ibid.
322 *It was not so showy:* Ibid.
322 *Mr. Adams's position:* DLA, Jan. 28, 1812, Reel 269 AFP MHS.
322 *The aspect of society:* Ibid.
323 *In Europe darkness and gloom:* WJQA, JQA to William Plumer, Sept. 8, 1811, IV, 211.
323 *out of this darkness:* Ibid.
323 *A letter full of woe:* DLA, Jan. 29, 1812, Reel 269 AFP MHS.
323 *[And] that of my brother-in-law:* Ibid.
323 *Mr. Adams's Uncle:* Ibid.
323 *And the dangerous:* Ibid.
323 *Full of mortal affliction:* Ibid., Jan. 31, 1812.
324 *How different will:* Ibid.
324 *He afflicts us in:* Ibid.
325 *A circumstance which:* MJQA, Feb. 4, 1812, II, 335.
325 *to be removed to:* Ibid.
325 *had mentioned it:* Ibid., 335–36.
325 *It was much the:* Ibid., 335–36.
326 *spirit of delirium:* WJQA, JQA to William Plumer, Sept. 8, 1811, IV, 211.
326 *that Congress will have:* WJQA, JQA to AA, Jan. 1, 1812, IV, 284.

326 *that in France a:* MJQA, Feb. 4, 1812, II, 336.
326 *With regard to American:* Ibid.
327 *Today the impression:* Ibid.
327 *To make them consistent:* Ibid.
327 *But in truth, commerce:* Ibid.
327 *The Emperor Napoleon:* Ibid.
327 *Tranquility is not:* Ibid., 338.
327 *I was speaking to him:* Ibid., emphasis in original.
327 *And now as perhaps:* Ibid.

CHAPTER 45: INTERFERENCE

Page

329 *My lovely beautiful:* DLA, Feb. 12, 1812, Reel 269 AFP MHS.
329 *Ah! The fountain of:* Ibid.
329 *Everyone who sees:* Ibid.
329 *The Russians are very:* Ibid.
329 *Toward evening my:* Ibid.
330 *The emperor said he:* MJQA, Mar. 3, 1812, II, 345.
330 *always made it:* Ibid.
330 *not suffer from:* Ibid.
330 *On the contrary:* Ibid.
330 *He had then worn:* Ibid.
330 *A physician therefore:* Ibid.
330 *You are not of my:* Ibid.
331 *I had so long been:* Ibid.
331 *But there are now:* Ibid.
331 *And so it is:* Ibid., Mar. 19, 1812, 352.
331 *But are all hopes:* Ibid.
331 *At all events we:* Ibid.
331 *Then as Your Majesty:* Ibid.
331 *I wish it may:* Ibid., in French.
332 *In my walk before:* Ibid., April 9, 1812, 356.
332 *That the floods would:* Ibid.
332 *The emperor is to:* Ibid.
332 *Two days before:* WJQA, JQA to SOS, April 28, 1812, IV, 314.
332 *What was the precise:* MJQA, April 20, 1812, II, 361.
333 *I was perfectly sure:* Ibid., 361–62.
333 *And unless restored:* Ibid., 362.
333 *I thought their existence:* Ibid.
333 *Did I think Mr. Perceval:* Ibid.
333 *I believed he would:* Ibid.
333 *But as it is the:* WJQA, JQA to AA, April 30, 1812, IV, 322.
333 *In that case we:* Ibid.
334 *I expressly requested:* Ibid.
334 *But as far as I can:* Ibid., JQA to AA, May 28, 1812, 341.
334 *precious engagement:* Ibid.

CHAPTER 46: TOMORROW

Page

335 *soured and exasperated:* MJQA, June 19, 1812, II, 377.
335 *I asked him where:* Ibid., 379.
335 *Perhaps at Warsaw:* Ibid.
335 *They think because:* Ibid.
335 *But with such a man:* Ibid.

336   *The facts show:* Ibid.
336   *My own disposition:* Ibid., June 21, 1812, 379.
336   *A father of a:* Ibid.
336   *perpetual temptations:* Ibid.
337   *What with all the:* Ibid., 380.
337   *June 22, 1812:* Tim Blanning, *Pursuit of Glory*, 663.
337   *June 23:* John Powell, *Chronology of European History*, 780–81.
337   *June 24, 1812:* David Warnes, *Chronology of the Tzars*, 154.

CHAPTER 47: HEAVEN
Page
339   *We have lived:* WJQA, JQA to JA, June 29, 1812, IV, 358.
339   *The most powerful:* Ibid.
339   *I had flattered myself:* Ibid., 359.
340   *The Perceval policy:* Ibid.
340   *I am 45 years old:* MJQA, July 11, 1812, II, 387.
340   *hostage or a prisoner:* Ibid., 386.
341   *They prepare for illumination:* Ibid.,July 9, 1812, 386.
342   *On the 16th of June:* WJQA, JQA to AA, July 13, 1812, IV, 367.
342   *My principal anxiety:* Ibid., 368.
342   *I am uneasy lest:* Ibid., 369.
342   *My coachman this morning:* MJQA, July 22, 1812, II, 392.
343   *The official news:* Ibid.
343   *I walked before breakfast:* Ibid., Aug. 3, 1812, 395.
343   *I then flattered myself:* WJQA, JQA to AA, Aug. 10, 1812, IV, 388.
344   *In this hope I:* Ibid.
344   *After reading Mr. Foster's:* Ibid.
344   *I lament the declaration:* Ibid.
344   *no alternative left:* Ibid.
344   *How far the policy:* Ibid., 389.
344   *My own most fervent:* Ibid.
345   *Our horses ran without:* MJQA, Aug. 14, 1812, II, 397.
345   *Went into the country:* DLA, Aug. 3, 1812, Reel 269 AFP MHS.
345   *I had not expected:* MJQA, Sept. 10, 1812, II, 401.
345   *He professed to:* Ibid.
346   *I assured him that:* Ibid.
346   *But the violence:* DJQA, Sept. 11, 1812.
346   *My dear child:* Ibid., Sept. 12, 1812.
347   *Language cannot express:* Ibid.
347   *Her mother, fond:* Ibid., Sept. 13, 1812.
347   *could not keep:* Ibid., Sept. 14, 1812.
347   *A gleam of voluntary:* Ibid.
347   *The Lord gave:* Ibid., Sept. 15, 1812.
347   *My dear wife:* Ibid.
348   *My child gone to heaven:* DLA, Sept. 12[15], 1812, Reel 269 AFP MHS. Note: JQA Diary documents death on Sept. 15.
348   *Believing in the:* DJQA, Sept. 15
348   *I endeavor to:* Ibid., Sept. 17.
348   *As life is:* Ibid.

CHAPTER 48: ENEMY WITHIN
Page
349   *My landlord, Mr. Strogofshikoff:* MJQA, Sept. 25, 1812, II, 405.
350   *The courtiers were as:* Ibid.

350 *It had occurred to the:* MJQA, Sept. 21, 1812, II, 402.

350 *Was [Adams] aware:* Ibid.

351 *I answered that it:* Ibid.

351 *I was very sure that:* Ibid.

351 *For myself, I so:* Ibid.

351 *He thought an indirect:* Ibid., 403.

351 *To a mutual friend:* Ibid.

352 *It is feared that:* Ibid., Sept. 30, 1812, 409.

352 *offensive to the emperor:* Ibid., Sept. 29, 407.

352 *His [Alexander's] spirit:* Ibid., Sept. 30, 409.

352 *Women! Women! Women!:* Ibid., Sept. 29, 1812, 407.

352 *It was unquestionably:* Ibid.

352 *The time of real danger:* Ibid., Sept. 30, 1812, 409.

353 *They are to go:* Ibid., Oct. 9, 1812, 411.

353 *We shall have scarcely:* Ibid.

353 *I have procured:* DLA, Oct. 22, 1812, Reel 264 AFP MHS.

354 *[S]till my mind:* Ibid., Oct. 23, 1812.

354 *Bitter reflection adds:* Ibid.

354 *a little [of] the sameness:* Ibid., Oct. 24, 1812.

354 *I visited the theatre:* Ibid.

354 *But on my return:* Ibid.

354 *It has been my:* Ibid., Oct. 25, 1812.

354 *And I suffer'd myself:* Ibid.

354 *I am peculiarly unfortunate:* Ibid.

355 *For those I love:* Ibid.

355 *I feel what a:* Ibid.

355 *There is something:* Ibid.

355 *In Mrs. Adams I:* Ibid.

356 *Suffering from the:* Encyclopedia of the War of 1812, s.v. "William Hull," 248.

357 *There are scarcely:* MJQA, Oct. 27, 1812, II, 418.

CHAPTER 49: IMPRESSMENT

Page

358 *About noon this:* MJQA, Oct. 27, 1812, II, 418.

358 *The passions of almost:* Ibid., Nov. 4, 1812, 420.

358 *I know not how:* Ibid.

359 *The trade is beyond:* Ibid., Nov. 10, 1812, 422.

359 *[F]or the impressment:* Ibid.

359 *Yet the same members:* Ibid.

360 *My thoughts have:* DLA, Nov. 6, 1812, Reel 264 AFP MHS.

360 *My babe's image flits:* Ibid.

360 *Necessity alone induced:* Ibid.

360 *I was playing with:* Ibid.

361 *We descended a flight:* Ibid., Nov. 11, 1812.

361 *Methought I got:* Ibid.

361 *With the usual inconsistency:* Ibid.

361 *I was left alone:* Ibid.

361 *And I raised my eyes:* Ibid.

361 *I struggle in vain:* Ibid., Nov. 6, 1812.

361 *My heart is buried:* Ibid.

CHAPTER 50: RETREAT

Page

362 *[T]here was a report:* MJQA, Dec. 8, 1812, II, 430.

362 *We afterwards, in the:* Ibid.
363 *It is the greatest victory:* Ibid., Nov. 25, 1812, 422.
363 *Joy and triumph:* Ibid., 423.
363 *It is now morally impossible:* Ibid., 422–23.
363 *performed their prostrations:* Ibid., 423.
363 *The emperor, on leaving:* Ibid.
364 *The crisis is great:* Ibid.
364 *It is long since:* DLA, Nov. 27, 1812, Reel 264 AFP MHS.
364 *How often when:* Ibid.
364 *We behold here:* Ibid.
364 *The character of this:* Ibid.
365 *The first was the:* MJQA, Dec. 7, 1812, II, 427.
365 *peculiarly agreeable to:* Ibid.
365 *I believe the emperor's:* Ibid., Dec. 3, 1812, 426.
365 *I had not, but that:* Ibid., Dec. 7, 1812, 429.
365 *Upon the chief:* Ibid.
365 *sense of independence:* Ibid.
365 *It was not exactly:* Ibid.
366 *few foreign seamen:* Ibid.
366 *The American sea service:* Ibid.
366 *And they have no:* Ibid., 430.
366 *he, the count, would:* Ibid.
366 *The news of the:* Ibid., Dec. 9, 1812, 430.
367 *Kitty has been:* DLA, Dec. 5, 1812, Reel 264 AFP MHS.
367 *To me there is:* Ibid.
367 *I know myself:* Ibid.
367 *one who loves:* MJQA, Dec. 24, 1812, II, 435.
367 *The reliance of man:* Ibid.
368 *The Emperor Alexander:* DLA, Dec. 5, 1812, Reel 264 AFP MHS.

Chapter 51: Dry Bones

Page
369 *They tell me that:* DLA [ca. Mar. 27, 1813], Reel 264 AFP MHS.
369 *In vain I reason:* Ibid.
369 *The emperor's birthday:* MJQA, Dec. 24, 1812, II, 435.
370 *I sent for my landlord:* Ibid., Mar. 17, 1813, 452.
370 *It has, indeed, constantly:* WJQA, JQA to SOS, Oct. 2, 1812, IV, 392.
371 *I still retain it:* Ibid.
371 *[Strogofshikoff] conversed with:* MJQA. Mar. 17, 1813, II, 452.
372 *As to the question:* Ibid., 451.
372 *This is the strangest:* Ibid.
372 *As Sir Francis is:* Ibid.
372 *He very stoutly contends:* Ibid., 450.
373 *Sir Francis appeared:* Ibid.
373 *We have at length:* DLA, April 4, 1813, Reel 264 AFP MHS.
373 *To hear from them:* Ibid.
373 *I scarcely can define:* Ibid.
373 *My health, the climate:* Ibid.
373 *I have just closed:* Ibid.
373 *pang of my bursting:* LA to AA, April 4, 1813, Reel 415 AFP MHS.
373 *Had you witnessed:* Ibid.
374 *How happens it that:* MJQA, May 11, 1813, II, 467.
374 *I knew not how:* Ibid.
374 *There had once:* Ibid.
375 *reminded me of the resurrection:* Ibid., April 3, 1813, 454.

375 *It was certain that:* Ibid., April 10, 1813, 460.
375 *Napoleon might be:* Ibid., 459.
375 *We were told that:* Ibid., May 13, 1813, 467.
376 *The situation of things:* Ibid., June 1, 1813, 469.
376 *Napoleon and his army:* Ibid., June 7, 1813, 471.
377 *He then showed:* Ibid., June 15, 1813, 473.
377 *in very handsome:* Ibid.
377 *The report of Messrs:* Ibid., 474.
377 *I presumed that:* Ibid.
377 *In a government:* Ibid., 474–75.
377 *did not think:* Ibid., 474.

CHAPTER 52: ESCAPE
Page
381 *It required a violent effort:* "NRF," Reel 268 AFP MHS.
381 *We got over and reached:* Ibid.
381 *Here I had to wait three:* Ibid.
382 *I was obliged to produce:* Ibid.
382 *The man appeared to be:* Ibid.
382 *He thought the carriage very:* Ibid.
382 *I cannot rely [at] all:* LA to JQA, Aug. 30, 1814, Reel 419 AFP MHS, emphasis in original 485.
382 *Although I do everything:* Ibid., Aug. 19, 1814.
384 *With this prospect:* MJQA, April 28, 1814 II, 602.
384 *Upon the canvas I never look:* JQA to LA, Aug. 9, 1814, Reel 419 AFP MHS.
384 *As I have written:* Ibid.
384 *At present I do not think:* Ibid.
384 *liberal and highly pacific:* Ibid., 486.
385 *If they choose to play:* WJQA, JQA to LA, Sept. 9, 1814, VV, 120, 7487.
385 *with increased vigor:* JQA to LA, Aug. 9, 1814, Reel 419 AFP MHS.
385 *We came suddenly upon:* "NRF," Reel 268 AFP MHS.
386 *Baptiste . . . began to assume:* Ibid.
386 *I intimated to him:* Ibid.
386 *great desire was to return:* Ibid.
386 *The performance of this:* Ibid., emphasis in original.
386 *was much more respectful:* Ibid.
387 *Mr. Bailey said he would:* LA to JQA, Aug. 5, 1814, Reel 419 AFP MHS.
387 *The excursions and:* JQA to LA, Sept. 2, 1814, Reel 419 AFP MHS.
387 *Really mon ami:* LA to JQA, Sept. 4, 1814, Reel 419 AFP MHS.
387 *I should never even:* Ibid.
387 *I am fully sensible of:* Ibid.
388 *But when events are totally:* Ibid.
388 *The situation of our country:* Ibid.
388 *You will now my dearest:* WJQA, JQA to LA, Aug. 9, 1814, V, 74.
389 *I most sincerely wish:* LA to JQA, Nov. 22, 1814, Reel 420 AFP MHS.
389 *My troubles never end:* LA to JQA, Dec. 6, 1814, Reel 421 AFP MHS.
389 *The season of the year:* Ibid.
390 *Everything around us:* "NRF," Reel 268 AFP MHS.
390 *the fearful remnants:* Ibid.
390 *had not been unprotected:* Ibid.
390 *houses half burnt:* Ibid.

Chapter 53: American Phoenix

Page

391 *He seems to think:* John Wesley, 1775, *Oxford English Dictionary.*

391 *resembling an eagle:* Phoenix, *Oxford English Dictionary.*

391 *They that wait:* Isaiah 40:31, King James Version.

391 *Faith is the phoenix grace:* Phoenix grace, *Oxford English Dictionary.*

392 *humble the Yankees:* WJQA, JQA to LA, Aug. 16, 1814, V, 84.

392 *It is impossible:* Ibid., 82.

392 *Your fears of bad news:* LA to JQA, Sept. 10, 1814, Reel 420 AFP MHS.

392 *You are hereby:* H. Adams, *The US During the Administration of Madison*, 126.

392 *That proclamation of:* LA to JQA, Sept. 10, 1814, Reel 420 AFP MHS.

392 *When our landsmen have:* WJQA to LA, Aug. 26, 1814, V, 104.

393 *Alas there are a few Washingtons:* LA to JQA, Aug. 30, 1814, Reel 419 AFP MHS.

393 *There is a report in town:* LA to JQA, Sept. 13, 1814, Reel 420 AFP MHS.

393 *I could almost wish:* LA to JQA, Oct. 16, 1814, Reel 420 AFP MHS.

393 *The melancholy situation:* Ibid., Oct. 18, 1814.

394 *in the best readiness:* JM to John Armstrong, July 2, 1814, *Writings of James Madison*, VIII, 1808–19.

394 *No, no! Baltimore:* H. Adams, *The US During the Administration of Madison*, 121.

394 *The newspapers contain:* JQA to LA, Oct. 7, 1814, Reel 420 AFP MHS.

395 *They left their:* Ibid.

395 *Shall this harbor:* George, *Terror on the Chesapeake*, 107.

396 *seat:* Ibid.

396 *The destruction of the:* JQA to LA, Oct. 7, 1814, Reel 420 AFP MHS.

396 *The same British officers:* Ibid.

397 *Boston is still exposed:* Ibid., Oct. 4, 1814.

397 *If it cannot be produced:* Ibid.

397 *The news of the destruction:* LA to JQA, Oct. 25, 1814, Reel 420 AFP MHS.

397 *I felt my exile:* Ibid.

397 *I trust in God:* Ibid., Nov. 6, 1814.

Chapter 54: Queen of Hearts

Page

398 *The evening was setting:* "NRF," Reel 268 AFP MHS.

398 *miserable common:* Ibid.

398 *One woman made her appearance:* Ibid.

398 *They answered doggedly:* Ibid.

399 *According to this plan:* Ibid.

399 *As I always had provisions:* Ibid.

399 *bore the mutilating:* Ibid.

399 *To my utter astonishment:* Ibid.

399 *The Cossacks! The dire Cossacks:* Ibid.

400 *There is scarcely a metropolis:* JQA to LA, Oct. 4, 1814, Reel 420 AFP MHS.

400 *The army of Napoleon did:* Ibid., Oct. 7, 1814.

400 *atrocious:* Ibid., Oct. 11, 1814, 508.

400 *the most execrable barbarities:* Ibid.

400 *It is said that the:* LA to JQA, Nov. 6, 1814, Reel 420 AFP MHS.

400 *Armstrong defends himself:* JQA to LA, Oct. 25, 1814, Reel 420 AFP MHS.

401 *The forces under Sir Alexander:* WJQA, V, 148n2.

402 *We may hope, therefore:* Ibid.

402 *It must indeed:* WJQA, JQA to LA, Oct. 14, 1814, V, 160.

402 *The nature of our government:* LA to JQA, Nov. 25, 1814, Reel 420 AFP MHS.

402 *we just might hold up*: Ibid., Nov. 5, 1814.
402 *We left Küstrin*: "NRF," Reel 268 AFP MHS.
402 *One of the postilions*: Ibid.
403 *My heart thrilled*: Ibid.
403 *Memory how ineffably*: Ibid.
403 *The carriage needed repairs*: Ibid.
404 *George's growth has been*: AA to JQA, May 1, 1814 (cited by JQA to LA Aug. 9, 1814), Reel 419 AFP MHS.
404 *said to me of our sons*: WJQA, JQA to LA, Sept. 9, 1814, V, 121.
404 *the luxuries*: "NRF," Reel 268 AFP MHS.
404 *forgetting in the lapse*: Ibid.
404 *I had had no small*: JQA to LA, Aug. 30, 1814, Reel 419 AFP MHS.
405 *Mr. Charles, who is*: LA to JQA, Dec. 30, 1814, Reel 421 AFP MHS.
405 *Pray tell me what fair lady*: Ibid.
405 *Do not fancy I am jealous*: Ibid., emphasis in original.
405 *She was a charming woman*: "NRF," Reel 268 AFP MHS.
406 *Countess Apraxin was*: Ibid.
406 *After tea she took the*: Ibid.
406 *She said that I was*: Ibid.
406 *I delivered your message*: LA to JQA, Mar. 5, 1815, Reel 422 AFP MHS.
406 *That when I had achieved*: "NRF," Reel 268 AFP MHS.
406 *That this circumstance*: Ibid.
407 *I laughed and thanked*: Ibid.
407 *I responded I was certain*: Ibid.

CHAPTER 55: KING OF SPADES

Page
408 *That fair lady is*: WJQA, JQA to LA, Jan. 24, 1815, V, 273.
408 *You must not be*: Ibid.
409 *The king, however, asked*: MJQA, Feb. 7, 1815, III, 151.
409 *Louis has only to discern*: JQA to LA, Oct. 18, 1814, Reel 420 AFP MHS.
409 *The great difficulty*: Ibid.
410 *After a very troublesome*: LA to JQA, Mar. 5, 1815, Reel 422 AFP MHS.
410 *be dispatched as*: "NRF," Reel 268 AFP MHS.
410 *Everything looked much*: Ibid.
410 *The Princess Louisa*: Ibid.
411 *The great people*: Ibid.
411 *Her husband and sons*: Ibid.
411 *When we were at Berlin*: JQA to LA, Nov. 22, 1814, Reel 420 AFP MHS.
412 *succeed in Vienna*: WJQA, JQA to LA, Nov. 4, 1814, V, 177.
412 *I think the President*: King, *Life and Correspondence of Rufus King*, Jan. 17, 1814, 364.
412 *The great effort of Lord Castlereagh*: Ibid., Nov. 18, 1814, 196.
412 *The great effort of Talleyrand*: Ibid.
413 *I fear the Emperor of Russia*: WJQA, JQA to LA, Oct. 4, 1814, V, 149.
413 *Early in the morning*: "NRF," Reel 268 AFP MHS.
413 *was as little altered*: Ibid.
413 *I quitted its*: Ibid.
414 *My lovely beautiful babe*: DLA, Feb. 11, 1812, Reel 269 AFP MHS.
416 *My friends in Berlin had*: "NRF," Reel 268 AFP MHS.
416 *In the evening after dark*: Ibid.
416 *And if you take up one*: JQA to CFA, Sept. 13, 1814, Reel 419 AFP MHS.
417 *But if you take out*: Ibid.
417 *A rumor had arrived of*: "NRF," Reel 268 AFP MHS.
417 *jokes, as he was known*: Ibid.
417 *I started with astonishment*: Ibid.

CHAPTER 56: "THE STAR-SPANGLED BANNER"

Page

418 *I went to bed very tired:* "NRF," Reel 268 AFP MHS.

418 *My purse was there:* Ibid.

418 *Last week . . . I was informed:* JQA to LA, Mar. 18, 1815, Reel 422 AFP MHS.

418 *No farewell but a welcome:* Ibid.

419 *Wherever we stopped to change horses:* "NRF," Reel 268 AFP MHS.

419 *At about a mile before:* Ibid.

419 *My heart throbbed:* Ibid.

419 *Conceive my horror:* Ibid.

420 *I was much questioned:* Ibid.

420 *took great pains to point:* Ibid.

420 *It was a very remarkable fact:* Ibid.

420 *At this place I observed:* Ibid.

420 *Feeling very uneasy:* Ibid.

422 *Through the clouds:* National Monument and Historic Shrine, *Fort McHenry.*

423 *No, I shall eat my supper:* Rukert, *Fort McHenry: Home of the Brave,* 24.

423 *The noble baron should:* JQA to LA, Oct. 25, 1814, Reel 420, AFP MHS.

423 *Heaven has not deserted us:* LA to JQA, Nov. 15, 1814, Reel 420 AFP MHS.

CHAPTER 57: ANTEBELLUM

Page

424 *We had never before taken:* JQA to LA, Nov. 8, 1814, Reel 420 AFP MHS.

424 *But our deliberations:* Ibid.

425 *a post-office between us:* WQJA, JQA to LA, Sept. 30, 1814, V, 148.

425 *In the instructions that we:* JQA to LA, Nov. 25, 1814, Reel 420 AFP MHS.

425 *For the first time:* Ibid., Nov. 29, 1814.

425 *We are now in sight:* Ibid.

426 *asked me, formally:* Ibid., LA to JQA, Nov. 25, 1814, Reel 420 AFP MHS, 541, emphasis in original.

426 *I speak of it as doubtful:* JQA to LA, Dec. 9, 1814, Reel 421 AFP MHS.

426 *I'd write you from:* LA to JQA, Mar. 17, 1815, Reel 422 AFP MHS.

426 *night and day:* Ibid.

426 *My two servants requested:* "NRF," Reel 268 AFP MHS.

427 *Here was a situation:* Ibid., emphasis in original.

427 *He was very polite:* Ibid.

427 *My position was so unpleasant:* Ibid.

427 *I insisted that it would:* Ibid.

427 *He [the banker] advised on the:* Ibid.

428 *the only creature he could:* Ibid.

428 *He had though so young:* Ibid.

428 *At the same time he:* Ibid.

428 *From want of judgment:* LA to JQA, Oct. 16, 1814, Reel 420 AFP MHS.

429 *It will at least be a:* Ibid.

429 *On Saturday last:* JQA to LA, Dec. 27, 1814, Reel 421 AFP MHS.

430 *I consider the day:* Ibid., Dec. 30, 1814.

430 *I therefore now write you:* Ibid., Dec. 27, 1814.

430 *I hope neither you:* Ibid.

430 *Consider the astonishment:* LA to JQA, Jan. 20, 1815, Reel 422 AFP MHS.

430 *I fear I shall be much:* Ibid., 548

CHAPTER 58: VIVE!

Page

432 *Napoleon had been:* "NRF," Reel 268 AFP MHS.

432   *He had been tried:* Ibid.
432   *I heard an exclamation of horror:* Ibid.
432   *Wagons of every description:* Ibid.
432   *said the country:* Ibid.
433   *Soldiers of the fifth:* Coote, *Napoleon and the Hundred Days,* 134.
433   *The public spirit in Paris:* MJQA, Mar. 15, 1815, III, 171.
434   *It is ascertained:* Ibid.
434   *I saw in various parts:* Ibid., Mar. 11, 1815, 167.
434   *From their ashes:* Shakespeare, *Henry VI,* Part 1: Sir William Lucy, act 4, scene 7, lines 92 and 93.
434   *The day at Strasbourg was:* "NRF," Reel 268 AFP MHS.
435   *We immediately entered into engagements:* Ibid.
435   *As he had rendered me good:* Ibid.
435   *We drove up to a miserable place:* Ibid.
435   *Dupin took the opportunity:* Ibid.
435   *heard threatening conversation:* Ibid.
436   *There were many bitter anathemas:* Ibid.
436   *Dupin told me:* Ibid.
436   *The waiter said that I:* Ibid.
436   *told me that the people:* Ibid.
436   *I went out half an hour:* MJQA, Mar. 19, 1815, III, 172.
437   *No appearance of anything:* Ibid., 172–73.
437   *"Vive le Roi":* Ibid., 173.
437   *most violent,* Ibid.
437   *They had not a hope:* Ibid.
437   *They left the palace:* Ibid., Mar. 20, 1815, 173.
437   *There was a great crowd:* Ibid.
437   *He says that divine Providence:* Ibid., 174.
438   *We had gone about:* "NRF," Reel 268 AFP MHS, 557.
438   *The first notice I had:* Ibid.
438   *Presently I heard these wretches:* Ibid.
438   *At this moment a party:* Ibid.
438   *I sat in agony of apprehension:* Ibid.
438   *A general officer with:* Ibid.
439   *God in his great mercy:* Ibid.
439   *called out, that I was an:* Ibid.
439   *At which the soldiers shouted:* Ibid.
439   *vive les Americains:* Ibid.
439   *If we attempted:* Ibid.
439   *He told me my situation:* Ibid.
440   *[W]henever they shouted:* Ibid.
440   *He complimented me:* Ibid.
440   *In this way we journeyed:* Ibid.
440   *At twelve o'clock at night:* Ibid.
440   *Madame Babet really:* Ibid.
441   *He told me that in:* Ibid.
441   *I had better not:* Ibid.
441   *This news startled:* Ibid.
441   *The crowd of people:* MJQA, Mar. 20, 1815, III, 176.
441   *The front of their helmets:* Ibid., Mar. 21, 1815, 176.
442   *The royal arms were removed:* Ibid., 177.
442   *I was again on:* "NRF," Reel 268 AFP MHS.
442   *My courage was fast oozing:* Ibid.
442   *He came up very politely:* Ibid.

442   *arrived in perfect safety:* Ibid.
442   *When I returned home:* MJQA, Mar. 23, 1815, III, 178.
443   *was perfectly astonished:* "NRF," Reel 268 AFP MHS.

EPILOGUE: THE BIRCHES OF BOSTON

Page
444   *If we go to England:* WJQA, JQA to AA, Dec. 24, 1814, V, 247.
444   *Mr. Gallatin is appointed:* MJQA, April 5, 1815, III, 182.
445   *The emperor of Russia:* Ibid., Mar. 29, 1815, 181.
445   *I saw him, but not distinctly:* Ibid., 182.
446   *The forty-eighth year:* Ibid., July 11, 1815, 250.
447   *When I retrace:* "NRF," Reel 268 AFP MHS.
448   *I was carried:* Ibid.
448   *A moral is contained:* Ibid.
448   *I had others under:* Ibid.
449   *Years have rolled on:* Ibid.
450   *And when it is his will:* Ibid.

Bibliography

Adams, Charles Francis, ed. *Memoirs of John Quincy Adams: Comprising Portions of His Diary 1795–1848*. Vol. II. Philadelphia: J. B. Lippincott, 1874.

Adams Family, *Adams Family Correspondence*. Vol. 10: January 1794-June 1795, Edited by Margaret A. Hogan, C. James Taylor, Sara Martin, Hobson Woodward, Sara B. Sikes, Gregg L. Lint, and Sara Georgini. Boston: Belknap Press of Harvard University Press, 2011.

Adams, Henry. *The US During the Administration of Madison*. New York: Charles Scribner and Sons, 1890.

Adams, John. *Diary and Autobiography of John Adams*. Vol. I. Edited by L. H. Butterfield, Leonard C. Faber, and Wendell D. Garrett. Cambridge, MA: Belknap Press, 1961.

———. *Works*. Vol. II. Edited by Charles Francis Adams,. Boston: Little Brown, 1850.

Adams, John Quincy. *Diary 23, 1 January 1795–12 May 1801, 5 August 1809–30 April 1836, page 218* [electronic edition]. *The Diaries of John Quincy Adams: A Digital Collection*. Boston, Mass.: Massachusetts Historical Society, 2004. http://www.masshist.org/jqadiaries.

———. *Writings of John Quincy Adams, 1801–10*. Vol. III. Edited by Worthington Chauncey Ford. New York: Macmillan, 1914.

———. *Writings of John Quincy Adams, 1811–13*. Vol. IV. Edited by Worthington Chauncey Ford. New York: Macmillan, 1914.

———. *Writings of John Quincy Adams, 1814–16*. Vol. V. Edited by Worthington Chauncey Ford. New York: Macmillan, 1914.

Adams Family Papers, 1639–1889, Microfilm 608 Reels Boston: Massachusetts Historical Society, 1954–1959. Reels 264, 268–69, 409, 410, and 419–22.

Allen John, and William Davis Ticknor. *Anecdotes of the Apprehension and Murder of the Duke d'Enghien and Reputation of Caulaincourt's Defense*. In *New Monthly Magazine*, Vol. I, 513, 1814, 513-5.

Ames, William E. *A History of the National Intelligencer*. Chapel Hill: University of North Carolina Press, 1972.

Amelekhina, Svetlana A., and Alexey K. Levykin. *Magnificence of the Tsars: Ceremonial Men's Dress of the Russian Imperial Court, 1721–1917*. London: V & A Publishing, 2008.

"American Statement." *Salem Gazette*, April 25, 1775. In *American History Told by Contemporaries*. Edited by Albert Bushnell Hart. Vol. II, 546–48. New York: Macmillan, 1919.

Antonov, Borisa. *Russian Tsars*, Ivan Fedorov, 2005.

Arch, Nigel, and Joanna Marschner. *Splendour at Court: Dressing for Royal Occasions Since 1700*. London: Unwin Hyman, 1987.

Arnt, Ernst Moritz. *The Life and Adventures of Ernest Moritz Arndt, the Singer of the German Fatherland*. Boston: Roberts Brothers, 1879.

Bemis, Samuel Flagg. *John Quincy Adams and the Foundations of American Foreign Policy*. New York: W. W. Norton, 1973.

Berlin Decree, November 21, 1806. In *Correspondence de Napoleon I*. Vol. XIII, 551–57, translated by James Harvey Robinson. University of Pennsylvania Translations and

Reprints. http://www.napoleon-series.org/research/government/diplomatic/c
_continental.html.

Blanning, Tim. *The Pursuit of Glory: Europe 1648–1815*. New York: Viking, 2007.

Borneman, Walter R. *1812: The War That Forged a Nation*. New York: HarperCollins, 2005.

Bowman, Ebenezer. *Removal of Pickering from the Office of Secretary of State*. May 21, 1800.
Papers of the War Department 1784–1800, Roy Rosenzweig Center for History
and New Media, George Mason University. http://wardepartmentpapers.org/.

Bozonelis, Helen Koutras. *Primary Source Accounts of the War of 1812*. Berkeley Heights, NJ:
Enslow Publishers, Myreportlinks.com, 2006.

British Order in Council, November 11, 1807. In *American State Papers: Documents, Legislative
and Executive, of the Congress of the United States. Class I: Foreign Relations. Selected and
edited under the authority of Congress*. Washington, DC: Gales and Seaton, 1832–61.
http://www.napoleon-series.org/research/government/diplomatic/c_continental
.html.

Coburn, Frank Warren. *The Battle Of April 19, 1775, in Lexington, Concord, Lincoln, Arlington,
Cambridge, Somerville And Charlestown, Massachusetts*. Lexington: Published by the
Author, 1912.

Coote, Stephen. *Napoleon and the Hundred Days*. Cambridge, MA: Da Capo Press, 2007.

Coxe, Tench. *A Series of Tables of the Several Branches of American Manufacturers Exhibiting
Them in Every County in the Union So Far as They Are Returned in the Reports of the
Marshals and of the Secretaries of the Territories and of Their Respective Assistants in the
Autumn of the Year 1810*. In *Book 2 of the Third Census*. Philadelphia, PA: A. Cornman,
1814.

Craig, W. J., ed. *As You Like It*, Act 2, Scene 7, Lines 147–50. *The Complete Works of William
Shakespeare*. London: Oxford University Press: 1914. www.bartleby.com/70/.

———. *Hamlet*, Act 3, Scene 1, Line 66. *The Complete Works of William Shakespeare*.
London: Oxford University Press: 1914. http://www.bartleby.com/70/.

Cutter, William Richard, ed. "Captain Benjamin Beckford." In *Genealogical and Personal
Memoirs: Relating to the Families of Boston and Eastern Massachusetts*. Vol. IV, 1853. New
York: Lewis Historical Publishing Company, 1908.

"Deaths: Preliminary Data 2009." *National Vital Statistics Reports* 59, no. 4 (March 2011).
http://www.cdc.gov/nchs/data/nvsr/nvsr59/nvsr59_04.pdf.

Decree of 1810. British Navy, Army, and Colonial Troops of the Napoleonic Wars. http://
napoleonistyka.atspace.com/Britain_and_British_forces.htm.

Dictionary of American Fighting Ships. s.v. "President," Vol. 5, 1970, http://www.hazegray
.org/danfs/frigates/presiden.htm.

Documents upon the Continental System. In *American State Papers: Documents, Legislative
and Executive, of the Congress of the United States. Class I.: Foreign Relations. Selected and
edited under the authority of Congress*. Washington, DC: Gales and Seaton, 1832–61.
http://www.napoleon-series.org/research/government/diplomatic/c_continental.html.

Dodge, Theodore Ayrault. *Napoleon, a History of the Art of War: From the Beginning of
the Peninsular War to the End of the Russian Campaign, with a Detailed Account of the
Napoleonic Wars*. Boston: Houghton, Mifflin and Company, 1907.

Encyclopedia Britannica Online, s.v. "Alexander I," http://www.britannica.com
/EBchecked/topic/14004/Alexander-I.

———. s.v. "Battle of Borodino," http://www.britannica.com/EBchecked/topic/74349
/Battle-of-Borodino.

———. s.v. "Battle of Jena," http://www.britannica.com/EBchecked/topic/302522
/Battle-of-Jena.

————. s.v. "Battle of Leipzig," http://www.britannica.com/EBchecked/topic/335470 /Battle-of-Leipzig.

————. s.v. "Charles-Maurice de Talleyrand, prince de Benevent," http://www.britannica .com/EBchecked/topic/581601/Charles-Maurice-de-Talleyrand-prince-de-Benevent /7103/During-the-Revolution.

————. s.v. "Denmark," http://www.britannica.com/EBchecked/topic/157748 /Denmark/33883/The-economy-and-agricultural-reforms.

————. s.v. "Eastern Orthodoxy," http://www.britannica.com/EBchecked/topic/177174 /Eastern-Orthodoxy.

————. s.v. "Elba," http://www.britannica.com/EBchecked/topic/182104/Elba.

————. s.v. "fjord," http://www.britannica.com/EBchecked/topic/209177/fjord.

————. s.v. "Holy Roman Empire," http://www.britannica.com/EBchecked/topic/269851 /Holy-Roman-Empire.

————. s.v. "Jutland," http://www.britannica.com/EBchecked/topic/308955/Jutland.

————. s.v. "Legion of Honour," http://www.britannica.com/EBchecked/topic/335043 /Legion-of-Honour.

————. s.v. "Louis Bonaparte," http://www.britannica.com/EBchecked/topic/72710 /Louis-Bonaparte.

————. s.v. "Mikhail Illarionovich, Prince Kutuzov," http://www.britannica.com /EBchecked/topic/325629/Mikhail-Illarionovich-Prince-Kutuzov.

————. s.v. "Russian Orthodox Church," http://www.britannica.com/EBchecked /topic/513815/Russian-Orthodox-church.

————. s.v. "Smolensk," http://www.britannica.com/EBchecked/topic/550073/Smolensk.

————. s.v. "Treaties of Tilsit," http://www.britannica.com/EBchecked/topic /595909 /Treaties-of-Tilsit.

Encyclopedia of World Biography. 2nd ed. Vol. VII. Detroit: Gale, 1998, s.v. "Henry IV."

————. 2d ed. Web. Detroit: Gale, 1998, s.v. "Napoleon I."

Ferrero, S, S. Pretta, S. Bertoldi, P. Anserini, V. Remorgida, M. Del Sette, C. Gandolfo, N. Ragni. "Increased Frequency of Migraine Among Women with Endometriosis. In Human Reproduction." Vol. 19(12): Oxford, UK, December 2004, 2927–32. http:// www.ncbi.nlm.nih.gov/pubmed/15513980.

First Ladies National Library. http://www.firstladies.org/biographies/ s.v. "Abigail Adams Biography."

————. http://www.firstladies.org/biographies/ s.v. "Dolley Madison Biography."

————. http://www.firstladies.org/biographies/ s.v. "Louisa Adams Biography."

Fort McHenry National Monument and Historic Shrine. *Fort McHenry.* Baltimore: National Park Service, US Department of the Interior, 2010.

Garraty, John A., and Mark C. Carnes, eds. "John Quincy Adams." In *American National Biography.* Vol. I. New York: Oxford University Press, 1999.

————. "John Armstrong, Jr." In *American National Biography.* Vol. I. New York: Oxford University Press, 1999.

George, Christopher. *Terror on the Chesapeake.* Shippensburg, PA: White Mane, 2001.

Google Maps Distance Calculator. Daft Logic. http://www.daftlogic.com/projects-google -maps-distance-calculator.htm.

Gray, Edward. *William Gray, of Salem, Merchant: A Biographical Sketch.* Cambridge, MA: Riverside Press, 1914.

Heidler, David S., and Heidler, eds. *Encyclopedia of the War of 1812.* Annapolis, MD, Naval Institute Press, 1997.

History of Christiansøe, http://www.christiansoe.dk/oens-historie.html.

Hooks, Jonathan. *Redeemed Honor: The President-Little Belt Affair and the Coming of the War of 1812.* In Volume 74, Issue 1, Pages 1–24, Spring 2012, http://onlinelibrary.wiley.com /doi/10.1111/j.1540-6563.2011.00310.x/full#fn20.

Howard, Jeremy, and Yuri Belinsky. *National Geographic Traveler: St. Petersburg.* Washington, DC: National Geographic, 2007.

Ingersoll, Charles Jared. *Historical Sketch of the Second War Between the United States of America and Great Britain: Declared by Act of Congress, the 18th of June, 1812, and Concluded by Peace, the 15th of February, 1815.* Philadelphia: Lea and Blanchard, 1849.

Jefferson, Thomas. *The Jeffersonian Cyclopedia.* Edited by John P. Foley. New York: Funk & Wagnalls, 1900.

Ketcham, Ralph. *James Madison: A Biography.* First paperback ed. Charlottesville, VA: University of Virginia Press, 1990.

King, Charles R., ed. *The Life and Correspondence of Rufus King, Comprising His Letters, Private and Official, His Public Documents and His Speeches.* Vol. V, 1807–16. New York: G. P. Putman's Sons, 1898.

King, David. *Vienna, 1814: How the Conquerors of Napoleon Made Love, War, and Peace at the Congress of Vienna.* New York: Harmony Books, 2008.

Kutler, Stanley I. *Dictionary of American History.* 3rd ed. Vol. VIII. New York: Charles Scribner's Sons, 2003.

Leavitt, Judith. *Brought to Bed: Childbearing in America, 1750–1950.* New York: Oxford University Press, 1986.

Loudon, Irvine. *Death in Childbirth: An International Study of Maternal Care and Maternal Mortality, 1800–1950.* New York: Oxford University Press, 1992.

———. *Medical Care and the General Practitioner, 1750–1850.* New York, Oxford University Press, 1986.

———. *Western Medicine: An Illustrated History.* New York: Oxford University Press, 1992.

Madison, Dolley Payne. "From James Madison Aug. 23, 1814." In *The Selected Letters of Dolley Payne Madison.* Edited by David B. Mattern and Holly C. Shulman. Charlottesville and London: University of Virginia Press, 2003.

Madison, James. "To John Armstrong, July 2, 1814." In *Online Library of Liberty: The Writings of James Madison.* Vol. VIII, 1808–1819. http://oll.libertyfund.org /title/1939.

March of Dimes. "Miscarriage." http://www.marchofdimes.com/baby/loss_miscarriage .html. October 2008.

Massachusetts Historical Society, Adams Family Timeline, 1735–1889, Boston: Massachusetts Historical Society, 1954–1959. http://www.masshist.org/adams /timeline.cfm.

McGrew, Roderick E. "Bloodletting." *Encyclopedia of Medical History.* s.v. In New York: McGraw-Hill Book Company, 1985.

———. "Midwifery." *Encyclopedia of Medical History.* New York: McGraw-Hill Book Company, 1985.

———. "Puerperal Fever." *Encyclopedia of Medical History.* New York: McGraw-Hill Book Company, 1985.

Milan Decree, December 17, 1807. In *Correspondence de Napoleon I.* Vol. XVI, 192–93. Translated by James Harvey Robinson. University of Pennsylvania Translations and Reprints. http://www.napoleon-series.org/research/government/diplomatic/c _continental.html.

Miniño, Arialdi M. and Sherry L. Murphy. "Death in the United States in 2010." In *NCHS Data Brief*, no. 99. July 2012. Centers for Disease Control and Prevention. http://www.cdc.gov/nchs/data/databriefs/db99.pdf.

Nagel, Paul C. *Descent from Glory: Four Generations of the John Adams Family*. Cambridge: Harvard University Press, 1999.

———. *John Quincy Adams: A Public Life, a Private Life*. Cambridge: Harvard University Press, 1999.

———. *The Adams Women: Abigail and Louisa Adams, Their Sisters and Daughters*. Oxford University Press, 2002.

Napoleon: The Myth, the Battles, the Legend. DVD. BFS Entertainment, 2001.

Napoleon's Final Battle. DVD. National Geographic, 2006.

Napoleon's Road to Moscow. DVD. Kultur Video, 1999.

NaPro Technology, *Recurrent Spontaneous Abortion (Miscarriage)*, http://www.naprotechnology.com/abortion.htm.

National Institute of Allergy and Infectious Diseases, National Institutes of Health. *Group A Streptococcal Infections*. http://www.niaid.nih.gov/topics/streptococcal/Pages/Default.aspx.

National Institute of Neurological Disorders and Stroke. National Institutes of Health. *Febrile Seizures Worksheet*. http://www.ninds.nih.gov/disorders/febrile_seizures/detail_febrile_seizures.htm.

National Park Service, *Russian Passport Accession for Louisa Catherine Johnson Adams*. Adams National Historical Park. Quincy, Massachusetts, January 28, 1815.

Neville, Peter. *A Traveller's History of Russia*. New York: Interlink Books, 2006.

Nichols, John. "Obituary Count Nicholas Romanzoff." *The Gentlemen's Magazine, Vol. 139*. Indiana University: E. Cave, 1826, 271–72.

Noyer, Anne Marguerite Petit. *The Correspondence of Madame du Noyer*. Translated by Florence L. Layard. London: Richard Bentley and Sons, 1890.

Paine, Robert Treat, Jr. "Boston Patriotic Song." Library of Congress. http://memory.loc.gov/diglib/ihas/loc.natlib.ihas.100010462/default.html.

Pezzola, John. *Battle of North Point 1814*. In *The War of 1812*. http://www.warof1812.ca/northpoint.htm.

Pitch, Anthony S. *The Burning of Washington: The British Invasion of 1814*. Annapolis, MD: Naval Institute Press, 1998.

Portrait of Benjamin Beckford (1758–1811). Beverly Historical Society & Museum, Beverly, MA.

Powell, John, ed. "Battle of the Nations." In *Chronology of European History: 15,000 BC to 1997*. Vol. II, 1478–1898. Pasadena, CA: Salem Press, 1997.

———. "Battle of the Austerlitz." In *Chronology of European History: 15,000 BC to 1997*. Vol. II,1478–1898. Pasadena, CA: Salem Press, 1997.

———. "Catherine the Great's Instruction." In *Chronology of European History: 15,000 BC to 1997*. Vol. II, 1478–1898. Pasadena, CA: Salem Press, 1997.

Rambouillet Decree, March 23, 1810. http://www.napoleon-series.org/research/government/diplomatic/c_continental.html.

Rice, Melanie. *DK Eyewitness Travel Guide: St. Petersburg*. London: Dorling Kindersley, 2007.

Rukert, Norman G. *Fort McHenry: Home of the Brave*. Baltimore: Bodine & Associates, 1983.

Rumiantzov, Nicholas. "The American Philosophical Society and the Epoch of Alexander I of Russia." *Proceedings of the American Philosophical Society* 94, no. 6 (Dec. 22, 1950): 565–71.

Schofield, Robert E. *Charles Willson Peale and His Philadelphia Museum, 1784–1827*. In *American Studies* 30, no. 2 (Fall 1989). https://journals.ku.edu/index.php/amerstud/article/viewFile/2470/2429.

Schom, Alan. *One Hundred Days: Napoleon's Road to Waterloo*. New York: Atheneum, 1992.

Shakespeare, William. *Henry VI,* part 1, act 4, scene 7, lines 92–93 http://shakespeare.mit.edu/1henryvi/full.html.

Seal, William. *The President's House.* Vol. I. Washington DC: White House Historical Association with the cooperation of the National Geographic Society, 1986.

Sonneborn, Liz. *The Star-Spangled Banner: The Story Behind Our National Anthem.* New York: Chelsea House, 2004.

Supplementary Observations. *US Census 1810, Book 2 of the Third Census.* Philadelphia, PA: A. Cornman, 1814.

The Napoleon Series. *France: Decrees on Trade, 1783–1810,* http://www.napoleon-series.org/research/government/france/decrees/c_decrees1.html.

———. *Franco-Russia Diplomacy 1810–12,* http://www.napoleon-series.org/research/government/diplomatic/c_rufrdip1.html.

———. *The Finances of France. Transcribed, with notes, by Tom Holmberg* http://www.napoleon-series.org/research/government/france/finance/c_finances1799.html.

Titen, A. *Migraine Is Associated with Menorrhagia and Endometriosis.* In http://www.ncbi.nlm.nih.gov/pubmed/16618258.

Trager, James. *The Women's Chronology: A Year-by-Year Record, from Prehistory to the Present.* s.v. 1796–1815 New York: Henry Holt, 1994.

US Department of Defense. *Active Duty Personnel, 1789 Through FY 1995, Table 2.* http://siadapp.dmdc.osd.mil/personnel/M01/fy95/SMS211R.HTM.

US Department of Health and Human Services. Child Health USA 2011. "Maternal Mortality" http://mchb.hrsa.gov/chusa11/hstat/hsi/pages/208mm.html.

US National Library of Medicine. *Encephalitis.* http://www.ncbi.nlm.nih.gov/pubmedhealth/PMH0002388/ 2012.

———. *Hyponatremia.* http://www.ncbi.nlm.nih.gov/pubmedhealth/PMH0001431/.

US State Department. Office of the Historian. *Biographies of the Secretaries of State: Timothy Pickering,* http://history.state.gov/departmenthistory/people/pickering-timothy.

———. Office of the Historian. *Diplomatic and Consular Posts, 1781–1997,* http://www.state.gov/www/about_state/history/faq.html#consular.

Ward, A. W., G. W. Prothero, and Stanley Leathes, eds. *The Cambridge Modern History: Napoleon.* Vol. IX. London: Cambridge University Press, 1906.

Warnes, David. *Chronicle of the Russian Tsars.* London: Thames and Hudson, 1999.

Wende, Peter. *A History of Germany.* New York: Palgrave Macmillan, 2005.

Wills, Garry. *Henry Adams and the Making of America.* Boston: Houghton Mifflin Harcourt, 2005.

Wu, Meng-Hsing., Chun-Wun Lu, Pei-Chin Chuang, and Shaw-Jenq Tsai. "Prostaglandin E2: The Master of Endometriosis?" In *Experimental Biology and Medicine.* Online: The Royal Society of Medicine Press, June 2010 Vol. 235 No. 6, 668–677 http://ebm.rsmjournals.com/content/235/6/668.full.

Xu, Jiaquan, Kenneth D. Kochanek, Sherry L. Murphy and Betzaida Tejada-Vera, and Centers for Disease Control and Prevention. "Deaths: Final Data for 2007." *National Vital Statistics Report* 58, no. 19, May 10, 2007. http://www.cdc.gov/nchs/data/nvsr/nvsr58/nvsr58_19.pdf.

Index

About the Author

A FREQUENT GUEST ON THE FOX NEWS Channel and national media commentator, Jane Hampton Cook is the author of seven books, mostly on American history topics. Her passion is to bring stories to life and make history memorable and relevant to today's news, current events, issues of faith, and modern-day life. Jane served President George W. Bush as a webmaster for five years, including two years in the White House and three in the Texas governor's office. Her love for US history skyrocketed when she discovered that historical stories about the White House, presidents, and first ladies were among the White House website's most popular pages. Inspired by these stories, she received a fellowship from the Organization of American Historians and the White House Historical Association to conduct historical research on the White House. With a bachelor's degree from Baylor University and a master's degree from Texas A&M University, she can both sic 'em and gig 'em. Jane hopes each new book is increasingly worth reading, each speech worth hearing, and each TV segment worth remembering. A member of the National Press Club, she lives with her husband and two sons in Fairfax, Virginia. For more information, go to www.janecook.com.